PROFESSIONAL SKILLS AND PRACTICE

Oxford University Press, the world's leading academic publisher, offers you a tailored teaching and learning solution with this custom text which contains chapters selected from OUP texts.

This custom text has been compiled for Birmingham City University

Please bear in mind that any cross-references will apply to chapters in the original book rather than to chapters within this custom text. If you would like to follow up on any of these references, please consult the original work in which the chapter appears. See www.oup.com for the full catalogue of OUP books.

Each page in this custom text has two sets of page numbers for ease of use. The page numbering of the original books is included to enable correct citation and reference back to the book from which the chapter is taken. There is also consecutive page numbering throughout this custom text in a shaded band at the bottom of each page.

The authors of this custom text are responsible only for the ideas expressed in their own writing and not for any views that might be expressed by authors of other chapters.

PROFESSIONAL SKILLS AND PRACTICE

Compiled from

Legal Systems and Skills
Scott Slorach, Judith Embley, Peter Goodchild, and
Catherine Shephard

Legal Skills, Fourth edition
Emily Finch and Stefan Fafinski

Employability Skills for Law Students
Emily Finch and Stefan Fafinski

A Practical Approach to Criminal Procedure,
Fourteenth edition
John Sprack

Legal Ethics
Jonathan Herring

OXFORD
UNIVERSITY PRESS

OXFORD
UNIVERSITY PRESS

Great Clarendon Street, Oxford, OX2 6DP,
United Kingdom

Oxford University Press is a department of the University of Oxford.
It furthers the University's objective of excellence in research, scholarship,
and education by publishing worldwide. Oxford is a registered trade mark of
Oxford University Press in the UK and in certain other countries

This custom text © Oxford University Press 2014

The moral rights of the authors have been asserted

Impression: 1

Public sector information reproduced under Open Government Licence v1.0
(http://www.nationalarchives.gov.uk/doc/open-government-licence/open-government-licence.htm)

Crown Copyright material reproduced with the permission of the
Controller, HMSO (under the terms of the Click Use licence)

Published in the United States of America by Oxford University Press
198 Madison Avenue, New York, NY 10016, United States of America

British Library Cataloguing in Publication Data
Data available

ISBN 978-0-19-873277-8

Printed in Great Britain by
CPI Group (UK) Ltd, Croydon, CR0 4YY

Compiled from:

Legal Systems and Skills
By Scott Slorach, Judith Embley, Peter Goodchild, and Catherine Shephard
ISBN 9780199676194
© Oxford University Press 2013

Legal Skills, Fourth edition
By Emily Finch and Stefan Fafinski
ISBN 9780199664498
© Emily Finch and Stefan Fafinski 2013

Employability Skills for Law Students
By Emily Finch and Stefan Fafinski
ISBN 9780199663231
© Emily Finch and Stefan Fafinski 2014

A Practical Approach to Criminal Procedure, Fourteenth edition
By John Sprack
ISBN 9780199651955
© John Sprack and Christopher J Emmins 2012

Legal Ethics
By Jonathan Herring
ISBN 9780198703457
© Oxford University Press 2014

CONTENTS

Communication

Learning objectives

After studying this chapter you should be able to:

- Appreciate the need for good communication skills.
- Describe effective communication skills.
- Practise and develop these skills during your legal studies and in everyday life.
- Practise techniques to help you deliver effective presentations.
- Appreciate what makes a good advocate.
- Prepare effectively for a moot.
- Communicate effectively in one to one and group situations.

Introduction

This is the first of two chapters on communication skills. Chapter 11 discusses specifically communication in the form of writing and drafting. This chapter deals with other forms of communication, including verbal and non-verbal communication. Of all the skills referred to in this book, it is these with which you will be most familiar. From the moment you were born, even before you could speak, you could communicate your need to feed, sleep, or play.

As you progress through your legal studies, seek employment opportunities and then start developing your career, communication skills will be fundamental. They are the primary means by which you impart what you know and what you think. *How* you communicate not only dictates the extent to which a recipient will understand what you are attempting to communicate: it will also result in the recipient forming a view of your ability to communicate.

There are a range of situations in which you will need to employ verbal and non-verbal communication skills during your studies: contributions in tutorials and seminars; making presentations; competing in a moot; being involved in pro bono or similar initiatives; vacation placements or other work experience schemes. They will be a fundamental part of the interview process as you look to develop career opportunities. In providing professional advice and services, lawyers have to communicate with clients, other lawyers, officials of public bodies, and a range of other professionals. Their communication skills will be employed in diverse situations, such as interviews, meetings, telephone calls, negotiations, presentations, and court appearances. These skills, even advocacy, have generic qualities that are transferable. That is, they can be employed in other contexts and careers. The requirements or job specification for nearly every profession and career will stipulate 'communication skills'. This chapter is therefore designed to help you develop and strengthen your communication skills. As these skills develop during your 'work'—your studies and career—you should also notice that they develop in your non-working life too.

Reading about communication skills, in isolation from practising these skills, may, at times, appear a little basic. However, it is a fundamental communication skill to be able to communicate complex ideas in a way that is easy to understand, and there is no value in dressing them up as more complex than they actually are. Like most skills, developing your communication skills predominantly requires some preparatory thought, the application of common sense, and subsequent reflection. This chapter aims to reflect that.

It would be unrealistic to ignore the requirement of a level of self-confidence. It is often the case that, when faced with a real recipient of their communication, in a situation where there is a little pressure and where they may have to think 'on their feet', the communication skills of both students and professionals are the first things to suffer. Unfortunately this also tends to be the first thing the recipient notices and, in professional circumstances, can result in criticism. A good level of self-awareness, reflective practice, and simply recognising the importance of communication skills will help you to develop the confidence to avoid these situations. Confidence is, to a large extent, a function of familiarity: this chapter has therefore been written on the basis that the more familiar you become with the basics early on, the more confident you will become in your communication.

Finally, remember that communication is a basic human interaction, and is what allows us to develop relationships of all types. To explore and become further aware of the variety of ways that communication can take place, both verbally and non-verbally, whether intentional or not, can be a fascinating and enriching experience.

10.1 What are communication skills?

The term 'communication skills' refers to several different skills which you use together to allow you to convey effectively information, opinion, and advice, and to receive the same from others.

10.1.1 Non-verbal communication

Before you even begin to speak, you communicate through your body language. When dealing with any complex issue or difficult situation, we may be deep in thought, or nervous. This can have a major effect on our eye contact and body language. Naturally pleasant and outgoing people can look distracted, or even severe and unapproachable. Even accomplished, talented professionals can find themselves unable to look anyone in the eye or offer a firm handshake. The good news is that much of this can be overcome through awareness, preparation, practice, and experience. The first step is to be aware of what you should be aiming for.

Eye contact

Eye contact is extremely powerful. In Western cultures, avoiding eye contact can be deemed to be a sign of dishonesty, which is obviously a particularly bad message for anyone, and particularly a lawyer, to communicate. Conversely, good eye contact can be very reassuring, instil confidence, be persuasive, and also allow you to pick up on cues others are making with their eyes. Eye contact is therefore important: if you struggle with it, and many do, then it is something to work on. You can practise making good eye contact in everyday life. Experimenting with eye contact in situations where you are comfortable can help develop the skill, so that you can then deploy it when you are outside your comfort zone. A good tip is to focus just behind a person's head to begin with. This helps to practise the habit and gives the other person the impression of eye contact. When you are comfortable doing this, progress to looking at their eyes, which has the added advantage of allowing you to read the eye signals they are communicating. Do take care to avoid becoming locked into eye contact. Being able to break off eye contact, and then seamlessly re-establish it, is another skill you can practise and master.

If you have Autism or Asperger's Syndrome, you may find eye contact particularly challenging. Even if you have learned to make eye contact, it may be that you still do not pick up on any cues from other people's eye contact. In this case, simply being aware of the importance of eye contact, and the messages it conveys, can be helpful. You may, for example, feel comfortable where appropriate to explain that just because you are not making eye contact does not mean you are not listening or paying attention to what someone is saying. This in itself is demonstrating a high level of self-awareness and good communication skills.

Body language

Our bodies can betray feelings that we would prefer to keep to ourselves. To some people, this is not desperately important. If the bass player in a band comes across as surly, hyperactive, or very shy, no one will use this to judge her ability to play guitar. However, in contrast, a lawyer must project a professional persona at all times. We need to be particularly alert to, and actively manage, the messages our bodies may be sending. Folding your arms looks defensive and hostile. Any persistent habits, such as foot jiggling, pen tapping, hand waving, hair flicking, or pacing around can detract significantly from what you are saying. Poor posture, including staring at your feet, sends the message that you are not interested. Scowling suggests you are unapproachable. A nervous demeanour can communicate itself to recipients such that they become nervous on your behalf, which can, in turn, impair the communication you are trying to make.

Part of being an effective communicator is being self-aware. We all do something inadvertently, but not all of us are aware of that fact. Painful though it may be, the best way to identify this is to ask someone you trust to be brutally honest, or alternatively record and analyse yourself. This latter technique is an established form of teacher and media training. Smartphones make this process much more accessible than it used to be. Simply recording yourself talking about your favourite subject for five minutes is likely to reveal what aspects of your body language may let you down. Failing this, watching yourself in a mirror can also help.

So far we have discussed inadvertent body language, but it is also worth considering how to use body language deliberately to send messages to others. During a negotiation, for example, you may wish to convey that you are open to hearing what others have to say. A relaxed, open position, smiling and with palms open (but in a natural position) can convey this very effectively. Nodding and making eye contact can denote that you are listening to what is being said. When you want to make a point firmly, putting your palms together and pointed subtly towards the person to whom you are making that point can help display conviction.

Appearance

It is a fact of life that some people will judge you by your appearance. Compare a lawyer who arrives at a meeting driving a Porsche and wearing a bold pinstriped suit, to a lawyer who arrives driving a Fiesta and wearing polyester. Consider the interview candidate who wears scuffed shoes and has a button missing from his jacket. Have you made a judgment about them already, before they have started to speak? Without advocating that you change your personal style, it shows good self-awareness at least to consider the impression your appearance might convey to others, and whether it aligns with the image you want to convey.

Any judgment that people may make is, of course, a first impression, which may be refined or even dramatically changed by what you go on to say or do (see the film *Legally Blonde*). That said, there is the risk that others might adhere to the adage that 'first impressions never lie' and you will find yourself fighting an uphill battle to retrieve a situation. Chapter 12 gives some tips as to how to you might dress for interviews or the office for the first time if you are unsure (see 12.1.3).

10.1.2 **Verbal communication**

Verbal communication includes not just what you say, but also how you say it. As a lawyer, your legal knowledge and skills are vital to ensure that what you say is technically correct. However, communication should not only be correct, it should also be effective. A client receiving legal advice is likely to assume that every lawyer would have delivered the same advice, in terms of the law. The client is much more likely to judge the lawyer on *how* the advice was delivered, as it is this which ultimately determines the effectiveness of the communication. Let us consider some factors which can affect the effectiveness of verbal communication.

Jargon

Lawyers should avoid jargon wherever possible when communicating with non-lawyers. Most will not understand what is being talked about, and why should they? You would not appreciate a doctor telling you that you have had a vasovagal syncope when instead she could have explained simply that you had fainted and why.

Tone

The tone of verbal communication is very important. It can help you to convey a range of messages: empathy, sympathy; humour; whether something is problematic. If you are not communicating face to face, for example when using the telephone, very subtle changes in tone can be important. Does your tone indicate that you are pleasant and smiling, or that you are grumpy or bored? You may find that when you are concentrating on something you can slip into a monotone. Make sure you vary the tone of your voice to add interest. Note, that people tend to 'mirror' emotions and so if you are pleasant to them, they are more likely to be pleasant to you.

Accent

Provided that you are clear in your speech, having an accent should not pose a problem in communicating. If you do think that your accent may cause difficulties with clarity, however, then simply slowing down your speech can help. Remember that colloquialisms (or slang phrases) are not appropriate in any professional office. So, for example, while it is fine to speak clearly with a Newcastle accent, it would not be fine when speaking to a client to refer to a good outcome as 'canny' (unless of course that client was a fellow Geordie).

Mannerisms

Just as you may do things inadvertently which affect your communication, you may also say things inadvertently. Asking for feedback or listening to a recording of yourself can also be helpful in revealing these traits. Common examples are saying 'erm' frequently rather than simply pausing. You may have a word you use frequently to punctuate or to fill a gap, such as 'ok', 'yeah?', 'hmm, hmm', 'fine', 'great', or 'like'. You need to eliminate this as soon as you can, because it can be very irritating, distracting, and often quite inappropriate. It is not entirely uncommon to hear a lawyer respond to a long tale of woe, be it death or impending insolvency, with a positive-sounding 'great', to the bewilderment of the client and the embarrassment of everyone else in the room.

10.1.3 Listening skills

Everyone likes to be listened to. If you can show someone you are listening they will automatically be predisposed towards you. The term 'active listening' refers to the fact that it is not enough that you are actually listening; you must be *seen* to be listening too. Body language is clearly important here and, as mentioned above, nodding and eye contact convey that you are listening. You should also react appropriately to what is being said, for example by laughing at jokes. Generally you need to show that you are engaging with what is being said. The person who is speaking will appreciate these signs and will remember those people who helped him to feel comfortable when speaking. This is true for large groups as well as for small groups. Presenters love a nodder.

Remember also that if you are speaking, you are not listening. Do not be tempted to chat through a presentation. The presenter *will* notice. Also, take care not to interrupt someone who is speaking. This is a common error on the part of lawyers, who tend to like to be in control and, being bright individuals, often pre-empt what is about to be said. Often, they think that they have thought of a solution before they have really listened to a problem in full, then interrupt the client to present that solution. Lawyers need to be open to hearing what clients are trying to tell them (and this includes listening to their feelings as well as their words). Test your discipline not to interrupt. In a suitable situation, try to concentrate *only* on listening to someone and digesting what he is saying (rather than, say, appearing to listen whilst actually rehearsing in your head what you are going to say next). You will be surprised at the value of the further information which may be revealed to you, and the other person will feel infinitely more valued by being allowed to have his say.

10.1.4 **Confidence**

Lawyers, like all professionals, need to inspire confidence. This is easier if you are confident yourself. If you are not confident in your own abilities, you are unlikely to persuade others to have confidence in you. Confidence is not the same as arrogance or brashness, however, and the line is a fine one to draw. It can help if you can think of someone you admire who inspires confidence and use them as a role model. What is it that they do which impresses you? How do they strike the right balance between confidence and arrogance? Then consider how you might incorporate some of their talents into your own communication skills.

Experience would dictate that those people who come across as truly confident often would not consider themselves to be naturally confident. However, they are people who are aware enough to understand that, to succeed, they need to project confidence. As with most skills, the more you practise looking and sounding confident, the more adept you will be at it, until you are so good it begins to come naturally.

10.1.5 **Communications skills**

Example 1

The following example paints a scene that you can observe or listen to daily in any shop or call centre in the country, and which provides the most basic illustration that knowledge alone does not equip you to achieve your objectives. (Of course, if you have worked in retail, it is also an example of how you could use your work experience to date, however apparently mundane, to show a professional employer what you have learned from it.)

Let's imagine that you bought a T-shirt last month. Yesterday you washed it for the first time and it has shrunk. You take it back to the shop where you bought it. From your study of law, you know that you have a statutory right, under the Sale of Goods Act 1979, to return faulty goods, and that this right is separate from any store policy in relation to the return of goods.

Consider the following two scenarios:

Scenario 1

Shop assistant:	Hello, can I help you?
You:	*Folds arms* I'd like to see the manager please. I'm appalled by what's happened to this T-shirt. It's clearly not of satisfactory quality or fit for purpose. I'm studying law. I know my rights. I want to speak to someone in charge so I can get my money back. And I'm not happy that I've had to make this journey into town. *Scowls*
Shop assistant:	Do you have a receipt?
You:	*Rolls eyes, raises voice* A receipt is completely irrelevant in these circumstances. I am not using your returns policy. This is about my rights as a consumer under the Sale of Goods Act. A T-shirt at this price should not have shrunk like this.
Shop assistant:	Yes, but I need to see how much you paid for it if I'm to refund you.
You:	*Avoids eye contact* Oh, I see. Yes, here it is. *Quietly* Thanks.

(continued . . .)

> ## Scenario 2
>
> | | |
> |---|---|
> | Shop assistant: | Hello, can I help you? |
> | You: | *Gives eye contact, smiles* Hello. I'm sorry to bother you, but I wonder if you could help me with a problem I've had with this T-shirt I bought here. As you can see, it has shrunk. |
> | Shop assistant: | Oh, yes. It does seem a little small! How did you wash it? |
> | You: | *Nods, gives eye contact, still smiling* I followed the instructions on the care label to the letter, but it went in a size 12 and seems to have come out a size 2. *Smiles* The receipt is here. I bought it a month ago for £20, but obviously I only discovered the problem when I washed it for the first time, and that was yesterday. |
> | Shop assistant: | I see. Unfortunately as you bought it a month ago I think we can only give you a replacement. |
> | You: | *Gives eye contact, still smiling* I wonder if you might be able to check that for me? I thought that if the T-shirt is clearly faulty then under the Sale of Goods Act you could still give me my money back, regardless of the store policy. I'm sorry; it is just that I cannot really spare the time to come back in if the same thing happens again. |
> | Shop assistant: | In the circumstances, yes we can refund you. I'm sorry you've had a problem with it. |
> | You: | *Gives eye contact, still smiling, audible so others can hear* Thanks so much for your help. I really appreciate it. Have a good day. |

Let's analyse how communication skills made a difference here. In both scenarios you achieved your aim of obtaining a refund. However, in Scenario 1 it is unlikely that either you or the shop assistant found the experience to be a positive one. Contrast that with Scenario 2. The shop assistant was helpful and received good feedback. You both achieved what you set out to achieve, remaining pleasant and cheerful. The relationship between the two of you was positive: you would be highly likely both to go back to that shop and to speak positively of the experience to others. If we translate this snapshot of daily life into a professional scenario, remember that many lawyers rely on repeat work or word of mouth to receive their next instructions. Someone with the skills shown in Scenario 2 is likely to be considerably more successful in this regard than the person in Scenario 1.

You had the same technical knowledge of the law in both scenarios. In Scenario 2 it was your communication skills, underpinned by that technical knowledge, which made the difference. At the beginning of the exchange you made clear that you intended to be pleasant. You did this through choosing your words carefully and thinking about your body language. You used humour to engage with the shop assistant. You listened to him and remained courteous throughout. You were no pushover; you did assert your knowledge to your advantage, but only as and when necessary, and without arrogance. Finally, you remembered to say thank you, and did so genuinely and with conviction.

10.2 Using communication skills

We noted in the introduction the range of those scenarios when you will use communication skills during your studies. We also considered the communication skills required in professional life and the scenarios in which they are used. The following sections of this chapter consider a number of these scenarios. Some are set in the context of your studies (e.g. mooting) and some are set in the context of professional legal practice (e.g. advocacy). However, all provide guidance on communication skills, and how you can develop and use them to good effect. The guidance is intended to help you make your first attempt in any of these situations a positive experience.

10.3 Presentations

10.3.1 Purpose

During your legal studies, you will most likely be asked to present on a legal topic. The purpose, as with essays and other written pieces of work, is for you to demonstrate your understanding of and opinions on a particular area of law. In addition, unlike written work (unless you are asked to read it out), you will be informing your peers about the law and your opinions.

There are several reasons why you might deliver a presentation in legal practice. One is to pitch for new work. In effect this presentation is to sell the firm to a client, and the stakes are high as a good presentation can secure high-value work from a reliable client over a sustained period of time. Another reason is to deliver training, either internally to trainees, your colleagues, or other departments in the firm, or externally, perhaps to clients or institutions such as a law school. In this type of presentation you need to convey your message clearly and succinctly in a way which will appeal to your audience. Finally, you may be delivering a presentation in order to recruit new trainees, in which case your presentation needs to fulfil both the selling and training criteria. It is quite common for junior lawyers to be involved in any of these types of presentation.

 Essential explanation

Larger clients put their legal work out to competitive tender, which is sometimes referred to as a **beauty parade** (because it involves law firms showing how attractive they are in order to win the competition). This involves a panel of people from each firm presenting to a panel of people from the client as to why they are the best firm for the job. This presentation is known as a **pitch**. Lawyers and members of the firm's business development team will invest a significant amount of time preparing the pitch and tailoring the selling message to the client.

Law firms visit universities to advertise their graduate vacancies, with a view to recruiting the best candidates to work for them. This is known as the **milk round**, to reflect the atypical position that the employers are delivered to the students at their universities, just like milk is delivered to people at their homes. Most firms no longer recruit directly in the milk round but instead will advertise why they are a good place to work as a lawyer and encourage students to apply using their centralised and uniform (often online) application process.

The following guidance is not particularly complicated. As noted above, often communication skills are often simply the application of common sense, together with some thinking ahead. Part of this is considering your audience: the guidance below should be adopted or adapted as appropriate depending on the size and nature of your audience, and your familiarity with them. Nothing will enhance your presentation skills more than actually presenting. The more familiar and comfortable you become with presentation skills, the more you will be able to concentrate on the subject matter of that presentation without losing your audience.

10.3.2 **Structure**

Your presentation should have a clear structure with a definite beginning, middle, and end, which makes it easy for your audience to follow. You should share this structure with your audience. This is a technique known as **signposting**. It might seem obvious to you, but your audience will appreciate it.

Beginning

Even experienced and professional presenters can feel nervous before starting. However, you need to develop a veneer of confidence as this is your chance to make a good impact. Chapter 12 discusses techniques to control nervousness (see 12.10.3), and you should experiment with these to discover what works best for you. Note, however, that a little nervousness is a good thing as it will produce adrenalin to enhance your performance.

Employ good body language from the outset, smile and make eye contact with everyone in the room if possible. Remember that people like to mirror, so you must be enthusiastic and energetic if you want your audience to react to your presentation in this way. Introduce yourself, and any other presenters, very clearly. Now is the time to check that everyone can hear you, to avoid the embarrassment of someone asking later if you can speak up, or, worse, getting to the end of your presentation only to discover that no one has heard a word you have said.

The best presentations are interactive; they engage the audience and make them active contributors rather than passive observers. Depending on the size and nature of your audience, you may wish to set the interactive tone from the outset by asking them to introduce themselves. If appropriate for the audience in question, you may wish to have name cards or badges for them; it can be very impressive if you can refer to them by name when you interact with them during your presentation.

In terms of content, here you will let the audience know what is in store. It is good practice to set out the specific aims of the presentation, namely what you hope your audience will be able to do at the end of your presentation, as a result of it. One model which can be adopted for the aims is SMART. This provides that your aims should be:

- **S**pecific: clear and unambiguous.
- **M**easureable: capable of being measured against objective criteria.
- **A**chievable: can be accomplished by your audience.
- **R**elevant: suitable for and of appeal to your audience.
- **T**ime-appropriate: achievable within the time frame of your presentation.

The learning objectives at the beginning of each chapter of this book are examples of SMART objectives. Consider how your lecturers use learning outcomes, which are aligned with what your assessments will test, to help you to prepare, consolidate, and revise your class work. You should seek to help your audience in a similar way, to help them to place your presentation in context.

Middle

This is where you will deliver the bulk of the content of your presentation. You need to use all of the communication skills discussed in this chapter to keep your audience engaged during this period. Be succinct, use humour where appropriate, continue to use effective body language, and provide examples that are tailored to and will appeal to your audience.

 Practice tip

Thinking about your audience is the key to preparing and delivering a good presentation. Throughout, their needs are paramount. A presentation should not be generic. For example, an employment lawyer should not be able to use a presentation delivered to employees, as a presentation for employers. This would indicate that it was not tailored to the needs of the audience. Employees, for example, will be interested in learning about their rights, and how to enforce them against their employer. Employers will be more interested in hearing about how they as employers should act in a way that does not infringe those rights of their employees. Both presentations will cover the same law, but the emphasis needs to be different to engage the different audiences.

Having tailored the content of your presentation to your audience, you should consider how else to appeal to it. Address your audience directly. If you are presenting to employers, say 'You, as employers, will need to bear this cost' rather than, say, 'This cost is borne by employers'. You are looking to produce 'light bulb moments'; when what you say truly resonates with your audience. Involve your audience at this stage wherever possible. Ask them questions. Ask their opinions. Give them a short time to discuss something with the person next to them. Do anything and everything to keep them engaged. Just as varying the tone of your own voice can add interest, a change of presenter can also renew your audience's enthusiasm. Think about whether there is a timely point in your presentation when a change of presenter might be well received.

Do not be afraid of reiterating your key messages. The maxim 'say what you're going to say; say it; then say it again' is a good one (see 'Performance' at 11.1.1 for its application in written communications). As a minimum you should deliver your key message three times. Signpost in the introduction what you intend to say. In the middle, say it, then, at the end, summarise what you have said.

Relax, smile, be yourself, and try to enjoy the experience.

End

This is the stage where you must draw everything together. Summarise the key points of your presentation. Remind your audience of the aims of the presentation and check whether they have achieved those aims, in an interactive way if possible. Leave the audience with a good lasting impression. Ask if they have any questions. If they do not, do not end on that note. Wrap up the presentation properly and enthusiastically, signposting clearly that it has come to an end. If appropriate, ensure everyone has your name and your contact details and make clear you are available for one to one questions afterwards. It is common for audience members to be shy about asking questions in front of others, but relish the chance to speak to you one to one.

10.3.3 Timing

You will usually be given a target time frame for delivery of the presentation. You must make sure that it does not run significantly under or over this time frame, so practise your presentation in advance to check the timing. You can add some flexibility to the final presentation by preparing some extra items that you can bring in, and identifying some items that you can cut out, if necessary.

10.3.4 Visual aids

Often you will be given the option of preparing visual aids. Visual aids have several advantages. They can:

- help to focus your audience by:
  - highlighting key points;
  - appealing to visual learners;

 Essential explanation

People learn in different ways, and these ways are referred to as **learning styles**. If you prefer to read a book rather than listen to a presentation on the same topic, like lecturers to use slides or write on a whiteboard rather than just speak, and find it helpful to distil information into a mind map or diagram, then you are likely to be what is known as a **visual learner**. If conversely you would much rather attend a lecture to listen to a speaker, or download a podcast, then you may be an **aural learner**. There are other learning styles on which further reading is suggested at the end of this chapter.

- add interest to your presentation;
  - images and catchphrases can appeal to your audience;
  - however, choose them wisely as some can detract from the professional quality of your presentation;
  - check the copyright position when using images;
- act as your prompt:
  - this allows you to dispense with any other prompt (such as a script);
  - however do not overload the slides; this should not be their primary purpose (and do not read out the slide contents verbatim—if they are visual aids, they are for the *audience* to read);
- give the audience something else to look at other than you.

Used well, slides can add significant impact to a presentation. However, you must use them with caution. Many presenters use slides poorly, and 'presentation' is frequently misinterpreted as 'slide show'. Remember to use slides to supplement what you say, not to replace it. These are the hallmarks of a *poor* presentation, and they may already be familiar to you:

- put everything you want to say on the slides;
- create lots of slides;
- fill each slide with as many words as you can;
- add some token clipart;
- choose your favourite colours, regardless of whether they are easy to read;
- fail to proof-read the slides properly;
- do not leave enough time to familiarise yourself with the projection equipment;
- progress too many slides at once and leave the audience hanging while you work out how to go back one slide;
- read out the slides, and read from the screen so that your back is facing the audience and they cannot see or hear you.

Compare the two slides at Figure 10.1. They both convey the same messages in the same basic font and colour. However, even using these basic tools, you can see that the slides look very different. The first slide is a good visual aid. It captures key points and lets the audience know what is to come. It has been proof read properly. This slide needs a good presenter to embellish these key points.

The second slide attempts to convey the entire message in full sentences. It will need to be read out because the audience towards the back of the room may not be able to read it. The rest of the audience will not be listening to the presenter while they are reading the slide. This will probably not be a problem however, because the presenter may not be audible as she will be facing the screen to read the slide. As they will be focusing all of their attention on this slide, the audience will notice the inconsistent use of full stops, the erroneous comma, and the misspelling of reliant.

Which slide do you prefer? This may depend on whether you are considering the slide from the perspective of the presenter or the audience. From the audience's perspective, the first slide is clear, readable, and prepares them to listen to the presenter. The second slide could be a good note to take away (if corrected), but the presentation is likely to add little to it.

From the presenter's perspective, the second slide does provide a safety net in terms of content. However it will actually detract from her ability to use the communication skills set out in this chapter. The first slide provides a decent prompt, but will encourage the presenter to be familiar with the content of the presentation and to employ effective communication skills to engage the audience.

The second slide is attempting to fulfil not only the role of slide, but also of script and notes. A good presenter should not rely on a script, and a slide is not the ideal way to provide notes. If you would like your audience to have a note to take away, then prepare a separate note for them. Most software packages have a function to allow you to prepare and print notes next to the slides.

Visual Aids	How to prepare an effective visual aid for your presentations

• **Not too much text**
 	
• **Not too full**
 	
• **Key points only**
 	
• **Add interest**
 	
• **Supplement presentation**
	• Try not to prepare too many slides.
	  - This will detract from your presentation
	• It is not a good idea to write in full sentences on the slide
	  - Your presentation will add the detail
	• Restrict what you say on the slide to the key points of your presentation
	  - Otherwise you might as well just mail the audience the slide set
	  - You are adding nothing to the presentation if you just turn up and read the slides
	• Try to make your slides as interesting as possible
	  - Law firms tend to have a house style layout for slides, but links to websites and video clips can add verve to your presentation.
	• Images can also help to make your presentation memorable
	  - Although query whether they might make it memorable for the wrong reasons
	• As a basic rule, imagine you could not use your slides. If you would still be able to present, then your slides are supplementing your presentation. If you would have to cancel, you are too reliant on your slides and are delivering a slide show not a presentation,

Figure 10.1 Examples of good and bad slides

10.3.5 Scripts and prompts

If you read from a script it will severely inhibit your ability to use the communication skills discussed in this chapter, including eye contact and body language, and is bound to detract from your presentation. The audience will definitely notice this. They will not definitely notice if you omit to mention one esoteric point because you were not reading from a script. On balance, the risks of reading from a script far outweigh the risks of jettisoning a script and being prepared for a few minor omissions. Never read out a pre-prepared presentation.

The best presenters do not use separate prompts either. Instead, as discussed, they will rely on a basic prompt from the visual aids they have prepared for the benefit of the audience. If you really cannot do without a prompt, restrict yourself to bullet points on cards or to using the slide software's notes facility.

10.3.6 Setting up the room

The layout and set up of a room can make a difference to your presentation. You need to consider this from the audience's perspective. Set out below are a number of factors to consider. Having the right set up can be as important as preparing the presentation: however good the presentation, it can be ruined if the room and facilities do not 'work'. As a presenter, you should take responsibility both for checking in advance and at the time of the presentation that the set up meets your requirements.

Will the audience hear you?

Test the acoustics. Consider whether there is likely to be any background noise. Check if there is a microphone you can use. If the audience are struggling to hear, they will switch off. Always ask the audience at the beginning of the presentation if they can hear, and encourage them to let you know during your presentation if they can no longer hear you. Also remember to ask the audience to turn off their mobile telephones, and always remember to switch off your own.

Will the audience be able to read your slides?

We have discussed what you can do to make your slides readable. However, the layout of the room may prevent the audience from reading even the best slides. Check if there is anything impeding the audience's view, or whether people at the back are too far away, and change the layout of the room accordingly. Take hard copies of the slides with you in case you cannot overcome any problems with audience members being able to read the screen.

Will you be able to interact?

The best presenters engage with their audience. This can be difficult to do if you are far away from them, or on a stage. Do what you can with the room to make it as intimate as possible. When you have exhausted the possibilities for this, there are other steps you can take to interact. If everyone sits at the back of the room, encourage them to come to the front before you start. If you are on a platform or stage, leaving it from time to time, to walk among your audience, can be very effective. In a large room, you will need a wireless microphone and a mouse to do this most effectively, so that the audience can still hear you and you do not have to return to the stage to progress your slides.

Do the audience need anything?

In professional situations, it is usual to leave at least a pen and some paper for each member of the audience, in case they arrive unprepared for taking notes. (Most law firms have branded pens and paper for this purpose, which help with business development, as do business cards, brochures, and other publications.) You may have prepared a handout for use during the session, so it is helpful to put this out in advance too, and to leave copies on spare chairs for any latecomers. If you have prepared notes to take away, consider whether you want to give these out at the beginning or the end. The risk with the former is that the audience will read them rather than listen to your presentation.

Delivering in unfamiliar premises

If you are delivering a presentation at someone else's premises, perhaps as part of an interview process or for business development purposes, do not assume you have no control over the layout. If you can show that you are putting the needs of your audience first, then your enquiries are likely to be well received by the person who has control of the room.

Always arrive well in advance of your presentation too. You will need to factor in time for some or all of the following: taking longer to get to the venue than you thought; going to the toilet; checking your appearance; setting up (sometimes completely re-arranging) the room; dealing with any IT glitches; writing up any information on a whiteboard or flip chart; and checking you have all the equipment and materials you need.

10.3.7 Equipment

You may be asked what equipment you need, or told what equipment will be available. The following list of equipment is a good guide as to what you might need: most items have already been referred to above. There is certainly no magic to them; however, if your presentation relies on any of them and they are not there, it can be difficult to work around their absence. Thinking about what you need and checking in good time that it will be there reduces the risks.

- Laptop or computer;
- memory stick loaded with presentation (even if a copy is pre-loaded onto the computer, as back-up);
- projector and screen;
- cordless mouse;
- cordless microphone;
- flipchart;
- whiteboard;
- marker pens;
- pens and paper for the audience;
- handouts or other materials;
- name cards or badges.

10.3.8 Preparation and developing your skills

As discussed, recording yourself and critically appraising your performance is the best way to prepare for a presentation. In the absence of any recording equipment, you can always present to a mirror. Check any bad habits, such as waving your arms about or playing with your hair. Seek feedback from others too. It can be helpful to seek the opinion of a non-lawyer as well as from another lawyer.

Think about someone—a lecturer, a colleague, or someone on television who you think presents well. Watch them. What are they doing (or not doing) that makes them so good? Do not make the mistake of thinking what they are doing is spontaneous. It will not be. To be a good presenter takes rigorous practice. It is not by chance that television presenters stand in the correct place, look at the correct camera, and deliver an effortless joke which is absolutely suitable for their target audience. Talented presenters practise. Now think of someone who you consider to be a poor presenter. What are they doing (or not doing)? Why do you think they continue to do this, even as a professional? As with most performance skills, observation and reflection will show you what works and what does not, as well as a reserve of ideas about what will work best for you.

10.4 Advocacy

10.4.1 What does an advocate do?

A barrister or a solicitor can be an advocate. Broadly, an advocate is someone who appears in court to argue her client's case before a judge. As you will no doubt be aware from watching television dramas, the role of an advocate is to persuade the court to find in their client's favour. However, they must be aware at all times that although they represent the client, they do so as an officer of the court. This means that advocates cannot mislead the court to help their client (e.g. by presenting evidence which they know is untrue). They must be ethical and maintain professional standards.

 Practice tip

A reference to **court** may conjure up a specific image in your head. The layperson often thinks of a court as comprising a judge—in full wig and gown—and a jury, all sitting in a room with wooden panels. However, in practice, this is not always the case. Serious criminal offences will be tried before a judge and jury, while less serious offences and most civil cases are heard before a judge sitting alone. Court dress differs depending on the court in question, with full wigs retained mainly for ceremonial purposes. Tribunal judges and magistrates generally wear suits. Many court-rooms are now more modern in decor.

In brief, advocates will:

- present evidence to the court (witnesses can provide evidence in written form or they may attend court to give oral testimony);
- present the relevant law, as it applies to that evidence (referred to as legal submissions). This typically involves inviting the court to apply the law as it was found to be in previously decided cases where the principles are similar to the present case;
- ask the court to find in favour of their client.

10.4.2 What makes a good advocate?

The role of an advocate involves presenting the client's case to the court. The guidance in this chapter on effective communication and presentation skills is very relevant in the context of advocacy. Making good eye contact with the judge, varying the tone of your voice, and speaking clearly, succinctly, and at an appropriate volume and pace (usually the pace at which you would normally speak) are all skills required of an effective advocate.

However, we need to consider some of these skills specifically in the context of advocacy, given that there are some key differences between presenting and being an effective advocate. For example, questions during or after a presentation tend not to be adversarial. With advocacy, however, you can expect someone to be ready to dispute or call into question what you have said.

 Practice tip

Legal work can be categorised as **contentious** or **non-contentious** work. Contentious work involves the resolution of disputes, some of which may result in proceedings in court (or other dispute resolution forums), and non-contentious work does not. As you progress in your legal career, it is usual to find that you prefer one type over the other, however many lawyers do not discover this until they have progressed quite significantly through a training contract or pupillage (and some not even by then).

The practice of corporate and commercial law are examples of non-contentious legal work. Litigation (sometimes called dispute resolution) is clearly an example of contentious work. Some departments can involve both contentious and non-contentious work, such as employment law, where you may be drafting an employment contract (non-contentious) or defending a claim for unfair dismissal (contentious).

Case analysis

This is a skill vital for contentious lawyers, as it provides an analysis of the fundamental aspects of a dispute. It is vital to the preparation for any formal proceedings in a court or other forum, and hence to advocacy. It is also, in relation to your legal studies, an approach which you can apply in developing your problem-solving skills (see Chapter 9).

You need to analyse the facts of your client's case well. You will have to establish what you need to prove, and how you can prove it. This will involve using your legal reading, research, and problem-solving skills (see Chapters 7, 8, and 9) to find not only the relevant law which will help you, but also any relevant law which your opponent may seek to rely on. Thus, part of case analysis involves anticipating your opponent's arguments and planning how you would answer them in favour of your client. Detailed knowledge of any cases or regulations likely to be referred to in court is vital.

Case analysis therefore requires you to identify:

- Who is the claimant?
- Who is the defendant?
- What is the loss that has been suffered?
- What is the relevant law (e.g. contract law or the law of tort)?
- What is the relevant cause of action (e.g. if tort, is it nuisance, trespass, negligence)?
- What are the necessary elements of that law (e.g. with negligence this would include a duty of care, breach of that duty, and causation)?
- How does that law apply to the specific facts of your case?

Example 2

Let's consider an example where there has been a breach of contract and one party (the claimant) considers that it has suffered a loss of around £500,000 due to the breach. This party seeks legal advice on the matter, and its solicitor advises that it has an excellent chance of recovering this amount if they take the other party (the defendant) to court. The defendant then offers the claimant an out of court settlement of £300,000. The claimant refuses. The matter goes to court and the court awards the claimant just £100,000 in damages, and also orders the claimant to pay some court costs. The claimant then considers whether it has a case against its solicitor for damages based on negligent advice. Analysing the case:

- *The claimant* in this negligence action is the claimant in the original breach of contract action, who had suffered a contractual loss and sought advice from its solicitor on how to recover the loss.
- *The defendant* is the solicitor who advised on the claimant's chances of success in litigating the breach of contract.
- *The loss* the claimant has suffered can be estimated as the difference between the £300,000 it was offered to settle (but rejected in the belief that it would receive more by going to court) and the £100,000 (less court costs) it eventually received.
- *The relevant area of law* is the law of tort.
- *The relevant cause of action* is negligence.
- *The necessary elements of that law* are duty of care, breach of that duty, and causation.
- You would then *apply this law* to the specific facts of the question, to establish and explain whether:
  - the defendant solicitor owed the claimant a duty of care;
  - the solicitor breached this duty with the advice given to the claimant;
  - any breach of duty actually caused the claimant to suffer the loss identified above.

As the claimant's advocate your role would be to:

- present the claimant's factual evidence to the court (to satisfy the court that your client did in fact receive clear advice from the defendant to litigate against the other party to the contract); and
- present legal argument to satisfy the court that as a matter of law the claimant is entitled to a remedy in the law of tort, because:
  - the defendant owed the claimant a duty of care;
  - the defendant breached that duty of care by advising the claimant that it had excellent prospects of recovering its entire loss through litigation;
  - the advice to litigate did cause the claimant to suffer the loss identified above.

Preparation

As with a good presenter, good advocates will make the task before them look entirely spontaneous, but it will not have been. Preparation and rehearsal, so that you are familiar with all aspects of your case analysis, are essential if you are to assimilate and process information quickly in court. There will of course be occasions where an opponent raises something that takes you completely by surprise, and you will have to react spontaneously and 'think on your feet'. However, this should be the exception and not the rule.

Court-room etiquette

This is the name for the series of conventions that have developed over time regarding how advocates should present their case in court. They should not detract from your communication skills: the conventions are simply to be learned and adhered to. The most important principles are set out below.

Language

As an advocate you represent your client, but you are not the client. Your role is to submit the relevant law and evidence to the court, not to offer a personal view on the case. Take care that when you make submissions to the court you do not use language which suggests that you have adopted the client's case as your own. In particular, avoid subjective language such as 'I think', 'in my case', and 'in my opinion' and instead learn to adopt objective phrases such as 'it is submitted' and 'it is the claimant's case that'.

How to address the court

How an advocate addresses the judge will depend on the type of judge who is sitting. For example, you should address a District Judge who sits in the county court as Sir or Madam. Typically you should address a High Court or Court of Appeal judge as My Lord or Lady. The website of the Judiciary of England and Wales explains in detail how to address judges (see 'Further reading' at the end of this chapter).

Other advocates should be addressed as 'my friend' or 'my learned friend'.

Dress

Advocates should wear smart, professional attire that is navy blue or black. In criminal courts they must wear a wig and gown, but this is not the case in all courts. You would not require a wig in family court proceedings, and increasingly judges are allowing advocates to remove their wigs during civil cases (especially in the summer months).

The art of persuasion

A significant part of the role of advocates is to persuade the judge, and jury if appropriate, to decide in favour of their client. A good advocate will have the power of persuasion. This is often discussed as if it is an inherent talent. To some degree this is correct. You probably already have some idea whether you are naturally adept at persuading others to see your point of view. If so, then this is a good foundation on which to build in order to be a successful advocate. However, the power of persuasion is really a skilful combination of good communication and presentation skills together with effective case analysis, preparation, and knowledge of court-room etiquette referred to above, all of which can be practised and honed.

Although within the formal setting of a court-room, an advocate will use verbal and non-verbal skills to communicate with the judge, other advocates and, in some cases, a jury. Thus, variation of the voice, correct pace, and eye contact can all be employed. As noted above, these skills are all part of the skill of persuasion: the judge (and jury) need to be able to hear, understand and feel sufficiently confident in what is being said in order to agree with it.

As with presentations, reading out notes will neither engage nor inspire confidence, so is highly unlikely to be persuasive.

Visiting the court

The advocacy employed in most courts and other dispute resolution forums is rarely of the type often portrayed in television and film court-room dramas. To improve your understanding of the skills required of an advocate, and assist you in developing your own advocacy skills (see also 'Mooting' at 10.5), a visit to a court is highly worthwhile.

The vast majority of our courts are open to the public and you should visit at least one during your studies to enhance your understanding of how the law works in practice. Court visits offer you a valuable insight into what practising advocates do on a daily basis. You will be able to observe how lawyers use the law and apply it to the facts of the case, how a judge reaches a conclusion, and the court procedure generally.

You should take care to comply with the rules of the court that you visit. There is a link to a helpful guide to visiting court in 'Further reading' at the end of this chapter. The reception staff and court ushers will be happy to help you when you arrive at the court. You should simply explain that you are a law student and would like to observe the court proceedings.

10.5 Mooting

10.5.1 What is a moot?

A mooting competition, referred to as a moot, is a fictitious court hearing. Generations of law students have used mooting to help them develop both their knowledge of the law and their advocacy skills. It involves presenting to the court the legal arguments that relate to a particular written problem provided to you in advance. Typically, moots are presented as appeals, so you present to an appellate court. This requires you to accept the facts and issues as they are presented in the written problem and focus exclusively on presenting legal arguments (also known as **submissions**). You should aim to participate in a moot during your studies. This is another way you can demonstrate to a prospective employer that you have developed the skills referred to in this chapter. The process of mooting may also reveal to you whether you enjoy contentious work or prefer non-contentious work (see 'Practice Tip' at 10.4.2).

Example 3

Example 2 regarding the negligent solicitor could be presented as a moot problem. You would be given the facts of the problem in writing. Appeal cases are based on an error on a point of law and you would be told what the grounds for the appeal are. If you represent the claimant (now referred to as the appellant because it is bringing the appeal), you need to persuade the Court of Appeal that the judge at first instance made an error in law and should have found in favour of the appellant. If you represent the solicitor defendant (now known as the respondent because it is responding to the appeal), then you need to persuade the Court of Appeal to the contrary.

10.5.2 **How a moot is structured**

You will receive the written moot problem in advance of the moot and you will be told whether you represent the appellant or the respondent. In most national competitions there will be two grounds of appeal, so your team would comprise two people who take one ground each, thus testing team-working skills too (see 12.2). There will be moot rules which need to be carefully observed. These will include rules about how long you have to make your submissions and the maximum number of legal authorities on which you can rely.

You and your partner will then undertake case analysis and preparation, as described above in relation to advocacy. You will research the moot problem and prepare your legal submissions either to support or oppose the grounds of appeal. This will involve deciding which authorities you wish to rely on and why you say they are relevant and binding.

Some moots require you to present a written summary of your submissions (known as a **skeleton argument**) in advance of the moot. A skeleton argument is exactly what the name suggests. It is the bones of the argument and you will put the flesh on those bones through your skilful advocacy in the moot. Typically a skeleton argument will comprise one page that details your basic submissions and the cases or other authorities that you will rely on. You may be asked to take copies of those authorities to the moot for use by the judge and your opponent.

When the moot begins, the team representing the appellant will present their submissions first and answer any questions that the moot judge may have arising out of those submissions. The team representing the respondent will then make their submissions. When they have finished, the team representing the appellant will often be given a very short amount of time to reply to the submissions for the respondent. The moot judge will then give a judgment on the law and, in a competitive moot, declare the team whose submission the court found most persuasive to be the winner.

10.5.3 **Mooting skills**

The judge will be judging your mooting skills, which are very similar to those you require to be an effective advocate, as referred to at 10.4. These include your ability to:

- analyse your case well (including the grounds of appeal);
- work as a team;
- manage your time;
- present your submissions effectively;
- structure your arguments;
- think on your feet;
- use court etiquette.

Note that it does not necessarily follow that the team that succeeds in the appeal will win the moot. One team may have the law on their side, for example.

As with advocacy, case analysis is key. You should pay particular attention to this because it is an area in which students can struggle. If you can show that this is a particular area of strength for your team, you will have a distinct advantage. You can do this in the following way.

- Present authorities which are binding on the moot court.
    - For example, if you are in the Court of Appeal, a decision by the House of Lords or the Supreme Court will bind the court, but a High Court decision will not. There is further guidance about this at 5.2.1.
- Be prepared to summarise the facts of the authority.
- Be able to explain which **principle** of law the authority establishes and why you consider that the authority should be followed or distinguished.
    - Students tend to focus their legal research efforts on trying to find a case with similar **facts**, but as Chapter 8 explains, finding a case which establishes or distinguishes a similar legal **principle** is the key.
- You must read the whole authority and not just the headnote in order to build a persuasive argument.
    - This is critical.
    - The judge or your opponent may highlight passages of a judgment which are less helpful to your client, and you must be able to deal with this.

10.6 Face-to-face communication

Many law programmes offer opportunities to become involved in pro bono schemes or law clinics. A small but growing number offer programmes or modules which involve client-based scenarios or simulations. These programmes offer you valuable experience in developing face-to-face communication skills. These skills are the foundation of the majority of professional relationships, whether with clients or other professionals. The guidance given below is in the context of a lawyer meeting with a client for the first time. If any of your law programme activities involve you in meeting real-life clients, you will be able to employ the various techniques described. Similarly, if you undertake work experience or a placement, you will be very likely at least to see these skills in practice, if not practise some yourself. Note that much of the above can also be said in relation to the telephone communication skills discussed at 10.7.

If you do not have any of the above opportunities during your studies, the guidance shows you how you can focus on practising skills such as listening and note-taking, so that when the time comes to meet a client for the first time, you will find the process easier. It will also develop your understanding of the communication skills which are important for developing professional relationships: this understanding and any relevant experience, in any context, is a topic frequently explored in job interviews. While the guidance below is set in the context of a first meeting between a lawyer and client, it goes without saying that the communication skills employed are applicable to face-to-face meetings in a range of other professional contexts.

10.6.1 **First meeting: introduction**

Your first meeting with any client is pivotal. If you make a good impression, this could be the basis of a long and mutually beneficial working relationship. If you make a poor impression, you are unlikely to see them again, and may have damaged your own and your employer's reputation. As you gain experience, first meetings will come naturally to you and you may vary more the particular structure or format employed. However, experience shows that as a student practising this skill, or trainee or junior lawyer trying it for the first time in practice, it can be helpful to follow a structure to ensure that you remember everything you need to do. This will free you to concentrate on listening to clients and communicating well with them. The flowchart at Figure 10.2 breaks down the meeting into manageable sections and will help you to structure your meeting logically. You can annotate it and take it into a meeting with you. The following commentary will help you to think about how you can communicate best at each stage. (Note that before qualification this skill is often referred to as 'interviewing and advising'. However this focuses exclusively on what the lawyer is doing and does not really capture the point that the client plays a pivotal role too. Few practising lawyers would refer to 'interviewing' a client, except in very specific circumstances.)

Most clients will be meeting you in the hope that you can solve a legal problem for them. The guidance set out in Chapters 8 and 9 is therefore relevant here too. Remember that Chapter 11 provides guidance about how to communicate with a client in writing. The guidance below focuses on a face-to-face first meeting with a client of a law firm, but as noted in the introduction to this paragraph, much of it transfers equally well to other professions and activities.

10.6.2 **Prepare for the meeting**

Preparation is essential for any professional meeting: any failure to understand either the objectives of meeting, the issues involved, and the subject matter in question, will become very obvious to any other party involved. As the objective of the current meeting is to advise a client with a legal problem, you should analyse what you know about the problem in advance of the meeting, identify the relevant facts, and find all relevant law (subject of course to any instructions and considerations about incurring costs).

Without suggesting that you read from a script in the interview itself—this would severely inhibit rapport between you and the client—you can and should prepare many aspects of the first client meeting in advance. Examples of questions are given below, but you can think of others which reflect your own personal style.

10.6.3 **Begin the meeting**

As with a presentation, the beginning of a meeting is crucial. The client will form an immediate impression and you want it to be a good one. You should arrive on time and be professional and confident from the outset, to reassure the client that she is in good hands and has chosen her adviser wisely. The client may also be nervous at this stage, so do what you can to put her at ease. A question about her journey to your office, or the weather, and taking

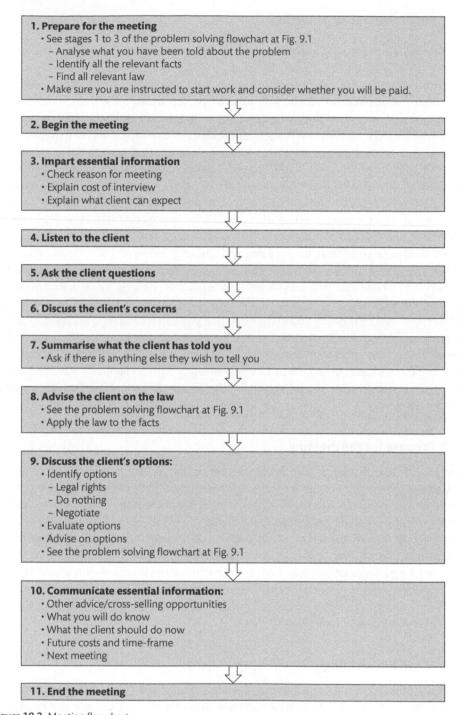

1. Prepare for the meeting
- See stages 1 to 3 of the problem solving flowchart at Fig. 9.1
  - Analyse what you have been told about the problem
  - Identify all the relevant facts
  - Find all relevant law
- Make sure you are instructed to start work and consider whether you will be paid.

2. Begin the meeting

3. Impart essential information
- Check reason for meeting
- Explain cost of interview
- Explain what client can expect

4. Listen to the client

5. Ask the client questions

6. Discuss the client's concerns

7. Summarise what the client has told you
- Ask if there is anything else they wish to tell you

8. Advise the client on the law
- See the problem solving flowchart at Fig. 9.1
- Apply the law to the facts

9. Discuss the client's options:
- Identify options
  - Legal rights
  - Do nothing
  - Negotiate
- Evaluate options
- Advise on options
- See the problem solving flowchart at Fig. 9.1

10. Communicate essential information:
- Other advice/cross-selling opportunities
- What you will do know
- What the client should do now
- Future costs and time-frame
- Next meeting

11. End the meeting

Figure 10.2 Meeting flowchart

time to listen to her answer while using appropriate body language, can help her to settle in to what may be an unfamiliar or even intimidating environment for her.

It is at this stage that you will set the tone for your meeting, and establish a rapport with the client. It can be difficult to judge how formal or informal to be with clients before you know them well. You are aiming to behave professionally, and if you are over-familiar, or not familiar enough, this will fall short of professional behaviour. As a general rule, it is good advice to start on the more formal side. It is easier to do this, then become more familiar, than to start off in a way the client considers to be over-familiar and then have to recover from that position. Apply this to how you address the client. If you begin with 'Mr', 'Mrs' or 'Miss', say, Shephard, they can always reply 'please call me Catherine'. This is much more comfortable than the alternative, where you greet the client as Catherine and she replies, 'please call me Miss Shephard', which can cause an awkwardness that can distract. Make a mental note of the name the client wishes to be called, use that name throughout the meeting, and note it on the client file for future reference.

Remember that you need to introduce yourself. Clearly state your name, and your status or role.

10.6.4 Impart essential information

There are a few essential pieces of information which, for practical reasons or to fulfil your ethical and professional conduct obligations, you must deal with at a very early stage of the meeting.

Double-check the client's reason for the meeting

First, you must make sure that you are the right person to help this client, by checking why she has come to see you. Usually when clients book their first appointment they will give whoever they are speaking to at the firm an idea of why they need an appointment. However, misunderstandings can occur at this stage and so it is always worth checking why the client is there. The potential downside to this is that the client might take this as a cue to tell you absolutely everything about the issue she has come to see you about. You should manage this risk by closing the question, such as 'I understand you have come to see me today with a view to setting up a business, is that right?' By structuring your sentence in this way you are encouraging the client to answer simply 'yes' or 'no'.

 Essential explanation

A **closed question** is one that can be answered with the word 'yes' or 'no'. An **open question** is exactly what the name would suggest, a question which leaves it open to the client how to answer the question. Asking open questions followed by closed questions is known as the **funnel down** technique. Conversely asking closed questions followed by open questions is known as the **funnel up** approach.

Explain the cost of the meeting

The next information you must give to the client is about the cost of the meeting. Some firms do not charge for first meeting, in which case you can say this. However, assuming your firm is charging, then for ethical and practical reasons the client needs the opportunity to walk away at an early stage, and you also need to fulfil your obligations in this regard under the **Solicitors Code of Conduct**.

Many lawyers can feel embarrassed talking about costs at all, but particularly early on. They think it can give the (false) impression that they are only concerned about money and not about helping the client with the law. This is interesting, because client feedback often reflects the exact opposite, namely that clients think lawyers focus overly on the technicalities of the law at the expense of client service, which includes giving information about costs. Think also about whether lawyers' fears about discussing costs are actually well founded. When you go into a shop, you do not wait until you reach the checkout before you know what you have to pay. You know before you select the product from the shelf, because the seller will have clearly labelled it with its price. Similarly, when you go to the dentist, he does not say I will fill your tooth and then we can discuss what it will cost. He will tell you beforehand, so you can make an informed choice as to whether to have your tooth filled or not. So, the client will expect you to discuss what the meeting will cost, and to discuss it before the meeting is in full swing.

You should explain that you charge on a time basis. Then let the client know your hourly rate and how long you expect the meeting will last. This will allow you to provide an estimate for the cost of the meeting. You then need to ask the client if she is happy to proceed on that basis. The client is now in an informed position as to whether she wishes to pay for your advice or not, before you have given it.

 Essential explanation

The **Solicitors Regulation Authority**, which regulates the profession, publishes a **Code of Conduct** which solicitors must follow. Chapter 1 of the Code sets out obligations regarding client care. It includes obligations about fee arrangements, including discussing with clients whether the outcome will justify the expense and risks, clearly explaining your fees, warning clients about other fees for which they will be responsible, and providing this information in a clear and accessible form. Students learn about this Code during their vocational stage of training, but useful information can be found on the SRA website (see 'Further reading' at the end of this chapter).

Explain what the client can expect to happen in the meeting

Finally, remember that while you have a clear idea of what will happen in the meeting, the client may not. It can be helpful in terms of reassuring the client and building rapport just to give her a brief outline of what will (e.g. you will listen to what she has to say, ask a few questions, consider the issue and give some advice which you will follow up in writing) and will not (e.g. decide to go to court, make any final decision) happen in your meeting.

10.6.5 **Listen to the client**

You are now ready to listen to the client's issue. It is a good idea to use the funnel down technique for this (see 'Essential explanation' at 10.6.4). As discussed, lawyers have a tendency to pre-empt what a client is about to say. This is not helpful, because the lawyer must give accurate, tailored advice on the client's actual issue, rather than the issue the lawyer thinks the client has. Consider, for example, a client who mentions he has come to see you about a partnership. It is impossible to pre-empt what the client wants at this stage. He may want to set up a partnership, exit from a partnership, or even enter into a civil partnership. Remember that everyone likes to be listened to, so do not think the client will be wondering why you are not speaking. He will enjoy being given the opportunity to explain his issue fully to you.

Prepare a good open question, for example 'Now please could you tell me about the issue you have come to see me about today', to signal to the client that this is his cue to tell you everything. Use your active listening techniques, discussed earlier (see 10.1.3), to encourage the client to continue to speak. You may need to practise your 'poker face', as clients can sometimes disclose information at this stage that is unexpected, salacious, or downright alarming, but you must maintain a professional demeanour at all times.

You will want to take notes, but bear in mind that this can inhibit rapport and may also prevent you from properly digesting what the client is saying (think of taking notes in a lecture and not knowing what you have written about until you read them through after the lecture). Depending on the complexity of the information being imparted at this stage, it can be a good idea to resist taking notes at the very start. If you must take notes at this stage, try to make sure you do so in a way which avoids these problems.

Do not interrupt the client. At best, you will come across as rude; at worst you may prevent the client from telling you a pivotal fact. If, on reflection, you think that you have a tendency to interrupt, then resisting the urge to do this is something you can practise in your conversations with friends and family.

10.6.6 Ask the client questions

When the client has answered your initial open question, you will probably need to ask further questions. Following the funnel down technique, you should continue to ask open questions to begin with, and then move on to closed questions. Good open questions are:

'Could you tell me some more about ...?'
'What in particular is the problem with ...?'
'How does everyone else feel about ...?'

The reason for the funnel down approach is that it should capture more information. For example, if you ask the closed question, 'Are you worried because of X?', then a client may say yes. However, if you had asked the more open question, 'Why are you worried?', the client may answer 'X, Y, and Z'. The closed question did not reveal the existence of Y and Z, but the open question did. Y and Z might be absolutely crucial in determining the advice to give.

Also bear in mind that your client is unlikely to be the only person involved in the issue. You need to remember to ask questions about other people, who they are, whether they are in a position of strength or weakness, and how they might affect your client's position. Be inquisitive and explore all aspects of what the client has told you. You can adopt good habits now of asking questions of people rather than talking about yourself (which many lawyers are guilty of). You may be surprised by the results.

You should start to take notes at this stage if you have not already. You may think that you will remember all the information until you return to your desk, but frequently you will be diverted into something else on the way back, and by the time you do return to your desk your head will be full of other information. Chapter 11 provides some guidance as to how to

only need to explain the options carefully, but you should also be clear about the advantages and disadvantages of each option (see 9.3.3). Only then can you help the client to choose the option that suits him best (see 9.3.4). The problem-solving model at Figure 9.1 will help you with this.

10.6.11 **Communicate essential information at the end**

Once again, you need to remember to impart some information towards the end of the meeting for both ethical and practical reasons, and to meet your professional conduct obligations.

Can your firm help with anything else?

Chapter 15 explains that a law firm is a business, and you should recognise that having a new client in front of you is a business development opportunity. This is a key chance, if appropriate, to 'cross-sell' the services of another department, or to obtain some further work from the client for your department. Use this stage of the meeting to:

- enquire whether the client has any other issue that he would like to discuss with a solicitor (e.g. if you have just advised on business acquisition, does the client need advice with more personal matters such as a will);

- discuss anything the client has raised at the meeting which you think may merit further attention from a legal perspective (e.g. if you have just advised on a business acquisition of a property rental company, you might ask if the client is interested in being introduced to your talented property law colleague).

 Practice tip

Firms are very keen to encourage **cross-selling**. This is where a solicitor in one department in the firm identifies and takes opportunities to promote to clients the work done by solicitors in other departments of the firm. Historically, partners' profit-sharing arrangements did not motivate partners to do this, as a partner in one department would see no personal benefit if a partner in another department brought in more fees. In fact, sometimes this could jeopardise a partner's position, as by promoting the success of a colleague, the partner risked looking less productive. Unbelievably, this led to situations where, for example, a large insurance company client of the property team may not have even been aware that the firm had expertise in advising on insurance law. However, cross-selling is now encouraged and often incentivised.

Let the client know what you will do now

You will always follow up the first client meeting with a letter, confirming the advice you gave in the meeting, following up anything else you promised to deliver and reminding the client of anything you need from him. Tell the client this; it will reassure and impress him. It is worth checking the client's contact details at this stage, and how he prefers to be contacted.

Let the client know what he should do now

Even though you will include this in your letter, remind the client now of anything he needs to do. If he agreed to meet someone with a view to attempting to negotiate a matter himself, make sure he is clear as to what he needs to do and when. Be clear about any deadlines in relation to anything he has agreed to do.

Discuss future costs and time frame

You need to link this back to the options you discussed earlier in the meeting. It is unlikely that the client will have selected a firm option at this stage, but if he has, you can tie your time frame and costs estimate into that. If the client has yet to choose a way forward, then go through each option and give your best estimate. If you do not have enough information to come up with a meaningful estimate at this stage, remind the client of your hourly rate and that you will keep him up to date with the costs incurred in the meantime.

Discuss your next meeting

It may be that the client has decided to do nothing further for the moment, in which case you will not need a next meeting. However, if a meeting is needed, then now is a good opportunity to be proactive and discuss when and where might be appropriate.

10.6.12 **End the meeting**

Just as it is important to create a good first impression, it is also important to leave the client with a good lasting impression. Bring the meeting to an end within your estimated time frame, if at all possible. If the meeting overruns, this will have costs implications. Be clear, both verbally and with your body language, that the meeting is coming to an end. Give a firm handshake, make good eye contact, and walk with your client back to reception. Part with a closing comment about how pleased you are to have met the client, and make sure he has your name and contact details by giving him your business card.

10.7 **Communicating by telephone**

Much of the guidance of how to communicate face to face applies equally when communicating by telephone. However, it is worth giving some consideration specifically to the skills required to develop a professional telephone manner.

10.7.1 **Why telephone skills are important**

Notwithstanding that text messaging and email may have overtaken telephone conversations as a way of communicating in your personal life, and the internet enables a panoply of bookings to be made that would previously have been made by telephone, telephone skills remain important in developing professional relationships and providing services. They are skills required by trainees and junior lawyers from day one. It is common for many first interviews to take place and initial instructions to be given by telephone. It is also a means by which transactions and matters are progressed, either on a one-to-one or telephone conference basis.

In light of this, take every opportunity to practise a professional telephone manner; complaints tend to remain the preserve of telephone call centres rather than being dealt with online, so next time you make a complaint, see if you can distinguish yourself by making your point clearly and firmly yet politely.

Try not to become too dependent on email. It may feel like an easy way of avoiding having to think on your feet, but the fact is that some matters are better handled by speaking to a client. Delivering an unpalatable message, such as that you are not going to meet a deadline, is the kind of matter that it is tempting to deal with by email so that you do not have to deal with the client's immediate reaction. However, it is precisely this kind of issue which is better handled by telephone. It is much easier to avoid errors in tone by telephone; emails can often be misconstrued and if the subject matter is delicate this can be exacerbated. Also, if you can call a client to deliver an unpalatable message, you will demonstrate to that client that you are an honest and confident lawyer with good communication skills, and most clients will appreciate this.

10.7.2 Begin and end a call with confidence

This sounds obvious, and again it is not complicated, but it is commonly performed quite poorly.

If you are making a call, introduce yourself properly, stating clearly and in an appropriate tone who you are, the capacity in which you are calling, and the reason for your call.

If answering a call, the common practice is to give your name along with the greeting. You will find that many firms encourage all their employees to answer with a uniform greeting, and to pick up within a certain number of rings. You may also be expected to pick up a colleague's telephone if it has been ringing without being answered.

When ending a call, make sure everyone is clear what needs to happen after the call, that everyone has the contact details they need, and that you leave a good impression.

Listen to how the professionals you encounter (on work experience, during pro bono work, and suchlike) do this, and emulate those you are impressed by.

10.7.3 Listening skills

The importance of these skills is set out at 10.1.3. On the telephone, it is more difficult to demonstrate that you are actively listening. When the other person is talking, particularly if she is providing a series of facts, the occasional 'yes', 'okay', or 'mm-hmm', provided it is not obtrusive, indicates that you are listening and taking in what is being said. The other aspect of listening skills on telephone calls is that not interrupting, and responding appropriately, become even more crucial.

10.7.4 Tone

We have already explored the effect of first impressions. On the telephone, your voice will be the thing you are judged on, so consider what impression you want to give, and make sure your tone conveys this. This is particularly important when recording your voicemail greeting. So many people sound at best flat and indifferent, and at worst cold and hostile. It may sound trite, but if you smile while you record your message, this will come through in that message.

10.7.5 **Clarity**

Ensure you pace your speech carefully and avoid jargon. Mobile telephones can also present problems in this regard. If the caller comes in and out of range, and you cannot hear properly, do not be embarrassed to say that you really cannot hear her. This is one instance where it is professional to interrupt.

10.7.6 **Taking a telephone message**

If you do pick up a telephone for colleagues, take care about what you might imply about them. Saying that they are still at lunch, or you do not know where they are, or that they have not arrived at the office yet, may be true but the caller may draw adverse inferences. It is standard practice simply to say 'I'm sorry, X is not at his desk at the moment, can I help you or would you like to leave a message?' If you take a message, make sure you take the caller's full name (ask her to spell it if necessary), the capacity in which she is calling, her contact details, the time she called, and establish what she is expecting in terms of a response and by when. If the client opts to ask you to help instead, do not be afraid to say that you do not know something but you can find out.

10.7.7 **Call processing skills**

How adept you are at using the features of a telephone will impact on how professional the caller perceives you to be. Dropping callers while transferring them is particularly frustrating for them. If you do not know how to operate the telephone system, ask someone to show you as soon as possible. As a minimum you should learn how to pick up a call that is not being answered, how to transfer a call, and how to join another caller into a conference call.

 ## Summary

- Communication skills are fundamental, both in education and employment.
- Communication skills include verbal and non-verbal communication skills, listening skills, and having confidence.
- Always consider the effect of your communication from the other person's perspective.
- You will need good communication skills when delivering presentations, as an advocate, when mooting, meeting clients and other professionals, and talking by telephone.
- First impressions and last impressions are particularly important.
- Communication skills are basic skills, but they are often forgotten in times of stress, which is often when you need them most.
- Clients may make the decision as to whether to give further instructions based upon their experience of their lawyer's communication skills.

What the professionals say

What do I value in a lawyer? As a client I expect all of our professional advisers to understand our business and to use their expertise to provide advice tailored to us and our strategic vision. I'm looking for the ability to listen, to work together to solve problems and create solutions, and to advise clearly and concisely in a way that resonates with me and on which I can act. For lawyers particularly to become 'go to' trusted advisers, they not only have to know the law, that's a given, but they also need the skills to deploy that knowledge effectively. It shouldn't be a chore to speak to a lawyer or to understand what they are advising, and if it is, clients will vote with their feet.

Chris Morris, CEO at The LateRooms Group

 ## Thought-provoking questions

1. What do you do in terms of body language that you need to pay attention to? What effect might this have on your communication skills?

2. Have you ever asserted your consumer rights? Did you achieve your aim? Having read this chapter, is there anything you would do differently next time?

3. What is your preferred learning style? What would you do in a presentation to make sure you appealed to those in the audience who have a different learning style from you?

4. Who do you admire for their communication skills? Can you articulate precisely what it is that they do that you admire? Is this transferable into what you do now, as a student, or will do later, as a professional?

 ## Further reading

P. Honey and A. Mumford, *The Manual of Learning Styles* **(Maidenhead: P. Honey, 1986)**
– a useful source of further information on learning styles (see 10.3.4).

D. Kolb, *Experiential Learning: Experience as the Source of Learning and Development* **(Englewood Cliffs, NJ: Prentice Hall, 1984)**
–a useful source of further information if you wish to explore your own preferred learning style.

Judiciary of England and Wales website: http://www.judiciary.gov.uk
–a useful resource for students who wish to learn more about court etiquette (see 10.4.2).

Solicitors Regulation Authority website: http://www.sra.org.uk/solicitors/handbook/code
–contains a wide range of material for students and trainees but if you navigate to the 'For solicitors' section you can familiarise yourself with SRA Code of Conduct (see 10.6.2).

Andrew Gillespie, *The English Legal System* **(Oxford: OUP, 4th edn, 2013) Online Resource Centre: http://www.oup.com/uk/orc/law/els/gillespie_els4e/**
–visit the Online Resource Centre and click 'Visiting Court' under 'Student Activities' for useful tips that you can use in planning your first court visit (see 10.4.2).

David Pope and Dan Hill, *Mooting and Advocacy Skills* **(London: Sweet & Maxwell, 2nd edn, 2011)**
–a helpful short mooting and advocacy guide (see 10.4 and 10.5).

 For the authors' reflections on the thought-provoking questions, additional self-test questions, podcasts offering a variety of perspectives on legal systems and skills, and a library of links to useful websites, visit the free Online Resource Centre at **http://www.oxfordtextbooks.co.uk/orc/slorach/.**

Presentation skills

17

INTRODUCTION

This chapter will draw upon some of the material covered in previous sections of the book that focused upon helping you to locate and understand the law (Part 1) in order to prepare and deliver an effective oral presentation. This will start by outlining some guidelines on preparing a presentation, including selecting an appropriate topic and making decisions about the use of supplementary materials such as handouts or PowerPoint slides. The chapter will then move to consider issues relating to the delivery of the presentation, including matters such as timing, combating nerves, and engaging the interest of the audience.

Many students are reluctant to give an oral presentation. For some students, this aversion is so extreme that they will avoid taking optional subjects that include a compulsory presentation element, even if the subject is otherwise one that they would like to study. These feelings are entirely natural; an oral presentation focuses the attention of many people on a single person which makes it a very nerve-wracking situation even for otherwise confident students. However, the ability to present information orally is a core skill for most professionals, not just those working within the law, so it is essential that you overcome any qualms about addressing others. Like anything else, the prospect of giving a presentation is daunting only until you know that you can do it proficiently. Many people are not natural speakers and will always quail at the thought of addressing even a small audience, but the fear does recede with practice so it would be extremely valuable if part of your university development included some attempts to overcome your anxiety about public speaking. This is particularly important given the growing tendency amongst prospective employers to require a presentation from applicants for work placements and training contracts. This chapter aims to equip you to prepare and deliver an easy-to-follow and engaging presentation.

LEARNING OUTCOMES

After studying this chapter, you will be able to:

- Select an appropriate topic that fits within the constraints of your course

- Conduct effective research into your presentation topic

- Construct an organized and flowing presentation

- Prepare some appropriate visual aids and use them effectively

- Understand the importance of practising the presentation

- Deal with common problems associated with nerves

- Deliver a comprehensive and engaging presentation

- Take questions from the audience with confidence

- Reflect upon your performance in order to strengthen future presentations

17.1 The presentation process

For most people faced with the need to deliver a presentation, the focus is on the actual delivery of the material. It is usual to think of 'the presentation' as the time-slot in which the material is communicated to the audience. Whilst this is clearly an important time, most of the work required for an effective presentation will be complete before you get to your feet in front of your audience. Planning and preparation are essential prerequisites of a good presentation and yet this 'behind the scenes' activity tends to receive very little attention.

Most students accept that they have to do *something* before standing up and speaking, but there seems to be general uncertainty as to what form this preparation might take and how exactly it prepares you to speak for the required amount of time.

One of the problems seems to be that students omit an essential stage of presentation preparation, treating it as a two-stage process (see Figure 17.1).

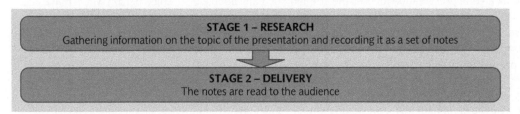

Figure 17.1 Two-stage presentation process

Although this approach does serve the purpose of transmitting the information to the audience, this is not necessarily packaged in a particularly palatable form. In fact, many student presentations are extremely boring because of the way in which the material is delivered: listening to someone read their notes for ten minutes is not in the least engaging for the audience and it can be very off-putting for the presenter to look around and see a distracted and bored audience.

To overcome these problems, it is valuable to insert a further stage in between research and delivery (see Figure 17.2).

As you will see, by inserting a middle step in the process, the end stage is also different and as a result the presentation is far more engaging for the audience.

It is important to consider a fourth stage that takes place after the presentation is complete. This stage involves a period of review in which the presenter takes stock of the way in which the presentation was received and seeks to identify examples of good and bad practice. The reflection stage maximizes the learning impact of the presentation and should enable you to strengthen future performances (see Figure 17.3).

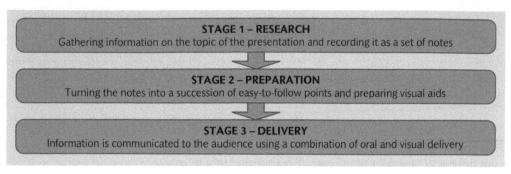

Figure 17.2 Three-stage presentation process

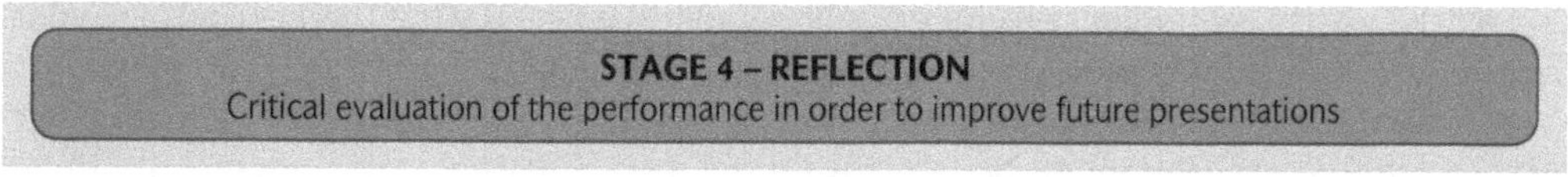

Figure 17.3 The reflection stage

Each of these stages will now be considered in turn to guide you through the process of preparing, constructing, and delivering a presentation as well as providing comment on the reflection stage.

17.2 Research stage

It is always tempting to see the delivery of the presentation itself—the end product—as being of primary importance. After all, it is this that determines the success (or otherwise) of the presentation, irrespective of whether success is measured in terms of the response of the audience or, in the case of an assessed presentation, the mark awarded. However, an effective end product is only possible if the groundwork has been done properly; it is for this reason that the 'five Ps' are often used to emphasize the importance of the pre-delivery stages of a presentation (see Figure 17.4).

Figure 17.4 The 'five Ps'

17.2.1 Choosing a topic

In some instances, particularly if the presentation is part of assessed coursework or is a compulsory non-assessed part of a course, the topic of the presentation will be allocated to you. Although this gives you no scope to choose your subject matter, it does ensure that you have a workable presentation topic that gives you a clear direction for your research. This means the topic 'fits' within the time allocated (or is capable of 'fitting' within it), that there is sufficient material available for you to research the topic, and that it is sufficiently linked to the relevant course material.

In the absence of a predetermined topic, you will have to choose an area of law upon which to base your presentation. This can be a tricky business as the success or otherwise of your presentation may depend upon the choice of subject matter, so give it some serious thought and take the following factors into account.

17.2.1.1 Time frame

Choosing an appropriate topic will depend upon the time frame available for your presentation: obviously, a greater level of detail is expected in a forty-five-minute presentation than would be the case in a ten-minute slot at the start of a tutorial. Never try to cram too much information into the time available. Content overload is a major weakness in a presentation as it tends to leave the audience reeling; it is better to leave material out than to overload your audience with too much information delivered at high speed.

For example, if you have to deliver a thirty-five-minute presentation on employment law, your initial decision might be to focus on sex discrimination. After some preliminary research, you are likely to discover that this is too broad to cover in this time frame. You will therefore need to select a smaller issue such as pregnancy-related dismissals or discrimination on the basis of sexual orientation. It may help to phrase your presentation title as a question—for example, 'how effective has the English law been in protecting postoperative transsexual people from discrimination?' and ask your lecturer if they feel that the topic will fit within the time frame of the presentation. If your lecturer offers an opinion on the breadth of your topic, do take this into account; they have a clearer idea of the material available and the amount of detail that is appropriate for the time frame of the presentation. Setting the boundaries of your presentation too wide or too narrow can have adverse consequences on its overall success.

- **Too wide:** you will struggle to fit all the information into the time available, so will end up either rushing your delivery, leaving out relevant material, or taking too superficial an approach
- **Too narrow:** you will run out of things to say or fill up time by repeating points or including superfluous material that weakens the focus of the presentation

17.2.1.2 Assessment criteria

If the presentation is assessed, students should check the assessment criteria to determine what attributes are regarded as important and what weight is given to them. Is there an equal emphasis on both content and presentation style, for example, and is there any credit available for the use of visual aids?

This can be useful in helping you to select a topic. For example, if credit is available for demonstrating independent research skills, selecting a topic that is covered in detail in the textbook is not going to enable you to demonstrate this skill, so your presentation will not attract a great deal of credit for this element. It may help to make a list of the desirable characteristics of a successful presentation from the assessment criteria and note how your topic will satisfy these characteristics.

It is essential that you know what you are aiming to do and even if it feels as if the answer is to 'survive the presentation', the ultimate answer will probably be to 'get a good mark in the presentation'; the latter is more likely if you have the assessment criteria in mind from the outset.

17.2.1.3 Aim

Make sure that you are clear about what you are trying to achieve in your presentation. If you have been given a title, what does it suggest about the aim of your presentation? Is it to introduce the topic, to give an overview, or to deal with a particular issue in depth? If you are unclear, seek clarification from your course materials or by asking your lecturer.

If you have free rein to select your own topic, it will add focus to your presentation and make the preparation process easier if you identify a clear aim to be achieved by your presentation. Keep this to the forefront of your mind when researching and planning your presentation. When delivering it, remember to tell your audience what your aim is from the outset as this will give them clear guidance on what to expect from your presentation.

17.2.1.4 Audience

Although you may have subjective aims in mind when delivering a presentation, such as obtaining a good mark, not looking foolish in front of your friends, or impressing a prospective employer, the predominant aim of any presentation is to communicate something of value to the audience. To be able to do this, you need to have some idea of what the audience wants, needs, or expects from your presentation. In other words, in order to choose a appropriate topic and select content at a suitable level, you need to understand how much your audience already knows about the subject matter.

If you are presenting to your peer group as part of an assessment, you have the advantage of knowing exactly what level of prior knowledge they have about your topic and this will help you to select an appropriate level of depth. Equally, your assessment may specify the level of expertise of your audience by providing instructions such as 'imagine you have been asked to deliver a thirty-minute presentation to senior partners at your law firm that updates them on a recent development in employment law' which will help you to determine what sort of depth is required and this in turn will be useful in selecting an appropriate topic.

17.2.1.5 Available material

You will need to make sure that there is sufficient source material available to enable you to research your presentation topic thoroughly. This means that you need to be able to identify a range of source books, articles, reports, and cases on your chosen topic and be able to obtain them in good time to prepare for your presentation. The increasing availability of online resources may help here, but remember the importance of ensuring that material that you encounter online comes from a reputable academic or professional source.

You will find some valuable guidance on evaluating the source of online materials contained in chapter 7. Remember that anyone can post anything on the Internet, so you should not rely on material for academic purposes unless it comes from a reputable source.

17.2.1.6 Interest and popularity

If you have free choice, it is also useful to take into account any interests of your own within the subject as it is always easier to research something that interests you and your enthusiasm for the topic will communicate to the audience, making your presentation more engaging.

It can also be sensible to take into account any information you have about the choice of topic made by other students. This can be significant if there is an entirely free choice of topic for an assessed presentation as it will be difficult to make your treatment of a topic seem original and interesting if it covers the same material as ten other students have already presented. In short, overlap with topics chosen by others will make your presentation seem uninspired even if it is the result of a great deal of hard work and independent research. If you are committed to presenting on a popular topic, try to find an unusual slant on the material.

17.2.2 Researching the topic

Once you have a clear idea of the topic of the presentation, you can start with the research.

17.2.2.1 Start early

Try to leave as much time as possible to do this before the presentation date in case it is difficult to acquire of some of the material that you need. That said, it is also important to know when to stop the research and start the construction of the presentation as both take time and both make an important contribution to the finished product. Aim for a roughly equal division of the time available between research and construction; you can always go back to research if you find you have overlooked something once you start to put the presentation together.

17.2.2.2 Be focused yet flexible

Achieve a good balance between keeping your focus and being receptive to new material. If your topic was allocated to you, there is far less flexibility to pursue different avenues of research but if you have some element of choice, take some time to follow up potentially interesting side-issues as they may change for the better the slant of your presentation. Remember, however, that if you change the focus of your presentation, you will need to change the title to reflect this. If you were required to submit a title in advance, you should check to find out whether changes are permissible.

17.2.2.3 Be effective in your note-taking

Remember, there is little to be gained by copying reams of material from books and journals, but do ensure that you have a clear and complete record of the sources you have used. Although you are presenting your material orally, you may still be required to produce a bibliography or a research journal and, of course, you may wish to include quotations or extracts from these sources on any handout that you produce to accompany your presentation, in which case you will need to be able to provide full bibliographic details.

In particular, you should take care to keep a note of any ideas you have during the research process about how the material could be used in the presentation. Try to devise a note-taking strategy that allows you to differentiate between factual material and your ideas, for example by dividing your page into two columns or by using different coloured ink to highlight your thoughts.

You will find more information on note-taking in chapter 9 that deals with study skills.

17.3 Preparation stage

Once you have conducted your research into your presentation topic, you will probably feel somewhat overwhelmed (a) by the volume of material that you have gathered, and (b) by the prospect of turning it into a presentation. These feelings are not unusual, but can lead to two of the key issues that limit the effectiveness of student presentations:

1. trying to cover too much information in the time available; and,
2. reading from a set of notes that are not suited to oral delivery.

Both of these problems can be resolved by judicious selection of material and by planning a structured presentation that is not exclusively reliant upon oral delivery but which makes use of visual aids.

17.3.1 Selection of material

It is always tempting, having devoted time and effort to conducting research, to try to make use of all the interesting facts that you have discovered. However, it is important to ensure that you do not exceed the time allocated for your presentation: in fact, if the presentation is assessed, you may actually lose marks for failing to work within the time frame stipulated. Equally, a hurried presentation that skims over a great deal of material is very difficult for the audience to follow and is likely to be a negative factor if your presentation is assessed.

Formulating a question that you will answer in your presentation is a good way to identify your focus and select relevant material as it tends to identify the 'job' that the presentation is trying to do. Once you are clear about what you are trying to achieve, you can sift through all the material you have gathered in order to eliminate that which is not relevant. As with essay writing, remember to judge the relevance of material in relation to the issue, not the topic: in other words, try not to think 'is this about provocation?' or even 'is this about the reasonable man in provocation?' but rather 'does this help me to explain the policy of the law towards the characteristics attributable to the reasonable man in provocation?'. The more specific you are in framing your issue, the easier you will find it to decide whether material is relevant.

Practical exercise

The following exercise can be used to help you determine the relevance of the material to your presentation.

1. Write your title at the top of a blank sheet of paper (or at the start of a new document).
2. Make a bullet point list of all the points that you could include.
3. Review the list, grouping similar points together and eliminating any repetition or overlap.
4. Draw three columns headed: essential, peripheral, and irrelevant and allocate each of your points to one of the columns, remembering that the question of relevance is determined by reference to the specific details of your presentation title and not to the general topic of the presentation.
5. Use this as guidance when determining the content of your presentation, starting with material that you have categorized as essential. If you still feel that you have too much information, you should repeat the exercise, this time using the three columns to divide up the points that you initially categorized as essential.

 A worked example of this technique can be found on the Online Resource Centre. You might find it useful to take a few moments to look at this example and read the accompanying notes to ensure that you have a good insight into the prioritization of the material.

17.3.2 Organization of material

Once you have made a preliminary selection of the material you want to include in the presentation, you need to consider the order in which your points will be made. Bear in mind that your presentation should follow a logical progression, it should 'tell a story' and, like all good essays, it should have a beginning (introduction), middle (the bulk of the presentation, divided into a series of issues), and an end (conclusion) (see Figure 17.5).

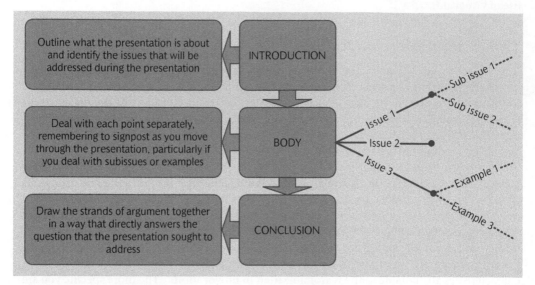

Figure 17.5 Organizing the material

17.3.2.1 Introduction

The introduction and conclusion should be succinct, clear, and straightforward. The introduction should outline the topic to be discussed, explain the structure and duration of the presentation (including any time allocated for questions at the end), and tell the audience why the topic is important and/or interesting. In essence, the introduction should give the audience an understanding of what is to follow and give a clear and concise account of the question that the presentation will address and the reason that this is important.

17.3.2.2 Main body

The body of the presentation can be more complicated to organize, so keep in mind the argument that you are going to advance and break this down into a series of issues and subissues. Bear in mind that one point should lead into another and that you should take care to select examples that demonstrate the point you are making and do not distract from the flow of your presentation. You may want to experiment with more than one potential structure to ensure that you find the most effective way to organize your material.

For the audience listening to the presentation, there are two tasks that need to be carried out simultaneously. First, the listeners have to digest the point you are making and, secondly, they have to slot this into the bigger picture of the topic as a whole. This can be difficult, so it is essential that you help your audience to follow the structure of the presentation with clear signposting; phrases such as 'there are three points of importance here and I shall discuss each in turn' or 'this is a powerful argument but there is an equally compelling counterargument that we must now consider'. Signposting explains to the audience how each piece of information relates to that which precedes and follows it and how it fits into the broader topic, so it is an important consideration and one which can contribute to the success of your presentation.

17.3.2.3 Conclusion

The conclusion should provide a brief summary of the material covered and a direct answer to the question addressed in the presentation. Try to think of a way to make the central message of the presentation stick in the mind of the audience by identifying a maximum of three points that you want them to remember and highlighting these.

 You will find some examples of possible wording for introductions and conclusions on the Online Resource Centre where there is also advice on using signposting phrases that can help to guide the audience through the main body of the presentation.

17.3.3 Using visual aids

Research into the psychology of effective communication has indicated that people take in more information from visual images than they do from listening. Therefore, it is a good idea to ensure that your presentation engages the eyes as well as the ears of the audience by using visual aids, whether in the form of a handout, use of an overhead projector or a PowerPoint presentation, or by writing/drawing on a whiteboard or flipchart as the presentation progresses.

Effective use of visual aids can achieve the following four objectives (see Figure 17.6).

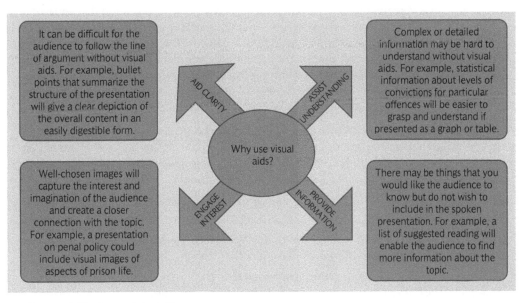

Figure 17.6 Effective use of visual aids

1. **Aid clarity:** a successful presentation is one which can be followed by the audience with ease. Visual aids can add clarity to a presentation by helping the audience to follow the line of argument and see links between the different topics. Look at the figure above which outlines the benefits of visual aids. It has immediate impact in communicating that there are four factors to be taken into account whilst Figure 17.5 on the structure of the presentation makes it apparent that there are three stages but that the second of these is the more complex and detailed. Diagrams, graphs, illustrations, flow charts, and other devices

add clarity, so visual aids can have a positive impact on the comprehensibility of your presentation.

2. **Assist understanding:** an oral presentation is a series of spoken words that are constantly replaced by others. The audience has to listen, understand, and keep pace with what you are saying and this may be a struggle, particularly if your presentation is dealing with complex issues. Visual aids will provide a written or pictorial source of reference that the audience can use to help them make sense of what you are saying and to remind themselves of the key points. Equally, it is often said that 'a picture paints a thousand words', so you may find that your audience is more able to understand if you complement your words with illustrations.

3. **Engage interest:** giving the audience something to look at whilst you are speaking can be an excellent way of engaging their interest and, if the images are well-chosen, of capturing their imagination. Most people tend to take in information more readily by observation than they do by listening, so using visual images can really enhance the impact of your presentation. That said, a presentation that is littered with gratuitous illustrations that have only a tenuous link with the material in question will act as a distraction as the audience ponder the connection between the content of the presentation and the seemingly irrelevant illustration.

4. **Provide additional information:** in a limited time frame, you may not be able to cover all the information that the audience needs about a topic or you may have additional points of interest that were not directly relevant to the content of the presentation that you would nonetheless like to communicate to the audience (perhaps the issues that were in the third column when you categorized your material) that could be listed on a handout as 'further thinking'. Be sure to give careful thought to including additional information on a handout, however; visual aids are supposed to supplement the spoken word and your presentation is supposed to be a self-contained exposition of a topic, so it is not good practice to use the handout as the repository for all the material that you did not have time to include.

Although there are clear benefits to using visual aids, you should do so only if you are prepared to devote effort to their preparation, as shoddy and ill-prepared visual aids will give a wholly negative impression to the audience. You must also take responsibility for ensuring that you are able to use your chosen visual aids during the presentation:

- Do not leave the production of the handout until the hour before the presentation in case you have printer problems or cannot find a photocopier

- Make sure that the room is equipped with an overhead projector or PowerPoint facilities and check prior to the presentation to make sure that they are operational

- Have a back-up plan in case anything goes wrong with the visual aids. What will you do, for example, if the bulb in the projector blows during the presentation?

- Ensure that the visual aids are visible! It is all too common to find material crowded onto a handout, presumably in order to use as little paper as possible, or to see PowerPoint presentations using a small font size which means that the audience struggles to read the content

- Consider the use of colour to enliven your presentation. Stick to two or three colours, however, as too much colour will be a distraction and make the visual aids look chaotic. It can be very effective even if you just use coloured paper for the handout

The following section will outline the main types of visual aid that you may wish to use in your presentation and comment on how they can be used to good (and bad) effect. Further on in the chapter, you will find suggestions on how to use these aids during the delivery of the presentation (see section 17.4).

17.3.3.1 Handouts

You should always prepare a handout to accompany your presentation unless you are told not to do so by your lecturer. Even if you are using one of the other visual aids such as PowerPoint, it is still a good idea to provide a handout. A good handout should enable the audience to follow the structure of your presentation and should give a snapshot of the content that they can supplement with notes if they choose to do so. Moreover, you can include information on the handout that needs to be communicated accurately but that the audience may not be able to note down during the presentation, such as definitions, quotations, statutory references, and case citations.

As such, a handout is a guide and a source of essential information. It should not be overloaded with detail and it should never be a word-for-word copy of your presentation—why would the audience bother to listen if they have been given a transcript of the presentation? A room full of people who are clearly paying no attention when you speak is very off-putting for a presenter, so make sure that you use your visual aids to increase engagement with the audience rather than to distract them or give them an excuse not to listen. Remember, visual aids supplement, rather than replace, the spoken word.

Part of the skill in putting together a handout is thinking about how the information looks on the page. This requires that careful thought is given to the appearance and size of the font used and how the information is spaced out on the page. Think about your own views, positive and negative, of the handouts given to you by lecturers by way of guidance.

Practical exercise

The following exercise can be used to help you to appreciate the qualities that characterize a good handout and the factors that render a handout less useful to the audience.

1. Take a few minutes to read through the handout shown in Figure 17.7.
2. Make a note of the things that you consider to be the strengths and the weaknesses of the handout. You will see that three of the weaknesses have been noted already to give you a start but there are many more points to note remaining.
3. Is there anything lacking that you would want to see included?
4. How useful do you find the handout?
5. Draw out your own version of the handout with a view to making it more user-friendly.

 You will find an improved version of the handout on the Online Resource Centre with some commentary on its merits that you may like to compare with your own thoughts.

17.3.3.2 PowerPoint

PowerPoint (or its Mac equivalent, Keynote) is an excellent visual aid and one that you should certainly try to use if it is at all possible. Not only does it have a range of features, such as the opportunity to incorporate sound and video clips, that are not available with other visual aids, it has the added advantage of improving your computer literacy skills by giving you experience of a new, and increasingly widely-used, package. If you are not familiar with PowerPoint, most institutions run courses on its use and, besides, it is very easy to pick up by experimentation as it is based on a template into which you insert text, images, and other features.

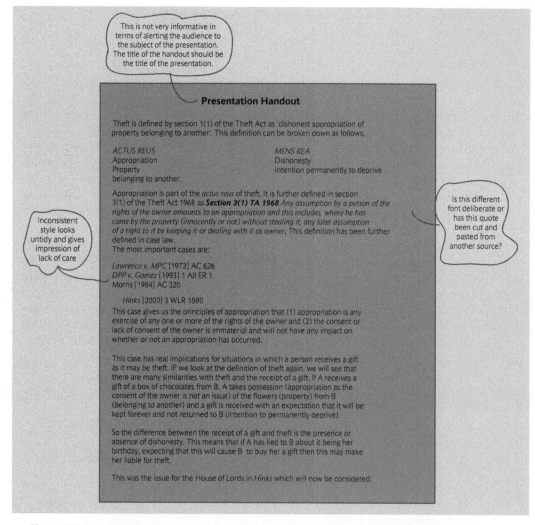

Figure 17.7 An example of a handout concerning theft

If you decide to use PowerPoint, you should ask your lecturer if the room in which you are due to present is suitable for you to do so; if not, it may be possible to arrange a change of venue if you give sufficient warning of your intentions.

There is some disagreement about how many PowerPoint slides should accompany a presentation with some suggesting an approach based on slides per minute of presentation, for example one slide every two minutes. Not only is this rather onerous in long presentations, it is also rather unrealistic; you should use as many slides as you need to communicate your point to the audience. The following points may help you to plan the slides you need to accompany your presentation:

- **Title slide:** this tells the audience who you are and what you are going to talk about.
- **Presentation outline:** this should be used during your introduction as you explain to the audience what points you are going to cover and in what order.
- **Content slides:** the general rule is that there should be one slide for each major concept or idea that you introduce to the audience. You should be relatively sparing with the amount

of words used on each slide and remember to keep the font size large: visual aids are not useful if they cannot be read by the audience.

- **Summary slide:** this corresponds with your conclusion and lists the points that you have covered to demonstrate the way that your ideas fit together. It may be spread over several slides if you want to include an 'implications' or 'future directions' section in your presentation.

- **Any questions?:** however much you hope that nobody will ask any questions, most presentations require you to allow time for questions and it is certain that your lecturer will ask something even if nobody else does.

You will find two sample PowerPoint presentations on the Online Resource Centre with some comments of the choice and layout of the material.

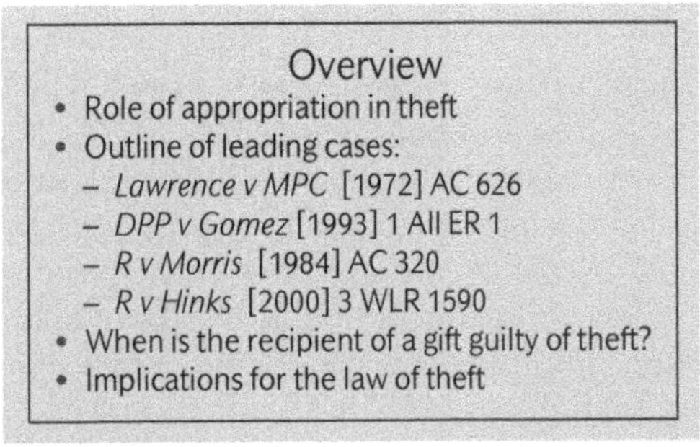

Figure 17.8 An example outline slide

17.3.3.3 Overhead projectors (OHPs)

Until the recent growth in popularity of PowerPoint, OHPs were the main visual aid used during presentations. Most lecture and seminar rooms will have an OHP whereas the facilities to use PowerPoint may not be available in the room in which your presentation is due to take place. If you do plan to use an OHP, it is advisable to visit the room before the presentation and make sure the equipment works, as blown bulbs are a common hazard. It is also a good idea to familiarize yourself with the operation of the OHP prior to the presentation. Make sure you have enough acetate sheets and the correct pens and plan out the spacing of the content carefully: the general rule is no more than seven points of seven words on each sheet. If you are going to print the content, make sure you use a sufficiently large font (no less than 18 point) and one that is relatively plain, such as Arial, as this is easier for the audience to read. If you want to include diagrams or graphs that are copies from books or other sources, make sure that these can be reproduced at an appropriate size and that any change of size does not blur the content.

17.3.3.4 Whiteboards and flipcharts

If there is a whiteboard in the room, you may like to use this to note information as the presentation progresses, because this can give quite a dynamic feel to the presentation. It can be particularly useful if you want to show the links between points, such as the overlap between the branches of state in relation to the separation of powers, or if you want to provide a visual depiction of the development of a topic such as noting a chronology, for example.

There are, however, a number of pitfalls for the unwary or inexperienced user of a white-board. You need to ensure that your writing is sufficiently clear to ensure that it can be read by all of the audience and you must remember that writing takes longer than speaking, so you may feel ill-at-ease with the silence whilst you are using the whiteboard. Of course, you can speak whilst writing but this means that you are facing away from your audience and you might find it hard to do two different things at once, particularly if you are finding the delivery of the presentation stressful.

Flipcharts are not used very often during student presentations, possibly because they are rarely available, but they can be very effective. Unlike a whiteboard presentation, your materials can be prepared in advance, although there is also the flexibility to write/draw as your presentation progresses. Make sure that your writing is sufficiently large and clear and do not go overboard on the use of colour: one main colour and one accent colour should be sufficient. As with handouts, do not try to crowd too much material on a single sheet of paper—it can be a good idea to plan out the content of each sheet in pencil first to see how it looks before using marker pens. One of their key advantages is that the paper can be annotated lightly in pencil to give you reminders of things to do and say that cannot be seen by the audience during the presentation.

As you can see, there are a range of visual aids available to support your presentation. Although the preparation of visual material can be quite time-consuming, the positive impact that it has on the presentation generally makes it a worthwhile exercise. Many students find that preparing a thoughtful and polished selection of visual aids makes them feel more confident about their presentation; if nothing else, it gives the audience something else to look at, so diverting attention away from the speaker.

Although there is much to be said in their favour, do not feel pressured into using visual aids if you do not feel comfortable in doing so. Some students feel that having to use an OHP, for example, makes them very self-conscious during the presentation whilst others find that worries about whether PowerPoint will work properly add to the overall anxiety that accompanies the presentation. Overall, it is preferable not to use visual aids, other than a handout, if they are going to be more of a hindrance than a help.

17.3.4 Practice

The most important element of preparation is practice. Most people are not used to speaking in public, so it is inevitably something that is going to need a little bit of practice.

17.3.4.1 Why practise?

You must practise your presentation several times over to ensure that:

- The presentation fits within the time allocated to it
- The order of the material is appropriate and one point runs smoothly into another
- There are no tricky words or phrases that trip up your tongue
- You familiarize yourself with the appropriate pace at which to speak
- You become accustomed to hearing your own voice
- You know how and when to use any visual aids
- You identify and eliminate any distracting habits

Many of these points will be more readily addressed if you practise in front of an audience. For example, you may think that your pace of delivery is appropriate but only someone who is listening can tell you whether that is the case. Equally, if you have any odd habits, such as fiddling with a pen or flicking your hair, you are likely to be unaware of this unless it is pointed out to you. Finally, a third party can give you feedback on the most important element of all: whether your presentation makes sense to the audience.

17.3.4.2 What to practise?

Although the obvious answer to this question would seem to be 'the presentation', it is not necessarily useful to devote too much practice time to the actual presentation. There are two separate facets to a good presentation: (1) the subject matter, and (2) the presentation style.

Although you will want to practise the actual presentation for the reasons noted in the preceding section, you should not neglect to practise in order to strengthen your presentation style. Until you are a seasoned public speaker, it might be an idea to practise the two separately, particularly if you are asking an audience of your peers to comment on your presentation as they may be tied up with commenting on the content rather than style.

Practical exercise

The following exercise can be used to help you to practise your presentation style. You will find that it will also help you to work on issues such as the organization of the content of the presentation and incorporating signposting.

1. Choose something that you know extremely well as the topic for a five-minute presentation. There is no need for it to have any academic merit as the essence of a good presentation is the communication of information, irrespective of the nature of that information. Suitable topics could be (a) good pubs in your home town; (b) favourite sporting activities; or (c) your first term as an undergraduate student.

2. Prepare a presentation on the topic. The idea of the exercise is to evaluate your presentation style, but this will not work if you treat it as a freeflow speaking activity in which you spill forth thoughts without structure. Use some of the techniques suggested in this chapter to help you to structure and organize your presentation.

3. Ask a couple of friends to observe your presentation and comment upon your style. Try to emphasize to them that you want honest and constructive feedback: it is much easier for your friends to say 'that was great' as they do not want to upset you, so you may need to convince them that you want to hear an objective review of the strengths and weaknesses of your technique. It can help to give them a feedback table and ask them to write comments as they may find this easier than voicing any negative views to you in person.

4. Make a list of the strengths and weaknesses that your audience noted. Ask them for suggestions as to what they think would improve on areas of weakness. Reflect upon your own experience as a presenter: how did it feel when you were delivering the material? What things would you change in future presentations?

5. Rework the presentation taking these observations on board and ask your friends to watch it again or present to a different group of friends. The aim is to determine whether you have improved on your previous performance.

 You will find video clips of students presenting on the Online Resource Centre. Have a look at these and note your own comments of the strengths and weaknesses of their presentation styles.

Once you have some general insight into your presentation style, it would be useful to practise the actual presentation to work on issues associated with the content. Remember to practise with the visual aids that you plan to use to make sure that you can use these without interrupting the flow of your presentation.

Having considered the mechanics of putting together a presentation, all that remains is to consider how to deliver it to the audience with clarity and confidence.

17.4 Delivery stage

This is the stage of the process that you probably think of as *the* presentation. Having followed the steps outlined in relation to preparation, you should have a presentation in a clear and accessible form, supplemented by carefully constructed visual aids. This section will go through some of the factors that will influence the success of the actual delivery of the presentation.

17.4.1 Delivery style

Your main objective in giving a presentation is to communicate an idea to the audience. This means that they need to be able to understand you. It is your job to make sure that you deliver your presentation in such a way that it is capable of being understood and, more than that, that it is packaged so that the audience *wants* to listen. As such, you will need to take the following points into account.

17.4.1.1 Engage with the audience

One of the worst ways to deliver a presentation is to read it to the audience from a prepared script. It leads to a flat and uninteresting delivery, which is very boring for the audience and it often causes the presenter to speak far too quickly. Reading a script also means that you have little or no eye contact with the audience as you have to focus your attention on the page.

The best way to avoid reading a script is not to write one in the first place. There really is no need as you will be familiar with your subject matter and you can ensure that you remind yourself of the order in which the points need to be raised by using cue cards. This frees you to look at the audience (collectively rather than any particular individual) and your delivery will be more natural as a result. Cue cards should be numbered (in case you drop them) and contain short reminders of each key point. Do not be tempted to divide your script into chunks and write these on cue cards as you will find that you merely read from those instead.

It is important also to remember that good written language and good spoken language differ dramatically. Speech tends to involve shorter sentences and more readily understood language than written communication, so if you write a script, the chances are that it will not be in language that is suited to oral delivery.

It is also easier to engage the audience if you replicate the variations in pace and tone that occur in natural speech. Try to make sure that you sound as much like yourself as possible in ordinary conversation, taking into account the need to pace your delivery. It can help to include instructions to remind yourself of these points on the cue cards. Write appropriate phrases such as 'pause', 'slow down', and 'look at the audience' on the cue cards but make sure that you do so in a different colour so that you do not confuse it for the text of your presentation. Nobody wants to engage the audience by making them laugh when you read out 'change the slide' from the cue cards!

Hopefully, you will have gained an awareness of these issues from your practice sessions.

17.4.1.2 Timing, pace, and volume

During the planning stages, you should have taken steps to ensure that your presentation fits within the time allocated to it. Remember that the audience will find it difficult to digest complicated material, so you will need to reduce your speed of delivery so that it is slower than ordinary speech. This can feel strange and it is not uncommon for speakers to start at a measured pace but to pick up speed as the presentation progresses until they are going too fast for the audience.

You will also probably find that you need to speak at a slightly louder volume than you would in ordinary conversation. Your voice will project better to those at the back of the room if you remember to face the audience. This is particularly important when using visual aids: even experienced speakers tend to look at their materials rather than the audience and this can really muffle the voice, so should be avoided.

17.4.1.3 Signpost your presentation

Telling the audience what you are doing makes it so much easier for them to follow the development of your argument. It is good practice to ensure that you start each fresh point with an explanation of how it relates to the rest of your material. If you think about it, there are only three options:

1. **It picks up on something said earlier in the presentation.** Try using phrases such as 'you may remember that I explained this at the start of the presentation' or 'referring back to the definition that I outlined earlier'.
2. **It is one of a series of points.** You can remind the audience of this by using a phrase such as 'the second point to consider here is ...' or simply 'secondly'.

3. **It is a move to an entirely new issue or perspective.** Advise the audience of the change by using phrases such as 'having outlined the position under English law, we now need to consider how this has been altered by membership of the European Union' or 'that concludes the discussion of dishonesty so I'll move on to consider issues relating to appropriation'.

It also helps your audience to follow your presentation if you signpost your use of visual aids with simple phrases such as 'this slide lists the four characteristics of an easement' or 'you will find the definition set out in full halfway down the first page of the handout'. Although this may seem like stating the obvious, you must realize that what is obvious to you—who is so familiar with the content and structure of your presentation—is not obvious to the audience. Moreover, it is important to remember that the audience will regard your presentation favourably if you have made life easy for them, so giving frequent clues as to the location of key information or the relevance of a particular point to the overall topic will always create a good impression.

17.4.1.4 Using visual aids

Visual aids are there to support your presentation but they can only do so if you use them effectively.

- Make sure that your handout, slides, or other materials follow the order of your presentation; if you have made last-minute changes to your content, you should check to see whether this necessitates alterations in your materials
- Practise using any equipment so that you are confident you will be able to operate it during the presentation
- Think about where you are going to stand in relation to the equipment. You do not want to block the screen or to have to keep walking across the room to change your slides
- Do not use visual aids as a substitute for speaking, by, for example, telling the audience to read a PowerPoint slide or section of a handout. One of the worst comments that could be made about your performance would be 'lousy presenter but a competent projectionist'
- Talk to the audience and not to the visual aids. Even the most experienced speakers make this mistake, as they look at their own PowerPoint slides or the material they have written on the whiteboard when they are explaining the points, rather than looking at the audience.

17.4.2 Combating nerves

Nerves are a problem for many students who are faced with the prospect of making a presentation. Even students who are confident of speaking out during group discussion in tutorials tend to find the prospect of standing in front of the group and speaking somewhat daunting. One of the best ways of overcoming nerves is to try and isolate what it is that is causing anxiety—knowing what the problem is takes you halfway towards overcoming it. Common fears include the following:

17.4.2.1 Presenting inaccurate material

This is such a common worry and yet it is one that should really not trouble you. If your research and preparation has been thorough, the content of your presentation should be accurate, so there should be no cause for anxiety on that front. Even if it is dreadfully inaccurate, it is extremely unlikely that other students will notice and even less likely that they will point it out. Your lecturer should not interrupt during the presentation, particularly if it is an assessed component of the course, although they may speak to you afterwards if they feel that you have missed the point or made mistakes regarding the law.

If you are particularly worried about inaccuracy—for example, if you feel that you may have misinterpreted the law or missed a vital point—it would be perfectly acceptable to approach your lecturer, explain your worries, and ask them to look at your planned content to ensure that there are no dreadful errors or omissions. If the presentation is assessed, your lecturer may not be able to do this, in which case you could cooperate with other students in the group, asking them to check your work for accuracy and agreeing to do the same for them in return.

17.4.2.2 Forgetting what to say

Thorough research and preparation will have made you extremely familiar with the subject matter, so, provided you have a note of the order in which you want to make points, it is extremely unlikely that you will forget what to say. You should be able to explain all the key concepts in your presentation without relying on any particular form of words. However, this fear tends to lead students to write a full script, which they intend to follow to the last word. As discussed earlier, reading a script (or reciting a memorized script) is not effective as it leads to stilted delivery, a fast delivery pace, and lack of engagement with the audience. Try making a numbered list of the points that you want to make and explaining each of them out loud without any further notes or prompts. The more you practise doing this, the more fluent you will become and this should help your fear of 'drying up' during the presentation recede.

Rather then merely forgetting what to say, you may fear that you will be incapable of speaking; that you will open your mouth but no words will come out. This is a common fear but an exceptionally rare occurrence. If you have never been incapable of speech at any time previously in your life, there is no reason to think that it will happen during your presentation. Of course, the stress of the situation may make your mouth dry—that is an entirely explicable physical response to fear—so make sure that you have some water with you to sip during the presentation. You should practise your opening sentence as often as possible—write it out on cards and pin them up at different places around your room so that you see them all the time; once the first sentence is out, the rest will follow on naturally.

17.4.2.3 Being visible and/or being judged

Probably the most frequently expressed concern arises from the visibility attached to the delivery of a presentation. Most student discussion takes part within a group where there is far less emphasis on any particular group member and where any lack of knowledge is readily concealed. A presentation removes these safety features and focuses uninterrupted attention on one person for a protracted period of time. This visibility and focus renders the speaker vulnerable to the criticism of their peers and it is probably this factor that induces the most anxiety: in fact, you could say that the three points listed above are merely specific examples of the overriding fear of looking foolish in front of others.

There are a couple of points to note here. First, do not imagine for one moment that every member of the audience is actually paying attention. The only person that you can guarantee is actually listening to what you say is the lecturer—even your friends are probably letting their minds drift whilst maintaining expressions of encouragement or polite attention. Secondly, even if people are paying attention, they are doing so out of interest in what you are saying, not because they want to criticize you. In fact, most people will be willing you on to succeed, knowing that they have either survived the experience or have their own presentation to give later that term, so it is really a mistake to assume that there is any negative judgement being directed towards you.

Overall, then, most presentation anxiety arises from a concern about looking foolish in front of others. Most of the reasons that you might feel foolish, such as inaccurate material or forgetting what to say, can be overcome with careful preparation and by practising the presentation several times beforehand. Other factors that might cause concern, such as inability to operate the equipment, can also be addressed by practice. Ultimately, most people do not have to speak in front of others very often, so a presentation is unknown territory and it is human nature to fear the unknown.

You can take various steps to minimize this prior to the presentation, such as ensuring that you become used to speaking out in front of other students by contributing to tutorial discussion. Some students find that the best way to appear confident is to pretend to be confident. They watch those who they consider to be confident presenters and emulate their behaviour. Other students take a contrasting approach by starting the presentation by confessing that they are feeling very nervous.

Practical exercise

The following exercise can be used to help you to practise your presentation style. You will find that it will also help you to work on issues such as the organization of the content of the presentation and incorporating signposting.

1. Have a think about your fears about giving a presentation. Try to articulate these as precisely as possible and note them as a list of numbered points on a sheet of paper.

2. Deal with each numbered point in turn and ask yourself (a) why you think that this will happen, and (b) what the outcome will be if it does happen. For example, you might be afraid that you will run out of time and not be able to deliver all of your presentation. This could result in loss of marks in an assessed presentation.

3. Think of at least two ways that you could stop the problem from arising. For example, you could practise the presentation several times to make sure that it fits within the time allocated and you could review the content to consider which points could be omitted if you run short of time on the actual day.

4. Consider how you will deal with the outcome of your feared situation occurring. In other words, address not just the consequence but the consequence of the consequence! For example, if you run short of time you will lose some marks as a result but it is unlikely to make the difference between a pass and fail, besides which it is unlikely that the course is assessed 100 per cent on the presentation.

By tackling your fears directly, you will be able to think of ways to prevent them from occurring and also realize that the consequences of their occurrence are not actually as bad as you imagine.

17.4.3 Dealing with questions

Most presentations conclude with a period of time for the audience to ask questions. It is probably fair to say that even the most confident presenter has some qualms about dealing with questions. This is because it is actually the only part of the presentation that you cannot control. If the presentation is assessed, the ability to deal with questions assumes a particular importance because it gives the marker an indication of the depth of the speaker's background knowledge. Try to take into account the following points to help you deal with questions:

- Listen to the question. Concentrate on what the person asking the question is saying rather than worrying that you will not know the answer
- Ask them to repeat the question if you did not follow it or to reword it if you did not understand it
- Take time to think about the answer to ensure that you have something sensible to say rather than saying the first thing that pops into your head just to fill the silence
- Be honest. If you do not know the answer, say so
- Do not talk for too long in answer to any particular question. It will come across as if you are rambling which will detract from the overall impression of your oral presentation skills. Think about your answer and make a couple of succinct points.

17.5 Post-presentation stage

You may think that your task is complete as soon as the final question has been answered and you have taken your seat with a sense of relief and achievement but there is another stage of the process which is frequently overlooked in its importance and that is the post-presentation reflection.

17.5.1 Why reflect?

You should reflect upon your performance in order to ensure that you gain something from the activity, so that you will be a more effective and confident presenter on the next occasion. You may think that once was enough and that you will never be called upon to present again but you cannot be sure of that, so it will maximize the learning potential of the activity if you set aside a little time to reflect upon how the presentation went and what, if anything, you would do differently if you were able to repeat the presentation the following day.

Try and formalize this process a little by making notes so that you have a record of your thoughts whilst they are still fresh in your mind. It will not help you improve in the future if, two years down the line when you need to give a presentation as part of an application for a training contract, you have difficulties calling to mind the topic of your presentation let alone your views on its strengths or weaknesses.

17.5.2 Seek feedback

The process need not take long and you can make use of any feedback that you have been given by your lecturer and by the audience. If the lecturer gave you feedback at the time, it might well have been based as much on content as it was on style and it may have been sanitized a little if there were negative aspects to the presentation, so that you did not feel embarrassed in front of the audience. It would be worth sending the lecturer in question an email to request more tailored feedback. Remember that you will receive a specific answer if you ask a specific question, so rather than saying 'could you give me some more feedback on my presentation?' try asking your lecturer to list three things that they liked about your presentation style and three things that they think that you should change. You may also receive written feedback at some point, particularly if the presentation was assessed.

It may be useful to consider in advance how to elicit the most useful feedback from your audience. Why not prepare a form to distribute at the beginning of the presentation and ask the audience to complete the forms and leave them behind at the end of the presentation? This could take a simple format that could be quite general, to give the audience the ability to note their own thoughts, or it could ask specific questions. Remember, however, not to ask too much of the audience as they are there to listen and learn rather than to provide you with a detailed commentary on your presentation technique.

FEEDBACK FORM

Thank you for attending my presentation on 'The Evolution of Appropriation in the Offence of Theft'

Please take a few moments to note your thoughts about this presentation:

What were the good aspects of the presentation that you enjoyed or thought were useful?
1.
2.
3.

What aspects of the presentation did you think were less good and which you found unhelpful?
1.
2.
3.

Figure 17.9 An example feedback form

CHAPTER SUMMARY

The research stage

- Take care to formulate a presentation topic that takes account of the time frame within which the presentation must be delivered, the availability of material, the aim of the presentation, and the requirements of the assessment criteria

- Start your research as early as possible to ensure you have time to identify and obtain relevant material and make sure that your note-making is effective

- Strive to find an original or interesting slant on the material to ensure that the presentation is interesting, particularly if you are aware that other students are covering the same topic

Preparing the presentation

- Content overload is a major problem for many presentations. Select your topic and the content of the presentation carefully to ensure that you do not try to cram too much material into the time available

- If you are having difficulties in making a decision about the content, try ranking each point on the basis of its relevance to the question that your presentation is seeking to answer

- Make sure that your presentation tells a story by giving it a clear introduction, a series of interrelated points within the body of the presentation, and a conclusion that draws together the issues raised and provides a succinct answer to the question posed by the presentation

- Always prepare a handout unless explicitly told not to do so. This should contain a skeleton of the presentation to give the audience an insight into its structure and content as well as noting any detailed information such as quotations that the audience could not be expected to note down during the presentation

- Give careful thought to the selection and presentation of visual aids to ensure that they complement, rather than replace or distract from, the presentation

- Practise, preferably in front of an audience. Present on everyday topics to practise your delivery style and then practise the actual presentation to ensure that it fits within the time frame and that everything flows smoothly

Delivering the presentation

- Try to adopt a style of delivery that is engaging for the audience to listen to and follow. Take particular care with the timing, pace, and volume of your presentation and remember that good spoken English differs enormously from good written English

- Never read from a prepared script. If to recollect the content of the presentation poses a problem, use numbered cue cards with key words and phrases noted that will jolt your memory

- Signposting is essential to enable your audience to follow the line of your argument and to understand how each point relates to others in the presentation. Use a signposting phrase in relation to each new point raised

- Anticipate issues that will cause you to feel nervous and try to formulate a means of pre-empting any problems that you fear may arise. Remember that most people suffer from presentation nerves

- Be prepared to answer questions from the audience. Listen carefully to what is being asked and take a moment to think about the answer before launching into a response

Review and reflection

- Presentations are increasingly required as part of the job application process, so take advantage of this opportunity to become a more accomplished presenter by reflecting upon your performance. Try to be honest with yourself about your limitations as a presenter and find ways to strengthen areas in which there is room for improvement

- Be active and precise in seeking feedback from others about your qualities as a presenter and remember that asking precise questions tends to elicit precise answers

- Circulating a feedback sheet and inviting the audience to complete it is a really valuable source of feedback, as written feedback tends to be more objective, hence more useful to your review of your performance, than face-to-face comment

Employability

Learning objectives

After studying this chapter you should be able to:

- Appreciate the skills law firms are looking for in prospective trainees.
- Begin to develop these skills yourself.
- Understand how to show prospective employers that you have these skills.
- Understand the skills involved in working effectively with others.
- Prepare effectively for an assessment day at a law firm.

Introduction

Chapters 7 to 11 consider the essential legal skills which all lawyers need, whether they are in practice or not. This chapter focuses on the additional skills you will require if you intend to embark on a career in the practice of law particularly, although it is important to recognise that law graduates are found in a variety of sectors other than law (including accountancy, banking, finance, the civil service, the police, government, the armed forces, management, journalism, and academia) and rest assured these skills are eminently transferable and will be useful wherever your career takes you.

In today's competitive marketplace, employability skills are key. Law students tend to prioritise the acquisition of legal knowledge over the acquisition of legal skills, but this is not a good idea. This is because employability skills play a pivotal role in distinguishing a good lawyer from an average one, from both an employer's and a client's perspective.

The term 'solicitor' is an umbrella term to describe professionals who practise all areas of that broad and diverse subject known as law. You cannot possibly arrive at a law firm on day one of your training contract armed with a comprehensive knowledge of the specific area of law you intend to practise. Law firms understand this and will help you to supplement your existing legal knowledge as they train you on the job for practice in a particular legal sector. Clients, rightly or wrongly, will assume you have that legal knowledge. But although there is a limit on how much you will impress your employer or the client with your legal knowledge on day one of your training contract, it is possible to impress on day one with polished employ-ability skills. By learning these skills early, you can stand out from your peers when you enter the world of professional practice. It is quite a transition between being a student and being a professional. This chapter will help to ease that transition for you when it comes, by showing what you can be doing now to prepare for professional life.

The term 'employability skills' includes all those skills which make you a covetable employee. Of course, it includes technical competence in law, which in turn requires the skills covered in this book, namely being able to read and understand the law, undertake legal research, solve legal problems, draft competently, and communicate effectively, both orally and in writing. However, effective lawyers deploy a host of other skills which we will consider in this chapter.

12.1 Personal characteristics

Effective lawyers share similar characteristics. They have a positive attitude to their work, approach work in a business-like manner, act with professionalism, and reflect on their work to develop their practice. These characteristics come more naturally to some rather than others, however the good news is that they can be learned and improved with practice, like any other skill. As a first step it is important simply to appreciate that they are vital components of a good lawyer. Eventually, most lawyers find they can demonstrate the following qualities when things are going well. However, law is a rewarding but demanding profession. It involves working under pressure, often during long and sometimes unsociable office hours. A really good lawyer will be able to show the same qualities when things are not going as well.

Law firms will be looking for evidence of these characteristics when they consider your application form and during the interview process. Let's explore further what they are and how you can show that you have them when you apply for a job. Work experience is excellent in terms of really bringing these points home. Spending time in any professional environment is a great idea at this stage, and will demonstrate clearly the points set out below.

12.1.1 Attitude

It is important to demonstrate that you have a positive attitude to your work. One of the most important things to show is enthusiasm, even (particularly) when you are given something to do which is relatively mundane. Taking responsibility for your own work, being proactive in identifying other work that might be required and being willing to do that work and showing commitment to your work are also examples of taking a professional approach to your work. The key point to bear in mind is that you must show that you are someone with whom other people would want to work. Lawyers work closely together and the hours can be quite intense. Being flexible, approachable, and having a sense of humour even when things are going wrong will count significantly in your favour. Do not underestimate how the personality of work colleagues can significantly affect life in the office. If you come across as someone who would enhance the experience rather than detract from it, you will make yourself a covetable employee. You can get into good habits now, by recognising when you are tired, stressed, or just cannot be bothered, and making a particular effort to try your best at these times. Try out different coping mechanisms to get you through these difficult periods, and find what works for you. Something as simple as going for a walk, listening to music, or taking a break and having a cup of tea can make a difference. Talk to others. Too many students isolate themselves when they feel overwhelmed, but if you talk to others you will tend to find (and it can be comforting to know) that everyone has concerns; some are just better at dealing with them than others. You can learn from your fellow students; consider who has an attitude you admire and would like to emulate, and talk to them about their coping strategies. Ask your tutors if they have any advice regarding any issues you are facing; they are likely to have advised many students with similar problems. You will continue to experience these feelings in professional life; there are just never enough hours in the day, so start now to discover what will help you through.

12.1.2 Approach

You must approach your work in a businesslike manner. Examples of behaviour which evidence this are being organised, demonstrating a high capacity for work, being resilient under pressure, self-aware, diligent, and paying attention to detail. In other words, you need to show that you are 'a safe pair of hands'. Of course, what you are doing right now, being a law student, lends itself to evidencing that you have these skills, but the fact is that some students are much more adept than others at organising their work. This is something you can improve immediately to make sure you are one of the good ones. Time management is crucial. You must be able to multi-task and achieve a balance between your work and social life, and this is no less true once you are a professional. It is not sustainable in the long run simply to work all the time at the expense of a social life. You can help yourself by being familiar with your timetable; importing it into your smartphone is best, so you always have it with you, but if this is not possible at least stick a copy on the fridge. Maintain a 'to-do' list; again you can do this on a smartphone so it is always with you. Set alerts to make sure you do not forget key events or deadlines. Ask your tutor how many hours a week the course demands of you, and timetable that into your diary, factoring in non-timetabled activities such as preparation, consolidation and revision, so you can then clearly ring-fence some leisure time. Start your work early, so you have time to look over it with a fresh perspective before the deadline. Know what you have to do, where you have to be, and when.

12.1.3 Professionalism and ethics

There is an understanding that professionals behave in a certain way. This behaviour includes being polite, approachable, reliable, honest, dependable, punctual, and dressing and behaving in an office-appropriate manner.

If anyone helps you, it sounds obvious but say thank you. This is equally the case if the help is by email. It is increasingly common for students and trainees simply not to reply to tutors and lawyers who respond to their queries by email. A quick email in reply just to say thank you will never be a waste of anyone's time.

Reliability, honesty, and dependability are particularly important qualities for a profession like law where professional ethics are held in high regard. Clients may need to disclose quite sensitive information to you so they must be able to trust you. Indeed the Solicitors Regulation Authority (see further 6.3), which regulates the profession, may not admit you as a solicitor at all if you have in your record certain matters which suggest that you are dishonest. Further information on this is set out in their Suitability Test which they publish on their website (details of which are set out in the 'Further reading' section below). It is important to realise that anything you do now which suggests dishonesty could impact quite seriously on your ability to join this profession, where honesty is valued above all else. So, for example, if you are found guilty of plagiarism, or are caught on a train without a valid ticket, this may have more serious consequences for you than for, say, your housemate studying the history of art (provided he is not planning to go on to convert to law by studying the Graduate Diploma in Law).

As Chapter 15 explains, a solicitor charges on a time basis (see 15.1.6). A client will not tolerate a solicitor taking longer than necessary over work, or keeping the client waiting unnecessarily. If you are a student who tends to be late to lectures on a regular basis then take heed and adopt good habits sooner rather than later.

In terms of dress, it can be difficult to pre-empt what is office-appropriate if you have not been inside a law firm before. Bear in mind that generally law firms are relatively conservative places. You have a working lifetime to express yourself through your clothes once you are more familiar with the firm and its culture. Initially however, as a rule of thumb it is a good idea to err on the side of formality if you are at all unsure. It is better to be too formal at first, and become less so, than to be too casual and have to smarten up. The look you are aiming for is that of a polished professional. The following guidelines may help:

- sober black, grey, or navy blue suits will never be out of place;
- for men, shirts should be light-coloured and long-sleeved, preferably without a pocket;
- women have more latitude in terms of colour, but should avoid anything too revealing;
- shoes should be polished;
- men should be cleanly shaved;
- hair should be clean and tidy;
- avoid anything 'novelty', including ties, socks, cufflinks, and jewellery;
- it is a good idea to wear your suit in the house for a practice run first, to identify any scope for a wardrobe malfunction.

Bear in mind that you will meet professionals during the course of your studies. They will visit your university and you will meet them at law fairs, while doing pro bono work and on vacation schemes. You should think carefully about how you can demonstrate that even at this stage you have the attributes of a professional. Like it or not, you will make an impression when you meet these people, and you need to give some thought as to what impression you want to make, then dress and act accordingly. Think carefully before making any permanent alterations to your appearance, such as having a visible tattoo or stretching the holes of your pierced ears. Something that you will feel comfortable sporting in the student union may make you feel very uncomfortable when you speak to lawyers at a law fair or enter a law firm for a vacation placement. Nor should you worry about your friends' reactions, for example, if you choose to wear smart clothing to a law fair. Have the confidence to be guided by your own instinct.

That said, law firms are not looking for clones and you should not be afraid to let your personality come through in your dress, provided you still fall within the description of a polished professional.

12.1.4 Development

Law firms are constantly looking for ways to improve, so that they can beat the competition. As an employee, the firm will expect you to operate a **reflective practice**, which means that you should reflect on your work at regular intervals and learn from your experiences, good and bad, to inform your practice going forward. This involves taking responsibility for your own learning and development, reflecting on your performance and learning from mistakes, seeking and accepting feedback and advice, and being willing and able to learn new skills.

Generally a supervising solicitor will be understanding if you make a mistake once, however she will be considerably less understanding if you make the same mistake again. The skill is to learn from your mistakes. This is one reason why it is important to secure a training contract where you will be given lots of practical experience. The sooner you are free to make mistakes, the sooner you will learn from them, and you will be a more impressive lawyer at an early stage in your legal career.

Reflective practice is something you can start to develop now, as a student. Analysing our own mistakes is never a comfortable exercise, but it pays dividends. When asked for their views, it is common to hear students say they would like more feedback on their

Example 1

The following example might help you to understand why law firms value the characteristics discussed above, but it is equally relevant to any other work experience you might undertake, such as working at a magazine publishing house (although the copying may be of slightly more glamorous documents).

Imagine you are a solicitor. It is 6pm. You are going to be working late and you have cancelled your plans for the evening. You ask your trainee, James, if he can copy the 150-page document which you will need to append to the document you will be drafting later in the evening. James' body language suggests he is not overly impressed with your request. He replies, 'OK, although I warn you I am not very on the ball when working late.' You leave your office for a while and return to find a pile of papers on your desk, and that James has left for the evening. The papers appear to be the photocopied document.

At 11.30pm, after several hours of drafting, you finish your document. However, when you try to append the copy document to your draft, you find that pages 148–50 are not in the pile of papers on your desk. You look for the original document, but it is not with the papers on your desk. You find it on James' desk, next to a half finished cup of coffee. Unfortunately pages 148–50 are also missing from the original document. You go to the photocopier and find that the lights on the copier are flashing to indicate a paper jam. You open the photocopier and fish out the original pages 148–50. You reset the copier. The copier is out of paper. You refill the copier. Finally you are able to add the photocopies of pages 148–50 to the appendix, email it to its destination, and go home at midnight.

As the solicitor in this scenario, what is your opinion of James? Consider again the personal characteristics which law firms value. Has James demonstrated any of them? Which ones has he definitely not shown? Analyse specifically what you would have liked him to have done differently. Now read the following:

Imagine you are a solicitor. It is 6pm. You are going to be working late and you have cancelled your plans for the evening. You ask your trainee, John, if he can copy the 150 page document which you will need to append to your document when you have finished drafting it. John looks up from his work, smiles and replies, 'Yes, of course'. You leave your office for a while and return to find two piles of papers on your desk, one with a label 'copy' and one with a label 'original'. John returns to your office with two cups of coffee, one of which is for you. He explains that he has counted the pages and two pages appear to be missing, so he is going to find them. Ten minutes later John returns with the two missing pages and puts them into the appropriate piles in the right place, explaining with a smile that he had just won a battle with the photocopier. He asks if you need anything else. You say no, thank him and say he should go home as there will be a few late nights ahead this week.

If both John and James were looking for a job in your department, it is likely that you would recommend John over James. John has made your life easier than James did. It is interesting to note what John did to earn your support. He was pleasant, smiled, did not complain, made you a coffee, checked the copying, and extracted two documents from the photocopier. None of these things in isolation is particularly burdensome. However it is these little things which can make a big difference to someone who asks for your help. Note that you did not have to do any of John's work. In contrast, it would probably have been more efficient for you to have done the copying yourself rather than give it to James. James runs the risk that you will not trust him again, and as a result he will not gather the same level of experience during this seat that John will.

work. However it can be that students who receive a poor mark find this so disappointing that they are tempted to file the work away without paying attention to the feedback provided. No matter how painful it may be, you must try to read feedback objectively, and discuss anything that you do not understand with your tutor. If you change your perception and view this as a positive process, by which you can move forward, it can help. It can also be useful to keep a reflective log, which might be referred to in practice as a personal development plan. The simpler you make this the more likely you are to use it, so if could just be a notes page on your smartphone which highlights areas of concern, and the steps you are taking to address them, which you can reflect on and update regularly to chart your progress.

12.2 Team-working

In the past, the image of a lawyer was perhaps of a professional sitting alone in an ivory tower, bestowing knowledge of the law onto grateful clients. Those days are gone. To be a good lawyer, or indeed any other professional, in the modern world you need to have good people skills and be able to work well with others. This includes working with those with whom you do not have a natural affinity. This is especially pertinent for a trainee lawyer, who will work in at least four different departments of a firm during their two-year training contract.

 Practice tip

Trainees sit with different departments during their training contract of two years. The time spent with one department is referred to as a 'seat', and when a trainee moves to a different department, this is called a 'seat move'. The majority of firms offer trainees four seats each lasting six months, but some firms offer more seats over the two-year period. Arranging seat moves can be a stressful time, as several trainees may indicate an interest in the same seat, and not all will obtain their first choice. It is important to give your best performance in all seats, even if you are not seeking to qualify into that department. Do not forget that the partner in your current department may well be acquainted with the partner in the department you want to go to next, and a positive or negative referral from one partner to another, however informal, may be pivotal in deciding whether you secure your first choice of seat move or not.

Most candidates who apply for any kind of employment refer in their curriculum vitae to good team-working skills. It is useful to give some thought as to what this actually entails.

12.2.1 What is team-working and why is it important?

You should be able to identify some examples where you have worked as part of a team. Playing team sports, being a member of a committee, or working as part of any other team, be it during work experience in a law firm or waiting tables, will all help you to give context to help you demonstrate that you are a good team player. If you have not done so already, start to examine your curriculum vitae for any gaps you need to fill in terms of team-working, and undertake activities now to plug those gaps. For example, you may need to take part in some extra-curricular activities such as joining a sports team or society (law-related, such as mooting, or otherwise). However, you may also be able to use examples you had not thought of to date as 'team work' such as working in groups during your face-to-face teaching, or setting up your own study group and establishing ground rules to help it work effectively.

A common question asked of prospective trainees at the interviewing stage is what exactly team-working involves. Some of the vital skills are highlighted below, in the order 'abcdef' to help you to commit them to memory.

- **A**cknowledging the contributions of others in the team.
- **B**uilding good working relationships.
- **C**ontributing to the team.
- Being able to **D**elegate, and be delegated to, **E**ffectively.
- Knowing how to **F**unction well as a team, including in team meetings.

We will explore these skills further in this chapter, and you can reflect on which component skills you may already have, and which you may be able to develop.

12.2.2 **Roles within a team**

It is worth spending some time reflecting on the role you like to take in a team, whatever team that may be. Most people have a preferred role that they find themselves adopting over again. Consider the scenarios in which you have worked as part of a team to date. Are you a dominant member of the team, or do you prefer to work away from the spotlight? Do you help the team to stay focused and on task, or are you a constant source of diverse creative ideas? Do you like to consider the detail, or do you prefer to think strategically but leave the finer detail to others?

There are several assessment tools available to determine how you can work to your full potential in a team, including *Belbin Team Roles*, which analyses the team role which would suit you best, and the *Myers-Briggs Type Indicator*, which analyses your personality type. It is common for employers, including law firms, to use these assessment tools as part of staff team-building days, to analyse how they might deploy their employees' skills to maximum advantage. Both the assessment tools referred to above require a fee to be paid, however they also have some useful free information available on their websites and the addresses are set out in the 'Further reading' section at the end of this chapter.

Whatever your preferred role, an employer will expect you to be aware of the strengths and weaknesses of that role. For example, if you are a dominant team member, you will have no problem in demonstrating that you contribute fully to the team, but are you aware that you may inhibit a valuable but quieter member of the team from contributing to the discussion? If you can both (i) identify the potential disadvantages of your personality type and also (ii) devise steps to address them, you are demonstrating high-level team-working skills. Professional employers will also be looking for employees with leadership potential. Regardless of the role you tend to adopt within a team, it is possible to show that working in any role within a team has allowed you to develop your own leadership skills. Team-working provides opportunities to reflect on your own strengths and weaknesses, and those of others, and to devise strategies and develop communication skills which allow team members to participate in the team inclusively and in a way which plays to their strengths. It affords opportunities for you to practise how to identify a goal and work towards that goal effectively, and how to learn from the successes and mistakes you or others may make. If you can show that you have recognised these opportunities and learned from them, you will be able to demonstrate leadership potential, as they are all essential characteristics of a good leader.

12.2.3 Who might be in your team?

It is worth considering what teams you consider yourself to be working in at the moment. The number may surprise you. Team-working is an important skill for a lawyer because at any one time you might be working in several different teams. Let us consider the example of a trainee working in the commercial and corporate department of a law firm. What teams might she be working in? This is precisely the sort of question you may be asked at an interview. Simultaneously the trainee might be working in all of the following teams:

- **Team 1: trainee team.** The trainee may be one of an intake of several trainees. The trainees will support one another as peers and may work together in the same department or across other departments.
- **Team 2: department team.** The trainee is spending a finite period of time in the commercial/corporate department. During this time she must work effectively with the other trainees, fee-earners, partners, and secretaries in that department.
- **Team 3: transaction team.** The entire commercial/corporate department will not be advising on the same transaction (or 'deal'). Instead, a transaction team will be selected from the department to work on one particular transaction. Depending on the size of the transaction, this team will comprise one or more partners, fee-earners, and trainees.
- **Team 4: client team.** The transaction team may be advising a client which is a company. There will be a team of individuals at the company who are involved in putting the deal together, such as the company secretary (often a lawyer), the directors (who manage the company), and possibly a team of senior managers who are not directors. The trainee must be able to work with these people as part of a team.
- **Team 5: advisory team.** Typically the client will need other advice, in addition to legal advice, in order to complete the transaction. For example, the client's advisory team might consist of accountants, bankers, stockbrokers, and public relations professionals.

It is important to realise that you will not always have a natural affinity with those in your team. Nevertheless you will be expected to work seamlessly with these people as well as those towards whom you would more naturally gravitate. Law tutors may help you to develop these skills by encouraging you to sit with people other than your friends during workshops and seminars, and perhaps to adopt a role that would not be your first preference. This can help you to develop your team-working skills and will also help to prevent you always adopting the same role within a team (which you were encouraged to identify above). As part of the self-reflection process, and to work on the problem-solving skills referred to in Chapter 9, it is good to consider any problems you have or might experience while working as a team, and how you tried or might try to solve these problems. For example, you may come across someone who does not contribute to your group work. This may be for a number of reasons: perhaps he has not prepared, is shy, is reluctant to interrupt a more dominant group member, lacks confidence, does not understand the work, is tired, genuinely has a more pressing problem distracting him, and so on. How might you encourage this person to contribute? Should you? Does the reason that he is not contributing make a difference? How would you find out the reason? Should you? Get into the habit of learning from your experiences, and do not be afraid to admit that you handled a situation in a way you would not repeat. This is all part of your learning as a student, as much as reading *Donoghue* v *Stevenson*.

12.2.4 Negotiating decisions as a team

If there is no consensus in a team, how does it decide how to proceed? In a law firm, which has a hierarchical structure, it is often left to the most senior person to decide. This is not without merit, as she is often the most experienced team member. However, consider a partner who makes the decision that each of her junior lawyers should record one more hour of chargeable time each day. Clearly this is an example where she will need her team to buy in to the idea, or she could be left with no team to record any hours at all. Generally, teams functioning at a high level structure the decision-making process effectively and inclusively. With the arrival of alternative business structures (see Chapters 6 and 15), law firms are increasingly aware that they have to think like businesses, and they are looking to recruit people who might be able to bring business acumen into the firm. If team-working is an area which interests you, this is an area that lends itself to analysis outside the law firm bubble, and the following general team issues are worth considering. Negotiation itself is also a key skill for lawyers. You might like to try out some of the theory right now, as a student, in the teams you are currently in.

Aims and objectives

A team will have been brought together for a particular purpose, and it is worth making sure that all members of the team are aware of this purpose and the time period over which it must be achieved. Any plans for the team should be clear and divided into short-, medium-, and long-term plans.

Strategy

A well-managed organisation will have formulated and often publicly stated a clear strategy to achieve its aims and objectives. For example, a law firm may want to be known for the quality of its advice above all else, or it may wish to be defined as a cost-effective option. Decision-making within teams in the organisation must be consistent with the stated objectives and strategy.

Know-how

It is important to determine whether anyone in the team has any knowledge which would make them the best person to take a leading role in a particular decision. For example, if a team in a law firm is tasked with arranging a client marketing event, and you have a contact at a venue you think would be ideal, you should speak up. If your university law society is asked to start tweeting on a regular basis to raise its profile, and you have a particular interest in and experience of this, then again you should identify yourself as a team member with useful knowledge. Know-how does not always rest with the most senior member of the team.

Resolving disagreements

It is unlikely that all members of a team will agree with each other all of the time. The easiest way to move forward is to go with the majority. This is not always the best way, however, because it may be that there is a better way forward which could be identified by further debate. It can also encourage a competitive atmosphere within the team which can distort and obstruct the decision-making process. If the team can reach a position which every team member can live with and support, even if that decision does not reflect exactly the decision they would have made, this puts the team in a strong position. Each team member will have bought into the decision and will be able to engage with the process of taking it forward, as a team. You can see that, as referred to above, to reach this point a team needs a combination of individuals with different strengths to adopt different roles, for example someone to bring out the quieter members, someone with good powers of persuasion, a peace maker, and so on. Body language is also important in ensuring the team is functioning inclusively in negotiating a way forward.

12.3 Delegation

For a team to work most effectively, each member of the team should be working to their highest level. This involves the team members working together in a structured way, sharing

---

Example 2

In Shephard & Son, a partner charges £360 per hour, an associate £150 per hour, and a trainee £50 per hour. A client, Emma, has asked the planning team whether she can cut down a tree in her garden. The team needs to research the issue then provide some advice to Emma in writing.

The partner could do this. It would take her 15 minutes to research the law, and 10 minutes to draft the letter. The cost to the client would be £150 (£360/60×25).

Alternatively, the partner could delegate some of the task to the trainee. Let's assume that it would take the trainee 30 minutes to research the law and 30 minutes to draft the letter. The partner could then check and amend the work in 10 minutes. The cost to the client would be £110 (£50+(£360/60×10)).

Effective delegation has allowed the firm to charge competitively for the work for Emma, has freed the partner's time to work on a more complex problem for another client, and has given the trainee valuable experience.

the workload efficiently between them according to their training and experience. This is not restricted to law firms; consider, for example, why you have blood taken by a nurse but your appendix removed by a surgeon. It is particularly important however that lawyers work at an appropriate level, because clients pay each lawyer a different rate calculated specifically by reference to experience (see 15.1.6). If a senior lawyer with a high charge-out rate is doing basic legal work, there is a danger that the charge would be so expensive that the client would not pay it. Rather than 'write off' this time, which would adversely affect the firm's profits, it is better for more senior members of the team to delegate less complex tasks to the more junior members.

It can be very frustrating for both the person delegating and the recipient of the delegated task if this delegation is not done effectively. Unfortunately, poor delegation is very common. The following are common signs of poor delegation:

- Leaving a task until it is urgent before delegating it.
- Not giving enough thought about who to delegate to.
- Failing to give clear instructions as to what needs to be done.
- Not agreeing a deadline.
- Not being available to answer essential questions.
- Not passing on new information.
- Giving no feedback, or negative feedback with no scope to allow for learning from mistakes.

Why is poor delegation common? There are several contributing factors and understanding them can help you to be better both at delegating and being delegated to. Looking from the delegator's perspective, he may simply be too busy to have given enough thought to how to delegate effectively. Sometimes a delegator may feel too inhibited to delegate properly. He may be embarrassed at having to ask for help or worried about burdening other people. In some cases, there may be something on the file which the delegator would prefer others not to see, such as a complaint or a long delay on his part. From the delegatee's perspective, she may be inhibited and respond negatively to the delegator due to the fact she is already overloaded, or because of previous negative experiences of delegation, or simply because the work is not at the right level for her to take on.

Good delegation can avoid these problems, but it requires planning and forethought. The flowchart at Figure 12.1 will help you, as a guide to what to do if you are in the role of delegator, and to help you ask for appropriate guidance if you are a delegatee. As a student you may consider that you are more likely to be the delegatee, and this is true in terms of the role you will have while on work experience, or a law firm vacation scheme. However, if you think carefully you will probably be able to identify some times where you have taken, or should have taken, the role of delegator. For example, if your tutor gives you a group assignment to complete, how have you decided who is doing what and when? If you have held a charity cake sale, who has decided who will bake, who might sell some raffle tickets and who might be in charge of the money? On what basis were these decisions made? Whether you knew it or not, someone was delegating, and if you are going to be a good delegator it helps to realise this.

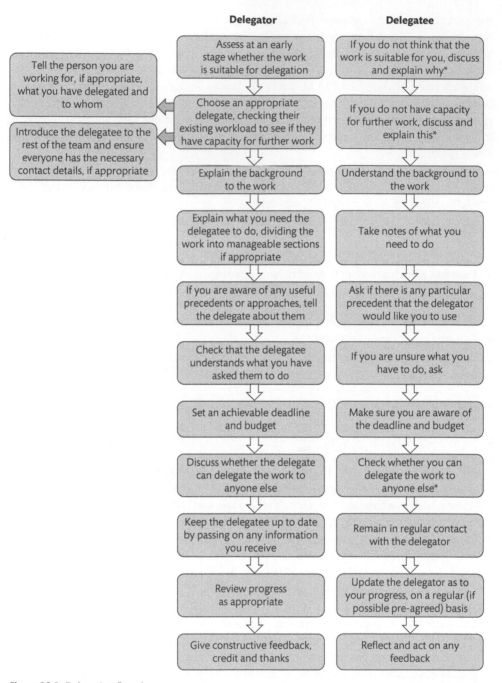

Delegator   **Delegatee**

Delegator	Delegatee
Assess at an early stage whether the work is suitable for delegation	If you do not think that the work is suitable for you, discuss and explain why*
Choose an appropriate delegate, checking their existing workload to see if they have capacity for further work	If you do not have capacity for further work, discuss and explain this*
Explain the background to the work	Understand the background to the work
Explain what you need the delegatee to do, dividing the work into manageable sections if appropriate	Take notes of what you need to do
If you are aware of any useful precedents or approaches, tell the delegate about them	Ask if there is any particular precedent that the delegator would like you to use
Check that the delegatee understands what you have asked them to do	If you are unsure what you have to do, ask
Set an achievable deadline and budget	Make sure you are aware of the deadline and budget
Discuss whether the delegate can delegate the work to anyone else	Check whether you can delegate the work to anyone else*
Keep the delegatee up to date by passing on any information you receive	Remain in regular contact with the delegator
Review progress as appropriate	Update the delegator as to your progress, on a regular (if possible pre-agreed) basis
Give constructive feedback, credit and thanks	Reflect and act on any feedback

Side notes (branching from "Choose an appropriate delegate..."):
- Tell the person you are working for, if appropriate, what you have delegated and to whom
- Introduce the delegatee to the rest of the team and ensure everyone has the necessary contact details, if appropriate

Figure 12.1 Delegation flowchart

* Take a cautious approach here. As a lawyer, you must be willing to take on challenging work in order to develop, and you must be willing to work hard. However, part of being a professional is also being able to manage your workload effectively, and knowing when to ask for help. If, for example, a supervisor mistakes you for someone else who is more senior, it would be appropriate to discuss that you are, say, a trainee. If you have been told by one supervisor that you should not take on any further work until you have completed a task for him, then again you would need to discuss this with the delegator. As ever, your tone and body language will be important here to make sure you do not come across as defensive, or simply saying 'no'.

12.4 Meetings

While initially you may have limited opportunities to change how meetings are run, it is nevertheless worth spending some time considering how meetings could be run most effectively, simply because meetings constitute such a considerable part of a lawyer's day. Lawyers will have external meetings (with clients, see 10.6) and internal meetings (with their colleagues).

12.4.1 Internal meetings

It will be probably be a while before you attend a meeting at a law firm or other professional office (although you may do so while undertaking pro bono work or on a vacation scheme or other work experience). However, as mentioned at 12.2.4 in the context of team-working, the arrival of alternative business structures (see Chapters 6 and 15) means that law firms are increasingly looking to recruit people who can bring business acumen into the office. If you are interested in this area, it is worthwhile considering how meetings can be run effectively while maximising profit.

While most businesses accept that external meetings should be run as efficiently as possible, typically internal meetings can be a significant source of frustration. It is a common complaint that businesses do not prioritise internal meetings, and law firms are no exception. While in theory they may appreciate that internal meetings should be on an equal footing with external meetings, it is not uncommon to witness lawyers who turn up late, allow themselves to be distracted and interrupted by their smartphones throughout the meeting, then leave early. Meetings can stray far away from the business they were called to discuss, or they may be called out of habit even though there is nothing to discuss. Internal meetings may fall into a regular pattern where each person repeats the same frustrating behaviour, be it one dominating voice, or someone complaining about the same old issue over and over again without suggesting any workable solution.

These issues may be familiar to you from meetings you have attended to date. However, when you factor in the cost of internal meetings in a law firm (by multiplying the time taken by their hourly salary, or indeed their hourly charge-out rate), it becomes clear that they are so expensive that solicitors particularly can ill afford to run them as they do.

Strategies to avoid some of these problems (and this could be the kind of question you might be asked in a law firm interview) include circulating an agenda in advance, establishing a practice of starting the meetings on time, nominating someone to chair the meeting to keep it focused and running to time, and restricting any record of the meeting to identifying the action required rather than recording exactly what everyone said. More creative ideas include conducting meetings with everyone standing up (to prevent meetings from running on too long) and imposing a time limit on contributions. These ideas obviously need to be implemented by someone with the power to force change; however as a student and a junior lawyer you can start as you mean to go on, develop your skills, and make a very good impression by thinking about how to make any meetings under your control (such as those of any club or society, or to organise the cake sale) run as efficiently as possible.

12.5 Client care

All businesses need to care for their customers, but some do this better than others. It is much more efficient to keep an existing, good client content than to lose that client and have to find another, but this is not always put into practice. For example, you might have experienced the frustration, as an existing customer of a bank or mobile phone company, of discovering that new customers are being offered better rates.

Without clients, businesses are nothing, and in an increasingly competitive marketplace all businesses, including law firms, need to keep their clients happy. When asked, law firms would say that they expect their employees to provide a good level of customer care, but anecdotally it would seem that many are yet to incorporate customer care into their training and development programmes. In the absence of any formal customer care training, the best guide is to consider the service you provide from a customer's perspective. This is good practice whatever the nature of the business. There are things you can be doing now to increase your understanding of customer care. If you have any experience of working in a service industry, such as in a shop, bar, or pro bono clinic, you will have a better understanding of what you can do to improve the customer's experience. Reflecting on this will help you to develop this skill now, and you will be able to showcase it on your curriculum vitae.

12.5.1 Common complaints (and how to avoid them)

Some of the most common complaints made by law firm clients are set out below, together with guidance to help you avoid being the lawyer they complain about. Again, this is exactly the sort of question that might arise in a law firm interview, but be aware that these complaints are not confined to law firms. Be alert to items in the news about customer care, and consider how they might transfer into areas relevant to your career.

Fees

Not surprisingly, bills can be a source of frustration for a client. A frequent complaint is that they are too high, but other complaints include that the bill arrived unexpectedly, contained obvious errors on its face, appeared to refer to work which was unnecessary or on which too much time had been spent, or included charges for disbursements (see definition) that seem very high or were unexpected.

 Essential explanation

A **disbursement** is a payment that the law firm has made on behalf of the client for goods or services. Examples include photocopying charges and fees paid to the Land Registry for land searches. They can amount to a significant proportion of a client's bill.

A good lawyer can help to avoid this by managing a client's expectations well. The bill should not come as a surprise to the client, nor should there be any surprises in the bill itself.

Jargon

Lawyers can become so used to using jargon or 'legalese' between themselves that they forget that a client will not understand what they are saying. Chapters 10 and 11 explain that all communication between lawyer and client should be clear and as succinct as possible. Clients will become frustrated if they cannot understand the advice they are paying for. A good lawyer can understand difficult legal concepts, but it takes a very good lawyer to be able to communicate those concepts clearly in a way that a non-lawyer can understand.

Listening

Everyone likes to be listened to and clients are no exception to this. Lawyers, like many other professionals, can be poor listeners, with a tendency to interrupt clients or make assumptions about what they think. As Chapter 10 sets out, this can have a catastrophic effect on the appropriateness of the work which a lawyer produces, but it can also leave the client feeling neglected and not valued. Asking lots of open questions, and listening to the answers without interruption, can help a client feel satisfied with your work. Chapter 10 explores this further.

Manner

It does not matter how technically brilliant you are if you have no interpersonal skills when it comes to delivering your advice. You need to develop a good 'bedside manner' with clients that is neither too patronising nor too abrupt. This will not be the same for each client. Once you know your clients and the work you will be doing for them, you can and should tailor your manner to suit. For example, advising a recently bereaved person may require a different manner to advising a company director on a multi-million pound deal. However, even this will depend on the individual concerned.

Keeping the client updated

Clients should not have to call you to find out what is happening with their matter. It is much better if you are proactive, and take the initiative to contact them, even just to convey a brief message that nothing has happened. It is particularly important to contact clients if they have tried to contact you. Failing to return a call is a common complaint. You may be able to think of an example from your own experience, such as trying to speak to your bank manager about a loan, and reflect on how it made you feel when your call was left unanswered. Admittedly as a lawyer it can be a difficult step to call a client to deliver an unpalatable message, such as your work is going to be late, or you have made a mistake in some way. However, experience dictates that clients will always appreciate an early and honest call rather than the alternative which is for them to wait, eventually call you and finally, when pressed, for you to confess to the delay or the error. Lawyers who covet the role of trusted adviser must develop good habits in keeping clients informed of everything they need to know, good and bad.

Poor-quality work

Chapter 11 explained that clients will judge you on the standard of your writing and drafting (often more so than the quality of your legal advice, which they will presume is accurate in the absence of any obvious error). Clients will complain about work which is clearly deficient in terms of spelling, grammar, and punctuation. Some errors which are undetectable using spell-check can actually cause offence. Consider the impact of 'Dear Gut' instead of 'Dear

Gus', or 'See you shorty' rather than 'See you shortly'. Common complaints surround poor use of punctuation (particularly the apostrophe) and sentence structure (particularly long letters with no paragraphs). While lawyers can argue that the work was actually of satisfactory quality given the circumstances in which it was done, for instance if they had to dictate a letter very quickly over the telephone, or draft a clause in the middle of the night, you can see that from the client's perspective these errors can be perceived as reflecting a generally substandard service.

Lack of continuity

Law firms are busy places and lawyers will be working for several clients at the same time. Client matters can also take a long time to resolve and even lawyers need holidays. It is a business reality therefore that from time to time you will have to pass work for one client to one of your colleagues. Most clients will understand this if the process is managed properly. However all too often, due to time pressure, the client is the last to know that someone else has taken over the work on his file, or will discover that the new lawyer may not have been brought fully up to date as to the progress on the file. Again, you might be able to reflect on your own experience; anyone who has had the experience of trying to contact a business only to find themselves passed from one person to another, having to explain the same issue to several different people, will appreciate how annoying this can be. Factor in that as a client of a law firm you are often paying by the minute for these repeated explanations and you will appreciate why this is a common client complaint. A few simple conversations, with the client and the lawyer you are handing over to, can remove these aggravating factors.

12.5.2 **Managing clients**

The key to good client relationships is to manage the client's expectations. For example, if a client is calling several times a day to check your progress, you clearly need to explain to her that you will provide a regular update and this will be a more cost-effective way for her to monitor your progress. Similarly, a client who expects you to be available to her or deliver work at unsociable hours needs to understand that this may be either unnecessary or may warrant a higher fee. The best time to discuss and establish all of this is at the outset, before the client instructs you.

12.5.3 **SRA Code of Conduct 2011**

You have read at 12.1.3 that lawyers must be aware of ethics (see also 6.3.4). The Solicitors Regulation Authority, which regulates the profession, has a Code of Conduct which solicitors must follow. Chapter 1 of the Code sets out obligations regarding client care. The Code reinforces the conclusions drawn above by placing an obligation on solicitors to provide clients with sufficient information about the services they require, how those services will be delivered, and how much they will cost. It also details how solicitors should make clients aware of their complaints procedure.

As referred to above, the Solicitors Regulation Authority also has requirements about how you must maintain confidentiality when dealing with clients. Students learn about this Code during their vocational stage of training, but useful information can be found on the Solicitors

Regulation Authority website, details of which are set out in the 'Further reading' section at the end of this chapter.

12.5.4 Feedback

It is good practice to seek feedback from any customer when you complete work for them. You may already have provided feedback to your university, for example on your course materials or the teaching you have received. This is so that the university can listen to your opinion, address any issues you raise, and ensure it continues to do everything that receives positive feedback. Thinking carefully about how you provide such feedback will develop your employability skills. For example, it is likely that you have been able to provide feedback anonymously to date, which has benefits in terms of freeing you to give your honest opinion, but has the drawback of allowing you to say things that you would not say to someone's face. When you enter the professional world your feedback will be attributable, so it is worth developing now the skill of providing feedback in a way that is constructive and which you would feel comfortable delivering face to face. As a professional, you will not just receive feedback but you will also have to give feedback to your colleagues and delegates, for example. Some businesses, including law firms, have formal procedures in place for this. Everyone likes to be asked their opinion, and indeed if business clients request feedback in their own business they may think it strange if you do not ask their opinion of your work at the end of the process.

12.6 Networking

Networking is a key skill for professionals, and although lawyers may have been relatively slow to embrace the need for this skill, it is now accepted that networking is part of a lawyer's job. Networking involves building new business relationships in order to generate business opportunities. Some people are very comfortable approaching and speaking to new people, and actively enjoy it, and to those people this skill will come more naturally. However for many lawyers, junior and senior, it is one that can take them outside their comfort zone. As ever, the keys to mastering this skill are preparation and practice.

There are networking opportunities everywhere and accomplished networkers will not only be able to identify these opportunities, but also work them to their advantage. As a student, you may encounter face-to-face networking opportunities through work experience, pro bono work, sitting in on court hearings, attending talks and law fairs, and also simply by socialising with your peers, who one day may be prospective and sought-after clients or employers. Social media such as Twitter and Facebook and the practice of blogging have also opened up networking opportunities online.

When you meet potential clients or employers, as the case may be, you want them to remember your name. If you have been given a name badge, wear it. It will be most prominent if you wear it on the side of your body you shake hands with. If you do not have a name badge, you need to develop another strategy to make sure the people you wish to secure as business contacts remember your name. If you have a business card, you can give them your card. Ask if they have a card, as not only do you want them to remember your name, you also need to remember theirs. If you are attending an event, it is helpful if you can see the attendee list in advance. Some event organisers are very good in this regard, and will send the attendee list, either directly to you or to the person in your organisation who has arranged your attendance. It is worth asking if one is available in advance. If it is not, there is often a sign-in sheet at the door of the event, and a quick glance can reveal whether there is anyone attending who you already know or who you would specifically like to make a business contact.

Then you need to start speaking to people. This is sometimes referred to as 'working the room'. It can be difficult to approach people, but remember that they too will be open to networking opportunities and are likely to welcome you. Use your communication skills, including good eye contact and body language, to signal to someone that you would like to join them.

Once you have the attention of the person you would like to meet, you need to be able to engage them. You can prepare in advance what you might be able to say if the conversation does not flow naturally from the outset. Remember that the other person is not privy to your preparation, so do not decide to talk about something so esoteric that, while impressive, will not allow the other person to participate in the conversation. The morning's headlines, or even something as simple as the good old weather, will be enough for most people to start the flow of conversation.

Another skill you will need is to be able to exit from a conversation. A good networker will seek to circulate as much as possible. Do not be inhibited about doing this (indeed the person you are speaking to will also want time to speak to others), but obviously there is a technique to exiting in a polite fashion. Classic techniques include excusing yourself to go to the toilet. Clearly however you cannot use this too many times. Going to get a glass of water or sandwich can also help you to exit in a polite fashion.

If you have been attending a talk, do not underestimate the value of staying behind to thank the speaker. Most attendees file out immediately, yet the five minutes after the talk can be an excellent opportunity for networking. Speakers will feel at ease, and will be happy to hear some feedback and answer questions which show that you have listened to and enjoyed what they had to say.

Remember to follow up the contacts you have made. Sending a short follow-up email, or, if appropriate, a short telephone call to say how you enjoyed meeting them, is a good idea. Social media, for instance the LinkedIn platform, can also be helpful to secure an ongoing contact, and this is explored further below. Use your instinct and skills to determine what it is appropriate to say in this follow-up communication. Depending on the individual concerned, and how your conversation went, sometimes it is not appropriate to do anything other than say thank you, while at other times a suggestion that you meet for coffee, or an expression of interest, such as in work experience or mentoring opportunities, can be appropriate and pay dividends.

Even reading this paragraph may have made your toes curl. To the uninitiated, networking can sound embarrassingly like you are trying to secure a date. In practice, take comfort from the fact that you will not be the only one in the room to be networking. It is now generally accepted that everyone in the room will be, or should be. Also appreciate the fact that most people will also feel a little out of their comfort zone. The more polished your networking skills, the more people will want to talk to you because, conversely, *you* will help to put *them* at ease.

Be aware that networking does not necessarily have immediate rewards. Do not feel frustrated if you attend an event and leave empty-handed, or people do not respond to your email. Networking will deliver benefits in the long term. It may only be after meeting someone for the fourth time, for example, that you feel comfortable in inviting that person to connect with you on LinkedIn, or to suggest you meet for a coffee. The only thing you can say with certainty is that if you do not attend events at all, you will definitely not extend your network.

You can practise your networking skills now. No matter how early a stage you are at in your career, you will already have a network you can access. Although they are likely to have no influence on getting you a training contract or other career just yet, your fellow students are excellent contacts as in the future they will go on to become lawyers and other professionals. The person you are sitting next to now might be the CEO of a company a law firm would love to bring in as a client in 15 years' time. Following the guidance in this book you can extend your current network to include alumni of your university and other legal professionals.

12.6.1 Law fairs

Law fairs offer a valuable opportunity to meet many firms under one roof. Many students choose to attend them, but often find themselves wandering rather aimlessly up and down many aisles of stands, perhaps managing to gather a few branded freebies on the way. Few students exploit their full potential.

At a law fair you will be able to speak to employees of many firms. Typically firms send a mixture of recruitment personnel, trainees, and other fee-earners. This is a huge expense for a firm, not least because the trainees and fee-earners are not fee-earning while they are at the fair. So think for a moment about why they bother to attend. They are hoping to attract good-quality candidates for training contracts. From this perspective, then, law fairs have the potential to be mini interviews where the firms have done all the work and come to meet you in one place. Put this way, it should be clear that no student considering a legal career should pass up the opportunity to attend a fair.

As many firms recruit years in advance, you should attend law fairs even in your first year of study. Although firms pay considerable sums to consultants to draft a set of values and to create a website which they feel reflects them uniquely, it is a common student observation that 'they all say the same thing'. The fairs offer a forum to meet and talk informally to firms and to get a real feel for their true culture and values.

The firms will be interested in meeting you. They will also expect you to be interested in meeting them. You need to prepare to make sure you leave the firm with a good impression of you and what you have to offer.

Preparation

The organisers of a law fair will circulate a list of attendees and a floor plan in advance of the fair. You need to study this to plan who to target, as the fairs are often so large you are unlikely to stumble across the firms you are looking for by accident. For example, if you are interested in working in a mid-sized regional firm which has a strong intellectual property presence, you need to work through the list in conjunction with a legal directory such as *Chambers and Partners* or the *Legal 500* and access to the firms' websites, and highlight those firms you would like to visit. Alternatively, if you have not yet narrowed your preference to that degree, you may like to make a varied selection of firms, from boutique practices to the largest Magic Circle firms, to start this process. Wherever you are in recognising where you want to practise, your aim should be to be able to produce a shortlist based on your experiences at the fair.

Presentation

Having drawn the conclusion that the fair offers an opportunity not unlike a mini interview, it follows that you should present yourself well. You will be making an impression on the law firms that you meet, and you should dress to convey the impression you would like to make. There is guidance at 12.1.3 about how to dress for an interview. You may feel more comfortable dressing in something a little more relaxed than a suit, however the guidance about general presentation in terms of your hair, shoes, and so on is just as applicable for law fairs.

Execution

Once you are at the fair, with a plan of action, you can expect to feel a little nervous. Take courage though, that the firms will appreciate that you might find the prospect of speaking to them quite daunting. If you can appear polite, well informed, and work on developing a veneer of confidence, this is all you need. The firms will want to speak to you, but this is easier for them if they have some information about you. Introducing yourself by name, shaking hands and telling them what you are studying, where, and what you are enjoying will help to start a conversation and strike up a rapport.

You should not ask questions you should already know the answer to. These include anything you could reasonably be expected to find on the firm's website. If you have prepared in advance you should already know the basics. This is not to say asking questions is wrong, far from it, but you should prepare questions which help to give you the edge in any subsequent application to the firm. For example, do not ask where the firm is based, or whether it has a property department (both of which you should have researched already), but, for example, you might ask whether the firm is planning to expand, geographically or strategically. Subtly show the firm that you have done your homework about them. Tell the firm what you are enjoying, and sound enthusiastic. Ask what you can be doing to impress in this area, give examples of what you are already doing, and what in the area has taken your interest.

After the fair, use the experience to prepare a shortlist of firms which you liked, and make a note of anything you learned which could help your application to that firm. A well-placed tweet can be helpful in putting a marker in the sand that you spoke to the firm, but be selective as the firms will be able to see who else you are tweeting.

12.6.2 **Mentors**

Having a mentor is a long-established and valued process by which you are guided by someone who has reached the place you are aiming for. The process has benefits for both the mentor and the mentee, and you will find that practising lawyers are often keen to take on the role of mentor. There are various ways of finding a mentor, and most universities have formal schemes which you can join. This is another valuable way to gain an insight into the profession, and learn valuable wider lessons about being a professional. Increasingly universities are harnessing their alumni network to help with mentoring current students, so this is a route you may be able to explore. Social networking may also lend itself to a more informal version of mentoring, as discussed above. Finally, do not forget the value in mentoring, and being mentored by, your fellow students. You will all have different skills and experiences to share and learn from, and appreciating at this early stage that you have something worthwhile to share will help you to reflect and identify your own individual strengths that you can showcase at interview.

12.6.3 **Work experience**

Employers will expect to see that you have sought and found work experience. Work experience will help you to develop your employability skills as well as give you an opportunity to impress those you are working with and learn what goes on in a law firm or in chambers. Mini-pupillages, vacation schemes, law tasters, opportunities to work as a paralegal, and other informal work experience are therefore things you need to seek out actively, and the sooner you do this, the better.

12.6.4 **Pro bono**

Pro bono means 'for the public good' and pro bono initiatives provide a superb opportunity to provide advice to real clients while helping members of society to access legal advice which they could not otherwise afford. There are numerous initiatives, covering the full spectrum of legal work. Universities often run law clinics in partnership with practice or charities, and there are also other external pro bono schemes, such as the Innocence Network UK. LawWorks is the Solicitors' Pro Bono Group. Together with the Bar Pro Bono Unit and the CILEx Pro Bono Trust, it forms part of the National Pro Bono Centre in Chancery Lane. Further information on pro bono is available online, for example on the website of ProBonoUK and on the Law Careers website. Further details are provided in the 'Further reading' section at the end of this chapter.

12.7 **Marketing**

Most businesses realise that they have to market the goods they are selling or the services they are providing, but some businesses will be more naturally adept at marketing than others. Lawyers do not tend to be natural salespeople. However, the market is now so competitive that everyone in the firm is expected actively to market their firm and bring in new business. In order to do this effectively, you need to understand the message that the firm wishes you to deliver. Most firms now have their aims, objectives, and/or strategy set out clearly on their website. When you join a firm, further information is likely to feature on the firm's intranet site. The earlier you are familiar with these selling messages, the better you will be at marketing. Of course the best form of marketing that you can deliver as a lawyer is to provide exceptional client service.

12.8 Information technology

There is no escape, you are likely to need sound IT skills wherever you work in today's world. From multinationals to local services such as your local car wash or gardener, businesses are using IT to increase their public profile and develop client relationships. The good news is that this is an area where youth is most definitely on your side. You are likely to have grown up around so much IT that your skills are well honed. Conversely, some of the partners in a law firm would not have had a single computer in their classroom during school and may have started out as a lawyer before mobile phones and the internet were in common use. You are therefore in a good position to dazzle them with your skills in this regard.

The firms will train you on their individual IT systems, which will include some or all of online time recording, dictation and precedent and information sharing systems. However the better you are with word-processing, spreadsheets, email, and typing, the more polished you will look and the more efficient you will be on arrival. Take advantage of the expertise you can tap into at university. Attend any courses you can which will polish your IT skills for the professional world.

12.9 Social media

Law firms are as alert to new business development opportunities as the next business and increasingly they are turning to social media platforms such as Twitter and Facebook to extend their reach. These platforms can also be useful networking opportunities for you as an individual. However, you must use them with care.

12.9.1 A word of caution

Remember that these are very public platforms, and you should not post anything on them which you would not be happy to say or show to a partner's face. Some professionals operate different Twitter accounts, one personal, and one professional. However, given the nature of the legal profession and the general availability of Twitter posts to the public at large, junior lawyers would be best advised to play safe and avoid using Twitter in a personal capacity. It is not uncommon for employers to check a prospective employee's Twitter feed. Clearly it is possible to use your feed to impress a potential employer if it evidences an interest in law or in other ways supports any claims you have made on your application form. However, your holiday snaps, or tweets about your latest big night out, might be best reserved for a more private forum. Facebook can be more private than Twitter, but you must take care to set your privacy preferences correctly, and choose your friends wisely. Again, given the potential for error it is advisable that you post only information that you would be happy for your employer to read.

12.9.2 Twitter

Twitter can be an effective networking tool if used correctly. By following firms and individuals in whom you have a professional interest, you can extend your professional network and access a wealth of relevant information, including employment opportunities. Tweeting itself improves your ability to summarise and distil information as you must restrict yourself to the limit of 140 characters. You can also increase your commercial awareness simply by following the right people then reading your timeline. Professionals, including employers and academics, tweet on a range of issues that can help you develop the skills in this book (see e.g. @missshephard which tweets about business law in practice, legal skills, commercial awareness, employability, law firms, and students). By re-tweeting or 'favouriting' tweets you can bring yourself to the attention of those you are following. However, if you are to do this you need to make a sustained effort. Several firms currently have a Twitter identity which is not managed on a regular basis, and this is revealed when they are copied into tweets which remain unanswered or are not commented on. If you no longer intend to maintain your account regularly, it is best to shut it down, otherwise you may well become known, but for the wrong reasons.

12.9.3 Blogging

A blog, or web log, is an online diary. There is extensive guidance available on the internet as to how you can create your own free blog. Maintaining a regular blog on a subject you are interested in, legal or otherwise, can help you to practise and improve your written communication skills and raise your profile among your professional network. You can use Twitter and Facebook to link to and promote your blog. Reading other people's legal blogs can also help to increase your own commercial awareness. Again, if you do decide to maintain a blog, take care to ensure the content is suitable for reading by a prospective employer.

12.9.4 LinkedIn

LinkedIn provides a professional social media platform on which you can showcase your curriculum vitae and capture your professional contacts, and it has been embraced by the legal sector. The process of putting together a profile will help you to focus your mind on your curriculum vitae, and the earlier you begin to think about your curriculum vitae the better it will be by the time you come to apply for a training contract. You will be able to link in to your peers immediately, and having your profile ready means that you are in a better position to capture any contacts you make while networking. The way the site works is that a standard message is sent to the contacts of your choosing, asking if they would like to connect with you. It is possible to personalise this standard message and this can be a good idea with contacts you are hoping to impress. As the site makes clear, however, you should only ask to connect to people you know well. As a rule of thumb, if the recipient will not be able to place you when your connect request arrives, you should probably not be sending them a contact request.

12.10 The application process

One of the reasons it is important to understand employability skills at an early stage in your studies is so that you will come across well when applying for a training contract or indeed any other graduate job.

Your careers adviser should have a wealth of information to help guide you through the law firm application process. You should consult a careers adviser, wherever you are studying, as soon as possible after you start your studies. Take as full advantage of the careers resources as you can. Find out any arrangements in place to contact alumni. Create a curriculum vitae the minute you start university and ask your careers adviser and personal tutor for help in identifying gaps and issues that you can work on while you are at university. Some tips about the application form and interview process are outlined below, to highlight how you can demonstrate your skills in the application process.

Further information is set out about presentations (12.10.4), group work (12.10.5), and socialising (12.10.6), which you may encounter on an assessment day or during any vacation schemes or work experience. It can be startlingly clear to an interviewer which candidates have not studied skills in a practical context, and which have. However, having read and engaged with the skills chapters in this book, you will be in a good position to show off your legal skills wherever you are currently in your legal career.

12.10.1 Timing your application for a training contract and vacation placement

The Law Careers website referred to in the 'Further reading' section of this chapter sets out firm specific application windows in relation to training contracts and work placements. The following will give you a sense of the general timescales of which you should be aware.

Larger law firms

The large law firms recruit two years in advance, so if you wish to apply to work for one of these firms you could be applying for interview in your *first year* of a two-year law degree or in your *second year* of a three-year law degree (hence the need to develop your employability skills now). If you manage to secure a training contract this way this would mean you could then complete your Diploma in Legal Practice immediately after your law degree and progress straight into your training contract.

Applications for both training contracts and vacations schemes tend to open in the autumn term, generally from October to December. Many vacation scheme applications close at the end of January, but some remain open as late as April. Training contract applications tend to close at the end of July. As the vast majority of these firms recruit from their vacation schemes, you should apply for both a vacation scheme and a training contract at the firm. Historically law firms did not take applications from first year students (on a three year degree) for vacation schemes, however this appears to be changing and more firms are introducing what they refer to as 'law tasters' for first year students.

You should look out for announcements that firms are recruiting to meet increased demand, as very occasionally the larger firms will realise they have under-recruited, perhaps as the market expands. Again, your careers adviser, Twitter, and your network of contacts will help in this regard.

Smaller law firms

Smaller firms recruit later, however the earlier you start to hone your employability skills, the better you will come across in any interview further down the line. These firms may recruit 12 to

18 months in advance, and may recruit trainees from their pool of paralegals. You should seek to obtain some work experience with these firms from your second year onwards, and if this goes well you may be able to secure part-time employment with these firms while you study. Generally these firms are more open to speculative applications.

12.10.2 **Application form**

The application form is likely to be the first impression you make on a law firm, so you need to make it stand out for the right reasons. Usually you will need to show that you have:

- a good academic record;
- good knowledge of the firm and the legal world (ideally referencing some work experience);
- the skills referred to in this book.

Many firms ask for forms to be typed and submitted electronically. Type in a word processing package first and apply a spelling and grammar check before you then cut and paste into the form. Despite the open acknowledgement that the application process for professional employment is highly competitive, it is all too common to find spelling and grammatical errors in submitted application forms. Firms receive huge amounts of forms and need to apply a filter system to identify which ones to reject. Those containing such errors typically will be rejected without further reading. You must not give the firms any easy excuse to reject your form. For firms which still require hand-written forms, it is obviously important that the form is legible and neatly presented. Follow any specific instructions, such as to write in capital letters using black ink. Failure to do so will help the employer narrow down the forms it needs to continue to read.

When composing the content of the form, of course you must highlight your strengths, but be aware that law firms remain relatively conservative places and so too many superlatives ('I am excellent at', 'I excel at') might dilute the overall effect. Analyse what you write from an objective perspective. If you are describing your academic results as excellent, consider whether they really are. Just because you describe results as excellent does not render them so. Be honest; identify what you think are your strong points and make sure your form highlights these strengths. Research the firm's stated objectives or strategy and make clear how your strengths will help the firm achieve its goals. Once you have identified your real strengths, do not be afraid to bring them to the interviewer's attention; it is not 'brash' or 'bragging', and you can be sure that the candidates before and after you will be drawing attention to what they do well.

It can come as a surprise to those new to the applications process that you also need to scrutinise your weaknesses. Is there anything in your record that stands out as being below your usual standard? If so, then you have two choices. You can either remain silent about it pending confirmation of an interview, or you can address the issue in the form. Whichever route you choose, be ready for an interviewer to ask you about your weaknesses. This is not necessarily a negative. Candidates who can show how they have learned from previous mistakes can make a very good impression. Those who refuse to acknowledge their mistakes will not come across well.

Don't be descriptive in your application. For example, if you worked in a bar in Corfu, say what you learned from it and how that will help the law firm's business needs, for example in terms of customer service, communication, language skills, punctuality, and complaints handling.

Analyse your form for any perceived inconsistencies, which you may need to explain either on the form itself or later if you are called for interview. For example, if you are applying to a corporate law firm, but your work experience to date has been with a high-street criminal practice, or you have chosen to study personal injury law, be prepared for an interviewer to question you about this. Again, it is not necessarily a negative, but being ill-prepared for what an interviewer considers an obvious question that your form raises will be deemed a negative.

12.10.3 Interviews

If you are called for interview you should feel a sense of achievement. You now have the opportunity to impress face to face. Naturally your communication skills (see Chapter 10) will be key in achieving this. First impressions count, so make sure you offer a firm handshake, look the part, pay attention to your body language and vocabulary, and are polite from the moment you arrive on the premises.

You are likely to feel nervous, but nevertheless you must be able to present with a veneer of confidence, both verbally and non-verbally. Try not to let nerves prevent your personality coming across. It is very easy for personable, enthusiastic individuals to turn unwittingly into overly intense, grim-faced interviewees. Remember that you want to convince the interviewer that she would like to work with you. Try to relax, smile, and make plenty of eye contact from the outset. You need to let your personality shine through the polished version of you that you are presenting to the interviewer. Never try to be someone you are not. It will be obvious to an interviewer and the chances are that the person you actually are is just as, or in fact more, appealing. Remember that you have been selected for interview on the basis of your application form, and this details all that *you* have achieved to date.

There are some techniques you can use to address the issue of nerves before an interview. Make sure that you arrive in good time. Aim to arrive at least an hour in advance, leaving plenty of time to allow for a late train or getting lost. When you arrive at the firm itself, you will be making an impression from the moment you open the door, so before you do that you may like to factor in some time to have a coffee nearby, where you can read through any notes, go through what you plan to say in your head, and check that you look presentable. If you can do all this 'off-site', the more professional and confident you will look when you arrive at the firm's offices.

Some students suffer more from anxiety than others. A certain level of anxiety can be helpful, as it can enhance your performance. However, if you know that anxiety is a particular problem for you, and can cause you to feel overwhelmed, you need to take steps to address this as it will inhibit your performance at interview. There are things that you can do to help. Regular exercise, relaxation, and talking to friends can all reduce stress levels which can lead to panic attacks, so try not to change your routine or isolate yourself in the run up to an interview, or spend too much time worrying about it. When you are at the interview, if you feel overcome, buy yourself some time by asking to be excused to go to the bathroom, practise good breathing techniques, and take a small bottle of water with you to sip as this can have a calming effect. Further guidance on how to control anxiety is set out in the 'Further reading' section at the end of this chapter.

During the interview process employers will be looking for good communication skills and in particular whether you can answer questions clearly, react appropriately, retain your composure, and listen to what others have to say. Your answers need to be fluent, comprehensive, and promote all those skills and experiences which, having read this book, you know that the employer is looking for. A good interviewer will help you to showcase your talents. However some interviewers do little in terms of guiding you through the process and simply ask open questions which leave it up to you to choose what to tell them. You need to be familiar with what you have written on your application form and show the interviewer that you (i) understand which skills they want you to have, and why, (ii) actually have those skills, and (iii) indeed can point to examples on your application form which prove this.

Do not be afraid of taking a moment to consider your answer before you speak. What can seem like a deafening silence to you is likely to sound simply like a natural pause from an interviewer's perspective. Remember that employers want employees to think carefully before they speak. Some employers will test whether you can do this specifically by asking you a question that you could not possibly have pre-prepared, for example 'what would you do with the Millennium Dome'? In fact, the actual answer to a question like this is unlikely to be of great import to the interviewer. Instead they will be looking to see how well you deal with the unexpected. If you did not pause for thought before such a question, your answer is unlikely to be good. You may start to stumble as you realise you need some thinking time, or in the heat of the moment you may simply say you do not know. This is not going to come across well. Instead, a candidate who responds by acknowledging that is an interesting question and requests a moment to think before answering is likely to come across well, even if ultimately his answer is not that feasible, such as 'I would turn it upside down and use it as a fairground ride'. You will not, of course be asked this example now as it was a topical question around the year 2000, but you can see how keeping up to date by reading a quality newspaper regularly, certainly in the month or so prior to interview, could give you an advantage in answering this type of question. Another example might be 'What should be done with the Olympic Stadium?', and there have been several press articles about whether the pitch is suitable for football club use, for example.

Conversely, make sure that your answers to any obvious questions, such as 'why law (or other profession)?', 'why this firm?', 'what is your main strength/ weakness?' or any question relating to the information on your application form, reveal that you have prepared well for the interview. Generally, you need to be prepared to talk about yourself, your interests, your strengths and weaknesses, challenges you have faced and how you tackled them, your team-working and leadership skills, what you are proud of, and precisely why the firm should choose you over another candidate.

You may also be asked questions about commercial awareness. Chapters 13 to 16 contain case studies and sample interview questions to get you thinking about how you might tackle these.

For all these questions the STAR technique can help you to structure your answer well:

- **S**ituation—give context.
- **T**ask—describe the challenge, why you were facing it, and the expectations of that challenge.
- **A**ction—describe what you did and how you did it.
- **R**esults—explain what they were and how you quantified them (e.g. did you obtain some recognition, make any savings?).

Being an impressive interviewee is a skill in itself, and as with all skills it improves with practice. Seek and take any opportunity to participate in a practice interview, and if possible record and review the practice interview yourself. Finally, remember that if you operate a reflective practice, then even if you do not succeed at interview, the process itself will have been a valuable one in terms of improving your interviewing skills for the next time. Remember you only need to succeed in one application to get into the profession, so stay positive.

12.10.4 Presentations

Chapter 10 considered the skill of presenting, and it is not unusual for an employer to test this skill by asking you to give a presentation as part of the assessment process (including on a vacation or other work experience scheme). This could be sprung on you when you arrive, or you may have been asked to prepare it in advance. The firm may set the title for you, or you might be able to select a topic of your own. Your audience may include other candidates, solicitors, partners, and/or members of the recruitment team.

You will usually be given a target time frame for delivery of the presentation. Practise your presentation to make sure it will not go on too long, and have extra items you can bring in, or items you can cut out, to give you some flexibility to hit the target timescale. Often you will be given the option of preparing visual aids. When preparing these, bear in mind how long the presentation is and keep them to a minimum; a slide show may help to put you in your comfort zone but it rarely makes for a good presentation. The best presenters do not use cards, but if you really cannot do without a prompt, restrict yourself to bullet points on cards and never read out a pre-prepared presentation.

When structuring you presentation make sure that it has a clear beginning, where you signpost the audience as to what is to come, a middle, and a definite end which draws everything together. In delivering your presentation, make sure you use the communication skills outlined in Chapter 10, and engage the audience by using effective body language (posture, eye contact, no distracting habits), looking professional (no leaning on the table or rushing around the room), projecting your voice (ask the audience if they can hear you), and trying to relax and smile. If you do not seem to be enjoying your presentation, the audience will really struggle to do so. Humour can be effective, but avoid being flippant and bear in mind you are unlikely to have had time to get to know your audience well. Remember to keep it simple. If you try to include too much detail you are likely to overrun. Include the essential information, and present it succinctly and clearly. Remember to try to relax, be yourself, and smile.

12.10.5 Group work

Assessment days can also include group exercises where the firm will test your team-working skills and how you work with others. You should bear in mind everything you have learned from Section 12.2 and seek to demonstrate you have these skills. Often the firm will have tasked particular employees to watch specific people. So the observer sitting at the back of the room might nevertheless be watching your every move. They will be looking to see what role you play in the group. You absolutely must make a contribution. However you must not be seen to dominate the discussion at the expense of the quieter members of the group. Showing that you have noticed someone who has not had the chance to contribute, and giving her the chance to speak (without putting her on the spot) will work in your favour. If you always take the easy role, such as writing up others' ideas without contributing any of your own, the observers will notice. They will also be looking to see how you handle any disagreements between the group members, and whether you have any powers of persuasion.

12.10.6 Socialising

Often lunch or drinks are factored into an assessment day (or vacation scheme) to allow you to meet the people who work there. Do not make the mistake of letting your hair down too much at these events. While they have more of a sociable element than the rest of the day, there is no doubt that you are still being assessed. Enjoy these occasions, certainly, as they represent another opportunity to show how well you fit with the firm, its employees, and culture. However the clever applicant will use them as an opportunity to find out more information about the firm and its people, particularly information which can be used later in the assessment day. A simple mention in passing of the name of a person who is interviewing you later can often turn up a few useful facts (e.g. 'she is *the name* in corporate at the moment', 'I hope you're a United fan', 'that's him over there', 'he's a man of few words'). Often those attending the lunch or drinks will be asked if anyone particularly stood out, so use your networking skills to your advantage (see Section 12.6) and circulate, wearing your name badge, making a good impression, to give you the edge over other good candidates who have not yet honed that particular skill.

You can practise this skill now by attending more formal events at university. You will find that drinks receptions after talks are good places to try out these skills.

Summary

- Technical ability is important for a lawyer, but the modern lawyer needs other skills, which are relevant to all businesses.
- Business skills such as client care, networking, marketing, and using IT and social media effectively are very important.
- Employers are not looking for clones. You need to show how your specific combination of skills will help the business to achieve its goals.
- A good team comprises individuals with complementary skills who work together effectively to achieve a common goal.
- Employability skills improve with practice and preparation.

Thought-provoking questions

1. What kind of personal characteristics would you like your colleagues to have? Consider ranking these attributes in order of importance, starting with those which you consider essential. Do you think you have these characteristics yourself? If so, are you able to show others that you have them?

2. What role do you tend to take when working in a group? Is this the role you like to take? What other role do you think you might flourish in?

3. If today you unexpectedly happened to meet a lawyer who works for a law firm you want to apply to, what would you say to him?

4. Think of a famous brand. How do you know about it? What did the company do to market its brand so well? What can a junior lawyer do to promote the firm's brand?

What the professionals say

What tips would I give a law student about employability? When it comes down to it, you can have the best legal knowledge in the world, but if you can't get on with people, they aren't going to trust you or engage with you. My mum advised me 'Do right by people and they do right by you' and it was sound advice for practice. Start the process now of learning 'people skills'. I'm passionate about pro bono work. If you have that on your cv, you have evidence that you got up and did something for someone else; that you've engaged at a human level. Pro bono also helps you to develop working relationships now at a level you are unlikely to be able to replicate until quite far progressed though your legal career.

Barry Matthews, Director of Legal Affairs at ITV plc

What did I learn from my work experience at ITV? I now understand the context in which law operates. As students we learn the law, but when I experienced law in practice I understood how it affected the client. The lawyers were in meetings sat next to and working together with people from all areas of the business, contributing to business ideas and saying things like, 'If you want to do that (commercially), then you have to do this (legally)'. I also learned that the skills I have acquired as a law student and in life are transferable into the workplace; it is not all about bestowing knowledge. For example I was acutely aware that I needed to be organised in everything I did, and I was reading and analysing documentation, such as file notes of meetings, and summarising information into timelines. I also undertook some legal research and drafted some terms and conditions. As a result I can now complete application forms with a better understanding of what employers expect from me as a lawyer. Rather than say, 'I am very interested in business law', I have clear examples to draw on to underpin what I am saying, for example 'I know that in team meetings that I would be expected to come up with creative solutions which not only work from a legal perspective but which also move the business towards its strategic goal and that aspect interests me because ...'. When I consider the application forms I completed before my work experience I can really see the difference work experience has made. It has really switched me on to an area of law I might otherwise have dismissed and made me enthusiastic and more informed about what lies ahead.

Serra Pheby, 2011 GDL student, The College of Law Manchester.

What advice would I give to mature students? It is easy to convince yourself that age and maturity may be viewed negatively by law firms. From my experience, nothing could be further from the truth. Your life experiences are attributes which will positively differentiate you from many of your legal contemporaries. Many of the skills which you have acquired to date will be transferable to your studies and later on in to practice.

In my first degree (pharmacy), which I studied straight after leaving school, I used to sit silently at the back of the lecture theatre, too unsure of myself to engage with the lecturers. By the time I came to study law several years later, I was determined to maximise the opportunity to learn. I was confident enough to ask questions and interacted with the tutors without fear of embarrassment. As a result, I really engaged with the subject and this undoubtedly came across during my training contract interviews.

During those interviews, I demonstrated to my potential employers how my experience as a pharmacist would benefit their business as a law firm. I already knew how to communicate effectively and behave professionally; I had acquired customer care skills; and I had background knowledge about the pharmacy sector which would benefit the firm's business. The bottom line is that many employers look for positive attributes in candidates which will differentiate them from all the other applicants clutching a 2:1. Work history, maturity and life experience are all positive differentiators for the mature student. Be prepared to use them confidently to your advantage.

To students who are not mature students, my advice would be to get stuck in to your studies and try not to worry too much about what others think. And invite the mature students to the odd party or two.

Richard Hough, Pharmacist and Associate Solicitor at Brabners Chaffe Street LLP

I attended a careers day at the university at the beginning of term. Some of the advice from the firms was a reality check, but the best thing I did was speak to the firms after they had finished their talks. I asked one of the firms if they might be interested in giving me some work experience, and they said they didn't really do this, but one of the lawyers gave me their card. I met the same person again at a pro bono fair a month later and following that I sent her a follow up email and she asked when I might be available. Around the same time I attended a law fair and talked to another representative of the same firm. She was really helpful and gave me some advice as to how to respond. I called the firm after the law fair, was given a telephone interview and I am now starting work experience with them in a month's time.

I have learnt that it is important to be proactive. My advice is to be prepared for rejection; do not let this dishearten you. Also ensure you start today what others will do tomorrow, and attend the careers days, pro bono events, law fairs, talks and other events that your university offers and publicises.

Mohammad Usman Choudhry, 2012 student, Postgraduate Diploma in Law, Manchester Metropolitan University

Further reading

Solicitors Regulation Authority website: http://www.sra.org.uk
—this sets out information relevant to the profession including the Suitability Test for prospective solicitors (see 12.1.3), and the Code of Conduct (see 12.5.3).

Belbin website: http://www.belbin.co.uk; Myers & Briggs Foundation website: http://www.myersbriggs.org
—these both contain assessment tools to determine how you can work to your full potential in a team (see 12.2.2).

Bruce W. Tuckman, 'Developmental Sequence in Small Groups' (1965) 63 *Psychological Bulletin* 384 (also available from http://dennislearningcenter.osu.edu under 'Research')
—this article provides further reading on team-working, and details a group development model by Bruce Tuckman which is commonly referred to in business.

Institute of Paralegals website: http://www.theiop.org
—if you are considering becoming a paralegal this website is a useful source of information.

LawWorks website: http://www.lawworks.org.uk; Innocence Network UK website: http://www.innocencenetwork.org.uk; ProBonoUK website: http://www.probonouk.net; National Pro Bono Centre website: http://www.nationalprobonocentre.org.uk
—these four websites all contain information about pro bono initiatives (see 12.6.4).

Law Careers website: https://www.lawcareers.net
—a resource for future lawyers, which works with the Law Society. Among other things it publishes information on pro bono (see 12.6.4), and on application deadlines (see 12.10.1).

Mind website: http://www.mind.org.uk/help/diagnoses_and_conditions/anxiety
—an online booklet on the causes of anxiety, its effects, and how to manage it.

For the authors' reflections on the thought-provoking questions, additional self-test questions, podcasts offering a variety of perspectives on legal systems and skills, and a library of links to useful websites, visit the free Online Resource Centre *at* **http://www.oxfordtextbooks.co.uk/orc/slorach/.**

Understanding employability skills

INTRODUCTION

In an uncertain job market, skills are your best security.[1]

The title of this book is *Employability Skills for Law Students*; but what do we actually mean by this? As a law student you will undoubtedly gain many practical, personal, interpersonal, and professional skills throughout your degree. The purpose of this book is to help you to:

- Understand the different type of skills employers are looking for when recruiting graduates

- Identify the skills which you will build by studying throughout your law degree, and participating in extra-curricular activities

- Take positive action to develop and add to your personal skills portfolio during your time at university

- Demonstrate effectively to employers the skills and attributes you possess, which will make you stand out from other graduates.

This chapter will begin by setting out our approach to the subject and then looking at the term 'employability skills' both in general and in the context of legal studies. After this, it will move on to explain just why these employability skills are so important and why you should take every opportunity to develop them throughout your time at university. Having set the scene, it will next give you a brief overview of some of the possible career pathways that can be pursued with a law degree before getting you to start thinking about the skills that you already have and spotting any gaps that might need to be addressed.

This chapter will be a valuable foundation for the rest of the book in helping you to understand what is meant by employability skills so that you can begin to understand why they are important and how you can develop them throughout your study of law. Remember that you are not just studying law to get a degree but to get a job and you need to be aware of what you should do to maximise your chances of getting the one you want. Overall, this chapter explains how this book will help you to emerge from your three or four years of study with the best chance of entering your chosen field of employment in an increasingly competitive market.

....

1. Donna Dunning, 'Top nine transferable skills' (2010) <**http://www.dunning.ca/blog/top-9-transferable-skills/**> accessed 19 July 2012.

Our approach

We have constructed this book around three key themes:

- **Maximising opportunities to develop skills.** Throughout this book you will find a variety of ways in which you will be able to develop your 'transferable skills'. These are generic skills that are equally applicable in a whole range of careers, such as problem solving skills and IT skills. Throughout your law degree you will grow these skills which will be useful across a range of different jobs and industries, not just those which are directly related to law. In essence, these are the skills that make you attractive to employers, and you should take every opportunity to develop them during your time at university.

- **Demonstrating skills to obtain employment.** As well as developing your skills to enable you to seek out job opportunities and successfully negotiate the appointment process, you will also need to demonstrate those skills to potential employers. This book will cover the process from the initial application form or CV, through to the face-to-face assessment at interview or assessment centre, so that you come to the attention of suitable employers and maximise your chances of getting the job you want.

- **Applying skills in the workplace.** Finally this book will cover the development and application of the particular skills that will ensure you are able to carry out the requirements of your desired job in a proficient and professional way; such as advocacy skills for working at the Bar or legal research skills for employment in academia.

The book is designed for *all* law students, regardless of their chosen career path or the stage of their university life. It is never too late to start developing your employability skills. Indeed, you should be developing them continually throughout your working life as it is virtually certain that you will change jobs at some stage between graduation and retirement and the skills you demonstrate to get your first job will be supplemented by those that you acquire throughout your career. So, you should not panic if you are not in your first or second year— there are still practical steps that you can take in order to enhance your skills and thus your prospects of success in the world of work. Your skills development will be more effective if it is done in a systematic way which this book is here to support.

Defining 'employability skills'

The term 'employability skills' means different things to different people. For some, it means everything that is involved in getting a job, for others, it is little more than interview technique or writing a good CV. For us, employability skills are those that make the link from learning to earning.

There are two formal definitions of employability skills that are widely adopted in higher education. The first is found in a report published jointly by the National Union of Students (NUS) and the Confederation of British Industry (CBI):

> A set of attributes, skills and knowledge that all labour market participants should possess to ensure they have the capability of being effective in the workplace – to the benefit of themselves, their employer and the wider economy.[2]

2. Confederation of British Industry and National Union of Students, 'Working towards your future: Making the most of your time in higher education' (May 2011) 14 <**http://www.nus.org.uk/Global/CBI_NUS_Employability%20report_May%202011.pdf**> accessed 19 July 2012.

This definition focuses on applying employability skills in the workplace. However, as previously explained, we think that employability skills go further than that, since they are also needed to obtain employment in the first place: you cannot be effective in a workplace without a job! Moreover, it does not focus specifically on graduate jobseekers. This second definition, from the Enhancing Student Employability Co-ordination Team funded by the Higher Education Funding Council for England includes these two missing aspects and is more in line with our view of employability skills:

> A set of achievements—skills, understandings and personal attributes —that makes graduates more likely to gain employment and be successful in their chosen occupations, which benefits themselves, the workforce, the community and the economy.[3]

Therefore, employability skills can be considered to be a range of skills and capabilities that virtually every employer is looking for in potential graduate recruits and an essential pre-condition for the effective development and use of other, more specialist or technical skills required for particular jobs. They are also a key underpin to your effectiveness at work.[4] However, since every employer is seeking such skills, you need to take every opportunity to develop your employability skills so that you can maximise your prospects of success in an increasingly competitive job market by demonstrating those skills to employers. Exploring these themes of development and demonstration of skills is the primary purpose of this book.

Types of employability skills

Just as there is no set definition of employability skills, there is no definitive list of what types of skills are included within the term. However, there are several skills that are commonly listed as key to overall employability. These include:

- Self-management
- Team working
- Problem solving
- Application of information technology
- Communication
- Application of numeracy
- Business and customer awareness.

You will see from this list the general nature of these skills. They are good examples of *transferable skills* which can be equally well applied to non-law as well as legal careers. For example, a barrister and a human resources manager will both be required to understand the needs of their clients and a solicitor and a management consultant will both benefit from a methodical approach to problem solving.

---

3. M Yorke, 'Employability in higher education: what it is – what it is not.' (Learning and Employability Series One, ESECT and HEA, 2006) 8 <http://www.heacademy.ac.uk/assets/documents/tla/employability/id116_employability_in_higher_education_336.pdf> accessed 19 July 2012.
4. Confederation of British Industry and National Union of Students, 'Working towards your future: Making the most of your time in higher education' (May 2011) 8, 11.

These transferable skills can be categorised under a number of broader headings:

- Practical skills: such as literacy and numeracy, problem solving and use of IT
- Personal skills: such as self-management, professional, and ethical behaviour and organisational skills
- Interpersonal skills: such as team working, written and verbal communication, customer service, and networking.

Although you may not yet realise it, not only will you have some of these skills already but you will also have the opportunity to develop them further during your studies as well as being able to add new skills to your portfolio.

Practical exercise: transferable skills

Think about the transferable skills listed in this section and how they might apply to a 'traditional' career in law as a barrister or solicitor.

By way of example to get you started, literacy and numeracy will be important to a barrister as they will need to draft accurate skeleton arguments and legal opinions that are precise and grammatically correct (literacy) and they will also need to submit invoices and deal with their accountant or the Inland Revenue (numeracy)!

☺ Compare your answers with those provided on the Online Resource Centre.

Practical legal skills

As well at these transferable skills, you will appreciate that there are, of course, specific practical legal skills that you will need in your portfolio, particularly if you are pursuing a career in one of the traditional legal professions. Therefore, we can add a fourth category to the list from the previous section:

- Professional skills: such as legal research, legal analysis, drafting, negotiation, and advocacy.

If you are planning a career in a part of the legal profession—or even considering it as a possibility—then it is obvious that you will need to develop the skills that will enable you to find, understand, and use the law in a work environment. However, if you do not intend to enter the legal profession but are studying law out of general interest as a good starting point for any number of non-law careers, these legal skills will still be useful to you in impressing potential employers. This is because these legal skills are simply more general skills that you will learn in a subject-specific context. To put it another way, you will learn how to conduct legal research as part of your law degree but if you take away the law focus then you have learned how to organise and carry out an effective research plan that enables you to identify and locate relevant information. This research proficiency can be deployed in any number of non-law settings. Similarly, advocacy and negotiation skills may seem to have a particular relevance to law but are really just different methods of oral communication that will be valuable to you irrespective of your career path. So whatever your career plans or your ultimate destination, legal skills will be an important part of your skills portfolio.

Skills acquired from legal study

The Higher Education Academy has produced a list of the skills that a graduate with an honours bachelor's degree in law will have. This is based on the benchmark for law produced by the Quality Assurance Agency (QAA) which describes the nature and characteristics of the law programme together with the attributes and capabilities that those with a law degree should have demonstrated.[5] The QAA stipulates that, by the end of a law degree, students should be able to:

- Demonstrate an understanding of the principal features of the legal system(s) studied
- Apply knowledge to a situation of limited complexity so as to provide arguable conclusions for concrete actual or hypothetical problems
- Identify accurately issues that require researching
- Identify and retrieve up-to-date legal information using paper and electronic sources
- Use relevant primary and secondary legal sources
- Recognise and rank items and issues in terms of relevance and importance
- Bring together information and materials from a variety of different sources
- Synthesise doctrinal and policy issues in relation to a topic
- Judge critically the merits of particular arguments
- Present and make a reasoned choice between alternative solutions
- Act independently in planning and undertaking tasks
- Research independently in areas of law not previously studied starting from standard legal information sources
- Reflect on own learning and proactively seek and make use of feedback
- Use English (or, where appropriate, Welsh) proficiently in relation to legal matters
- Present knowledge or an argument in a way that is comprehensible to others and which is directed at their concerns
- Read and discuss legal materials, which are written in technical and complex language
- Use, present and evaluate information provided in numerical or statistical form
- Produce word-processed essays and text and present such work in an appropriate form
- Use the World Wide Web and email
- Work in groups as a participant who contributes effectively to the group's task.

This list might seem quite daunting but try not to worry: it is likely that you have some of these skills already and you should remember that this is the list of skills that the QAA requires that your university cultivates in its law students so you can guarantee that there will be opportunities to develop these skills in the course of your studies. However, just because the law degree is designed to give you these skills, it is your responsibility to take the opportunities which arise to cultivate and develop them. It is not enough simply to sit back and assume that you will be sufficiently skilled to make yourself stand out in the job market. Remember that the QAA says that each law student should be equipped with these skills. You will have to take action in order to demonstrate your enhanced skills capability and really differentiate yourself as positively as possible:

....

5. Higher Education Academy, 'Student employability profiles: law' (September 2006) <http://www. heacademy.ac.uk/assets/documents/employability/studentemployability/student_employability_ profiles_law.pdf> accessed 19 July 2012.

I have done a number of things to make myself stand out from any other candidates who are applying for the same job. I have looked online at larger law firms to see what they are looking for in future employees and applicants for work experience. These law firms are all looking for the same qualities in an employee such as research, problem solving, team work and communication skills. In my second year module 'Legal Research and Reasoning' I enhanced and developed these skills by participating in presentations and various workshops.

To stand out more I have worked hard to make my CV look more appealing to the interviewer by doing some voluntary work and gaining some work experience. I have organised a charity football event for Overgate Hospice and I was also a marshal for their charity Midnight Walk. Last summer I worked for an insolvency company, Spencer Hayes, gaining experience in insolvency law and made valuable contacts. These contacts have enabled me to form relationships with higher management in a top law firm with offices based in the UK and overseas. I am now hoping to be accepted onto one of their graduate schemes once I have completed my law degree. By being involved in multiple football and rugby teams as well as being a student ambassador, I can demonstrate team working and communication skills to prospective employers and also show my willingness to get involved and to work.

Matthew, University of Central Lancashire

Practical exercise: building a reflective employability skills portfolio—self-assessment against QAA benchmark

As you work through this book you will find various practical exercises that invite you to reflect, review, and plan your skills development and to gather evidence that you have done so. You might find it helpful at this stage to get somewhere to keep all your employability materials together. This might be as simple as a ring binder with a set of dividers or, if you prefer to keep things electronically, a folder on your computer with various subfolders within it.

The first activity is to review your own current proficiency against the QAA benchmark skills in law. You will find a downloadable template to help you with this on the Online Resource Centre. Think about each of the skills in turn and then rate yourself as follows:

- I am confident that I can do this to a high standard

- I can do this to some degree but am aware that I could do it better

- I cannot do this at all.

This exercise will give you an initial self-evaluation snapshot of your capability in each of the QAA skills. You should repeat this exercise periodically so that you can chart your progress and skills development over time.

So far, you have discovered many of the skills which go towards making up the overall employability skills portfolio, which is shown graphically in Figure 1.1.

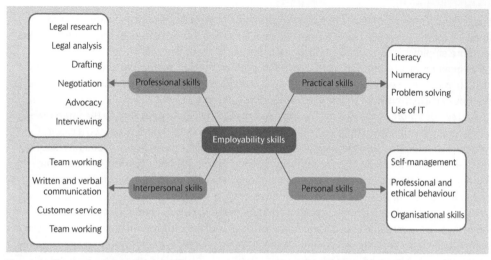

Figure 1.1 The employability skills portfolio

The importance of employability skills

While the importance of employability skills should be self-evident—they maximise your chances of getting the job you need to set you on your chosen career path desire—they are not always recognised as such by students as the following comment illustrates:

I've always been told to work hard and get good qualifications. Everyone has said that education opens doors, so the key to getting the job you want is to get as good a degree result as is humanly possible.

Sam, University of Northampton

However, as well the seemingly obvious benefit, there are broader reasons as to why employability skills are so valuable. First, as the CBI and NUS jointly recognise, they 'underpin success in working life'.[6] As you have already seen, employability skills are not just useful for getting a foot on the career ladder. They are valuable, and should be developed, throughout your working life so that you are able to seek out new job opportunities as your career develops. They also enable you to 'adapt to an unknown future'.[7] This is key. Not only should you be able to seek out new positions within your career, you should also be capable of taking your transferable skills and applying them equally well to a related as well as a non-related alternative:

6. Confederation of British Industry and National Union of Students, 'Working towards your future: Making the most of your time in higher education' (May 2011) 11 <**http://www.nus.org.uk/Global/CBI_NUS_Employability%20report_May%202011.pdf**> accessed 19 July 2012.

7. <**http://www.nus.org.uk/Global/CBI_NUS_Employability%20report_May%202011.pdf**> accessed 19 July 2012.

My first degree was in Natural Sciences, specialising in physics. That taught me – amongst other things – how to take a methodical and scientific approach to problem solving which I then applied in my first career in software and technology development. Some years later, I studied law and found that the same approaches served me well in legal analysis and drafting. The management skills I picked up during my time in the technology industry also help when dealing with publishers and writing plans. So all the skills I've developed over the years in various settings are still useful today.

Dr Stefan Fafinski (author)

Development of employability skills is also crucial for two further reasons. First, employers consistently state that they are not always satisfied with the employability skills of graduates as Figure 1.2 illustrates.

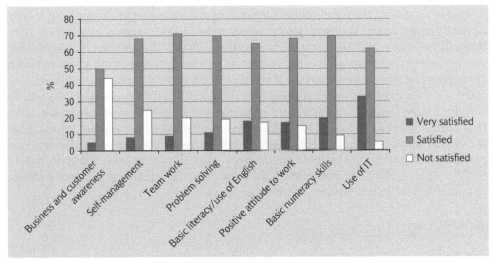

Figure 1.2 Employer satisfaction with graduate employability skills[8]

Similarly, 70% of employers said that they would like to see 'more effective development' of graduates' employability skills although they emphasise that it is up to students themselves to 'seize the opportunities available to strengthen their employability'.[9]

We need students who have more to offer than just academic brilliance. They need to be well-rounded individuals who will work well with others in our firm and, perhaps more importantly, with our clients. They should also be capable of understanding the world in which we work. So it's a package of skills that we're looking for.

Training partner, London

8. Confederation of British Industry and Education Development International, 'Building for growth: business priorities for education and skills—Education and skills survey 2011' (May 2011) 22 <http://www.cbi.org.uk/media/1051530/cbi__edi_education__skills_survey_2011.pdf> accessed 19 July 2012.
9. <http://www.cbi.org.uk/media/1051530/cbi__edi_education__skills_survey_2011.pdf> accessed 19 July 2012.

So, in summary, employability skills are important because:

- They help you to get the position you want
- They are highly desired by employers who want them to be developed further.

Doing a skills audit

The next chapter will help you to begin putting together a plan for developing the employ-ability skills that you need for success. Before that, though, you should spend some time thinking about the skills that you currently have as well as identifying the 'attainment gaps'[10] that you need to address: that is, parts of your skills portfolio that are either missing or need further development.

Think about the activities that you currently do or have done in the past. These do not have to be academic. They could equally be sporting or musical, or some particular favour-ite hobby or pastime, or to do with paid or voluntary work that you have undertaken. Then think about what skill or skills you use to carry out each of these activities. For instance, if you have done voluntary work in a charity shop, you might think of the associated skills of timekeeping and customer service. If you have been captain of your netball team, you could consider your leadership as a skill. You could also ask other students, friends, or family what they see as your skills: these are more likely to be the transferable skills rather than specific professional skills. It can be quite illuminating to see yourself as others see you. Be honest with yourself: there is nothing to be gained if you rate yourself as expert at everything. By being realistic about your current skills capabilities, you will give yourself the best opportunity to engage actively with your skills development and take personal responsibility for your future employment prospects.

Practical exercise: doing a skills audit

You will find a downloadable template to help you begin your skills audit on the Online Resource Centre. The skills that are listed on the template are just a starting point and you should feel free to add others if you wish. Then, as before, rate yourself against each of the skills. Unlike the last exercise, which used a very broad rating system with three possible options against each of the QAA bench-mark competencies, you should this time use a five point scale:

1—No current knowledge of the skill (no current competency)

2—Some awareness but not sufficiently competent to use the skill with confidence (partially compe-tent)

3—Familiar with and able to use the skill (competent)

4—Proficient with the skill and able to demonstrate this to others (highly competent)

5—Expert in the skill (fully competent)

So that you get used to demonstrating evidence-based skills, you should also use the space in the template to describe the evidence that you have to support your self-assessment of each of the skills.

---

10. Confederation of British Industry and Education Development International, 'Building for growth: business priorities for education and skills—Education and skills survey 2011' (May 2011) 11 <http://www.cbi.org.uk/media/1051530/cbi__edi_education___skills_survey_2011.pdf> accessed 23 July 2012.

If you do not have evidence at this stage, then you should just write a brief note or comment: you will be adding evidence as you build your portfolio of skills over time. You will find an example of a completed audit in Table 1.1.

You may also wish to complete these with a friend from your course, or with someone that you trust and who knows you well. Alternatively, you could compare your answers with a friend's responses and discuss them together. Sometimes others may offer a more constructive insight into you own skills than you are honestly able to do for yourself.

As you work through the remaining chapters in this book, you will find suggestions on how you could develop these skills. Note the actions that you are going to take in the 'Action plan' column. Remember to set a target date against each item if you can.

You will be revisiting this audit as part of your future personal development planning, so make sure that you put the date on your audit and keep your answers in the 'Reviews' section of your portfolio.

You will find information on personal development planning (PDP) in Chapter 2.

Table 1.1 Example skills audit

Skill	Self-assessment rating (1–5)	Evidence	Action plan
Practical skills			
Written communication skills	4	I normally get good feedback on clarity, grammar, etc in my assessed pieces of work.	
Numeracy	3	I hated maths at A-level and I'm pleased my phone has a calculator on it: but I can do mental arithmetic pretty well. I had to when the till broke at the Oxfam shop.	
Problem solving	4	When I did my Duke of Edinburgh expedition we had loads of practical problems along the way that we needed to solve.	
Use of IT	2	I'm ok with Word but still struggle with what to do if it doesn't quite do what I want it to. I can never format footnotes correctly.	
Personal skills			
Time management skills	3	I usually get my assignments in time but I do tend to leave things to the last minute.	

Skill	Self-assessment rating (1–5)	Evidence	Action plan
Professional and ethical behaviour	2	I have a basic understanding about things like client confidentiality but have never had to put them into practice.	
Organisational skills	3	I suppose I've got my own system for filing and finding things, but I'm not sure anyone else would be able to follow it easily.	
Flexibility	2	I often get really flustered if things don't go according to plan.	
Planning	3	I make lots of lists of things, but could probably be more effective to be honest.	
Decision-making	3	I guess I have to make decisions all the time, but I'm not convinced that I'm skilled at it.	
Interpersonal skills			
Team working	4	I love working with other people.	
Verbal communication	3	I don't mind speaking up in tutorials, but sometimes struggle to make myself clear.	
Customer service	4	I worked in the Oxfam shop in the holidays and much preferred being out at the front, rather than sifting through all the stuff out the back.	
Leadership	4	Again, my DofE helped me with leadership. It went along with team working.	
Professional skills			
Legal research	4	I think I am a good legal researcher. I can find and use case law, Acts and journal articles, but prefer the databases to using the law library.	
Legal problem solving	2	I am a bit unsure when I have to identify legal issues in a problem question—I worry that I go off on tangents...	

(Continued)

Table 1.1 *Continued*

Skill	Self-assessment rating (1–5)	Evidence	Action plan
Drafting	1	Don't even know what this means in practice!	
Negotiation	3	I had a go at the internal negotiation competition and found it really enjoyable. Would like to do it again next year.	
Advocacy	2	I had to do an assessed moot, but it didn't go very well.	
Knowledge of legal practice and procedure	1	I have never worked in any form of legal practice.	
Interviewing	1	We don't have the option of doing any client interviewing.	
Presentation skills	3	I don't mind doing presentations, so long as I'm prepared.	
Commercial awareness	1	I know that law students are supposed to know about this, but couldn't really explain what it means at the moment.	

Remember that this initial audit is the baseline for continued improvement: your skills will only improve from here. No-one is perfect! If you have been realistic in your assessment of your own competencies then you will undoubtedly have identified areas that would benefit from some development. You should return to complete this exercise again periodically as part of your personal development planning. This will show you that you have developed your employability skills which will, in turn, build the confidence that you will need to demonstrate those skills effectively and to realise your potential in the competitive job market.

The chapters that follow will help you build your employability skills and then use them to pursue your chosen career. As you work through the book, you will learn how to understand, identify, build, focus, and demonstrate your employability skills. The chapters are grouped around these themes, as shown in Figure 1.3.

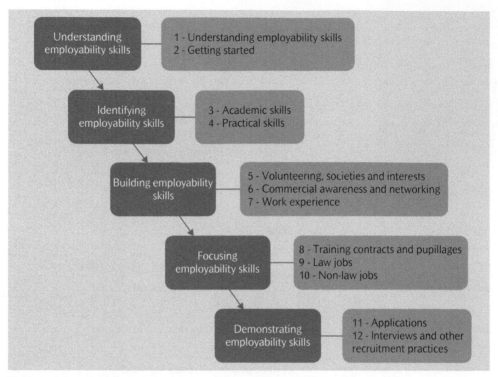

Figure 1.3 Structure of the book

A more detailed synopsis of each chapter is set out in Table 1.2.

Table 1.2 List of chapters

Chapter 2—Getting started	Helps you to build a plan for your skills development activities.
Chapter 3—Academic skills	Highlights the relationship between academic skills and employability skills so that you can maximise the value of the skills acquired through legal study for gaining employment.
Chapter 4—Practical legal skills	Reviews various practical legal activities that are available to you and demonstrates how you can develop both legal and transferable skills.
Chapter 5—Volunteering, societies, and interests	Considers the contribution that voluntary work, involvement in University societies, and your general spare time activities can make to your employability skills development.

(Continued)

Table 1.2 *Continued*

Chapter 6—Commercial awareness and networking	Focuses on two key development areas that you can use to make yourself stand out: awareness of the commercial world and building your personal network.
Chapter 7——Work experience	Covers all facets of work experience with particular emphasis on identifying placement opportunities and subsequently developing your skills through work experience.
Chapter 8—Training contracts and pupillages	Gives a comprehensive account of the steps involved in obtaining a training contract or pupillage with practical tips from former students and employers.
Chapter 9—Law jobs after graduation	Considers careers other than the traditional legal professions of barrister and solicitor, but which still offer some legal content.
Chapter 10—Non-law jobs	Looks at other career options that you can pursue with a law degree.
Chapter 11—Applications	Offers guidance on creating effective CVs and covering letters and completing application forms.
Chapter 12—Interviews and other recruitment practices	Outlines common approaches used in recruitment and offers a wide range of practical advice, including the importance of commercial awareness, that will help you perform to the best of your ability and highlight your employability skills.

WHERE NEXT?

You should by now have a clearer idea of what we mean by employability skills and why they are significant. Perhaps most importantly you should have an honest assessment of where you currently stand in terms of your own personal employability skills portfolio. The next step is to start planning not only for skills development but also for the practicalities of seeking employment including taking time to reflect on the sorts of career pathways you could explore with a law degree. This will be covered in Chapter 2.

Getting started

2

INTRODUCTION

Having explained what we mean by employability skills and why they are important, this chapter moves you on to start the planning stage: how do you get from where you are now to working in the career that you want to pursue? The chapter begins by considering one of the key questions that all law students must answer: to practise or not to practise? It then moves on to give an overview of the two traditional branches of the legal profession—solicitors and barristers—before explaining the stages in qualification, the employability skills that are essential in each and some insight into the likely competition and costs involved. After this, it introduces some of the alternative possible career pathways that can be pursued with a law degree on the strength of the transferable employability skills you will develop. The chapter then explains the idea of personal development planning (PDP) which gives you a framework within which to build an action plan of activities that will enhance your employability skills portfolio. Finally, the chapter will give you an initial timetable of actions to reflect on and consider and orientate you to the chapters later in the book, which will support you in achieving each step in the journey to employment.

You will develop two key plans in this chapter. The first will give you a structured means of developing (and documenting the development of) your employability skills while the second will serve as a useful reminder of the key stages and activities that you will need to do throughout your undergraduate studies. As there is much to do in addition to your academic legal studies, careful planning allows you to prioritise, focus on what is important and make informed decisions. In addition, this chapter should help you to realise that there are many different careers that can be pursued with a law degree, and that it is essential that you think carefully and objectively about the pathway that is right for you.

To practise or not to practise?

Having worked through the first chapter, you should now have an understanding of the nature and importance of employability skills and should be ready to start planning to develop them in pursuit of your chosen career. One of the most important decisions that you will need to make is whether or not you want a career in legal practice. If you complete your law degree with the intention to practise law, your only further decision—in terms of career path—is whether to qualify as a solicitor or a barrister. If, on completion of your studies, you have decided not to enter into legal practice then your choices are much wider as you have a choice of almost any career. Before we address the issues of the various career paths that are available, the very first question for you to consider is whether or not you do want to practise law. Remember that the world of legal practice is very different to the academic study of law so it really is advisable to ensure that you have opportunities to see the law in action to help you make a decision about your future career path.

The best way to work out whether or not you want to practise law is to get as much first-hand experience of the legal profession in operation as possible. This means finding opportunities for work experience and trying to ensure that this is as varied as possible: different size firms, different areas of practice, and gaining insight into the work of both solicitors and barristers. You will also find that court visits provide a useful basis to observe much of the daily life in legal practice.

You will find more detail on work experience in Chapter 7.

You may also want to give some thought to the following points that may influence your decision as they are often overlooked aspects of legal practice:

- **You need to be able to work with people who do not understand the law.** It should be obvious that people come to solicitors and barristers for legal advice because they lack legal knowledge but one of the facets of practice that is often a struggle for newly qualified lawyers arises from the need to talk to non-lawyers about the law in a way that they can understand. Remember that people often have entrenched preconceptions about the law that you will need to overcome and that many people are simply not able to grasp the complexities of the law and the way that it applies to their problem. Moreover, people who need legal advice do not appreciate what aspects of their problem are relevant to its legal resolution so you will need to listen to a mass of detail and be able to pick out the parts that have legal relevance in order to address their problems. And do not fall into the trap of thinking 'ah yes but I want to practise commercial law' as if this means that you will not have to deal with people—commercial entities are comprised of people so you will never conduct an interview with a company but with a person who represents that company and this, of course, raises a whole new set of problems.

- **You need to be both passionate and dispassionate.** It is hard work being a lawyer. You need to be passionate about the law because you will have to know your area of practice in a degree of depth that makes the work that you do as a student seem trivial and you will need to read about that area of law constantly to ensure that you are up-to-date with all new developments. You will also need a passion for the practical aspects of practice—an eye for detail, a determination to win, and a commitment to all clients irrespective of how pleasant or otherwise they are and their behaviour has been—combined with an ability to remain dispassionate as it is inevitable that you will lose cases, some of which you will have been convinced you could and should have won. You need to care about your clients whilst remaining at an objective distance from their problems: just as a nurse needs to treat a patient's injuries rather than weep for the pain they suffer, a lawyer needs to try to resolve a client's problems rather than agonise over the circumstances of the case.

- **You need to be robust.** As well as being passionate about the law, you should also remember that a law career is a lifestyle choice: you will also need to be competitive, driven, and determined as well as being capable of taking criticism and complaints. There is a lot of hard work: early starts and late finishes are commonplace.

- **Can you deliver bad news?** Imagine telling an injured client that their claim for compensation has been rejected, a prisoner who has protested his innocence that his appeal against conviction was not successful, or a parent that they have lost a custody battle and can no longer live with their children. As a lawyer, you will often be the bearer of bad tidings and need to be able to deal with the upset, disappointment, and frustration that this causes for a client. You will also need to be prepared for the client to blame you for the consequences of a lost case and to be able to carry on your own working life with confidence as you represent other clients.

Despite these considerations, law remains a rewarding and exciting career path that offers the opportunity to have a real and positive impact on the life of others. It offers an ongoing intellectual challenge in a setting where your skills, knowledge, and ability can be used to protect others and to resolve problems for people that they are not able to solve themselves. However, be aware that it is not a career that suits everyone and even if you are knowledgeable and passionate about the law, you may nonetheless lack some of the professional skills and personal qualities that are necessary to practise the law successfully.

The roles of solicitor and barristers have several employability skills in common: inter-personal skills, intellectual ability, written and oral communications skills, commercial awareness, and initiative. However, the differing nature of the roles means that solicitors need to have well-developed team working skills, since they may work with other members of a legal team on a case. They also engage in more direct client contact, and so must be able to develop and sustain long-term client relationships. Barristers are usually self-employed and therefore need to be more confident in working independently as well as part of a team. The nature of advocacy requires barristers to develop their oral presentation skills and the ability to think quickly in response to challenges in court. If you are considering a career as a practising lawyer, you should think about the types of activity you enjoy and how those fit with the basic requirements of the professions. For example, if you are not comfortable with public speaking, then you can either decide that you are not suited to advocacy and therefore that a career at the Bar is not really for you, or you can decide to take active steps to plan to develop your advocacy skills.

If you are still unsure, it is worth remembering that this is not necessarily a decision for life. Indeed some people find out that they are better suited to an alternative career once they are in legal practice:

I was in medical practice—not the 'injured in a trip or fall' kind—but dealing with cases where individuals had sustained life-altering injuries that required long-term specialist care and treatment. This involved working with all sorts of other professions to work out what each client needed and to predict how their capability would change in the future. I became fascinated by the work of occupational therapists—now that was a job that made a real difference to people's lives—and eventually gave up my career as a solicitor to retrain in occupational therapy. That was four years ago and I don't regret it for a single minute—the financial rewards may be less than legal practice but the personal and professional satisfaction of helping people on a hands-on basis is immense.

Huw, University of Reading (graduated 2004)

As you will have seen, there are many factors to consider when making the decision whether or not to pursue a career in practice, and it may even be that you change your mind over time. The next two sections in this chapter move on to look in more detail at the practising and non-practising options open to law graduates, starting with solicitors and barristers.

Solicitors and barristers

This section deals with the two 'traditional' branches of the legal profession— barristers and solicitors. Although many law students embark on their studies with a clear idea of what they want to do, it is useful to clarify the differences between the two options as there are sometimes misconceptions, particularly as some of the distinctions between the professions are beginning to become more blurred.

Solicitors have direct contact with their clients and provide expert legal advice on a huge range of legal matters. They can represent clients in the lower courts (magistrates' courts, county court, and tribunals). Once qualified, solicitors generally work in private practice in a firm although other options, such as working as an in-house legal advisor to a large non-law organisation, are possible.

Barristers are specialist legal advisers and courtroom advocates with rights of audience in all courts. The usual route to a barrister is through a solicitor. Solicitors are likely to be able to identify the most suitable barrister to deal with a particular case. However, members of the public may now, in certain circumstances, access a barrister directly (without first going through a solicitor) should they have an enquiry. In addition, organisations or individuals that have an identifiable area of expertise or experience can apply to the Bar Standards Board to be licensed to instruct barristers directly. Most qualified barristers are self-employed, working in a set or chambers, being a group of barristers in a building sharing office facilities, clerks and administrators (and paying a contribution towards their costs). There are also opportunities for employment in the government and private sectors. Barristers must also be members of one of the four Inns of Court: Lincoln's Inn, Gray's Inn, Middle Temple, and Inner Temple. These are the only institutions with the authority to call a person to the Bar, and students must join one of the four Inns before starting their professional training.

Solicitor-advocates are solicitors who have undertaken further specialist training post-qualification to enable them to represent clients in the higher courts (Crown Court, High Court, and Court of Appeal).

Routes to qualification

Having introduced the two branches of the legal profession, this section will outline the routes to qualifying as a solicitor or barrister. Although the professions are different, they both have a similar three-stage process to qualification, depicted in Figure 2.1 for the Bar and Figure 2.2 for solicitors:

- Academic. The academic stage requires a qualifying law degree or a non-law degree plus a conversion course known as the Graduate Diploma in Law (GDL).
- Vocational. The vocational stage requires successful completion of the Bar Professional Training Course (BPTC) for barristers or the Legal Practice Course (LPC) for solicitors.
- Professional. The final stage of training is a two-year training contract for solicitors, or a one year pupillage for barristers.

The GDL

The GDL is a mandatory qualification for students without a qualifying law degree to progress to the vocational (LPC) stage of training. The GDL covers the seven core foundations of legal knowledge that are required in a qualifying law degree along with the English legal system and legal research skills. The GDL is a very intensive and expensive course. You may also encounter the term 'CPE'. The CPE (standing for Common Professional Examination)

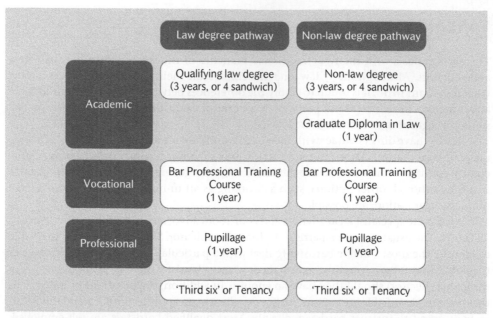

Figure 2.1 Routes to the Bar

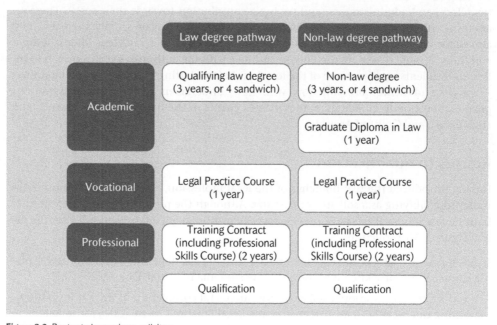

Figure 2.2 Routes to becoming a solicitor

was the forerunner of the GDL and was, for all practical purposes, the same qualification. The Solicitors Regulation Authority continues to use the term CPE.

The LPC

The LPC builds on the academic stage of training. In essence, it teaches how the core legal principles learned in the academic stage are used in practice. For instance, you will have been taught remedies for breach of contract during your studies, but the LPC will explain how to bring a contractual dispute to course. In addition it will build on your practical legal skills such as client interviewing and negotiation and teach new ones, such as drafting contracts and court papers and using practitioner research resources.

The BPTC

The BPTC (formerly known as the Bar Vocational Course or BVC) is a practical course that, according to the Bar Standard Board aims:

> to ensure that students intending to become barristers acquire the skills, knowledge of pro-
> cedure and evidence, attitudes and competence to prepare them, in particular, for the more
> specialised training in the twelve months of pupillage.

From 2013, applicants for the BPTC are required to pass the Bar Course Aptitude Test (BCAT) before an offer of a place on the course can be confirmed. The BCAT tests the core critical thinking and reasoning skills required for the BPTC. The aim of the test is to ensure that students undertaking the BPTC stand the best chance of success. Tests can be sched-uled from 1 March after applying for the BPTC and can be taken between 3 April and 31 July. The BCAT costs £150 for UK and EU students and £170 for students from the rest of the world. You pay at the point of scheduling your test.

Training contracts

The training contract is the last step in the process of qualifying as a solicitor. It is gener-ally a two-year full-time period of paid practical experience, typically undertaken in a firm of solicitors (although there are other organisations authorised to take trainees). Trainees must also complete the Professional Skills Course during their training contract. On suc-cessful completion, a solicitor can be admitted to the Roll of Solicitors and may apply for their first practising certificate.

See Chapter 8 for more detail on the training contract.

Pupillage

Pupillage is the final stage of training to be a barrister and combines the vocational training that you will have acquired with practical work experience in a set of barristers' chambers or with another Authorised Training Organisation (ATO). Pupillage usually lasts for one year and is formally divided into two six month periods, known as 'sixes', the first of which is non-practising.

See Chapter 8 for more detail on pupillage.

Competition and costs

In order to be as well-equipped as possible to make an informed decision regarding your future career aspirations, you need to appreciate two very important considerations from the outset: first that there is great competition for places in the traditional legal professions and second that the process of qualifying involves considerable cost.

Although it remains true that most students who embark upon a law degree intend to pursue one of the traditional legal professions of solicitor or barrister, not all graduate law students end up in such legal practice. In the year ending 31 July 2011, there were 8,402 new solicitors admitted to the Law Society Roll; of these, 5,441 started a training contract—around 65%.[1] Similarly, in the legal year 2009/10,[2] 1,432 students successfully completed the BPTC, of which 460 began pupillage—around 32%.[3] Therefore, one-third of students who completed the LPC and two-thirds of students who completed the BPTC did not manage to secure a place in legal practice. The attrition at each stage of the process is shown in Figures 2.3 and 2.4.

Entry to the traditional legal professions, then, is hugely competitive. To maximise your prospects of success, you will need to look carefully at the skills needed for your chosen branch of the profession and take every opportunity to develop them and gather evidence of that development to demonstrate to potential employers. The chapters in the rest of this book will support you in doing that.

As well as the prospect of stiff competition, you should also be aware of the costs of qualification over and above the costs associated with your first undergraduate degree. For non-law graduates, the cost of the full-time GDL varies, depending upon location, from around £3,500 to £9,500. The BPTC costs from around £12,000 to £16,500 and the LPC from around £8,000 to £14,000.

There are financial awards and scholarships available from a range of sources. In addition, some (larger) firms of solicitors will pay LPC fees and some chambers may allow pupils to take some of their pupillage award (payment) in advance.

See Chapter 8 for more detail on finding funding.

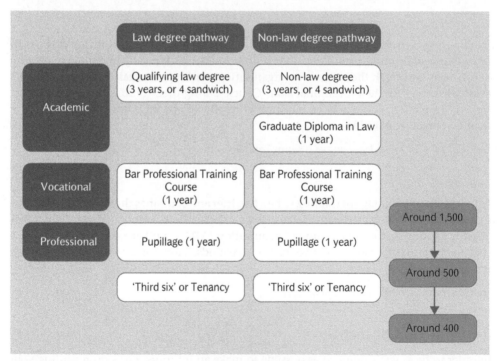

Figure 2.3 Routes to the Bar—attrition

1. Nina Fletcher, 'Trends in the solicitors' profession: Annual statistical report 2011' (May 2012, Research Unit, The Law Society) <http://www.lawsociety.org.uk/representation/research-trends/annual-statistical-report/documents/annual-statistical-report-2011---executive-summary-(pdf-1mb)/>.
2. The legal year runs from 1 October —30 September.
3. Bar Council Statistics <http://www.barcouncil.org.uk/about-the-bar/facts-and-figures/statistics/> accessed 23 July 2012.

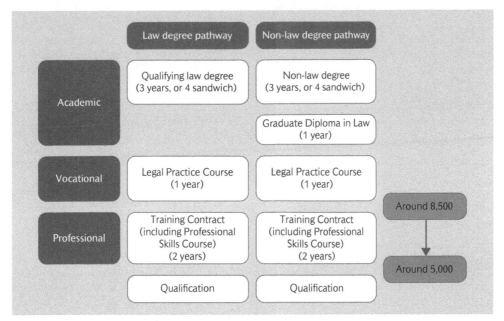

Figure 2.4 Routes to becoming a solicitor—attrition

Alternatives to the traditional professions

As well as the traditional legal professions already covered in this chapter, you should also remember that the transferable employability skills that you will acquire and develop throughout your law degree will also enable you to seek employment in many alternative fields. This section will give you an overview of some of the possibilities that are open to you. Remember, though, that this is not a definitive list!

Careers with a law degree can be broken down into four broad categories, depending on the extent to which the professional skills covered in Chapter 1 are used in everyday working life:

- **Law jobs.** This includes careers which involve working with the law, but not in the traditional professions, such as paralegal, licensed conveyancer, or law teacher.
- **Non-law work in a law context.** This section will cover careers in which the tasks performed are not legal in nature but are performed in a law environment such as a legal secretary (administrative work in a law firm) or a witness care officer (working in the criminal courts).
- **Non-law work with legal content.** This covers careers in which the understanding and application of a particular area of law is needed on a regular basis such as a social worker (who applies social welfare law) or a career in human resource management (using employment law).
- **Non-law work with no legal context or content.** This includes careers where there may be a legal framework that regulates how the job must be done, for instance the regulatory framework of professions such as dentistry and accountancy, but where this is very much a peripheral part of the role as well as careers with no legal basis whatsoever.

See Chapter 9 for more detail on law jobs, and Chapter 10 for the three different categories of non-law work.

These categories, and some example careers within each of them, are depicted in Figure 2.5.

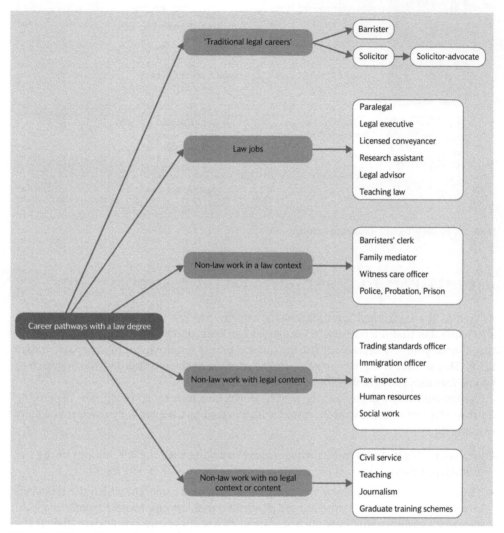

Figure 2.5 Career pathways with a law degree

Planning to develop your employability skills

Having introduced some of the career destinations possible with a law degree, the next step in getting started is to plan to develop your employability skills. The skills audit that you undertook in Chapter 1 should have helped you to highlight the areas in which you need to develop your skills. Chapters 3 to 7 will cover a wide variety of means in which you can develop your employability skills through your studies, undertaking practical legal skills activities, extra-curricular activities, and work experience. You should get into the habit of documenting and recording your skills development activities and building up a set of documentary evidence that you can use later on when you come to start completing applications. This involves going through a process called personal development planning.

Personal development planning (which is usually referred to as 'PDP') serves two important purposes. Not only does it enable you to reflect upon and build your employability skills, but it will also enable you to improve your academic skills while you are at university. Improved academic skills should help you to study more effectively and achieve improved results.

What is PDP?

In 1997, the Dearing Report[4] recommended that there should be 'a means by which students can monitor, build and reflect upon their personal development'. This recognised the views of some employers that they needed more information to differentiate between growing numbers of graduates over and above basic degree classification and transcript information. PDP was defined by the Quality Assurance Agency for Higher Education (QAA)[5] as: 'a structured and supported process undertaken by an individual to reflect upon their own learning and to plan for their personal, educational and career development'.[6]

The key points within this definition are those of planning, structure, and support.

Planning, action, review, and reflection: the PDP cycle

Effective PDP will involve you in a continuous cycle of activity, which can be depicted as shown in Figure 2.6.

As you can see, there are several stages in the process:

- Planning. Planning for PDP purposes requires you to set a list of targets and to work out how you can best achieve them. You have already considered your skills and abilities in the skills audit in Chapter 1 and thought about which of your employability skills are well developed, why that is, and whether there are any particular areas that you need to develop. Now that you have identified areas for development, think about how you can go about improving them. Chapters 3 to 7 will give you a whole range of suggestions as to how you can go about achieving this.

- Action. Having identified areas for development, you now need to engage in the process necessary to reach the planned targets. Start taking the steps that you considered useful after completing the planning stage.

- Recording. You should start compiling a set of evidence of the achievements that you have made while putting your plans into action and the activities that you have

---

4. The Dearing Report is actually a series of reports commissioned by the UK government into Higher Education in the UK. It is available online at <**https://bei.leeds.ac.uk/Partners/NCIHE/**>.
5. The body which checks standards in UK higher education institutions.
6. QAA, *Guidelines for Higher Education Progress Files* (2001) <**http://www.qaa.ac.uk/Publications/ informationAndGuidance/Pages/Guidelines-for-HE-Progress-Files.aspx**>.

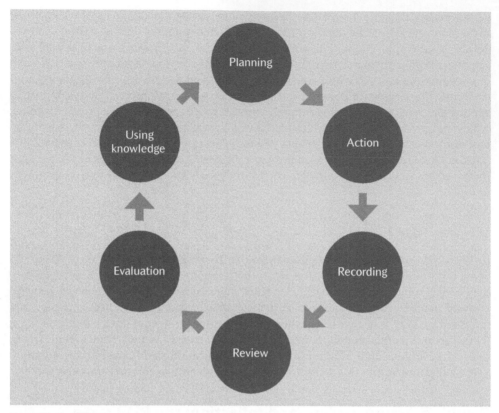

Figure 2.6 The PDP cycle

undertaken in doing so. In other words, you should compile a set of information that will not only help you to document the steps you have taken to grow your employability skills, but also help you in the next stage of the process.

- **Review.** So far you have come up with a plan, put it into action, and recorded evidence of how it is progressing. You should now review your plan in the light of the recorded evidence. Is the plan making the difference you wanted? Are you making progress towards the targets you identified for yourself in the light of your own evaluation of your strengths and weaknesses?

- **Evaluation.** This is an important stage in the process that requires you to pass critical judgement upon yourself and to reflect on your review of your plan to evaluate its overall success or otherwise.

- **Using knowledge.** By the time you get to this stage, you will have been through a whole cycle of PDP. You will now be in a position to plan future actions, and to identify if there are new areas for development, or whether you need to enhance existing areas further. This will inform the next stage of your planning process and the start of a brand new cycle of PDP.

Structure and support

The extent to which an institution provides structure and support for PDP will vary. You may be required to provide evidence of PDP by an academic or personal tutor throughout your studies. There may be a formal means of recording PDP either online, or in some sort of handbook. Alternatively, the arrangements may be more *ad hoc*, with less formal structure. You should see if your university has a member of staff responsible for PDP within law, and make contact with them. There may also be information provided in your student handbook, or PDP may be covered as part of a Legal Skills course or employability workshop. Whatever structure your university provides (and even if there is very little), you should take the time to go through the PDP process yourself, or with a group of friends, or suggesting that a more formal arrangement might be of benefit to students. All that is required is a desire to improve, self-reliance to take action for your own learning and career development, and the maturity to reflect critically on your own abilities. Practically speaking, evidence of PDP and the ability to describe your own PDP experience is something that will be of use to you in moving on to the next stage of your career, whichever route you choose to take.

⚫ On the Online Resource Centre, you will find a template that you can download and use to record your PDP activities and progress.

Putting your plan together

As well as your personal development planning which will enable you to identify areas for skills enhancement and to document your activities, you should also start to put together a checklist of activities to undertake so that you do not miss any key deadlines, or leave skills development activities too late for them to have any meaningful impact on your applications.

There are no absolutely hard and fast rules about when you should plan to do things—of course, every student is different and individual circumstances might dictate that certain activities may be easier to do at certain times. The two most important things are to put together a plan that works for you and to start now, regardless of what stage you are at in your studies. This should help you to avoid coming to the end of your degree and being lost as to what to do next:

....

I'm in my final year and I don't want to practise law. When I say this out loud, it is usually met with gasps of horror. 'What will you do?' I get asked as if there is no other career but law for me to follow. The truth is that I don't know what I'm going to do but I do know that I don't want to be a lawyer. I've enjoyed my degree but I just don't fancy working in the law so I'm looking around at other graduate opportunities. At the end of the day, this is far more sensible than doing the LPC just because I don't know what else to do, which is what some of my friends are doing. Am I making the right decision? It feels like the right decision for me but I guess you'll have to come back in a few years' time and find out whether things have worked out for me or not!

Mollie, Southampton University (2013)

....

The checklists that follow (see tables 2.1, 2.2, and 2.3) are also not exhaustive, but should give you a starting point as to the things that you should consider doing. You may wish to add to or amend your own personal plan as you work through the chapters in the rest of the book, but your initial checklist should sit alongside your PDP plan as a list of 'practical things to do'.

⚫ You will find downloadable versions of the tables that follow on the Online Resource Centre, which you can then edit and use in the way that suits you.

Finally, we cannot put together a checklist of practical steps towards every potential career that we discuss throughout the book. We have, therefore, concentrated on the two traditional branches of the legal profession, although there are many steps that will be transferable to other careers (such as 'put together a draft CV'). Where there is more information in this book, there is a cross reference to the relevant chapter. There are some important activities for you to consider that are outside the scope of this book, but they are still included in the checklists.

The advice for first year undergraduates is geared to building up a solid foundation in skills (see Table 2.1), before diverging in the second and third years (see Tables 2.2 and 2.3).

Table 2.1 First year checklist

When	What	Look at
First year undergraduate	Start to build your contacts within the legal profession	Chapter 6 on networking
	Join the university law society	Chapter 5 on building skills through social activities
	Get some legal work experience/volunteer work	Chapter 7 on work experience
	Get involved with practical legal skills activities (client interviewing, negotiation, mooting) at your institution	Chapter 4 on practical legal skills and Chapter 6 on finding opportunities
	Focus on your academic studies	Chapter 3 on academic legal skills
	Investigate pro bono opportunities through your institution	Chapter 6 on finding opportunities
	Think about doing some charity work or organising events	Chapter 5 on building skills through social activities
	Plan for/apply for holiday work	Chapter 10 on applications

Solicitor route

Table 2.2 Second and final year checklist

When	What	Look at
Second year—autumn term	Consider whether the solicitor route to practice is right for you	Chapter 2 for an overview and Chapter 8 for the realities of the training contract
	Think about your preferred area of practice	Chapter 8 for overview of the major practice areas

(Continued)

Table 2.2 (*Continued*)

When	What	Look at
	Look out for and attend law fairs and other career events	Chapter 8 on law fairs
	Draft your CV and have it checked	Chapter 10 on CVs
	Research possible LPC providers	
	Investigate funding options for the LPC	
Second year—Christmas holidays and spring term	Apply for vacation schemes	Chapter 7 on work experience
	Draw up a shortlist of firms of interest	Chapter 8 on training contracts
Second year—summer holidays	Apply for work experience	Chapter 7 on work experience and Chapter 10 on applications
	Compile a list of deadlines for your training contract applications	
	Apply for training contracts in good time	Chapter 8 on training contracts and Chapter 10 on applications
Final year—autumn term	Training contract interviews	Chapter 11 on interviews and other assessment methods
	Apply for the LPC	
Final year—spring and summer	Enrol with the Solicitors Regulation Authority as a student member	
	Focus on your final exams and getting the best degree classification you can	Chapter 3 on academic legal skills
	Continue training contract applications	Chapter 8 on training contracts and chapter 10 on applications
	Continue work experience	Chapter 7 on work experience and Chapter 10 on applications

Barrister route

Table 2.3 Second and final year checklist

When	What	Look at
Second year—autumn term	Consider whether the barrister route to practice is right for you	Chapter 2 for an overview and Chapter 8 for the realities of pupillage
	Think about your preferred area of practice	Chapter 8 for overview of the major practice areas

When	What	Look at
	Take part in mooting	Chapter 4 on practical legal skills and Chapter 6 on finding opportunities
	Draft your CV and have it checked	Chapter 10 on CVs
	Research possible BPTC providers	
	Investigate funding options for the BPTC	
Second year—Christmas holidays and spring term	Apply for mini pupillages	Chapter 10 on applications
	Undertake legal work experience	Chapter 7 on work experience
Second year—summer	Continue legal work experience	Chapter 7 on work experience
Final year—autumn	Join an Inn of Court	
	Apply for the BPTC	
	Make arrangements for the BCAT	
	Submit scholarship applications	
Final year—spring and summer	Submit pupillage applications	Chapter 8 on pupillage and Chapter 10 on applications
	Attend pupillage interviews	Chapter 11 on interviews
During the BPTC	Continue gathering as much work experience as possible; non-legal work experience can still be valuable and help fund studies	Chapter 7 on work experience
	Reapply for pupillage	Chapter 8 on pupillage and Chapter 10 on applications

WHERE NEXT?

This chapter has set out an overview of the possibilities that a law degree can open up for you. Where you go next in the book really depends on what stage you are at in your studies and in your plan. As you will have seen from the outline plans in the last section of this chapter, there are many different routes through the book. The important thing is to have a plan for what you need to do next and to stick to it.

7

BAIL AND REMANDS

The principal subject matter of this Chapter is bail, which may be defined as the release of **7.01** a person subject to a duty to surrender to custody at an appointed time and place. The time when a person bailed is to surrender to custody may be fixed when bail is granted or, in the case of a person sent on bail to the Crown Court for trial or sentence, it may be notified to him subsequently. The place where he is to surrender is either a court or a police station, usually the former. The granting of bail in criminal proceedings is governed by the Bail Act 1976.

A   REMANDS AND ADJOURNMENTS

The power of courts (especially magistrates' courts) to remand an accused person is closely **7.02** bound up with the power to grant bail. A remand occurs when a court adjourns a case and either bails the accused for the period of the adjournment or commits him to custody to be brought before the court on the adjournment date. As the above implies, remands are either on bail or in custody, by contrast with a simple adjournment, which does not entail the same restrictions. A magistrates' court has a general discretion to adjourn a case at any stage prior to or during committal proceedings or summary trial (see Magistrates' Courts Act 1980, (MCA) ss 5 and 10). It also has power to adjourn after summary conviction for the preparation of reports.

In fact, it is rare for a case of any gravity or complexity to be totally disposed of on the occasion **7.03** of the accused's first appearance. Either the prosecution will need time to prepare statements for committal, or serve advance information, or ensure that their witnesses are present for summary trial; or the accused will want an adjournment to apply for publicly funded representation, see a solicitor, and generally put his case in order. The only type of case likely to need only one appearance is where the accused pleads guilty to a relatively minor offence and the court does not consider it needs reports before passing sentence.

Assuming the magistrates do have to adjourn, they are always entitled to remand the accused. **7.04** However, if the offence is summary and it is an adjournment prior to trial, they have a discretion simply to adjourn without remanding. Similarly, if the offence is triable either way and the accused has not been remanded before and appears in answer to a summons (as opposed to having been charged and bailed from the police station), there is a discretion not to remand upon adjourning. In all other cases (e.g., offences triable only on indictment, those triable either way where the prosecution was commenced by way of charge, and all adjournments after conviction for reports), the magistrates must remand—i.e., grant the accused bail or remand him in custody. The difference between, on the one hand, simply adjourning and, on the other, adjourning and granting bail is that, in the former case, no adverse consequences flow from the accused failing to appear on the adjournment date, save that the offence will very likely be proved against him in his absence, whereas in the latter case he is under a duty to appear and commits an offence by not doing so. Normally, magistrates only adjourn without remanding in trivial cases, especially road traffic matters. The next section deals especially with the periods for which magistrates may remand an accused; the remainder of the Chapter deals with bail.

Periods of remand

Subject to what follows, when magistrates remand an accused in custody prior to committal **7.05** proceedings or summary trial, the period of the remand must not exceed eight clear days:

MCA, s 128(6). Usually it is simpler to make the adjournment and remand for a week, rather than using the full period allowed. The limitation on remands in custody is inconvenient when a period of several weeks or months is bound to elapse before the committal or summary trial can take place. Again, subject to what follows, the accused has to be brought before the court each week, even though the virtually foregone conclusion of his appearance is that he will be remanded in custody for another week. The pointlessness of his appearing in the dock just to be told that his case is further adjourned until such and such a date is accentuated by the fact that, since the decision of the Divisional Court in *Nottingham Justices ex parte Davies* [1981] QB 38, the defence have basically only been allowed one, or at most two, fully argued bail applications. Once they have exhausted those applications, they can only re-open the question of bail if fresh considerations have arisen which were not placed before the bench that originally refused bail. Obviously, if the defence are prevented from arguing for bail, the remand hearing turns into a charade. The decision in *Ex parte Davies* has been statutorily confirmed by the insertion in 1988 of Pt IIA in Sch 1 to the Bail Act 1976 (see 7.38 to 7.41).

7.06 In recognition of the unsatisfactoriness of successive remands in custody and the necessity for the accused's presence at each remand, the Criminal Justice Act (CJA) 1982 introduced several new subsections into s 128 of the MCA, the basic effect of which is to allow the accused to consent to being remanded in custody for up to 28 days without attending court. The system is that, on the first or any subsequent occasion when magistrates propose to adjourn prior to committal or summary trial and remand the accused in custody, they must, if he is legally represented in court, inform him of the possibility of further remands being made in his absence. If, and only if, he consents, they may then remand him thrice without his being brought to court. On the fourth occasion he must attend whether he wishes to or not. The possibility of custodial remand in absence does not arise if the accused is unrepresented or if he is a juvenile.

7.07 Although probably the bulk of defendants who will have to be remanded in custody for substantial periods do sooner or later agree to remands in absence, the Government apparently came to think that, given the pressures under which the prison service is currently working, it was unsatisfactory to burden the service with the task of bringing remandees to court when no useful purpose could possibly be served by that being done. Accordingly the CJA 1988 inserted a new section (s 128A) into the MCA which allows a magistrates' court to remand an accused in custody for up to 28 clear days, whether or not he consents. It enables a magistrates' court, once it has set a date for the next stage of the proceedings to take place, to remand an accused in custody for a period ending on that date, or for a period of 28 clear days, whichever is the less. Importantly, it does not apply on the occasion of a first remand in custody but only if at a second or any subsequent remand the court again decides to refuse bail. Section 128A thus dovetails with the statutory provisions about argued bail applications, because the defence has a right to make an argued bail application both on the occasion of the accused's first appearance in connection with the charge and (if bail is then refused) at the next hearing. Thus, it is only when the ration of argued applications has been used up that the court may remand in custody for up to 28 days. If they are considering an extended remand under s 128A, magistrates should have regard to the total period of time the accused would spend in custody if they were so to remand him (see para 9B, added to Pt 1 of Sch 1 to the Bail Act 1976).

Where magistrates remand an accused after conviction for the purpose of preparing reports **7.08** on him, the period of the remand must not exceed three weeks if it is in custody; four weeks if it is on bail: MCA, ss 10(3) and 30(1). Remands on bail prior to summary trial or committal proceedings may be for any convenient period. There is also a power in addition to s 128A to remand in custody for up to 28 days if the accused is already serving a custodial sentence for some other offence (see MCA, s 131(1)).

B   OCCASIONS ON WHICH A PERSON MAY BE GRANTED BAIL

The occasions on which a court or magistrate or police officer is faced with the decision to **7.09** grant or refuse bail are as follows:

(a) During the arrest and charge procedure at the police station, the question of bail can arise either as a result of the police charging the arrestee or as a result of their deciding that he should be released from the station without being charged. In the last resort, the decision on whether or not the arrestee should be bailed rests with the custody officer, although he will no doubt be much influenced by the views of the investigating officers. For details, see 3.29 to 3.30 and ss 37 to 38 of the Police and Criminal Evidence Act 1984 (PACE).

(b) A magistrate issuing a warrant for the arrest of the person named in a written information which has been laid before him should consider whether to endorse the warrant for bail: MCA, s 117—see 3.42 to 3.44. Similarly, a magistrates' court or the Crown Court on issuing a warrant may back it for bail: s 117 and Supreme Court Act 1981, s 81(4).

(c) A magistrates' court has jurisdiction to grant bail when:
   (i)   it remands an accused for the period of an adjournment prior to committal proceedings or summary trial: MCA, ss 5, 10(4) and 18(4)—see 7.08; or
   (ii)   it remands an offender after conviction for the period of an adjournment for reports under MCA, ss 10(3) or 30—see 7.08; or
   (iii) it commits or sends an accused to the Crown Court for trial on indictment or for sentence (MCA, ss 6(3) and 38 which provide respectively that committals for trial and sentence may be in custody or on bail); or
   (iv)   a person in custody is appealing to the Crown Court or the Divisional Court against one of its (the magistrates' court's) decisions: MCA, s 113—see 27.03 to 27.11 and 27.18 to 27.23.

The maximum periods for remands in custody prior to committal proceedings or summary trial have been explained at 7.05 to 7.08. A remand for preparation of reports following summary conviction may be for a maximum of three or four weeks depending on whether the offender is or is not in custody (see MCA, ss 10(3) and 30). Committals for trial or sentence in custody will be for whatever period may elapse until the case can be heard in the Crown Court. Because that period will certainly be one of several weeks and may extend to several months, the decision to grant or refuse bail on committal is a particularly important one.

(d) The Crown Court has jurisdiction to grant bail when:
   (i)   a magistrates' court has remanded an accused in custody and has issued a certificate to the effect that it heard full argument before taking the decision to refuse bail (see 7.45 for details); or

(ii) a person has been committed or sent to it for trial or sentence in custody or is appeal-
      ing to it against conviction or sentence by the magistrates; or

(iii) a person is appealing from it by case stated to the Divisional Court or is seeking judi-
      cial review of its decision; or

(iv) the appropriate Crown Court judge has certified that a case is fit for appeal to the
      Court of Appeal against conviction or sentence (see also 26.10 to 26.11).

The above powers to grant bail are contained in s 81(1) of the Supreme Court Act 1981.
The Crown Court also has inherent jurisdiction to grant bail during the course of a trial
on indictment and for the period of an adjournment for reports following conviction.
If the accused was on bail prior to the commencement of the trial and surrenders to
custody at the appointed time, it is normal practice to renew his bail for any overnight
adjournments. Bail may be withdrawn, however, where there is a real danger that he
might abscond (e.g., because the case is going badly for him), or interfere with witnesses
or jurors. When a custodial sentence would be the likely result of conviction and the
prosecution case seems strong, bail is often withdrawn once the judge has commenced
his summing-up. The *Consolidated Criminal Practice Direction*, para III.25 deals with the
principles governing bail during the course of a trial (for the website address, see the end
of this Chapter).

(e) A person charged with murder may not be granted bail, except by a judge in the Crown
     Court (Coroners and Justice Act 2009, s 115).

(f) The High Court has jurisdiction to grant bail when a person is appealing to it by way of
     case stated or seeking to quash a decision of the magistrates' court or the Crown Court.

(g) The Court of Appeal (acting through a single judge) has jurisdiction to grant bail both
     to a person appealing to it against conviction or sentence in the Crown Court, and to a
     person who, after an unsuccessful appeal to it, is further appealing to the House of Lords:
     Criminal Appeal Act 1968, ss 19 and 36.

C   PRINCIPLES ON WHICH THE DECISION TO GRANT OR REFUSE BAIL IS TAKEN

7.10   Section 4 of the Bail Act 1976 gives to an accused person what may usefully, if slightly inac-
       curately, be described as a right to bail. The section does not apply at all stages of the crimi-
       nal process, and, even if it does apply, the accused may be refused bail if the circumstances
       of his case fall within one of a number of sets of circumstances defined in Sch 1 to the Act.
       Nevertheless, the right to bail is of value to an accused because it emphasizes that it is for the
       prosecution to show a good reason why bail should be withheld, not for the defence to plead
       for bail as a favour to which the accused is not prima facie entitled.

7.11   There is a group of defendants who may be granted bail only if there are 'exceptional cir-
       cumstances which justify it'. This is the category covered by s 25 of the Criminal Justice and
       Public Order Act 1994 (CJPOA). That provision covers any person charged with murder,
       attempted murder, manslaughter, rape, attempted rape, or one of the serious sexual offences
       added by the Sexual Offences Act 2003, Sch 6, para 32, if he has previously been convicted
       in the United Kingdom of one of those offences, or of culpable homicide. Where the prior

conviction was manslaughter or culpable homicide, however, the provision applies only if the sentence imposed on that occasion was imprisonment or long-term detention. The current offence with which the accused is charged does not need to be the same as that for which he was convicted previously. The restriction on bail for accused in this category applies also on appeal against conviction.

In *R(O) v Harrow Crown Court* [2007] 1 AC 247, the House of Lords considered that s 25 is compatible with Art 5 of the European Convention on Human Rights, which guarantees the right to liberty. It did not cast a formal burden of proof upon a defendant to make out the exceptional circumstances allowing bail. In so far as s 25 appeared to do so, it should be 'read down' in accordance with s 3 of the Human Rights Act 1998, so as to ensure that it was consistent with Art 5 (the right to liberty). In *O'Dowd v United Kingdom* [2011] Crim LR 148, the European Court of Human Rights came to a similar conclusion, holding that there was good reason to require proof of exceptional circumstances before granting bail to someone who had been convicted of a similar serious offence previously.

7.12 Where a defendant is charged with murder, he may not be granted bail unless the court is of the opinion that there is no significant risk that he will commit (while on bail) an offence which would be likely to cause physical or mental injury to another (Coroners and Justice Act 2009, s 114, inserting s 6ZA in the Bail Act 1976).

Occasions on which there is a 'right to bail'

7.13 Section 4 provides that a person to whom it applies 'shall be granted bail except as provided in Schedule 1'. The section applies whenever a person accused of an offence appears or is brought before a magistrates' court or the Crown Court in the course of or in connection with proceedings for the offence. Thus, at his first court appearance before the magistrates and at all subsequent appearances before the magistrates or the Crown Court up to the occasion on which he is convicted or acquitted, the accused has a right to bail. Even following conviction, he still has a right to bail if his case is adjourned for reports prior to sentencing. He can also rely on the right to bail if, during these stages of the proceedings, he applies to the Crown Court for bail following a refusal of bail by the magistrates. There is no right to bail when:

(a) the custody officer is considering bailing an arrestee from the police station after he has been charged; or
(b) the magistrates, having summarily convicted an offender, commit him to the Crown Court for sentence; or
(c) a person who has been convicted and sentenced, whether by the magistrates or in the Crown Court, is appealing against conviction or sentence.

Of course, in all three of the above cases the police officer or court has power to grant bail, but there is no statutory presumption in its favour by virtue of s 4. In case (a), s 38(1) of PACE gives the accused something very similar to the Bail Act 'right to bail'. The subsection provides that a person who has been charged *shall* be released from the police station (either on bail or unconditionally) unless the custody officer reasonably fears that that would have one or more of a number of undesirable consequences (e.g., the arrestee absconding or interfering with witnesses—3.29 to 3.30).

Refusing bail for a defendant charged with an imprisonable offence

7.14 Schedule 1 to the Bail Act 1976 sets out the circumstances in which a person to whom s 4 applies (i.e., a person with a right to bail) may be refused bail. Schedule 1 refers to a person with a right to bail as 'the defendant'.

7.15 Part I of Sch 1 applies when the defendant stands accused or convicted of at least one offence punishable with imprisonment. He need not be granted bail if:

(a) the court is satisfied that there are substantial grounds for believing that, if released on bail, he would:
   (i)   fail to surrender to custody; or
   (ii) commit an offence while on bail; or
   (iii) interfere with witnesses or otherwise obstruct the course of justice whether in relation to himself or some other person; or
(b) he was already on bail at the time of the charged offence, which is indictable-only or triable-either-way; or
(c) the court is satisfied that he should be kept in custody for his own protection or, if he is a juvenile, for his own welfare; or
(d) he is already serving a custodial sentence; or
(e) the court is satisfied that lack of time since the commencement of the proceedings has made it impracticable to obtain the information needed to decide properly the questions raised in (a) to (c) above; or
(f) he has already been bailed during the course of the proceedings, and has been arrested under s 7 of the Act (arrest of absconders etc.—see 7.60 to 7.63); or
(g) he is aged 18 or over, there is drug test evidence of a specified Class A drug in his body, the offence is a Class A drug offence (or was caused or contributed to by a Class A drug) and he does not agree to undergo an assessment or a follow-up programme as to drug misuse or dependency.

When the Legal Aid, Sentencing and Punishment of Offenders Act 2012 (LASPO Act 2012), s 90 and Sch 11 come into effect, certain of the above exceptions to the presumption that bail should not be granted will not apply unless there is a real prospect that the defendant will receive a custodial sentence. This new test will increase the availability of bail. It is limited to non-extradition proceedings, and to adult defendants who have not been convicted. The exceptions which will be subject to the 'no real prospect test' are those set out in (a), (b), and (f).

7.16 Exception (b) above deals with the general position where the defendant is alleged to have committed an offence which is indictable-only or triable-either-way while on bail. Section 14(1) of the CJA 2003 introduced a new test where the offence for which bail is being considered carries a maximum sentence of life imprisonment. In circumstances where the offence appears to have been committed on bail and the defendant is aged 18 or over, he may not be granted bail unless there is no significant risk of his committing an offence while on bail. Section 14(2) states that in the case of a defendant aged under 18 who was on bail when the alleged offence was committed, the court can give particular weight to this fact when deciding whether he will be likely to re-offend if released on bail. Exception (f) above deals with the general position where the defendant has absconded during the course of current proceedings. Section 15 of the CJA 2003 again introduced a new test where the offence for which bail is being considered carries a maximum sentence of life imprisonment. In the case of an adult offender who has absconded during the current proceedings, he may not be granted bail unless there is no significant risk of his failing to surrender to custody. If he is under 18, the court shall give particular weight to the fact that he has previously absconded in the proceedings when deciding on bail. When the LASPO Act 2012, s 90 and Sch 11 come into effect, the exceptions to the presumption of bail summarized in (b) and (f) of 7.15 will be subject to the 'no real prospect test' detailed in that paragraph.

The above reasons for refusing bail are listed in paras 2 to 6 of Pt I of Sch 1. The one most **7.17** commonly relied upon is that set out in (a). It will be noticed that the wording of the reason is very precise. The court must be 'satisfied that there are substantial grounds for believing' that, if bail were granted, one or other of the undesirable consequences specified would ensue. A subjective belief that that is what would happen is not enough if it is based on flimsy or irrational grounds. On the other hand, the prosecution are not required to prove beyond reasonable doubt that the defendant would jump bail etc., or even to produce formal evidence to that effect. The question for the court is essentially a speculative one, not amenable to proof according to the rules by which disputed issues are normally resolved in a court of law. Thus, a prosecutor objecting to bail may state his opinion that it would lead to the accused absconding, or he may even, with a view to showing that there is a risk of interference with witnesses, recount to the court what a police officer has been told by a potential witness of threats the latter has received (*Re Moles* [1981] Crim LR 170). This was confirmed by *Mansfield Justices ex parte Sharkey* [1985] QB 613, where the Divisional Court accepted counsel's proposition that 'a bail application is an informal inquiry and no strict rules of evidence are to be applied'. However, para 9 of Pt I of Sch 1 does give the courts some guidance on how this informal inquiry should be approached by listing a number of considerations to be taken into account; para 9 only applies when the objection to bail is one of those presently being discussed—i.e., that the defendant would abscond, commit further offences or interfere with witnesses. The factors which it lists are described in 7.18. When the LASPO Act 2012, s 90 and Sch 11 come into effect, the exceptions to the presumption of bail set out in (a) of 7.15 will be subject to the 'no real prospect' test detailed in that paragraph.

First, there is 'the nature and seriousness of the offence and the probable method of deal- **7.18** ing with the defendant for it'. The more serious the charge the more likely it is that he will abscond because he will realize that conviction would result in a lengthy prison sentence. Secondly, the 'character, antecedents, associations and community ties' of the defendant are relevant. Under the heading of 'community ties' the court will be assessing how much the defendant has to lose by absconding. If he is a married man with a family living in his own house, he is less likely to abscond than a teenager with a room in a hostel. However, a person should not be refused bail simply because he is living in the latter type of accommodation—it is merely one factor which goes to indicate a lack of roots in the local community and there- fore a greater risk of jumping bail (see Home Office Circular, No 155 of 1975). The defend- ant's character and previous convictions are important in two ways. They may show that he is untrustworthy, and they may also show that, even though the offence charged is not intrinsically in the first rank of gravity, he is likely if convicted to receive a custodial sentence because, e.g., he will be in breach of a suspended sentence. Thirdly, the court may look at the defendant's past record for answering bail and/or committing offences while on bail. If he has previously been bailed and has not abused the trust placed in him, that is some reason for saying that he can be trusted on bail on the present occasion. Fourthly, the court should consider the strength of the prosecution case—the weaker the evidence seems, the stronger is the argument for bail. Unfortunately, the strength or weakness of the case will probably not emerge until later in the proceedings, by which time the defendant may have spent a considerable period in custody. Finally, where the court is satisfied that there are substantial grounds for believing that the defendant would commit an offence if released on bail, they should consider the risk that such an offence would be likely to cause physical or mental injury to anyone else. The list of relevant considerations in para 9 is not intended as an exhaustive one. One obviously important factor not mentioned in the paragraph is whether the defence can put forward sureties.

7.19   Reason (b) in 7.15 for refusing bail was added to the list by s 26 of the Criminal Justice and Public Order Act 1994 and amended by the CJA 2003 it will be amended once the LASPO Act 2012, s 90, comes into effect. It covers the position of the offender who is alleged to have committed a further offence while on bail. An accused who is in due course found guilty of that further offence can expect a harsher sentence as a result (see 23.22). But his bail prospects will also be affected. The court still has a discretion whether to grant him bail or not. In exercising that discretion, however, they need not regard him as having the right to bail. As a result, the refusal of bail will be easier, for in cases where there is a right to bail there must be substantial grounds for believing that one of the exceptions applies before bail can be withheld. In this context, 'substantial' means more than a subjective perception (*Ex parte Sharkey* at p. 625).

7.20   The other justifications in Sch 1 for refusing bail to a defendant with a right to bail call for little comment. Keeping somebody in custody for his own protection might be necessary where the offence charged has raised a great deal of local anger, as where it is alleged that the defendant sexually assaulted young children. If the defendant is a juvenile, bail can be refused in his own best interests even though he would not be physically endangered through being released (e.g., if he has run away from home, remanding him into the care of the local authority may be preferable to leaving him to fend for himself). Where the defendant is already serving a custodial sentence which will last until well after his next court appearance on the present charge, there is little point in going through the motions of considering a bail application. Lack of information on which to base a proper decision about bail is a problem when the defendant makes his first court appearance before the magistrates after being arrested without warrant, charged at the police station and thereafter kept in police detention. He may not have been able to consult with a solicitor or to arrange for one to be at court to make a bail application for him. Although the duty solicitor will no doubt be asked to assist, there will be little time for him to be given proper instructions (e.g., as to who might be prepared to stand surety). From the police viewpoint, they may not have been able to check on matters such as the defendant's address, identity and previous convictions. The magistrates are therefore allowed to 'play safe' by remanding in custody for a week or so, at the end of which the arguments for and against bail can be properly presented on both sides. Lastly, if the defendant has already been bailed in connection with the present proceedings against him and has had to be arrested for absconding or otherwise failing to comply with the conditions of his bail, the court is entitled to say the legal equivalent of 'once bitten twice shy' and refuse to set him at liberty again.

At the stage of an adjournment for reports following the defendant's conviction, there is   **7.21**
one additional possible reason for refusing bail, namely that the court believes it will not
be practicable to complete the report without the defendant being in custody. For example,
the court may have ordered medical reports, but the mental condition of the defendant may
make it obvious that he will not voluntarily attend at a hospital so as to be examined. The
court should therefore remand him in custody (or it may now have the additional option of
remanding him to a mental hospital—see 10.72 to 10.74).

Refusing bail for a defendant charged with a non-imprisonable offence

Part II of Sch 1 applies when none of the offences of which the defendant stands accused or   **7.22**
convicted is punishable with imprisonment. He need not be granted bail if reasons (c) or (d)
for refusing to grant bail to a defendant accused of an imprisonable offence apply in his case
(i.e., he should be kept in custody for his own protection, or he is already serving a custodial
sentence). Further, where he is arrested under s 7 of the Bail Act, bail may be refused only if
there are substantial grounds for believing that, if released on bail (whether subject to conditions or not) he would fail to surrender to custody, commit an offence while on bail, or
interfere with witnesses or otherwise obstruct the course of justice (Sch 1, Part 2, para 5 of the
Bail Act, as amended by CJA 2003, s 13(4)). There is no general power to refuse bail on the
grounds that he might abscond, but, if he failed to surrender to custody after being bailed in
previous criminal proceedings and the court therefore believes that, if now granted bail, he
would again fail to surrender, bail may be refused. It is very rare for a court to refuse bail if the
offences are non-imprisonable.

Custody time limits

Under s 22 of the Prosecution of Offences Act 1985, there are regulations which lay down   **7.23**
custody time limits (i.e., maximum periods during which the accused can be kept in custody
before trial). The regulations were originally in force in certain areas only, but have now been
extended to all parts of the country. They fix the following maximum periods for which an
accused may be held:

(a) 70 days between his first appearance in the magistrates' court and committal proceed-
     ings;
(b) 70 days between first appearance and summary trial for an offence which is triable either
     way (reduced to 56 days if the decision for summary trial is taken within 56 days);
(c) 56 days between first appearance and trial for a summary offence;
(d) 112 days between committal for trial and arraignment;
(e) 70 days between first appearance and the decision to send an indictable-only offence to
     the Crown Court; and
(f) 182 days between the date when an indictable-only offence is sent for trial and the start
     of trial.

Special rules apply to the accused's right to bail when the prosecution fails to comply with a   **7.24**
custody time limit. When the limit has expired, the exceptions to the right to bail listed in
Sch 1 to the Bail Act 1976 no longer apply (reg 8 of the Prosecution of Offences (Custody Time

Limits) Regulations 1987: SI 1987 No 299). The effect is to give the accused an absolute right to bail (other than in cases governed by s 25 of the CJPOA—see 7.11 and *R(O) v Harrow Crown Court* [2007] 1 AC 247). Further, the court is prevented, when bailing an accused entitled to bail by reason of the expiry of a custody time limit, from imposing a requirement of a surety or deposit of security or any other condition which must be complied with *before* release on bail. It may impose a condition such as a curfew, or a condition of residence or reporting, which has to be complied with *after* release. The prosecution can, of course, avoid these consequences by ensuring that the case is dealt with quickly, so as to avoid the expiry of the custody time limit. Failing that, it can apply for an extension of the time limit.

7.25 The application for an extension must be made before the custody time limit expires. In considering whether to grant an extension, the criteria laid down in s 22(3) of the Prosecution of Offences Act 1985 are applied. The court must be satisfied:

(a)   that the need for the extension is due to:
    (i)   the illness or absence of the accused, a necessary witness, a judge or a magistrate;
    (ii)   the ordering by the court of separate trials in the case of two or more accused or two or more offences; or
    (iii) some other good or sufficient cause; and
(b)   that the Crown has acted with all due expedition.

(For a detailed analysis of the case law on custody time limits, see *Blackstone's Criminal Practice 2012*, D14.6 to 14.35.)

D   REQUIREMENTS IMPOSED WHEN GRANTING BAIL

7.26 A defendant may be granted bail unconditionally, in which case he is not required to provide sureties before being released and, having been released, the only obligation he is under is that of surrendering to custody at the appointed place and time. Alternatively, s 3 of the Bail Act allows the police or the courts to attach requirements to a grant of bail.

7.27 One of the common requirements attached to bail is that of providing one or more sureties. Both the police when bailing an arrestee from the station and the courts may require sureties, but they should only do so if it is necessary to ensure that the defendant surrenders to custody (see s 3(4)). A surety is a person who undertakes to pay the court a specified sum of money in the event of the defendant failing to surrender to custody as he ought. The undertaking into which the surety enters is called a recognizance. If the defendant absconds the surety may be ordered to pay part or all of the sum in which he stood surety. This is known as forfeiting or estreating the recognizance. A surety whose recognizance has been estreated is dealt with as if he had been fined, so if he fails to pay the sum forfeited a means inquiry is held and, ultimately, he could be committed to prison. The possibly serious consequences of being a surety mean that no person proffered as a surety should be accepted as such unless he apparently has the means to satisfy his potential liability under the recognizance. On granting bail, the police officer or court fixes the number and amount of the sureties which will be required, and the defendant must remain in custody until suitable sureties in the stated sums have entered into their recognizances. If the sureties are not forthcoming the defendant, at his next appearance before the court or on an application to the Crown Court, may argue that the requirement for sureties should be varied or dispensed with altogether.

Note that a surety for an adult accused is responsible only for ensuring that the accused **7.28** attends court. He is not obliged to ensure that other conditions of bail (e.g., not to commit further offences) are met. Some magistrates' courts have been in the practice of asking for 'sureties for good behaviour'. There is no power to do this under the Bail Act 1976, so they attempt to remedy the deficiency by using their general powers to bind over under the Justices of the Peace Act 1361 and the Justices of the Peace Act 1968. There are two problems with this practice:

(a) Binding over to keep the peace is only of relevance where the court fears repetition, e.g., of an offence of violence. It can hardly be properly invoked in relation, say, to an offence of dishonesty.

(b) A court requiring a surety for good behaviour appears to be contravening the Bail Act 1976, s 3(3)(c) of which provides: 'Except as provided *by this section*...no other requirement shall be imposed [on the accused] as a condition of bail' (emphasis added).

The position as far as sureties for juveniles is concerned is different. By s 3(7) of the Bail Act **7.29** 1976, where the accused is a juvenile and his parent or guardian stands surety for him, the court may require that surety to ensure that the juvenile complies with any condition of bail imposed by virtue of s 6. Hence, the court can quite properly require the parent or guardian to be a surety for good behaviour. The recognizance under s 3(7) is, however, limited to £50.

A requirement for sureties does not involve the sureties or the defendant himself paying **7.30** money to the court as a pre-condition of his release on bail. The position is different, however, where the court requires that the defendant supply *security* for his surrender to custody (s 3(5)). Giving security means that the defendant or somebody on his behalf deposits money or other property with the court, which will be forfeited if he absconds.

Instead of or in addition to imposing a requirement for sureties or, where appropriate, a **7.31** requirement for the giving of security, a court may require the defendant to comply with such other conditions as appear necessary to ensure that he does not abscond, commit offences while on bail, or interfere with witnesses: (s 3(6)(a) to (c)). The court may impose conditions to protect the accused, or (if he is a child or young person) for his own welfare or in his own interests (Bail Act 1976, s 3(6)(ca) added by the CJA 2003, s 13(1)). A condition may also be imposed to ensure that the defendant attends an interview with his legal representative (s 3(6)(e)). By virtue of s 3(6), the defendant may be required, e.g., to report to the police station once a week or even once a day, to surrender his passport, to live at a certain address (e.g., his home address or, if he is of no fixed abode, a bail hostel run by the probation service), to report any change of address, or to be indoors by a certain time each night. Negatively, he could be ordered not to contact potential prosecution witnesses or not to go within a certain distance of where the victim of the alleged offence lives. More controversially, in *Mansfield Justices ex parte Sharkey* [1985] QB 613, a number of miners from Yorkshire involved in the strike of 1984–5 were required as a condition of bail not to picket otherwise than at their own pits, which were solidly for the strike anyway. They were awaiting trial on threatening behaviour charges, the alleged offences having occurred when they were taking part in the mass picketing of working pits in the East Midlands. The Divisional Court upheld the requirements on the basis that the defendants would otherwise have returned to the picket lines which, given that the picketing was 'by intimidation and threat' (per the Lord Chief Justice at p. 627), might have resulted in their committing further offences. *Ex parte Sharkey* was of interest not only for its political implications and the impact it had on the course of the miners' strike, but also for the Lord Chief Justice's comments on how probable the commission of further offences must appear if that is to be used as a justification for imposing conditions of bail. The court must perceive a real, as opposed to a fanciful, risk of unconditional bail resulting in offences being committed while on bail, but it need not have the 'substantial grounds' for its belief which it would have to have if it were minded to refuse bail completely for the same reason. Thus, the justices were entitled to impose the conditions even though the defendants were of previous good character and the only grounds for supposing they would commit offences if allowed to picket again was the justices' local knowledge of how the picketing was in general being conducted. The implication of Lord Lane's judgment was that those grounds would not have been substantial enough for a total refusal of bail.

7.32 *Ex parte Sharkey* was a case where the accused were charged with an imprisonable offence. In *Bournemouth Magistrates' Court ex parte Cross* (1989) 89 Cr App R 90, the point at issue was whether conditions could be imposed on bail for non-imprisonable offences. C was a hunt protester who was arrested for an offence under s 5 of the Public Order Act 1986 (non-imprisonable). He was bailed on condition he did not attend another hunt meeting before his next court appearance. He was arrested for alleged breach of this condition, and remanded in custody by the magistrates. On application for judicial review, the Divisional Court held that the condition had been validly imposed. The justices had been of the view that it was necessary to prevent the commission of further offences, and they were entitled to impose it by s 3(6) of the Bail Act 1976.

7.33 When a convicted defendant is remanded on bail for the preparation of reports on his physical or mental condition prior to sentencing, the Crown Court may and a magistrates' court must require him to make himself available for the necessary medical examinations (see Bail Act 1976, s 3(6), and s 30(2) of the MCA). When a juvenile has conditions attached to his bail, his parents (provided they consent) may be required to secure his compliance with the conditions, on pain of forfeiting a recognisance of not more than £50 (Bail Act 1976, s 3(7)). Otherwise sureties have no responsibility for ensuring that the defendant complies with any conditions of bail, other than the basic one of surrendering to custody at the appropriate time.

E   PROCEDURE AT AN APPLICATION FOR BAIL IN A MAGISTRATES' COURT

7.34 Most bail applications are made in the magistrates' courts. Essentially the procedure is that the court asks the defence whether there is an application for bail and the prosecutor whether there are any objections. Strictly speaking, the granting or withholding of bail is always a matter for the court, not for tacit agreement between the parties, but obviously if a bail application is unopposed the court is unlikely to raise objections, whereas if no application is made it will need little convincing that there are sufficient reasons for remanding in custody. Assuming, however, that there is an opposed bail application, the prosecutor outlines his objections. It is rare for the police officer in the case actually to attend court, but he should have completed a form contained in the CPS file stating why (in his view) bail is undesirable. Reasons commonly given are that the gravity of the offence charged and/or the accused's previous record make it likely that he will receive a custodial sentence if convicted; that he is currently appearing in other courts for other matters and that the present offences were committed while on bail; that he has past convictions for failing to appear after being granted bail; and that he knows the chief prosecution witnesses and, if at liberty, would be in a position to influence them. A list of previous convictions may be handed into the court and commented on in general terms but it is not normally read out in full (see *Dyson* (1943) 29 Cr App R 104). Following the prosecution objections to bail, the defence representative makes a speech countering those objections as best he can. He may, e.g., stress that the accused has a permanent address and strong community ties and so is unlikely to abscond, even though the charges are serious. If there are sureties available, it is sometimes helpful to call them so that the bench can appreciate the quality of the persons who are prepared to put money at risk on behalf of the accused. The more impressive the surety, the more likely it is that bail will be granted. On the other side of the argument, while it is unusual for a police officer to be called by the prosecution at the outset, the court may occasionally ask that a responsible investigating officer attend to elucidate the nature and strength of the case against the accused and—if one of the objections to bail is that enquiries are still being undertaken which may result in more serious charges against the accused or others—to explain the nature of those enquiries in general terms. Having heard the arguments for and against bail, and having considered the evidence of any witnesses called, the magistrates announce their decision.

Bail hearings have been much criticized for what is perceived as their cursory nature. One   **7.35** study of two busy London magistrates' courts put the average length of bail proceedings at six minutes, leading to a recommendation from Lord Justice Auld that 'magistrates and judges in all courts should take more time to consider matters of bail' (Auld Report, pp. 428–30).

In addition, the form taken by hearings related to bail has been questioned in the light of the   **7.36** Human Rights Act 1998, and the safeguards contained in Art 6 of the European Convention on Human Rights. The question may be posed in this way: to what extent should the safeguards in Art 6 apply in reviews of pre-trial detention guaranteed by Art 5 (the right to a fair trial and to liberty respectively). The question was examined in *DPP v Havering* [2001] 1 WLR 805. In that case, the need for formal evidence and procedures was rejected, in favour of a focus upon the quality of the material, with the accused given a right to cross-examine if oral evidence is presented. In *R (Malik) v Central Criminal Court* [2006] 4 All ER 1141, the Divisional Court considered that Art 6 (in so far as it requires a public hearing) may apply at bail hearings in the Crown Court, and that they should take place in public, unless the judge considers that it is necessary to depart from the ordinary rule of open justice. In *R (Thomas) v Greenwich Magistrates' Court* [2009] Crim LR 800, the Divisional Court stated that it was 'well-established' that strict evidential rules did not apply, with the result that a hearsay statement by a police officer was properly taken into account by the district judge, without the need to enquire into whether it satisfied one of the exceptions to the rule against the admission of hearsay evidence.

Whenever magistrates (or any court) refuse bail to an accused with a prima facie right to bail,   **7.37** they must state the reasons for their so doing (see 7.45 for details). In addition, para 9A was inserted into Pt I of Sch 1 to the Bail Act by the CJA 1988, requiring a court which grants bail to an accused charged with certain offences to give reasons and cause those reasons to be entered into the record of the court proceeding. The offences to which para 9A applies are murder, manslaughter, rape, and attempts to commit the same. The duty to state reasons where one of these grave offences is alleged is distinct from the restrictions on the grant of bail for a person who is charged with such an offence and has a previous conviction for a similar crime (see 7.11 to 7.12).

Successive bail applications

7.38   The rule that a remand in custody prior to committal proceedings or summary trial could not exceed eight clear days led in the past to defendants using each weekly appearance before the magistrates to renew a bail application. The same arguments for bail that had been pre-sented at perhaps numerous previous hearings would be re-presented, the magistrates would listen with as much patience as they could muster, and the result would almost inevitably be a further remand in custody. Eventually the courts devised a way of preventing these time-consuming charades. In *Nottingham Justices ex parte Davies* [1981] QB 38 the Divisional Court held that a decision by one bench of magistrates that bail should be refused was a finding to which *res judicata* or something akin to it applied, and the defence could not therefore re-open the question of bail unless they had some fresh argument to put forward which had not been before the magistrates who originally remanded in custody. Most courts interpreted this decision fairly liberally so as to allow the accused two bail applications, one on his first appearance after being arrested without warrant and charged, and a second when, perhaps a week later, the defence solicitors had had more time to consider the case, find potential sure-ties and generally marshal the arguments for bail. The CJA 1988 confirmed and clarified the decision in *Ex parte Davies* by inserting a new part (Pt IIA) into Sch 1 to the Bail Act.

7.39   First, Pt IIA states that it is the court's duty, having refused bail, to consider at each subsequent hearing while the accused remains in custody whether the decision ought to be reversed (para 1). But there is an element of unreality about this statement of principle because paras 2 and 3 then provide that, although the accused at the first hearing after that at which the court decided not to grant him bail may as of right 'support an application for bail with any argument as to fact or law whether or not he has advanced that argument previously', at subsequent hearings 'the court need not . . . hear arguments which it has heard previously'. Of course, although it is not expressly stated in Pt IIA of Sch 1, the accused may on his first appear-ance support a bail application with any relevant argument. The defence (perhaps through the duty solicitor) may argue for bail on the occasion when the accused is first brought before the magistrates in custody by the police, secure in the knowledge that—should their argu-ments fail—a second argued application may be presented a week later. However, should that second application also fail, any further argued application will be at the court's discretion unless the defence can point to some fresh argument (whether of fact or law) that has not pre-viously been aired. In *Blyth Juvenile Court ex parte G* [1991] Crim LR 693, the Divisional Court gave consideration to the question of what constitutes a fresh argument such as to trigger off the right to make a further bail application. The situation was that G, aged 11, was charged with the murder of the 18-month-old child whom she was baby-sitting. She was remanded into the care of the local authority for the protection of her own welfare, and it was ordered that she be held in secure accommodation. Various unsuccessful bail applications were made on her behalf, but an appeal against the secure accommodation order was successful. The justices were asked to hear a further bail application on her behalf, and refused on the ground that there were no changed circumstances. The fresh arguments put forward on G's behalf were that the passage of time had meant that feelings against her no longer ran so high; that there had been a change from secure to non-secure accommodation; that the move to some 46 miles from her home meant it was difficult for her mother to visit her; and that G had been assaulted by three other inmates. The Divisional Court allowed the application, and directed the justices to hear a further application for bail. The necessary change in circumstances need not be major, and it was sufficient in this case.

Once the defence have used up their argued applications, further remand hearings become **7.40** meaningless exercises. Although in theory the magistrates consider whether a remand in custody is necessary, in fact the decision is a foregone conclusion, and the 'hearing' consists in the chairman saying that the case of Z is adjourned to such and such a date, he being remanded in custody. In recognition of the pointlessness of the accused being present to hear the above take place, Parliament amended the MCA first to allow three successive remands in custody to take place in the accused's absence provided he consents and then to allow remands in custody for up to 28 days whether or not he consents so long as he has already been remanded in custody once (see 7.05 to 7.08).

What is the position if the accused consents to being remanded in his absence? In *Dover &* **7.41** *East Kent Justices ex parte Dean* [1992] Crim LR 33, D made no bail application on his first appearance, and consented to be remanded in his absence for three weeks. He appeared before the justices at the end of the three-week period, and wished to make a bail application. The justices decided that the hearing at which he had the right to do so was the first date on which he was remanded in his absence. Not surprisingly, the Divisional Court held that D had a right to make a bail application when he came before the justices at the end of the period of remand by consent.

Taking sureties

If the magistrates grant bail subject to the provision of sureties, and the necessary sureties are **7.42** present at court, they may enter into their undertakings before the magistrates. Section 8(2) of the Bail Act 1976 provides that, in considering the suitability of a proposed surety, regard may be had to his financial resources, character and previous convictions, and connection with the defendant (e.g., is he a relative, friend, neighbour etc?). Before he formally agrees to be a surety, it is normal practice to explain to him the nature of his obligations and the possible consequences to him of the defendant absconding. He is also asked whether he is worth the sum involved after all his debts are paid. If the sureties are not at court when bail is granted, they may enter into their recognizances subsequently before a magistrate, magistrates' clerk, police officer not below the rank of inspector, or (if the defendant has already been taken to a prison or remand centre) the governor of that establishment. Until they have done so, the defendant must remain in custody. If a surety attempts to enter into a recognizance before one of the persons mentioned above, but he declines to take the recognizance because he considers the surety unsuitable, the surety may apply to the court to take the recognizance.

7.43 To avoid the inconvenience to the sureties of their having to enter into recognizances every time the defendant's case is adjourned, the magistrates may make the sureties continuous. This means that on the occasion when bail is first granted the surety undertakes to pay the specified sum if the defendant fails to appear on any of the occasions to which his case is adjourned. If the offence charged is indictable the recognizance may be further extended to secure the defendant's appearance before the Crown Court should he be committed for trial: MCA, s 128(4).

7.44 Similar provisions to those described above apply when the Crown Court, Divisional Court or Court of Appeal grants bail subject to sureties. Continuous bail is particularly useful where, following the defendant's surrender to custody on the first day of his trial on indictment, he is granted bail for the overnight adjournments. If bail is made continuous the sureties only need to be present to enter into their recognizances on the occasion of the first adjournment.

Recording and giving reasons for decisions on bail

7.45 Section 5 of the Bail Act 1976 sets out some administrative procedures which must be followed when decisions on bail are taken. They are that:

(a) Whenever bail is granted (whether by a court or by the police) and whenever a court withholds bail from a defendant with a right to bail under s 4, a *record* must be made of the decision. A copy of the record should be given to the defendant on request.

(b) When a magistrates' court or the Crown Court withholds bail from a defendant with a right to bail (or grants bail but subject to conditions), it must give *reasons* for its decision. The reasons should be such as to help the defendant decide whether it is worth making an application for bail to another court (see 7.49 to 7.54). A note must be made of the reasons and a copy given to the defendant (unless the decision was taken by the Crown Court and the defendant is represented by counsel or solicitor who does not request a copy). As a result of the CJA 1988 it is now also necessary for the court to give its reasons for granting bail to defendants charged with certain offences (see 7.37).

(c) If a magistrates' court withholds bail from an unrepresented defendant, they must tell him of his right to make a bail application to the Crown Court.

(d) If a magistrates' court remands a defendant in custody after a fully argued bail application, they must *issue a certificate* confirming that they did hear argument. Where it was not the first or second argued bail application, the certificate must state the change in circumstances which persuaded the court to listen to renewed argument. A copy of the certificate must be given to the defendant. (Its significance will emerge at 7.49.) However, no certificate is required if the defendant was committed for trial or sentence in custody or had an application for bail pending determination of an appeal from the magistrates turned down.

Variations in the conditions of bail etc.

7.46 Where a court has granted bail either the prosecution or the defence may apply to it for a variation in the conditions of bail, or, if bail was granted unconditionally, the prosecution may apply for conditions to be imposed: Bail Act 1976, s 3(8). If the defendant has been committed on bail to the Crown Court for trial or sentence, an application for variation may be made to either the Crown Court or the magistrates' court. Should the court decide to vary or impose conditions a record must be made of its decision. If the defendant has a right to bail, reasons for the decision are required, and the defendant is entitled to a copy of the note of the reasons: s 5.

A magistrates' court which has remanded a defendant on bail to appear before it on a certain **7.47** date may, if it is convenient, appoint a later date for the defendant to appear and amend the recognizances of any sureties accordingly: MCA, s 129(3). This power to 'enlarge bail' is useful if, e.g., the court will not have time to deal with the defendant's case on the day originally fixed. Where a defendant who has been remanded in custody or on bail cannot be brought or appear before the magistrates on the day appointed because of illness or accident, the magistrates may further remand him in his absence, and a remand in custody may exceed eight clear days: MCA, s 129(1).

Reviewing bail on new information

What if the court grants bail, and information later comes to light which throws light on the **7.48** correctness of that decision? Under s 5B of the Bail Act 1976 (inserted by the CJ POA), the court may then reconsider the whole question of bail on the application of the prosecution. This power is only available if the offence is indictable-only or triable-either-way. The application must be based on information not available to the court (or to the police officer) who made the grant of bail which is now under review. If invoked, it enables the court to vary bail conditions, impose conditions for the first time, or remand in custody.

F APPLICATIONS TO THE CROWN COURT AND HIGH COURT CONCERNING BAIL

The Crown Court may grant bail to a defendant refused it by the magistrates if: **7.49**

(a) they remanded the defendant in custody (whether prior to committal proceedings or summary trial or after summary conviction and before sentence), and heard a fully argued bail application before deciding on the remand in custody; or
(b) they committed the defendant in custody to the Crown Court for trial or sentence; or
(c) they convicted him summarily, imposed a custodial sentence and refused to bail him pending determination of his appeal to the Crown Court: Supreme Court Act 1981, s 81.

Thus, in most cases a defendant whose bail application to the magistrates fails will have the option of making a further application to the Crown Court. So that there will be no disputes as to whether there has been an argued bail application, the magistrates must issue a certificate stating, if it be the case, that they refused bail after hearing argument (see 7.45).

Applications to the High Court for bail

An application to the High Court for bail is made to a judge in chambers. The procedure is set **7.50** out in Ord 79, r 9 of the Civil Procedure Rules 1998. It is to be followed when the High Court has jurisdiction under s 37 of the CJA 1948 to grant bail to a person who has applied to the Crown Court to state a case or who is applying to quash a Crown Court or a magistrates' court decision (see 7.09). The jurisdiction of the High Court to deal with appeals from the magistrates on bail matters was abolished by the CJA 2003, s 17 with effect from April 2004.

Applications to the Crown Court for bail

7.51　A defendant refused bail by the magistrates is usually able to make a further application to the Crown Court (see above). If, as will usually be the case, the defendant has been granted legal representation for the proceedings as a whole (or even if he was just granted it for the purpose of making a bail application to the magistrates) it will cover a Crown Court bail application. The application, which may be heard in chambers, is normally listed for hearing by a circuit judge or recorder.

7.52　Prior to April 2004, the position was that any appeal against *conditions* of bail imposed by the magistrates had to be made to the High Court and not to the Crown Court. Section 16 of the CJA 2003 created a new right of appeal to the Crown Court against the imposition of certain conditions of bail. The conditions which may be challenged in this way are requirements relating to the provision of a surety or giving a security, curfew, electronic monitoring, residence, or contact. Section 17 removed the power which the High Court had up until then to deal with such appeals, abolishing the jurisdiction of the High Court in respect of bail where it duplicated that of the Crown Court.

7.53　The procedure for applying to the Crown Court for bail is to serve written notice on the prosecutor of intention to make the application (Criminal Procedure Rules 2005, r 19.18). The notice must be served at least 24 hours before the application. The prosecutor must then do one of three things. He may either notify the appropriate officer of the Crown Court and the defendant that he wishes to be represented at the hearing of the application, or he may give notice that he does not oppose the application, or he may give to the appropriate officer, for the consideration of the Crown Court, a written statement of his reasons for opposing the application. A copy of the written statement must be sent to the defendant. Although he may be given leave to attend the hearing of the application, the defendant has no right to be present. If bail is granted subject to the provision of sureties, they may enter into their recognizances before an appropriate officer of the Crown Court or before any of the persons who may take a surety following a grant of bail by magistrates (see 7.42 to 7.44).

7.54　The above procedure is not applicable where a bail application is made during the course of the Crown Court proceedings (e.g., for bail during the period of an overnight adjournment). Such applications are made without notice to the judge trying the case. As a matter of practice, counsel waits for the jury to leave court before making the application.

Prosecution appeals against bail

7.55　The Bail (Amendment) Act 1993 confers upon the prosecution the right to appeal to the Crown Court against a decision by magistrates to grant bail. It is limited to cases where:

(a)　the offence is imprisonable; and

(b) the prosecution is conducted by the CPS, or by certain designated public prosecutors prescribed by statutory instrument; and

(c) the prosecution made representations against bail before it was granted.

The 1993 Act lays down procedural requirements with which the prosecution must comply **7.56** in order to exercise their right. They must give oral notice of appeal at the conclusion of the proceedings in which bail was granted, and before the defendant is released from custody. This notice must be confirmed in writing within two hours after proceedings end; otherwise the appeal is deemed to be disposed of. Pending appeal, the magistrates must remand the defendant in custody. The Crown Court, for its part, must hear the appeal within 48 hours (excluding weekends and public holidays). The appeal takes place by way of rehearing in the usual way and the judge may then remand the defendant in custody or grant bail with or without conditions.

This right to appeal against the grant of bail is distinct from the review of bail at the instance **7.57** of the prosecution (see 7.48). It is triggered immediately after the magistrates have decided to grant bail (whereas the power to review may take place some considerable time thereafter). The conditions for the exercise of the right to appeal are also somewhat different. Crucially, moreover, where the procedure under the Bail (Amendment) Act 1993 is used, the accused is kept in custody until the appeal is heard (whereas with the review procedure the accused will typically be at large). In *Allen v United Kingdom* [2011] Crim LR 147, the defendant was granted bail at the magistrates' court. The prosecution appealed while she remained in custody. The judge in the Crown Court refused to allow her to be present for the appeal. She applied to the European Court of Human Rights, claiming that her rights under Art 5 (the right to liberty) had been breached because she had not been allowed to be present. The Court held that there had been a violation. Although there was no general right for a defendant to be present at remand hearings, it was important that a defendant should be present at any proceedings at which liberty might be taken away. The appeal hearing fell within this category.

G   CONSEQUENCES OF A DEFENDANT ABSCONDING

If a defendant who has been granted bail fails to surrender to custody at the appointed time **7.58** and place, three questions arise for the court's consideration. There is the immediate question of how to secure the defendant's attendance before the court, and there are the further questions of how to deal with him for his breach of bail and how to deal with any sureties for breach of their recognizances.

Prior to discussing these questions, it is necessary to consider just what is meant by 'failing to **7.59** surrender to custody'. According to *DPP v Richards* [1988] QB 701, it means complying with whatever procedure the court prescribes for those answering to their bail. If the court operates a procedure whereby persons bailed are required to report to an usher, and are then allowed to wait in the court precincts until their case is called, a person who so reports has surrendered to custody. If he then goes away before the court calls his case, he has not absconded within the meaning of s 6 of the Bail Act 1976. (Note, however, that in these circumstances the court is entitled to issue a warrant under s 7(2) of the Act—see 7.60 to 7.62.)

Powers in respect of an absconder

7.60 Section 7(1) of the Bail Act 1976 provides that if a defendant has been bailed to appear before a court and fails to do so, the court before which he should have appeared may issue a warrant for his arrest. This is known as a bench warrant. Although it could be endorsed for bail, it is unlikely that the court would want to take the risk of the defendant again absconding.

7.61 In the circumstances which arose in *DPP v Richards* [1988] QB 701, s 7(2) can be invoked. This provides that, where a person on bail absents himself at any time after he has surrendered to custody but before the court is ready to hear the case, then the court may issue a warrant for his arrest. Where a person was arrested without warrant and bailed by the police to appear back at the police station, s 7 does not apply, but should the person fail to answer to his bail, the police will have power to arrest him without warrant (s 46A of PACE).

7.62 In order to prevent possible breaches of bail, a police officer may arrest without warrant a defendant whom he reasonably believes is unlikely to surrender to custody: s 7(3) of PACE. The power only applies if the defendant was bailed to surrender to the custody of a court. A police officer also has power to arrest a defendant whom he reasonably suspects of having broken, or reasonably believes will break, a condition of his bail. Thus, if it was a condition of bail that the defendant report to a police station, and he fails to report, he may forthwith be arrested without warrant. Similarly, if a surety notifies the police in writing that the defendant is unlikely to surrender to custody and that he (the surety) therefore wishes to be relieved of his obligations, the defendant may be arrested. A defendant who is arrested for suspected or anticipated breach of bail must be brought before a magistrate as soon as practicable and, in any event, within 24 hours of arrest (unless he was to have surrendered to custody within 24 hours in which case he is brought before the appropriate court). If the magistrate is of the opinion that the defendant has broken or is likely to break any condition of his bail, or is not likely to surrender to custody, he may remand him in or commit him to custody, or impose more stringent conditions of bail. Otherwise, he must release him on bail on the same conditions, if any, as were originally imposed. When the LASPO Act 2012, s 90 and Sch 11 come into effect, the magistrates will have no power to commit an adult defendant to custody under this provision if he has not been convicted in the current proceedings and it appears that there is no real prospect that he will receive a custodial sentence in those proceedings.

7.63 The CJA 2003, s 15(1) and (2) apply to cases where the offence carries a maximum sentence of life imprisonment and lay down that the court must refuse bail to an adult defendant who failed without reasonable cause to surrender to custody in answer to bail in the same proceedings, unless it is satisfied that there is no significant risk that he would so fail if released. In the case of a defendant under 18, the court must give particular weight to the fact that they have failed to surrender to bail in assessing the risk of future absconding.

The offence of absconding

7.64 In 1976 the Bail Act created a new offence of *absconding*. Section 6(1) provides that:

> if a person who has been released on bail in criminal proceedings fails without reasonable cause to surrender to custody he shall be guilty of an offence.

Similarly, an offence is committed if, having had reasonable cause for not surrendering at the time he should have done, the accused then fails to surrender as soon thereafter as is reasonably practicable (s 6(2)). An offence may be committed under s 6 even though the accused is acquitted of the offences that formed the subject matter of the proceedings in respect of which bail was granted. Moreover, it is always for him to prove, on a balance of probabilities, that he had reasonable cause for not surrendering when he ought. It is worth making the point that the breach of bail conditions in itself does not, of itself, constitute an offence, although the consequences of such a breach may be serious for the defendant, resulting, e.g., in more onerous conditions, or the withdrawal of bail altogether. Hence, in *R (Gangar) v Leicester Crown Court* [2008] EWCA Crim 2987; All ER (D) 112 (Oct), the five-month sentence imposed on the accused for breach of a bail condition was quashed as unlawful.

Section 6 of the Bail Act prescribes three methods by which an accused may be prosecuted **7.65** and sentenced for an offence of absconding. First, he may be tried summarily for the offence and sentenced by the magistrates to up to three months' imprisonment and/or a £5,000 fine. Although the Act appears to contemplate summary trial as a possibility even when the offence consisted in failure to surrender to the custody of the Crown Court, judicial interpretation of s 6 has subsequently decreed that magistrates should deal only with failure to attend at their own court.

Secondly, following summary conviction for a s 6 offence, the magistrates may commit the **7.66** offender to the Crown Court to be sentenced if *either:*

(i)   they consider their own powers of punishment to be inadequate; *or*
(ii) they are committing the offender for trial in respect of an indictable offence and they consider it preferable that the Crown Court should sentence him both for the absconding and (should he be convicted) the other offence.

The Crown Court's powers of sentence upon such a committal are 12 months' imprisonment and/or an unlimited fine.

Thirdly, failure to answer bail at the Crown Court can and should be dealt with by that court **7.67** as if it were a criminal contempt. This means that the Crown Court judge 'tries' the accused without empanelling a jury. The enquiry is semi-informal with the judge adopting whatever rules of procedure or evidence appear to him appropriate for giving the accused a fair hearing. If convicted, the accused is liable to the same penalties as if he had been committed for sentence for the offence following summary conviction (see 7.66).

Whether an alleged offence of absconding is tried summarily or dealt with as if it were a **7.68** criminal contempt, the only issue likely to be in dispute is whether the accused had reasonable cause for failure to surrender. The actual non-appearance can be established from the court records which are virtually incontrovertible.

The nature of the offence of absconding and the correct procedure for dealing with it were **7.69** analyzed in some depth by Watkins LJ in *Schiavo v Anderton* [1987] QB 20. Some minor clarifications of the judgment are contained in *Consolidated Criminal Practice Direction*, part 1, para 13). The effect of the judgment and Direction are summarized in the following propositions, which apply to bail granted by a court, rather than police bail.

(i) The offence of absconding is *sui generis* in the sense that it is neither summary nor triable-either-way, and the normal rules about commencing prosecutions by the laying of an information do not apply.

(ii) The offence should *invariably* be tried in the court at which the substantive proceedings in respect of which bail was granted have been or are to be heard. Thus, if an accused was remanded on bail prior to committal proceedings or summary trial, any alleged failure to answer to bail should be heard by the magistrates as the substantive proceedings (i.e., the committal or trial) are in their court. If, on the other hand, there was a committal for trial on bail, the Crown Court is obliged to deal with non-appearance as a criminal contempt. Contrary to earlier suggestions, it would never be right for the Crown Court to remit such a case to the magistrates for summary trial. The rule that magistrates should try summarily allegations of failing to appear before their court is, of course, without prejudice to their power to convict and then commit for sentence in the circumstances already described.

(iii) Since absconding is 'tantamount to the defiance of a court order', it is normally more appropriate for the court to initiate proceedings on its own motion without waiting for any formal information or charge to be preferred. However, the court should not act except upon the invitation of the prosecutor, who should consider whether proceedings are necessary or desirable in the light of factors such as the seriousness of the failure to appear and any explanations advanced by the accused. However, in practice in the magistrates' court the bench often asks the absconder why he did not appear. If his answer is satisfactory, no further action is taken. If it is not, the charge is put to the accused by the clerk.

(iv) According to the *Practice Direction* (para I.13.5) the courts should no longer automatically defer dealing with the offender for failing to surrender until the conclusion of the proceedings in respect of which bail was granted. Instead, they should deal with him as soon as practicable, taking into account the seriousness of the original offence, the likely penalty for breach of bail, and any other relevant factors. If the disposal of the bail offence is deferred, it is necessary, in the event that the accused is found guilty, to consider imposing a separate penalty, which will normally be custodial and consecutive to any other custodial sentence. In addition, bail will usually (but not invariably) be revoked in the meantime. If the original offence is unlikely to result in a custodial sentence, then trial in the absence of the defendant may be the pragmatic solution.

(v) If the accused denies absconding, the prosecution should conduct the proceedings and call the evidence in the normal way, notwithstanding that the proceedings are, in a sense, initiated by the court (see (iii) above). But, since proof of the actual failure to surrender to custody will come from the court's own records, the role of the prosecution representatives is likely to be confined to cross-examining the accused about any reason for non-appearance which he puts forward.

7.70 As far as police bail is concerned, the failure to surrender cannot be said to be in defiance of a court order. There is therefore no compelling reason for the court to act of its own motion, and any failure to surrender should be dealt with by charging the accused or laying an information.

7.71 The CJA 2003, s 15(3), which came into effect in April 2004, disapplied s 127 of the MCA (which prevents summary proceedings from being instituted more than six months after the commission of an offence) in respect of offences under s 6 of the Bail Act. It provides that such an offence may not be tried unless an information is laid either within six months of the commission of the offence, or within three months of the defendant's surrender to custody, arrest, or court appearance in respect of that offence. This ensures that a defendant does not evade prosecution for absconding merely by keeping out of the way for more than six months.

Estreating a surety's recognizance

Where bail was granted subject to a surety being provided, and the defendant absconds, the court before which he was due to appear must: **7.72**

(a) order that the recognizance of the surety be estreated (i.e., that he has to pay the sum in which he stood surety); and

(b) issue a summons to the surety requiring him to appear before the court to show cause why he should not be ordered to pay the sum promised

> (MCA, s 120, as amended by the Crime and Disorder Act, s 55). The court should then consider the means of the surety, and the extent to which he was to blame for the defendant absconding—e.g., did he, on first having reason to suspect that the defendant would abscond, give written notice to the police and ask to be relieved of his obligations as a surety? Failure to consider these matters may lead to the quashing of a decision by magistrates to forfeit a recognizance: *Southampton Justices ex parte Green* [1976] QB 11. However, the presumption is that the defendant's absconding will lead to the surety having to pay the whole sum in which he stood surety. As it was put in *Horseferry Road Magistrates' Court ex parte Pearson* [1976] 2 All ER 264:

> The surety has seriously entered into a serious obligation and ought to pay the amount which he or she has promised unless there are circumstances in the case, relating either to means or culpability, which make it fair and just to pay a smaller sum.

The above principles have been confirmed in numerous more recent cases, including *Uxbridge*   **7.73**
Justices ex parte Heward-Mills [1983] 1 WLR 56 and *Warwick Crown Court ex parte Smalley* [1987] 1 WLR 237. *York Crown Court ex parte Coleman and How* [1987] Crim LR 761 provides an example of the kind of exceptional case in which it is unfair to forfeit the whole recognizance. C and H stood surety for C's son who had been committed for trial at York Crown Court. They telephoned him at regular intervals to remind him of the trial; they arranged for other relatives to accompany him to court on the actual day; and they received a message that he had arrived. Unfortunately, the case could not commence until the afternoon and, during the wait, the accused's nerve broke and he absconded. The Divisional Court held that C and H had done everything they practically could to secure proper surrender to custody and so should not have lost the entire amount of their recognizances. However, May LJ stressed what had earlier been said by McCullough J in *Ex parte Heward-Mills* (above), namely that 'the burden of satisfying the court that the full sum should not be forfeited rests on the surety *and is a heavy one*' (emphasis added).

The point was underlined in *Maidstone Crown Court ex parte Lever* (1994) *The Times*, 7   **7.74**
November 1994, where the remarks of Lord Widgery CJ in *Southampton Justices ex parte Corker* (1976) 120 SJ 214 were quoted with approval:

> The real pull of bail...is that it may cause the offender to attend his trial rather than subject his nearest and dearest who had gone surety for him to pain and discomfort.

7.75 The surety's obligation is extinguished once the defendant surrenders to the court. After such surrender, the surety is no longer at any risk of being estreated (unless, of course, the surety is renewed). In *Central Criminal Court ex parte Guney* [1996] AC 616, the House of Lords held that, where a defendant was formally arraigned, the arraignment amounted to a surrender to the custody of the court, so as to extinguish the liability of the surety. Neither the agreement of the parties nor the order of the judge could deprive arraignment of its legal effect.

H   DETENTION OF A DEFENDANT WHEN BAIL IS REFUSED

7.76 The arrangements for detaining a defendant who is refused bail are as follows:

(a) If he has attained the age of 21, he is committed to prison.

(b) If he is aged 17 to 20 inclusive he is committed to a remand centre, provided that one is available 'for the reception from the court of persons of his class or description': CJA 1948, s 27. If a remand centre is not available he is committed to prison.

(c) If he is under 17 he is committed to the care of a local authority: Children and Young Persons Act 1969, s 23.

(d) By the Children and Young Persons Act 1969 (CYPA), s 23, courts have additional powers to remand children between 12 and 16, to local authority secure accommodation. For remand to secure accommodation, the following conditions must be satisfied:

    (i) the juvenile must be charged with, or have been convicted of:
      a violent or sexual offence, or
      an offence punishable in the case of an adult with 14 or more years in prison, or
      one or more imprisonable offences amounting to a 'recent history of repeatedly committing imprisonable offences while remanded on bail or to local authority accommodation'; and

    (ii) the court must be of the opinion that only a remand to secure accommodation would be adequate to protect the public from serious harm from him, or to prevent the commission by him of imprisonable offences.

When the LASPO Act 2012, s 91 comes into effect, the relevant age in (b) and (c) above will be 18 rather than 17. There will also be certain changes of detail in relation to the conditions laid down for remand of those under the age of 18 to local authority or youth detention accommodation (see ss 92 to 97 and Sch 12).

7.77 When a magistrates' court has power to remand a defendant in custody it may instead commit him to police detention for a period not exceeding three days (24 hours in the case of a juvenile: CYPA, s 23(14)), provided that is necessary for the purpose of inquiries into offences other than the one charged: MCA, s 128(7). As soon as the inquiries have been completed the defendant must be brought back before the magistrates, who will either bail him or, more probably, remand him in custody to prison or remand centre. Whilst in police detention, he is entitled to the same safeguards as is an ordinary arrestee (e.g., there must be periodic reviews of the propriety of continuing to detain him). Presumably, if the offences to which the inquiries relate are not serious arrestable ones, he should be charged or brought back before the magistrates within 24 hours, since an ordinary arrestee suspected of a non-serious offence would have to be released or charged within that period (see 3.25). However, s 128 is not clear on the point.

KEY DOCUMENTS

Bail Act 1976, as amended.

Parts 19 and 20 of the Criminal Procedure Rules 2005, available on the website of the Ministry of Justice: <http://www.justice.gov.uk/courts/procedure-rules/criminal>.

Forms relating to Bail, contained in annex D of the *Consolidated Criminal Practice Direction* and available on the website above.

Academic skills

3

INTRODUCTION

This chapter considers the contribution that academic activities make to your acquisition of the key employability skills. These skills have been explained in Chapter 1 where you were encouraged to undertake a skills audit to identify which skills you have and to what degree of proficiency and to note any gaps in your skills portfolio. In this chapter, you will be encouraged to think about the employability skills that you have developed as a result of your academic studies. It explains how each of the activities that you do as part and parcel of being a law student can be unpicked to discover important employability skills that can be expanded and developed to enhance your attractiveness to employers.

Think for a moment about the academic activities that you undertake on your degree: you write essays, answer problem questions, revise for and sit examinations, carry out research, learn how to reference, attend lectures and make notes, participate in tutorial discussion, and perhaps give a presentation or take part in an assessed moot. You may think that the link between these activities and your future employment lies solely in their contribution to your degree classification but this is not so: all of these activities have the potential to allow you to develop and strengthen the employability skills that you need to be able to demonstrate to prospective employers, irrespective of whether or not you are seeking work within the legal profession. This chapter shows you how to use your studies to showcase your skills and, crucially, highlights skills that are not triggered by your academic activities so that you are aware of the need to look elsewhere for opportunities to develop them.

Academic skills and employability skills

It can be difficult to see an immediate link between the academic skills that you develop through your study of the law and the employability skills that are valued by employers. Of course, it is obvious that you demonstrate your written communication skills by writing an essay but it may be less obvious how this can be used to impress a potential employer when you will not be required to write essays as a solicitor or barrister (or in most other careers if you are not destined for legal practice) and, in any case, all other law graduates will have the same experience of essay writing. Moreover, there are other employability skills that may seem to have no bearing on academic study. Sometimes it is the case that the employability skills are just quite well hidden within the academic activity and have to be teased out but it is true to say that not all employability skills are demonstrated by your studies. In any case, it is not suggested that you should rely on your studies to demonstrate any of the employability skills: rather, that you should start out by considering what skills you have developed during your studies and how you can build on this foundation and strengthen the skills by demonstrating them in action in some other setting. This will become clear as the chapter progresses.

Practical exercise: identifying skills

Make a list of all the study-related activities that you routinely do: this will include things like 'going to lectures', 'preparing for tutorials', 'answering problem questions', and 'revision'.

◑ Visit the Online Resource Centre where you will find a downloadable template containing the skills categories you have already encountered in doing the skills audit activity at the end of Chapter 1.

Think about the skills listed in turn. For each skill, review your list of study-related activities and decide if the activity does anything to help you build that particular skill. Some of these might be quite obvious; for instance, 'answering problem questions' clearly develops the professional skill of 'legal problem solving'. Others may be less immediately apparent.

You will probably find that by the time you have finished there is more of an overlap between academic skills and employability skills than you first anticipated.

The other reason that it is important to focus on your academic skills is that they are at the heart of one factor that will be influential to a prospective employer in any profession: your overall degree classification. Employers tend to be looking for students with a 'good' degree; that is, a 2.1 or a first. This means that it is essential that you think about your studies in order to identify areas of weakness and address these to maximise your prospects of obtaining a degree classification that will be most attractive to potential employers. Do not let this deter you if your academic performance is not as strong as it could be as it is still possible to get a training contract or pupillage with a 2.2 provided you can supplement your degree with a really strong collection of work experience that demonstrates your aptitude for legal practice, particularly if you do well on the LPC or BPTC.

In the sections that follow, you will find a discussion of each of the academic activities undertaken by law students and an explanation of how these develop key employability skills. The skills themselves will not be explained in any great detail so you may want to read this chapter in conjunction with Chapter 1.

Essay writing

As it is a popular method of assessment in law, it is inevitable that you will have had quite a bit of experience of writing essays during the course of your degree, both as formative and summative coursework and in examinations. It would be easy to assume that essay writing demonstrates written communication skills and nothing else but that would be to overlook the other processes that contribute to the finished essay. In order to extract the full range of skills from the activity, let's think for a moment about the things that you do in order to produce an essay:

• Identify the subject matter of the essay and conduct preliminary reading to get a feel for the topic

- Make a set of notes that captures the relevant points from your reading and eliminates irrelevant or peripheral points
- Conduct more detailed research to identify a range of relevant primary and secondary sources
- Extract information from the source material including useful quotations to incorporate into the essay
- Make a plan of the essay that establishes a working structure
- Start to write ensuring that the essay flows and makes sufficient links back to the question
- Refine and polish the essay until you have a finished version that is written in clear and eloquent language and is fully referenced.

Obviously the process is a little different for everyone but these are the basic stages that most people would incorporate into the essay writing process at some point. So what employability skills are involved in this process?

Written communication skills

Language is the primary tool of the trade for a lawyer. The ability to communicate information about the law—to clients, other lawyers, professionals in other fields, judges, jurors, and so on—is a central component of the daily work of solicitors and barristers. It should go without saying, then, that all prospective lawyers should have outstanding written (and verbal) communication skills.

This means that you should be able to do the following things:

- Write at a level of formality that is appropriate to the nature of the document and that is pitched at a suitable level for the recipient
- Construct documents and correspondence that uses words and punctuation in an accurate way so that your precise meaning is captured and no ambiguity arises
- Follow legal convention in the way that you refer to cases, statutes, and judges and in your use of legal terminology.

These skills are developed through your essay writing as you will need to adhere to the formalities of written language that are required within academic law and use terminology correctly. You will be expected to understand terms such as *inter alia*, *per incuriam* and *res ipsa loquitur* and to be able to reference a case, statute, statutory instrument, and the law of the European Union correctly.

Why is this important?

No law firm or chambers (or employer in any other profession) will rush to recruit an applicant who lacks written communication skills.

Within the legal profession, an employer would be concerned that you would not be able to draft legal documents with the required degree of precision. For example, a Canadian contract dispute about the placement of lampposts focused on the meaning of one sentence in a 14-page document and the misplacement of a single comma in that sentence ultimately cost Rogers Communications over one million dollars. As this example demonstrates, a lawyer who does not understand the nuances of language, the shades of meaning between different words and the impact on the meaning of a sentence created by punctuation would be a dangerous (and costly) liability in practice. So try not to be exasperated when your lecturers pick up on your misuse of punctuation in your essays: they are not being pernickety, they are trying to help you to reach the standard of written communication that will be expected of you in practice.

Employers in every profession will be unimpressed by poor use of language in communications with clients and other people outside of the organisation. It reflects very badly on the firm if correspondence is ungrammatical, inappropriate in style, or badly punctuated. Many people associate poor written language skills with incompetence or laxity, neither of which are characteristics that any professional organisation will want to convey to its clients or business partners.

Do you have good written communication skills?

Look for evidence in the feedback that accompanies essays that have been marked by your lecturers that will enable you to understand whether or not you have sufficient proficiency in written language. If you have been told that your meaning was not always clear, that your writing style was not appropriate, or that you are too long-winded then there is work to be done on your written communication skills.

- If your written communications skills are strong then find a way to demonstrate this to prospective employers over and above pointing to your prowess at essay writing. Perhaps you could make regular contributions to the student newspaper or to a blog about life as a law student. Alternatively, you could enter one of the essay writing competitions that are aimed at law students such as the Times Law Award or the UK Supreme Court Blog Essay Competition.

- If your written communication skills are not strong then find a way to improve them. Ask your lecturers for help when you receive your essay marks, visit the study skills advisor in the library, or attend a course aimed at helping students to improve their writing. There should be plenty of resources available at your university.

- Demonstrate your written communication skills in your application. There should be no need to say 'I have excellent written communication skills'; your use of language and command of grammar and punctuation should speak for itself in your application. A surprising (and alarming) number of applications are marred by poor spelling, grammar, and punctuation and are doomed to failure as a result as the employer will either think that you cannot do these things properly or that you cannot be bothered to check that you have done them properly. Neither of these situations will make an employer want to invite you for interview or take your application further.

Use of information technology

Given the prominence of information technology in all facets of professional life, potential employers will require you to possess a high degree of competency in the use of various forms of information technology. In legal practice, for example, you will be expected to file court papers electronically, to create legal documents that comply with particular formatting requirements, and to use databases to locate cases and legislation.

You should be able to see parallels between these tasks and things that you do as part of the process of essay writing. For example, many universities have presentation requirements for formative and summative coursework that specify that you must use a particular font and formatting style or that the pages of the document are numbered as well as requiring that your essay is accompanied by a bibliography or table of references. Although the presentation requirements for legal documents may differ to those of an essay, the pro-cesses for creating a document in a particular style will be familiar to you. The process of saving and uploading legal documents will not be dissimilar to the electronic submission of coursework to the university virtual learning environment and the same legal databases that you use to locate primary and secondary resources for your essays will be used in practice.

Time management skills

Every employer will be looking for employees with good time management skills. Employees who are able to manage their time stay in control of the work and are more productive in achieving work targets and objectives. This is particularly important in professions where you are expected to work unsupervised and organise your own working day in the way that best enables you to achieve your objectives. The legal profession is particularly demanding in terms of the pressures of time: you must arrive at court on time, file court papers within a time limit and be punctual and prepared for client meetings.

How long does it take you to write an essay?

Writing a coursework essay is a good test of your time management skills. You have a regu-lar pattern of commitments upon your time with the structure of lectures and tutorials and coursework interrupts this by requiring additional work over and above the ordinary flow of academic life. This has to be fitted in with your other work commitments and extra-curricular activities that you take part in on a regular basis.

But do you know how long it takes you to write an essay? The answer, unfortunately, for many students is that they start writing when everyone else does and continue until its finished, staying up later and later at night if the essay is not going well and the deadline is looming. If you work out how long it takes you to carry out the various tasks involved in essay writing, you will be able to make a realistic estimate of the time that it will take you and select a start date that will avoid the last-minute panic that leaves you with the sense that your essay could have been much better if only you had more time.

In legal practice, people will often give you a task and ask you how long it will take you to finish it. They will need to know when they can expect the task to be complete so that they can plan their own work around it so you will not be popular if you either under- or over-estimate how long you will take to complete your work. You need to have an idea of how long it takes you to do things so practise this with your essay writing and not only will you improve your time management skills but it should help you to work more efficiently towards the essay submission deadline.

Practical exercise: honing time management skills

Look at each of the activities that could be involved with writing an essay and estimate how long (in hours) you would spend on each. Ignore any activities that you would not do and add any others that are not listed. This will give you an approximate idea of how many hours you need to devote to your essay.

- Reading around the topic
- Searching for cases and articles in legal databases

- Reading cases and articles and making notes
- Discussing the essay with your friends
- Looking for inspiration on the Internet
- Planning the structure of the essay
- Writing a first draft
- Redrafting, polishing, and reflecting
- Creating a bibliography.

So you now have an estimate of how long it will take you to write an essay. Does it seem realistic? How does it compare to the time that you usually take? The next time that you write an essay, time each of the stages and compare how long you actually take with how long you thought you would take. This will help you to plan your time more effectively in the future.

By using strategies such as this to estimate how long you will need to complete tasks, you will be honing your time management skills and gaining a greater insight into your own productivity. You will understand what tasks you can undertake quicker and which ones take you longer to complete. Remember that time management is a personal skill so an awareness of your own working habits is essential to utilising this skill effectively. You will be managing your time at both high and low levels. High level time management will involve 'big' tasks, such as 'complete essay' and 'prepare for contract law tutorial'. Within each of the big tasks, you will have series of sub-tasks, like those listed in the practical exercise on essay writing. You should plan and allocate time for each of these individually.

You will need to be able to manage your time effectively once you start to make applications for work experience, training contracts, and pupillages as the application forms ask challenging questions so can be quite time-consuming to complete. Employers will not even read a late application so there is no leeway on the deadline, however good the reason.

Legal research

When you enter legal practice, you will not be expected to know the law but you will be expected to be able to find the law. In other words, the purpose of your law degree is to provide a foundation of understanding of key concepts in law and of the operation of the legal system and to equip you with the skills to find, understand, and use the law. The ability to conduct research that will enable you to identify and locate primary and secondary sources of law—statutes, statutory instruments, bye laws, regulations, case law, official reports, and articles published in academic journals— is crucial. You will have gained experience of finding these sources as you conducted research for an essay although you may find that other activities, such as writing a dissertation or taking part in a moot, provide a better example of your legal research skills (discussed later in the chapter).

Other skills involved in essay writing

The previous sections have covered the main skills involved in essay writing but there are others that merit at least a mention even though you should be able to find a better way to demonstrate them than by reference to your essay-based coursework:

- **Problem solving.** It is possible that you will have encountered a problem when writing at least one of your coursework essays which you will have had to have solved in order to complete and submit it. For example, Jade from Bournemouth University tells of her two-hour drive to another university library to get hold of a particular book that she felt was essential for her coursework.

- **Planning, organisation, and flexibility.** To complete the essay in time, you will need to work out what source materials you need and ensure that you get hold of them. You will need to plan your work and plan the structure of the essay. You will need to be adaptable if your plans do not work and make changes that improve your chances of success.

- **Team working.** Have you been required to produce a group essay? These are quite a common approach to assessment as universities are conscious of the need to ensure that undergraduates get opportunities to develop this important employability skill. Working on a group essay would be a good example of your ability to collaborate with others to achieve a shared goal and may also demonstrate leadership and decision-making if you took control of the group to coordinate the different contributions and to ensure that the group produced the finished essay within the timeframe allowed.

Practical example: group essays

We were allocated to groups of five for our assessed Legal Skills essay and it was clear after our first attempt at a meeting that my group was not going to work well. One girl never turned up and another didn't speak. One of the guys was really argumentative and wanted it all done his way and so we all went along with it. Our next meeting was a shambles as only myself and the silent girl had done the work that we were supposed to do and the third meeting never happened at all. It was clear that we were going to fail if something did not change so I took charge of the group. I worked out what still needed to be done and divided it into five tasks, which I allocated to group members with a deadline for completion. I emailed this to them and printed copies which I gave to them in person and sent chasing emails every couple of days which I copied to my contract lecturer so that he could see that I was trying to make sure that the essay was completed. I think that these four people now hate me with a passion but they all did their work, after a fashion, and I spent a lot of time turning it into the finished product. It was submitted in time and we got a reasonable mark but, more than anything, I realised that I did have leadership skills in me which I would never have believed before the group essay.

Saira, University of Surrey

Answering problem questions

Problem questions are a popular method of assessment in legal education and it is likely that you will encounter them in most subjects that you study as coursework and examination questions. They provide the opportunity to develop a number of key employability skills.

Legal problem solving

Have you ever wondered why problem questions are used to assess law students? It is because they offer an approximation of a key part of legal practice—offering legal advice to a client. It is a simulation of the situation that occurs when a client comes into a solicitor's office and sets out details of their problem as the solicitor sifts through the facts to isolate those that are legally relevant and gives advice based upon them. In the same way, you analyse the facts of a problem question, filter out the facts that have no relevance, and apply the law to those that remain in order to reach a conclusion as to the strength, or otherwise, of the fictitious client's case.

It is because legal problem solving is such an important lawyering skill that prospective employers will be interested to see evidence of your proficiency in this area. Of course, you could point to your prowess in answering problem questions in coursework and examinations but remember that this will not help you to stand out from other applicants (unless your marks are truly exceptional) because all law students will have experience of answering problem questions. As such, you should seek to build upon the foundation of legal problem solving skills that you have acquired in your coursework and examinations by finding other opportunities to demonstrate your ability to sift through facts and give legal advice:

- Client interviewing is an extra-curricular practical skills activity that simulates a first interview between a solicitor and client that requires the students taking the role of solicitor to elicit facts from the client with a view to offering some preliminary legal advice. You will find more details of this activity in Chapter 4.

- You may be able to find voluntary work that includes opportunities to use the law to resolve problems for other people such as working at the Citizens Advice Bureau, training as an appropriate adult or undertaking pro bono work. You will find information about those and other forms of law-related voluntary work in Chapter 6.

- The best way to see legal problem solving in action is to obtain work experience with a solicitor or barrister and observe their client conferences as this will give you insight into the use of questioning to elicit facts and the way in which legal advice is given in practice. There is guidance on all aspects of legal work experience in Chapter 6.

The other skills involved in answering problem questions have much in common with those outlined in the section on essay writing so, in order to avoid repetition, they will not be revisited here.

Dissertation

There is sometimes a temptation for students to view a dissertation as a long essay but the two pieces of work differ in a number of ways, with the dissertation posing a far greater challenge in terms of the skills required. Not only is a dissertation a longer piece of work—anything between 10,000 to 15,000 words—that requires far greater planning and organisation than a 2000 word essay, it also places far greater responsibility in the hands of the student to make the decisions that determine the success, or otherwise, of the piece of work. For example, the student decides on the research question, what to include and what to omit, how the work is to be divided into chapters, the extent of the research—everything in fact, albeit under the supervision of a lecturer. It is for this reason that a dissertation is often regarded to be the truest reflection of a student's ability and it is certainly a good way to develop and showcase key employability skills.

Legal research

Legal research is probably the skill with which the dissertation is most closely associated. Certainly, it provides a greater challenge to your research skills than almost any other activity that you will undertake during your time as an undergraduate and, as such, provides a perfect means of evidencing your proficiency as a researcher to prospective employers.

I am always interested to see a student's marks for their dissertation as our area of practice involves a great deal of research so it is essential that our trainees have excellent library skills and can get on with a piece of research under their own steam without asking for help every two minutes. A good dissertation mark says to me firstly 'this person can think for themselves' and secondly 'this person can research' and these qualities are so important that their application invariably finds its way onto my shortlist.

Training partner, Manchester

These quotations show that the two qualities most associated with a good dissertation performance is proficiency in research and an ability to work under your own initiative. There may be aspects of the subject matter of your dissertation that enable you to really emphasise these qualities:

- Did it involve the law of any other jurisdiction that required you to use unfamiliar databases or take into account the differences between two (or more) legal systems?

- Was it inter-disciplinary in any way?

- Was the subject something that was wholly unrelated to any law that you had covered on the syllabus of your degree?

Anything that takes you into unfamiliar territory will highlight your ability to conduct independent research. You may also want to consider whether you can make links between your dissertation and your future employment: perhaps the subject matter links to an area of specialism within the firm or it may be that you covered a topic that is of general relevance to legal practice.

Flexibility

A dissertation can require a great deal of flexibility as it gives you so much more choice about structure, content, and focus so it is likely that you will need to change your plans in light of feedback from your supervisor or due to the discovery of new articles that you find once you have started writing or the law itself may change. If you have already committed a great many words to paper, it can require a great deal of courage to make the change but it can be worth it if you realise that a different structure or approach would work better.

My dissertation was about youth offender panels and I always felt that there was something not quite right with it but I couldn't put my finger on what it was. Three days before I had to submit, I suddenly saw a way that it could be restructured so that it would work much better. My supervisor was rather wary but told me it was my decision but to make sure I kept a copy of the first version to fall back on if the restructuring didn't work or couldn't be done in time. It was hard work but I did manage to get it done and it eventually was awarded a mark of 67%.

Jordan, Birmingham City University

Employers will value employees who are flexible in their approach to work as they are more ready to adapt to changes that are made to the time, place, or method of working and can therefore fit in with the employer's requirements. Flexibility will enable you to respond to last-minute changes or emergency situations in a calm and unruffled way and to be happy to switch to an alternate course of action if the need arises rather than sticking with rigid determination to the original plan.

Time management

A dissertation is a long piece of work with a long deadline. Students often find it difficult to work out how to divide up the tasks involved in the dissertation so that they are spread out across the time available so it can prove to be a very good way of strengthening your time management skills. Some universities provide a timetable that students writing a dissertation are expected to follow but, in the absence of this, you will need to work out your own timetable. Your supervisor will be there to help you with this but do not expect them to manage the project for you.

Practical example: planning your time

It can be very difficult to create a timetable for your whole dissertation particularly if this is the first project with a high level of complexity that you have had to organise for yourself. Build up your time management skills gradually by setting yourself a goal—completing a first draft of the first chapter within two months is not unreasonable—and make a list of the things that you need to do in order to achieve this goal. Work out what order the tasks need to be done in and then set a deadline for each task. This will give you a timeline to follow that will take you towards your first goal.

Problem solving

Remember that this sort of problem solving refers to the more general ability to overcome setbacks and resolve difficulties rather than law-focused meaning of problem solving in the sense of answering a problem solving question. A dissertation is a complex project that requires you to do far more work under your own steam than is usually the case so it would be surprising if you did not encounter problems. It may be possible to use these to demonstrate your ability to work your way through difficulties that you encounter.

Practical example: identify and resolve problems

If you write 'I opted to write a dissertation in my final year which gave me an opportunity to develop my problem solving skills' on an application form, the prospective employer does not have sufficient information to make an assessment of the standard of your skills. You should be specific about the nature of the problem and give an indication how you went about solving it. For example:

- My supervisor told me to read three articles by a particular author but they are published in sociology journals and I don't understand the terminology. I borrowed a sociology dictionary from the library but still felt that I needed to do more to get to grips with the subject matter so asked if I could attend a lecture on social theory that was being given in the School of Sociology. This really helped me to get to grips with the unfamiliar material and I was able to incorporate different social theories into my dissertation.

As you can see, this provides far greater evidence of the student's ability to resolve problems than an unsupported assertion that the writing of a dissertation developed problem solving skills. Think about the following three problems, all of which are real problems encountered by recent students writing a dissertation. What would you do to resolve them and how would you use this to demonstrate your problem solving abilities to a prospective employer?

- There is an old Law Commission Report that I have to read for my dissertation as the extracts that are in the books don't provide enough detail but it isn't available online and the library copy is missing.

- One of the articles that I read for my dissertation made it clear that Australian law had taken a very different approach to the problem so I wanted to look at this in more detail and maybe have a comparative chapter but I don't know how to find Australian law.

- I've done a lot of reading and I know what I want to write but I don't know how to break it down into chapters.

- 🌐 You will find some suggested answers on the Online Resource Centre.

Professional and ethical behaviour

This category of skills relates to your ability to regulate your own conduct in a way that is appropriate to the circumstances and act in accordance with a moral code even when your behaviour is not under scrutiny and when there is little or no risk that contravention would be detected. It is essentially concerned with self-discipline and self-regulation. It is something that is of great importance within the legal profession but is a skill that few students are able to evidence.

You may be able to use your dissertation as evidence of your appreciation of the importance of professional and ethical behaviour if you collected data for your dissertation. Unlike other disciplines, law students tend not to collect data—by interviews or questionnaires, for example—for their dissertations, preferring to stick to library-based methods of research—that is, reading books, articles, cases, and materials. However, it may be possible to conduct interviews or administer a questionnaire or even conduct focus group discussions to collect data which can then be amalgamated with the literature in your dissertation. This sort of research has to comply with strict ethical guidelines and you would need to make an application for permission to go ahead with your research from the university Ethics Committee.

I wanted to carry out interviews with members of the child protection team in the social services department where I had worked before I started to study law as a mature student. As this involved conducting interviews with professionals working in a sensitive area, I had to obtain ethical approval. The application procedure was complex and I had to make several amendments to my proposal before ethical approval was granted. I was able to speak about this during my pupillage interview when asked about the resolution of ethical dilemmas and this led to an interesting discussion with a member of the interview panel about whether a system of regulation was any substitute for a strong personal sense of what is ethical.

Samia, University of East London

The other ethical issue that has some bearing on a dissertation is plagiarism. You will notice that you will be expected to complete a declaration that is submitted with your dissertation that declares that it is all your own work and that all sources have been fully acknowledged and referenced. This is because the dissertation offers more scope for inadvertent plagiarism than other types of coursework; when a piece of work is created over a period of six months or more, it can be difficult to keep track of your references and to remember whether the scribbled words in your notes were your own inspiration or a quotation from some long-forgotten source. It is very important to keep track of all your source material and to take particular care in noting the provenance of any quotations that you use in your dissertation as unattributed material could give rise to a suspicion of plagiarism. Of course, this applies equally to all other coursework that you produce as a student.

Practical example: academic integrity

You may be struggling to see the link between plagiarism and professional and ethical behaviour in legal practice. If so, then you are probably not aware that your university has an obligation to report all 'unfair academic practice' (as plagiarism is often known) to the Bar Standards Board or the Solicitors Regulatory Authority (depending upon your career path) where your lack of academic integrity is likely to be regarded as evidence that you are not suited to entry into the legal profession. It would also be very likely to feature in any reference regardless of the job opening and may even be indicated on your final academic transcript.

Other forms of assessment

This section completes the discussion of the skills involved in the different forms of assessment used during an undergraduate law degree by considering some of the less common methods of assessment that you may encounter.

Case note

It is often the case that students in their first year of legal study are asked to produce case note or case commentary, often as part of their assessment in a Legal Skills, Legal Methods, or English Legal Systems module. The objective of this activity is to make sure that students are able to read case law and extract relevant information from it. A case note is usually broken down into sections:

- Facts. This section tests your ability to distinguish the material facts, i.e. those which are legally relevant, from the background detail that sets the scene of the case.
- Law. The second section requires that you set out the legal provisions—from statute, case law, or a combination of the two—that governs the case.
- Held. Here you will be expected to state the outcome of the case. This usually includes a note of whether the decision upholds or reverses the ruling of the lower court.
- Analysis. This should be the longest section of your case note and it is where you move beyond picking details out of the case into a discussion of the implications of the judgment. It may be further divided into sections such as *ratio decidendi, obiter dicta* and academic commentary.

The ability to pick essential information out of a case and extract the legal principle is an important one for incipient lawyers to acquire. So your mastery of case noting will be useful in practice but does not offer a great deal of opportunity to demonstrate employability skills over and above those demonstrated by other methods of assessment.

Presentation

There has been an increasing move towards the use of presentation as part of the assessment strategy in recent years in acknowledgement that prospective employers in many professions are interested in applicants who can demonstrate strong verbal communication skills. Alternatively, it may be a requirement that students deliver a presentation in a tutorial but without it forming part of the formal assessment for the module. This may be made optional in recognition that some students would find the idea of speaking in front of their peer group awkward.

If you do get the opportunity to give a presentation, be sure to take it. Many employers within the legal profession have introduced presentations as a part of the recruitment process so it would be beneficial if you were to have some experience of presenting in less demanding circumstances. You will be able to demonstrate skills over and above verbal communication:

- Use of IT. Most presentations are accompanied by slides that capture key points. Take time to learn how to use presentation software and ensure that you produce slides that are professional but also visually attractive. You could try to master one of the mainstream packages such as PowerPoint or Keynote but there is also a lot of free software that will give your presentation an individual and polished feel such as Haiku. Remember not to get too carried away with images and animation though; your presentation has to be suitable for a professional audience.

- Time management. There is a different type of time management at issue in a presentation as you have to ensure that you cover all the material that is relevant to your topic within a set time. This has to be done without rushing—speaking too fast makes your presentation very hard for the audience to follow—or running out of time: it is very unprofessional to say 'that's it for now but you can catch up on the remaining slides in your own time'. So do not try to cram too much material into the time and practise to ensure that you can cover the points in the time available.

- Legal Research. If you are given an unfamiliar topic as the focus for your presentation, you will be able to demonstrate the strength of your research skills by finding relevant and complete information on the topic.

You will find information on delivering a presentation in Chapter 12.

Mooting

Some universities have incorporated mooting into their structure of assessment. This ensures that all students have the opportunity to take part in one of the greatest skills-building activities rather than leaving it as an optional extra-curricular activity. Mooting is an immensely skills-rich activity and it is one that is valued by prospective employers within the legal profession.

You will find a detailed discussion of mooting including a breakdown of the skills that it develops in Chapter 4.

Revision and examinations

The primary purpose of your revision is to ensure that you perform well in the exams and the primary purpose of the exams is for you to obtain the best mark possible to ensure that you achieve a good degree classification. However, the process of revising and the exam itself also provide opportunities for you to develop key employability skills:

- **Planning and organisation.** The revision period spans several weeks and so you will need to plan your revision carefully to ensure that you cover sufficient topics in all of the examined subjects. You will need to be organised to ensure that you have all the materials that you need in order to revise successfully. In the exam, you will need to plan your answers.

- **Written communication skills.** There are two separate processes involved here: you will need to have an effective approach to note-taking during the revision period and a clear and concise written style to capture your answers within the time available during the exam.

- **Time management.** This can be challenging during the revision period: many students report that they spend far more time on topics that they revise at the start of the revision period and then have to cram several topics into a single day as the exam date approaches. Make sure that you have a more balanced approach by creating your own timetable that spreads your work across the revision period and sets goals which are realistic and achievable. During the exam, the ability to manage your time is crucial to your success as you need to be able to complete the required number of questions within the time available.

- **Decision-making.** You will have to make decisions about which topics to revise and how many topics to cover as well as deciding which questions to answer from the exam paper.

- **Team working.** Working with other students can be a great way of sharing the workload and, for many students, discussing the law in a group can help to clarify areas of uncertainty and make the material more memorable. If you set up a revision group, this would be a good example of your ability to work in a small team.

Lectures and tutorials

The final academic activity to consider is the day-to-day business of student life of attending lectures and tutorials. The function of the lecture is to communicate a framework of knowledge about a subject to the students whilst tutorials give you the opportunity to explore particular aspects of a topic in greater depth by means of group discussion. As such, it may seem that their focus is on providing you with knowledge but do not overlook the skills that you are developing by attending lectures and tutorials:

- **Written communication skills.** Whether it is taking notes in a lecture or writing answers to tutorial questions, you will be developing your written communication skills. You may well use a word processing package so will also be using your IT skills.

- **Time Management, organisation, and planning.** You need to work out how long it takes you to prepare for each lecture and organise your time accordingly so that you can work around your timetable and other commitments. This may be a particular challenge if all of your tutorials are timetabled for the same day, for example, or if you have to divide your time between study and work or social activities.

- **Flexibility.** Even though tutorial questions tend to be set in advance, it is sometimes the case that you will have to adapt your preparation to suit an activity that the lecturer announces in the tutorial.

- **Team working.** You may work with other students to prepare for tutorials and it is often the case that lecturers allocate students to small groups with different tasks within the tutorial.

- **Verbal communication.** Tutorials require you to join in with discussion and to answer the lecturers questions so are an opportunity for you to develop your verbal communication skills.

- **Legal research and legal problem solving.** Most tutorials require preparation so you will be conducting legal research if you are finding cases, statutes, and articles and it is common for students to be given problem questions as tutorial preparation.

- **Presentation skills.** You may be asked to give a presentation in a tutorial (see the earlier discussion and Chapter 11).

Skills gap

This chapter has pointed out the employability skills that are involved in various aspects of your academic work so it should be clear to you that some skills are very well demonstrated by certain academic activities whereas others are demonstrated less well and others are not demonstrated at all.

You might find it useful at this stage to create a list or a table that divides the employability skills outlined in Table 3.1 into three categories so that you can see at a glance which ones are:

- **Demonstrated to a high degree.** These are the skills that you have developed to a high standard and where the evidence from your academic studies provides a good example of the skills in action that will be suitable to use to impress prospective employers.

- **Demonstrated to some degree.** These are skills that are either only demonstrated in a peripheral way and where you would like to expand the skill further and gain a better example of your ability or where the skill is highly developed but in a way that is common to many other students so you would like a more compelling example.

- **Not demonstrated at all.** These are skills that have not been developed to any meaningful extent by your studies.

By categorising your skills in this way, you have an idea of your skills gap: that is, the areas where you have not yet had the opportunity to develop a particular skill or where you would like an example of the skill in action other than your academic studies. You can then build upon this as you start to think about your other activities—extra-curricular skills activities, sports, voluntary work, and work experience. The aim is to develop all your employability skills to a high degree.

You will find more about personal development planning and addressing your skills gap in Chapter 2.

Table 3.1 Skills categorisation

High degree	Some degree	Not at all
Legal research and the assessed moot in contract (dissertation)	Written communication skills are good but want a better example than essay writing.	Numeracy
Team work (study group for final year revision and the group essay in ELS)	Problem solving skills have been developed but I'd like to have something that stands out more than problems finding materials for the moot.	Professional and ethical behaviour. Customer service Leadership
Verbal communication skills and presentation skills (tutorial presentation in public law and land law)	IT skills are good but I don't feel that I can do anything that other students won't be able to do.	Drafting Advocacy Negotiation
Knowledge of legal practice and procedure (writing a dissertation about the impact on legal practice of ABS was a stroke of genius!)	Time management skills are fine but need to make reference to all my other activities too.	Interviewing
	I'd like better examples than my studies for things like organisation, planning, decision-making, and flexibility.	

WHERE NEXT?

By thinking about the employability skills involved in academic activities, you will have a clearer idea of the skills that you already possess and your level of proficiency in them (see Table 3.2). You will also be aware of the skills that you will not get an opportunity to develop or demonstrate through your participation in academic activities. Armed with this knowledge, you can start to build your skills portfolio through your participation in other activities outlined in later chapters of this book. It is important to do this because your academic studies alone will not be sufficient to impress prospective employers, irrespective of whether you intend to work within the legal profession or in some other industry. So make a decision as to which employability skills you can demonstrate by reference to academic activities—you could use your dissertation to demonstrate legal research skills, for example, and a study group that you have set up as evidence of your team working skills—and which skills that you have developed through your studies need to be demonstrated in action in some other activity. For example, you might want to find some example of your written communication skills in action other than by reference to your coursework grades. Similarly, you will need to be conscious of the gaps in your skills portfolio where your academic skills do not give you the opportunity to demonstrate things like customer service or advocacy and look for other activities that will enable you to develop these important employability skills. You will find some good suggestions in Chapter 4 which covers practical legal activities such as mooting, Chapter 5 where the focus is on building skills through activities undertaken in your spare time, and Chapter 7 which looks at all aspects of work experience.

Table 3.2 Employability skills and academic activities

Skill	Lectures	Tutorials	Note-taking	Writing	Referencing	Essays	Dissertation	Problems	Revision and exams
Practical skills									
Written communication skills			x	x	x	xxx	xxx	x	x
Numeracy							x		
Problem solving						x	x	x	
Use of IT	x	x				xx	x	x	
Personal skills									
Time management skills	x	x				x	x	x	x
Professional and ethical behaviour							x		
Organisational skills	x	x				x	x	x	x
Flexibility		x	x				x		x
Planning	x	x				x	x	x	x
Decision-making							x		x
Interpersonal skills									
Team working		x				x	x		
Verbal communication		x							
Customer service									
Leadership									

(Continued)

Skill	Lectures	Tutorials	Note-taking	Writing	Referencing	Essays	Dissertation	Problems	Revision and exams
Professional skills									
Legal research	x	x			x	x	x	x	
Legal problem solving		x						x	x
Drafting									
Negotiation									
Advocacy		x							
Knowledge of legal practice and procedure					x				
Interviewing									
Presentation skills		x							

Commercial awareness and networking

6

INTRODUCTION

This chapter covers two aspects of employability that can really help students stand out from other applicants. The first of these is commercial awareness. Commercial awareness usually features very highly on the wish list of skills for a career in law, but it is a valuable transferable employability skill regardless of career path. However, many students are unsure about what the term 'commercial awareness' actually means, or how they should go about acquiring it, developing it, and demonstrating it. This means that by taking some proactive steps to build your commercial awareness you will greatly enhance your overall employability skills portfolio. This chapter will first explain what is meant by commercial awareness and go on to provide some practical advice on how to develop it. The second aspect is networking: building effective relationships with others inside and outside the professions. The second part of this chapter will explain why networking is important, and give some pointers on how you can start networking and how to make the most of it. It will give a brief introduction to LinkedIn: an online tool for professional networking, before closing with some practical advice on making the most of law fairs.

Commercial awareness is important, since all commercial businesses exist to make a profit and all self-employed people need to earn a living. Therefore, it does not matter whether you end up working in a law firm, in-house in another business, or at the self-employed Bar: you will need some awareness of the business world in which both you and your clients exist. Networking is important as it enables you to build a list of useful contacts and connections, within which you can find opportunities and establish relationships within the legal profession. Such relationships will stand you in good stead in your search for employment and beyond. In addition, your first-hand interaction with members of your network will enable you to hear directly what is going on in their businesses and therefore will also enhance your commercial awareness. The two activities therefore go hand-in-hand.

Commercial awareness

Put simply, commercial awareness requires some knowledge of the business or financial context in which firms, transactions, or situations exist and operate. Therefore, in order to demonstrate this, you will need to have a basic level of understanding of the factors that underpin and influence successful businesses: how they work, what their employees do, how they are organised, and the issues that they face.

Commercial awareness is important to careers on both sides of the traditional legal professions:

- As a solicitor, you will be providing legal advice that will have some sort of financial dimension (particularly if you become a commercial lawyer). At the very least you will need to be aware of what your clients need, why they need it, and how much they are prepared to pay for it. As your career progresses to more senior positions within the firm, you will become more deeply involved in decisions that will have a commercial impact on your own firm's business. If you demonstrate the capacity for developing new client relationships, or, in time, new products or services, then you will be a good acquisition for a law firm. Remember the Legal Services Act 2007 opened up competition in the legal marketplace and introduced alternative business structures (ABSs): as such, commercial competitiveness is crucial for all law firms. Firms of solicitors are traditionally structured as limited liability partnerships (LLPs). You can find out what this means on the Companies House website at **www.companieshouse.gov.uk/infoAndGuide/llp.shtml**.

You will find more on ABSs in Chapter 8.

- As a barrister, you will be responsible for the commercial aspects of your own practice and the impact of that on your chambers. Of course, commercial barristers will need to demonstrate higher standards of commercial awareness.

Many students will think that they are not commercially aware, but commercial awareness is an employability skill that can be developed just like any other, as your experience, research, and learning continues. In order to develop your commercial awareness, there are a number of activities that you can undertake:

- **Develop your knowledge of current business issues.** You can do this by reading a business newspaper (or the business section of a serious newspaper) regularly. Sign up for alerts from the financial websites, listen to radio financial programmes, or watch business programmes on television. This does not have to be dull. You can start to develop your interests in financial and commercial matters by focusing on stories that relate to your own interests. For example, if you are an avid football supporter, look to see what transfer or loan deals are being done in the January transfer window and start to think of the commercial aspects of each of them such as player salaries, investments by clubs looking for promotion or trying to avoid relegation, or the need for clubs in financial difficulties to sell players. Thinking about the commercial aspects of something that interests you should build your curiosity in other commercial areas and start to build your skills in analysing situations from a commercial perspective. When you next read a business article that interests you, think beyond the main business or financial effects to the legal, social, or political implications that could arise (or have already arisen). Analysing a few stories in depth is preferable to a superficial knowledge of many.

- **Develop your knowledge of the commercial issues facing the legal professions.** You can develop your knowledge of the commercial environment and pressures facing the legal community by reading the legal press and subscribing to news alerts from them. You should also consider how the general state of the economy may affect the professions and whether any proposed reforms may have a positive or negative effect.

Practical exercise: commercial awareness

Have a look at the story in Figure 6.1.

Home | News | In Practice | In Business | Features | Opinion | Blogs | Moving On

Peers pursue low-cost arbitration service

Monday 04 February 2013 by **John Hyde**

A group of four peers will this week make the case for an arbitration service for defamation cases.

In an amendment to the Defamation Bill to be debated tomorrow, the Lords want to follow the recommendation of the Leveson report and push forward a low-cost arbitration service.

Courts would be encouraged to take into account whether claimants or defendants have chosen to use the service when awarding costs and damages.

Even successful parties may be ordered to pay all the costs of proceedings if they have unreasonably refused to use an available recognised arbitration service.

The lord chief justice would establish a Defamation Recognition Commission to appoint an independent regulatory board to provide the service.

Figure 6.1 *The Law Society Gazette*

You will see that the story concerns a proposed arbitration service for cases that involve defamation. It mentions the impact on costs for both claimants and defendants and the introduction of a new Defamation Recognition Commission. Think about the commercial implications of this, should it go ahead, and then consider the following questions:

• What impact would this have on law firms that specialise in defamation cases?

• Is it right that the law should impose a financial penalty on those who refuse alternative dispute resolution?

☺ Compare your thoughts with those provided on the Online Resource Centre.

• **Understand how law firms operate.** You should make sure that you understand how firms of solicitors and chambers operate: how they are structured, how they find and retain clients, and how they make and spend their money. In anticipation of your interview, research the market/sector in which you are looking to be recruited, and the main competition. You can also gain useful insight by talking to practitioners at events or open days.

- **Think about your own commercial experience.** It is likely that you already have some awareness of commercial issues, even if you might think otherwise. If you have had work experience outside the law, then think about how the organisation that you have worked for is organised and how it operates. Who are its customers? What is it trying to achieve? How well does it manage? If you have helped to run a university society, you will have encountered objectives, members (customers), finances, and policies in some form: all of which are key components of a commercial operation. Even if you have just sold some textbooks via online auction, you will probably have made some commercial decisions—how many other similar books are for sale, how much have they sold for, where should you set your asking price, how much should you charge for postage and packing?

An important point to note is that there is a distinction between 'awareness' and 'knowledge': many students fret that they need to grasp the minute details of the commercial world, but, as a trainee or pupil, they will not be expected to know everything from the outset. So, employers will not expect you to have comprehensive commercial knowledge or fully developed commercial skills: these can only be achieved after substantial commercial experience. However, they will expect you to have a genuine and demonstrable interest and understanding of business issues, the concepts of the commercial world, and the context in which legal services are provided.

Some suggestions of sources that you can investigate and which offer useful insight are listed in Table 6.1. Not all of them will suit you, but do try some. As you read, watch, or listen, think about the commercial context/impact of the features you encounter, just as you did in the practical exercise earlier in this chapter.

Table 6.1 Some useful sources of commercial information

General press	*The Times* (the law supplement is published on Thursdays)
	The Daily Telegraph (particularly the Saturday edition)
	The Guardian (also has a law supplement)
	The Financial Times
	The Economist
	BBC News website (**www.bbc.co.uk/news**)
Legal press	*The Lawyer*
	Legal Week
	Law Society Gazette
Television	BBC News
	Channel 4 News (a longer format gives time for more in-depth reporting)
	Newsnight
BBC Radio 4/World Service (also on iPlayer)	Today Programme
	Global Business
	World Business Report

Networking

Love it or hate it (and opinion seems to be split amongst law students), networking is important. It gives you the opportunity to make an impression upon people who may, directly or indirectly, provide career opportunities to you. More than this, however, it is an important employability skill in its own right as the ability to make useful professional contacts thereby generating business or forging valuable mutually beneficial working relationships is a significant part of professional life. In essence, it is the skill of making the right impression and creating a network of professional contacts that can further your career or the business prospects of the organisation for which you work.

So how can networking help you as a law student and what opportunities exist for you to network within the legal profession?

Why network?

You already have a network. It is your family, friends, fellow students, lecturers, and anyone else that you associate with on a regular basis. It may be that you can use this network to create employment opportunities: perhaps a family member works as a solicitor or a lecturer will recommend you to one of their contacts for work experience. However, in order to find opportunities that will strengthen your career prospects more effectively, it would be useful to expand your network of contacts to include people working within the legal profession.

You may think that networking is unnecessary—surely the 'its not what you know but who you know' era has long gone and everybody has an equal chance to apply for work experience, training contracts, and pupillage. This is certainly true to a degree, particularly in relation to advertised opportunities but there are two ways in which networking can nonetheless be advantageous:

- It can alert you to opportunities that are not advertised. Not all firms routinely offer work experience and there are certain opportunities, such as shadowing a judge, that tend to be available if asked for but not advertised as such. Meeting people and asking them whether opportunities are available is a great way to create something that would not have otherwise existed.

- It can give you the edge over other candidates if someone at a firm or chambers can endorse your application on the basis of having some personal knowledge of you. It takes some of the gamble out of the appointment process if you have managed to create a positive impression on someone who works for the firm or chambers in question.

Practical example: the value of personal knowledge

Brian Clough, England footballer and controversial manager who led Nottingham Forest to consecutive European Cup victories in 1979 and 1980, once famously said 'we were a good team on paper. Unfortunately, the game was played on grass'.

This gap between how a person seems 'on paper' and how they actually perform in practice is a perennial problem for employers. As the chair of a pupillage committee at a London chambers put it 'students these days seem to get a great deal of help with their applications so it is very often the case that an applicant who appears brilliant on paper is considerably less so in person when they turn up for their mini pupillage'.

If you are known to somebody at the law firm or chambers to which you are applying for work experience, training contract or pupillage, they can comment on their experience of you as a person, confirming or contradicting the impression that you have given in your paper application. Therefore, it cannot hinder your prospects of success if you build up a series of contacts and use these to strengthen your applications. For example, if you are able to write 'I met Mrs James at our university pro bono dinner and she suggested that I apply to your firm for work experience due to my interest in employment law' then it implies that the person in question formed a favourable opinion of your capability and suitability. Of course, this may not be true and Mrs James may have said this to be polite but a quick question to her is all that is needed. A response 'oh yes, he was so well informed about recent cases and seemed very personable and enthusiastic' is likely to make your application stand out from another applicant who is equally good 'on paper' but who presents more of a gamble for the law firm because have no basis upon which to judge whether they will live up to the promise of their paper application.

Finding networking opportunities

You can network anywhere that you meet someone who is involved in the legal profession. There are obvious places to do this—you will always find solicitors, barristers, and judges at court—but part of your networking strategy should include ensuring that you are ready and able to network if you should have a chance encounter with a lawyer in an unexpected place. In essence, you should be able to get stuck in a lift with a lawyer for five minutes and come away having made a useful contact to add to your network (plus a promise of work experience if you have done really well).

This leads on to another facet of successful networking: you must ensure that you make a positive impression. This requires some prior thought and preparation. It is not enough (for most people anyway—some people are just naturally good at creating opportunities out of nothing with no prior thought) simply to bumble your way through a conversation with any solicitor you happen to meet and expect to come away with two weeks' work experience in your pocket! Bear in mind the following points as they will help you to network successfully and with confidence:

- Be able to start a conversation. It will usually be up to you to initiate contact so you need to be able to introduce yourself in a way that creates a good first impression. Practise your handshake and introduction until it feels natural and appears confident.

- Think about what you want to say about yourself. This will depend to a degree on the situation in which you meet the other person and what you want to achieve. For example, if you meet a barrister who has come to your university to judge a moot, it is not necessary to say 'I am a law student at the University of x' but you would want to say this if the encounter took place at court. Formulate some stock sentences that you can combine that capture who you are and what your interest is that are appropriate to the situations in which you might encounter lawyers. You will find some suggestions on the Online Resource Centre.

- Keep the conversation going. As it was you that initiated contact and are the one that wants something from the conversation, the onus is on you to keep it flowing. Moreover, it provides an instant demonstration of your verbal communication skills. Open questions are useful—these are questions that require information as an answer rather than a one word response so try questions such as 'what makes x a good place to work?' rather than 'is x a good place to work?' and 'what sort of work experience would be most useful?' rather than 'should I get more work experience?'. You can create a list of questions to help you maintain a conversation as part of your preparation for networking.

- **Ask for suggestions.** Remember that creating contacts is not the only purpose behind networking. It can also be a great source of inspiration and guidance in terms of your future career. All solicitors, barristers, and judges have already achieved what you want to achieve so do not be afraid to ask them for advice.

- **Build your network.** The person you are speaking to already has their own network of legal contacts so try to tap into it by asking for suggestions of other people that you could contact. You can then start your initial email by saying 'x suggested that I contact you because...' as this personal recommendation is more likely to elicit a positive response.

- **Remember names.** It is no good sending an email that starts 'I met someone who works at your firm who suggested that I get in touch with you and ask about work experience' because you have forgotten the name of your contact. An inability to name the person you spoke to does nothing to strengthen your approach and it looks very unprofessional.

- **Make contact.** Ask for a contact email address and get in touch with the person shortly after meeting them to thank them for their help and to follow up on any other relevant points: for example, you may have offered to send them your CV, asked for further information about a case they were handling, or asked for details of someone to contact about work experience. Keep your email short, polite, and relatively formal as well as ensuring that it is well presented and free from errors.

- **Keep in touch.** Make a note of who you have met and what it is that you want to achieve from networking with them and follow up your initial contact after an appropriate period of time. You could update them on significant achievements or on developments that are relevant to what you discussed, for example:

  ○ You may remember that we discussed my dissertation on family-friendly maternity policies as it was relevant to one of your cases. I am pleased to say that I have received first class marks for my dissertation, thanks in part to the sources that you suggested: please do let me send you a copy by way of thanks as it contains a summary of some recent European developments that might be of interest to you.

  ○ When we met, you suggested that I contact your associate, John Garvey, with a view to securing work experience given my interest in environmental law. I did as you suggested and am pleased to report that I will be working with him for six weeks over the summer. I wanted to let you know and to thank you for the suggestion.

- **Provide a point of reference.** Make life easy for your contact by providing a short statement that will help them to remember you. Something like 'you judged a moot at my university last week and we talked about European consumer law' or 'we met at your firm's open day and you suggested that I contact you about the case you are working on about criminal liability for sporting injuries'. If the person you contact cannot remember speaking to you, they are less inclined to answer so it can be useful to provide a reminder.

Tell us

We'd like to hear about your best (or worst!) networking experience. Tell us at finchandfafinski.com/get-in-touch or @FinchFafinski on Twitter.

The final point to consider is where you can go to meet people to add to your network of professional contacts. It can be a good idea to start in an environment where you feel comfortable as you are more likely to be calm and confident when meeting people in familiar surroundings. Does your university have a law fair where you can meet local solicitors and barristers or perhaps there are links between your law school and a particular local chambers or law firm that leads to some shared events? These events organised for your law school are the obvious place to start networking. Alternatively, you may find that local solicitors or barristers visit your school to give talks about the legal profession or to judge a moot or your student law society may arrange a visit to one of the Inns of Court. These are all good networking opportunities where the lawyers that you meet will be expecting to talk to students about the legal profession.

As you grow in confidence, you can expand the scope of your networking operation. Investigate the possibility of attending an open day or insight event at one of the large law firms. These are designed to give law students an insight into the operation, work, and ethos of the firm and are an excellent opportunity to meet practitioners and build contacts within the legal profession. They are often targeted at students in their first year so it is important to look out for these opportunities at an early stage of your studies.

Practical example: open days and insight events

Addleshaw Goddard has two one-day events for first year students held during the Easter vacation: one in London and one in their Leeds office. These provide students with an insight into the firm's practice areas and life as a trainee solicitor. There will be an opportunity to meet partners, trainees, and the graduate recruitment team and a session that helps students to think about the process of applying for a training contract with hints on how to make your application stand out from others.

DLA Piper host three one-day insight days for first year students during June each year. These introduce students to the firm and to life as a commercial lawyer. As well as offering an opportunity to meet partners, associates, trainees, and the graduate recruitment team, the days offer advice on how to develop commercial awareness and share the secrets of making a successful application.

Eversheds offer a different sort of experience to first and second year law students with their Big Deal event that takes place in March each year in their London, Birmingham, and Leeds offices. This gives students the opportunity to work in small teams on a simulated multi-agency international deal which includes experience of brokering an agreement, creating a marketing strategy, holding a press conference, and negotiating in the boardroom. Students work alongside experienced lawyers and the event is a great insight into the commercial reality of legal practice.

Court is an obvious place to meet legal practitioners but remember that they are there to work so they may be rather busy or preoccupied when you try to engage them in conversation. Watch proceedings and try to predict good times to approach people—this may be a matter of trial and error so try not to be daunted if someone you approach is brusque and does not want to speak to you but learn from this and time your future approaches differently. The added advantage about approaching a solicitor or barrister at court is that you can ask about the case that you have just seen them working on as a way of engaging them in conversation.

I was sitting in the magistrates' court out of interest one summer and there was a case about a lady who had been picking wild mushrooms and was charged with theft. I asked the solicitor who represented her about this as I was genuinely curious as I had thought that things growing wild did not fall within theft and he offered to have coffee with me and explain it. We had a really good discussion and I ended up with an offer of two weeks' work experience starting the following day without even having to ask for it!

A further opportunity for networking arises during any work experience that you have secured. Not only will you meet practitioners working for the particular firm or chambers but it is possible that you will meet other solicitors and barristers as you go about your work. Be sure to explain to them that you are a student on work experience and try to add them to your network. Express an interest in their work and ask if there is an opportunity for work experience with them. This can be a good strategy:

I spent the week of my mini pupillage at Snaresbrook Crown Court on a trial involving drugs and weapons. My advice is that you should get involved and be friendly with the other side—they may offer you a mini pupillage after if you show enough enthusiasm: it happened to me!

Practical example: networking schemes

Pure Potential organises events for students wanting an insight into the legal profession that includes networking advice and opportunities, guidance on applying for vacancies for vacation schemes and training contracts, as well as a visit to a leading London law firm. You will find further details on their website: **www.purepotential.org/events/pp-law**.

City Solicitors' Education Trust Summer School is a residential skills-training event to be held at Queen Mary University of London. It includes group and individual structured sessions on making a successful application, confident networking, and the commercial background to legal practice while providing business and social networking opportunities. Students will meet senior representatives and graduates from leading law firms as well as visiting the firms' offices. Further details are available online: **www.cset.org.uk/?page=cset-summer-school**.

City Law for ethnic minorities organises a two-day event to facilitate networking between eligible students and representatives of top City law firms. The event includes real business activities and law case studies to provide insight into the legal profession. It also includes the opportunity to meet graduate recruiters and develop essential skills and interview techniques for vacation schemes and training contracts. For further details, see: **targetjobsevents.co.uk/city-law-for-ethnic-minorities**

LinkedIn

There is a theory known as six degrees of separation which surmises that everyone is six or fewer introductions away from anyone else in the world. In other words, any two people can be connected through 'friends of friends' in a maximum of six steps. There is an associated game known as 'Six Degrees of Kevin Bacon' in which the goal is to link any actor to Kevin Bacon through no more than six connections (two actors are connected if they appeared in a film, television show, or commercial together). For example: Stefan Fafinski appeared with Professor Brian Cox on a show with the British Science Association in 2006; Brian Cox and Jonathan Ross appeared on Stargazing Live; and Kevin Bacon appeared with Jonathan Ross on Film 2005. Therefore Stefan's Bacon Number is 3 (Fafinski—Cox—Ross—Bacon).

LinkedIn (**www.linkedin.com**) is a social networking site for professionals. It enables individuals to create a profile and contact network and to grow it through introductions to the contacts of their contacts. It is essentially a professional manifestation of Six Degrees of Kevin Bacon.

However, this does not mean that you are instantly going to get connected to the managing partner of each of the major firms or the heads of chambers in the City. If you choose to use LinkedIn, there are some basic principles that you should follow:

- **Keep it professional.** LinkedIn exists as a professional directory. It has different norms to other social networking sites and you should use it in a way that reflects that standing.

- **Build your profile.** Add the details of your academic and employment history. Unlike a static CV, LinkedIn allows you to continually update your activities and to demonstrate the steps that you are taking to build your employability skills portfolio.

- **Build your network.** Start with people that you know: fellow students and academics. Add people that you meet both online and offline in whatever context. However, do not send out a huge number of speculative requests to connect with people that you do not actually know. Not only is this ill-mannered, but can be quite irritating for the recipient. If you build a good network, not only will this show that you are not afraid to network, but your network may also be useful to your employer in the future.

- **Seek recommendations.** LinkedIn allows you to receive recommendations for your work. Therefore if you have had a successful work experience, pupillage, or placement, ask if your employer would be willing to write you a positive recommendation endorsing your position on LinkedIn.

- **Join groups.** There are a huge number of interest groups on LinkedIn. You should consider joining those that are linked to your university and law school. Then look to see if there are relevant groups for legal areas in which you are interested or would like to work. If there is no group that suits exactly what you are seeking, then think about starting one: this will demonstrate entrepreneurial skills. Do not hold back from joining groups in areas outside the law: this will show that you can relate and engage with people with similar interests but different backgrounds.

Overall, LinkedIn is a useful networking tool, if used professionally and carefully. You can find us on LinkedIn at **www.linkedin.com/in/stefanfafinski** and **www.linkedin.com/in/dremilyfinch**.

Law fairs

Law fairs are a great networking opportunity for you to meet practitioners, current trainees, and graduate recruiters and to find out more about their firms. They are usually held on campus in the autumn term. Not only are they an opportunity for you to find out more, they also offer recruiters the first opportunity to meet you face-to- face in a setting that is a lot less formal (and intimidating) than an interview.

To make the most of a law fair:

- **Think about your practice area.** This chapter will have enabled you to have, at the very least, a rough idea of the sorts of areas that you would ultimately want to practise and why. If you are able to communicate this to recruiters from firms involved in those areas, then this will demonstrate that you have already started preparing for success.

You will find more detail on various areas of legal practice in Chapter 8.

- **Find out who's going and do some research.** You should find out what firms are attending and draw up a plan of those that you think will be most interesting for you to meet. There will probably not be enough time for you to talk to everyone, so be focused. When you know which firms you will be approaching, do some preliminary research into who they are and what they do. Even at this early stage, recruiters do not appreciate explaining what their firm does or giving out very basic information that could easily have been found on the firm's website homepage.

- **Be confident and personable.** Being armed with a little knowledge about your preferred areas of work and the firms you are meeting should give you some confidence. Always give your name, as firms often pro-actively approach impressive candidates after a fair. Try to be as natural as possible (for more advice on this, see the section in Chapter 12 on interview technique) and ask suitable questions about the firm. These could include the culture of the firm, the style of training and the structure of the training contract, or the opportunity for travel (but only for firms with overseas/multiple offices!). Whatever questions you prepare, ask them of all the firms you meet. That way you will have a consistent framework for evaluating them afterwards.

- **Talk to trainees.** Do not overlook the value in talking to current trainees. While you will want to be memorable to recruiters (for the right reasons), trainees will be able to give you first-hand accounts of the reality of training in that firm.

- **Be patient.** Law fairs can be quite chaotic places and queue jumping can happen. Stay calm, wait patiently, and be polite. These professional characteristics can—and are—noted by recruiters, just as negative behaviour is also noted.

WHERE NEXT?

By following the advice in this chapter, you should find that you have demystified two of the areas that students are often concerned about. Commercial awareness and networking are two key skills that, if properly developed and demonstrated, will greatly enhance your employability skills.

The next chapter looks at a more practical way of building your employability skills with concrete examples to back them up: work experience.

7 Work experience

INTRODUCTION

This chapter focuses on all aspects of work experience. It explains the importance of work experience for law students and the benefits to be gained as well as outlining the different kinds of work experience available. It covers work experience in a law firm, mini pupillages, and other less common opportunities such as marshalling a judge that will add variety to your work experience portfolio as well as outlining opportunities for law-related voluntary work. It includes advice on how to find and apply for work experience and how to make a good impression during your placement. The chapter concludes with guidance on how to find opportunities to undertake the various types of work experience including advice on how to write an effective speculative application.

Students tend to recognise that it is important that they gain work experience but often lack understanding of what work they should do, how to find it and, crucially, when to do it. This lack of awareness can lead to a situation in which students leave it far too late, only thinking about work experience in their final year when the reality of the end of the degree is looming. Of course, it is not too late but there is a limit to what can be done in a year, especially when this has to be combined with the demands of final year studies. This chapter will encourage you to think about work experience from the very first day of your degree (if not before) and explain what you need to be doing to ensure that you have a portfolio of varied and relevant work experience as well as a degree when you graduate.

Benefits of work experience

There is a strong link in most people's minds between work experience and employment. In other words, it is usual to think that the benefit of work experience is that it will help you to get a job or, in the case of law students, a training contract or pupillage as an interim step that will enable you to enter the legal profession as a qualified solicitor or barrister. Obviously, this is an important factor but work experience is not only valuable because it enhances your employability; there are a range of other benefits to be gained:

- Development of skills. Work experience with a solicitor or barrister will help you to understand how the law in practice differs from the academic study of law. You will start to develop the skills that you will need as a legal practitioner such as working under time pressure, dealing with clients, and other aspects of professional life. This will demonstrate to prospective employers that you have an aptitude for working within the legal profession and, just as important, the glimpse that it affords into legal practice will increase your confidence in your ability to do the job of a solicitor or barrister.

- **Career decisions.** How do you know that you want to be a solicitor rather than a barrister or that you want to practise commercial law in a large City firm rather than family law in a high street firm? You might think that you know what type of legal career you want but undertaking a diverse range of work experience will enable you to make a more informed decision about your future career objectives. This will help you to target particular vacancies that fit your desired specifications (size of firm, area of practice etc.) and this will strengthen your application as you will have a basis to demonstrate to potential employers that you are looking for a particular kind of practice based upon your work experience rather than blindly applying for every training contract.

- **Confidence.** In order to succeed at interview and other stages of the recruitment process, you need to come across as a person who is confident in the workplace and in your interactions with colleagues and clients. Few people achieve this confidence without experience in a professional environment. Work experience gives you the opportunity to become familiar with working practices within a law firm, chambers, or other workplace, to develop a professional outlook and to gain confidence in handling the situations and people that are part and parcel of employment in a professional setting.

- **Commercial awareness.** The business of working within the law is a world away from its study at university level. Work experience will enable you to understand the commercial reality of legal practice and give you an understanding of the operation of the legal profession. This is important because it is sadly often the case that academic success is not necessarily an indicator of potential to work effectively in an employment setting. Work experience gives you the opportunity to demonstrate that you can work well with others (colleagues and clients) and within the procedural parameters of legal practice.

- **Interview practice.** The process of obtaining work experience often mirrors the process of applying for training contracts and pupillages in that you will need to locate appropriate vacancies, complete an application form, and attend an interview. As with anything, you should get better at these things with practice so you are polishing your application and interview skills ready to apply for training contracts and pupillages every time you apply for work experience. You will learn what works and what does not work on the basis of your successful and unsuccessful applications and you may find that you receive feedback on your application and interview that helps you to improve subsequent performances.

- **Networking.** Work experience will give you the chance to make good contacts within the legal profession that might help you to find further work experience opportunities so you should strive to make a good impression on everyone that you encounter. You may also find that you further your prospects of gaining a training contract as a result of undertaking work experience as some of the larger law firms use their summer placement schemes as part of the recruitment process.

As you will see from this list, work experience offers benefits far beyond its role in bolstering your CV. It gives you insight into the world of legal practice that will enable you to make informed decisions about your future, strengthen your prospects for success with future applications, and gives both you and prospective employers confidence that you can operate in a professional setting. However, the most immediate driving force that should create an impetus for you to seek out work experience is that you will be competing for training contracts or pupillage places against students who have work experience. Do not put yourself at a disadvantage.

I was able to get various work experience placements though throughout my degree and also several mini pupillages. These helped in many ways. Firstly, I was familiar with an office environment before starting my job which made me feel much more confident on my first day. I was also able to gain an insight into how a law firm works in practice, first-hand experience of dealing with clients and attending court and colleagues and also an understanding of various legal terminology and procedures. Secondly, I was able to judge which career path I wanted to take by observing both solicitors and barristers at work. In short, work experience taught me a whole range of things that you simply cannot learn at law school.

Lizzie, law graduate

Practical advice: diversity in work experience

Keep these benefits in mind when making applications for work experience to ensure that you target a range of different opportunities to ensure that your work experience portfolio is diverse as this maximises your opportunity to develop the whole spectrum of employability skills. Try to find a mix of large and small law firms, City and provincial practices, and different areas of specialisation as well as working for different lengths of time: you will get a different insight into legal practice working for a month than you will for a week. Not only will this variety give you a breadth of experience that will impress prospective employers, you will gain a greater insight into the sort of work that you most enjoy which will help you to make decisions about your career path.

Don't panic

Are you worried about work experience? Perhaps the experience described in the following practical example sounds familiar to you:

Practical example: worried about work experience?

The whole work experience thing took me by surprise in my second year. Up until then, nobody had mentioned it all and then, all of a sudden, all of my friends were talking about what work experience they had lined up. I was the only person, or so it seemed, that hadn't done anything plus they were all telling me it was too late to do anything now. The received wisdom was that if I didn't have it by now, I wouldn't get any this year and if I didn't do it in my second year then I wouldn't get any in my final year. And, of course, without work experience then I had no chance of getting a training contract. So I felt as if my chances of a career in law were finished and I was only halfway through the second year of my degree. It was pretty depressing. Foolishly, I didn't do anything about it—largely because I didn't know what to do—but then, in the final year, I was talking about it to one of the lecturers. She told me that it was never too late and sat down with me for about an hour to put together a plan of action which I followed and, by return of email, I had my first piece of work experience! I ended up fitting five different pieces of work experience into my final year. And, yes, I did get a training contract so all the fear-mongers who said that it wouldn't happen because I didn't have work experience in a City firm in my second year were wrong.

Ryan, University of Law LPC

Unfortunately, Ryan's experience is not uncommon. Many students do not appreciate the need to start finding work experience until quite a late stage of their degree as not all universities are active in pointing this out to students. This can lead to a feeling that you have 'missed the boat' if everyone else has work experience and you do not but remember, it does not matter what point you are at in your studies—or even if you have already graduated—it is never too late to start looking for work experience. Do not measure your work experience (or lack of it) by comparison with other students: whether or not they have work experience is of no relevance whatsoever to your situation so concentrate on working out a strategy for finding work experience rather than worrying about what other students are doing. Similarly, try not to be too influenced by the urban myths that circulate about work experience: there is no magic time or type of work experience that will open the door to a training contract or pupillage. It is simply the case that the earlier you start, the more work experience you can acquire during your degree and this will have an obvious impact on the strength of your training contract and pupillage applications.

So if, like Ryan, you feel that you have left it a bit late, try not to worry. Despite not looking for work experience until a late stage of his degree, Ryan secured a fair amount of work experience in his final year and was successful in obtaining a training contract. You will be able to find work experience that will help you on the way towards a training contract, pupillage, or other career path of your choice if you follow the advice and guidance set out in this chapter.

Before then, though, we are going to look at three common reasons that students panic about work experience:

- I don't know how to get work experience
- I don't know what to do on work experience
- I don't have any work experience.

It is often the case that the third problem—not having done any significant work experience—is a consequence of one (or both) of the first two problems. Students often fail to acquire any work experience either because they simply do not know how to go about gaining work placements or they are so worried that they will not know how to do the work that is required of them that they avoid doing work experience altogether. Each of these problems has the potential to lead to the same outcome— you will complete your degree without work experience and be at a competitive disadvantage to other students in the competition for a training contract or pupillage. Even if you decide that you do not want to practise law, the lack of experience in a professional working environment may be a significant impediment to the development of any alternative career.

So how can each of these three problems be avoided or overcome?

I don't know how to get work experience

It is most unfortunate that so many students miss the work experience boat because they do not know how to go about securing work placements. It seems to be the case that universities differ enormously in the level of help that they give students with finding work experience and the degree to which they publicise the help which is available so it is important that you take the initiative when it comes to seeking out work placements:

- **Act sooner rather than later.** It is never too early to get work experience; in fact, some students do this whilst at school and turn up at university with three or four law-based placements under their belts. The sooner you start, the more experience you can acquire.

- **Ask everyone for help and advice.** If other students have work experience, ask how they obtained it. Ask your personal tutor for guidance and visit the careers service at your university. See if any one amongst your family and their friends has any useful contacts in the legal profession. If solicitors, barristers, or judges visit your university, try to find an opportunity to ask for their advice or, even better, ask for a day or week of work experience with them.

- **Find out what your university offers.** More and more universities are offering support to students looking for work experience so see what services are available and use them. There may be a database of work experience that you can search on the university website or there may be a person in the law school whose role it is to offer career guidance or someone within the careers service that specialises in law placements.

- **Do it yourself.** Do not rely on the university to provide work placements—a great many do not do this at all and, in any case, there are far more opportunities available than are made available through your university. Make it your responsibility to find your own work experience. Carry out a search on the Internet to find solicitors or barristers in the locality or area of specialism that interests you. There is no magic to this: just type 'solicitors in Guildford practising family law' or 'solicitors in Bournemouth offering work experience'. Get the name of a specific person and send them a short email introducing yourself and asking for work experience.

Practical advice: finding a named contact

If you are making speculative enquiries to a law firm where you have no existing contacts, it is important to direct your request to a particular person rather than using a general enquires form or email address. Look on the firm's website to see if they specify how enquiries for work experience should be made. In the absence of this, telephone the firm and ask for the name of the person to whom requests for work experience should be directed. Alternatively, look under the 'people' link on the firm's website to identify a particular individual with expertise in your chosen field and contact them directly.

I don't know what to do on work experience

For some students, fear of the unknown deters them from making an attempt to gain work experience. This is perfectly understandable: after all, work experience takes you out of your comfort zone as a university student and launches you into a pressured work environment full of busy people. However, it is self-defeating to let this uncertainty hold you back from undertaking work experience as you will never find out what a solicitor or barrister does unless you venture into the workplace. Moreover, without work experience, you are limiting your opportunities to develop and demonstrate employability skills which will be instrumental to your career prospects in the future irrespective of whether or not you practise law.

Practical advice: overcoming your fears

Think about what worries you about taking on work experience. Make a list and be as specific as possible—there's no point in listing something general like a concern about looking silly—you will need to work out what it is that you think that you could do (or not do) that would make you look

---

silly. Once you have a list, look at each item and think about how to avoid the problem from arising or how you would deal with it if it does arise. If you cannot think of solutions, book an appointment with a personal tutor or a careers advisor and ask for their help. Once you have worked out a strategy for dealing with problems, you should feel more confident about making a foray into the workplace.

⬤ Have a think about these common concerns about work experience expressed by law students and consider how you would advise someone to overcome them. You will find our suggestions on the Online Resource Centre.

- I don't know what to wear
- I'm worried that I'll make a mistake with something that will have serious consequences for a case
- I'm afraid that I won't know how to do something that someone asks me to do
- I might run out of things to do and just be hanging around getting in the way
- I might not understand what people are talking about when they discuss cases.

Tell us

Tell us about your concerns regarding work experience and what, if anything, you did to overcome your fears. Contact us at finchandfafinski.com/get-in-touch or @FinchFafinski on Twitter.

Most people feel nervous when going into a new and unfamiliar environment but try not to let this deter you from seeking work experience. After all, it is only by going into the workplace that you will come to understand what it requires of you and therefore become more confident. Everybody you encounter was once new to the firm and new to the practice of law so they will remember this and not expect you to have skills and knowledge beyond your experience. It is very unlikely that you will be asked to do anything particularly complex and if you are in any doubt whatsoever then you should always express this and ask for help. You are there to learn and the firm has offered you work experience to help you learn so do not be afraid to ask for help or clarification of your instructions.

Practical advice: an easy introduction

If you are really anxious and this is stopping you from trying to find work experience, try these suggestions to ease your way into a work placement.

- **Attend an open day.** Many firms have open days to inform law students about their work and to explain what they can expect to do during a work placement. This will give you a chance to see what a firm is like and get an insight into what you will be doing if you apply for work experience.
- **Start with shadowing.** Explain that you are inexperienced and that you would like to shadow a solicitor or barrister—that is, follow them as they go about their daily work—for a short time, even a couple of hours will do. This will allow you to get the feel of the firm and an idea of what work they might require from someone on work experience.
- **Go to court.** Dress smartly, sit in on a few cases, and identify the solicitors and/or barristers involved. At an appropriate time, start a conversation in which you tell them that you are a student and ask if they have ten minutes to tell you about the case over coffee. This will give you an opportunity to ask for a day (or more) of work experience with them.

Each of these three suggestions gives you some exposure to a firm by taking you into their offices or establishing a link with a solicitor before you apply for work experience. This will take some of the unfamiliarity out of the situation and help you to take your first steps in the legal work environment.

I don't have any work experience

Let's imagine that it is almost April in the final year of your degree. Your exams are looming and you have just been told the date of your graduation ceremony. Other students are boasting about training contracts that they have secured or have a list of impressive work experience that spans several pages of their CV. You, however, have no work experience at all.

Whilst this is not the best situation you could be in, all is not lost. You will have the summer vacation after graduation and before starting the LPC or BPTC to gain relevant work experience plus there will be opportunities available for work experience once you start to study for these professional qualifications. Moreover, you could always take a year out before commencing the next stage of your studies to work as a paralegal which will both give you an in-depth insight into the legal profession and earn money to pay for the LPC or BPTC.

See Chapter 9 for further details on working as a paralegal.

The sections that follow will provide guidance for all students, irrespective of the stage of your studies, on how to find work experience. Before then, you might find it useful to read the section on getting started as this answers some commonly asked questions about work experience.

Getting started

This section of the chapter will cover some preliminary matters about work experience that answers the three questions most commonly asked by law students such as:

- When should I start applying for work experience?
- What sort of work experience should I do?
- How much work experience am I expected to have?

Before addressing these questions, we will deal with a more fundamental issue which is to define what we mean by work experience in this chapter.

What is work experience?

There is a general and a specific answer to this question. In general, work experience refers to any experience of the world of employment so would refer to any full-time or part-time jobs that you have had irrespective of the nature of the employment or the industry within which you worked. It could also refer to unpaid employment such as voluntary work. So the answer to the question 'what work experience do you have?' could be 'I worked part-time for two years in the Student Union bar and I volunteered at a hostel for homeless people for three months in the summer as part of my Duke of Edinburgh award'. However, in this book and in the context of university life as a law student, work experience refers to a more specific type of activity: it is work undertaken, paid or unpaid and irrespective of its duration, in an environment that gives you insight into working life within the legal profession. This might involve:

- Temporary work on a part-time or full-time basis in a law firm
- A mini pupillage with a barrister

- A vacation scheme involving a structured placement of one or two weeks in a large law firm that usually takes place in the summer vacation prior to the final year of study
- Other work in a law firm
- A placement for a longer period, usually six months or one year, which forms part of the assessable component of the degree, often referred to as a sandwich year
- Voluntary work in a pro bono centre or advice centre
- Shadowing a judge or other legal professional for a day.

These are common forms of work experience undertaken by law students but are by no means the only activities that you could undertake. In essence, any work that gives you direct or indirect experience of working within the legal profession or dispensing legal advice will be relevant to your objective of maximising your employability within the legal profession at the end of your degree. Do not be afraid to look for work experience other than with solicitors and barristers: sometimes opportunities exist in unexpected settings:

I'd left it too late to apply for summer vacation placements so I applied for a job at the magistrates' court working with the victim liaison team. To be honest, I only did this because it paid quite well for a summer job and had a vague connection with law but it was fascinating. I learned an enormous amount about criminal practice and procedure and decided that I wanted to specialise in criminal law. Talking to the solicitors at the court was really helpful too and it was actually very easy to get work experience with those that I'd met at the courts so it turned out to be a really wonderful opportunity.

Stephanie, De Montfort University

Of course, you may decide that you do not want to practise law—sometimes students do this as a direct consequence of undertaking work experience and finding that it is not for them—but the experience of working in a professional environment and the skills you gain will be valuable irrespective of your ultimate career destination. If you are undecided about your career path, you may also find the section on non-law work experience later in this chapter useful.

In the next section, there is some guidance to help you to start planning the timing of your work experience. This is important as students (as the earlier examples illustrate) often fail to realise how early some applications need to be made, particularly for vacation placement schemes at large law firms.

When should I start applying for work experience?

Today.

Start planning your strategy for finding work experience right now. It is never too early to start making preparations for work experience and the earlier you start, the more opportunities there will be available to you. If you have left it rather late to arrange work experience (anything after the Easter vacation of your second year falls into this category) then you need to get moving on your applications as soon as possible. In the sections that follow, you will find advice tailored to the different stages of your academic studies.

Irrespective of whether you are in your first year or final year, you will need to think in a realistic way about how much time you have available to undertake work experience. Take into account the demands of your lectures and tutorials, the amount of private study required, and the timing of coursework and exams plus any paid employment commitments in order to reach a reasoned decision as to whether you could undertake work experience in term time. Even if you have only a few hours spare a week, it might be possible to find an opportunity that fits into your availability. Other than this, consider the three holiday periods: could you do one week at Christmas and another at Easter with more time devoted to work experience in the longer summer break? Making decisions about when you want to undertake work experience is an important factor in the timing of applications.

Another factor that ties in with your availability is the location of your work experience. If you are aiming to work in the holidays then it is likely that you will want to target law firms and barristers working near your home rather than in the vicinity of the university (assuming that you study somewhere other than your home town). This can be advantageous especially if you live in an area where there is no university offering a law degree as these firms are less likely to be overwhelmed with applications than firms located in areas where there is a university with a law school.

Tell us

Resolve to make one application for work experience every day for a month. One application a day will not take you long to research, compose and submit. Get in touch to let us know how many days it took you to achieve success. Tell us at finchandfafinski.com/get-in-touch or @ FinchFafinski on Twitter.

Hopefully, you are convinced that you should start making applications right away so in the next section you will find some guidance on the sort of work experience that you should aim to acquire at each stage of your studies. This is a suggested approach only, to help you to get started, it is not the only approach and the overriding principle is that all work experience is valuable.

What sort of work experience should I do?

As was explained earlier in this chapter, relevant work experience for those considering a career in the legal profession covers any time spent working with a solicitor or barrister as well as any other situation involving the giving of legal advice, the administration of legal rules, or participating in the operation of the justice system. This gives you a great deal of choice of potential work experience. However, the range of options available can be problematic in itself as many students say that they do not know what sort of work experience to undertake and that this uncertainty puts them off making applications.

• I didn't know what to do about work experience so I did nothing at all.

• It seemed like other students knew something that I didn't know about what to do and where to apply. People kept talking about placements they had done and I had no idea how to go about getting work experience myself so I felt more and more left behind.

• I knew we were supposed to get work experience but where from? Do I look for vacancies somewhere or approach firms directly and ask for work experience? If I approach firms directly, how do I know who to contact? Do I write a letter or send an email? I thought that there might be some sort of protocol involved that I'd breach by accident and make myself look silly.

The overriding theme from these quotations from law students is that they had grasped the general idea that it was important for them to gain work experience but that the specific details of how to go about finding and securing work experience were unclear to them. This uncertainty leads far too many students, as the first quotation here illustrates, to do nothing at all. In the sections that follow, you will find some suggestions of the sort of work experience that you should target in each year of your degree along with guidance on how to go about obtaining work experience.

First year

Many students do not think about work experience at all in their first year—after all, it seems like graduation and career choices are a long way off in the future—but it pays to start gaining work experience at the very earliest opportunity. Think about it like this: if you leave it until the second year of your law degree, you will be at a competitive disadvantage compared to other applicants at the same stage of their studies who have already gained work experience as employers are more likely to offer placements to students who have already demonstrated their commitment to a career in law and have proved that they can operate in a professional environment. In particular, you will find it difficult to get accepted onto one of the vacation placement schemes in your second year in the absence of any prior work experience that demonstrates your commitment to a career in law. However, you should not be deterred if you have no prior legal work experience as some firms are prepared to consider work in other environments as relevant work experience:

Work experience is always useful as it consolidates skills that you practise at university, but it doesn't need to be legal. A candidate who has been working part time through their studies or who has had a summer job, will also be using those competencies we are looking for in suitable applicants for the vacation scheme.

Amelia Spinks, Field Fisher Waterhouse

Although many firms operate a vacation placement scheme for second year students, very few have comparable schemes for students in the first year of their studies. There are some exceptions such as the Pathfinders scheme introduced by Linklaters in 2011 to provide work experience for first year law students.

Practical example: pathfinder at Linklaters

The Pathfinder scheme is a two-day programme created by Linklaters to provide first year law students with an early insight into the work of a global law firm. The programme introduces the firm's work, culture, direction, and strategy and provides opportunities for students to work with existing trainees as well as opportunities to develop important skills.

Day 1. Students attend a range of workshops aimed at developing team working, networking, and commercial thinking skills. There is an overview of the recruitment process from the Graduate Recruitment Team that includes hints and tips on applying for the summer vacation scheme and training contracts. The evening social event provides an opportunity for you to get to know others on a more informal basis.

Day 2. Students will shadow a trainee and observe work and life in a leading commercial law firm as well as receiving a personal impact master class which will help you to stand out from the crowd when making future applications.

You will find more information on the Pathfinder scheme at Linklaters on their website: www.linklatersgraduates.co.uk/our-schemes/pathfinder.

There are actually very few placement schemes that are open to students in the first year of their studies so you must be prepared to be proactive and find your own opportunities for work experience by making speculative approaches to law firms. This means that you need to contact a firm directly, usually by email although you could write a letter or telephone, and find out whether they will be prepared to offer you a period of work experience. You can either use the Internet to search for law firms in a particular location (near to your home or to the university is usual) or you can consult a directory such as the Legal 500.

Practical advice: your first application

Because you are in the early stages of your studies with no prior work experience, a solicitor or barrister is likely to have reservations about offering you work experience. You are unlikely to know what to do so it is possible that you will be more of a hindrance than a help in their busy day. Here are some suggestions to help you to make a successful application:

- **Ask for work of limited duration.** Stipulate the dates that you are available and ask for one or two days' work within those dates whilst indicating a willingness to work for a longer period should this be required. This strikes a nice balance between not posing too great a burden on a busy employer if you prove to be a hindrance whilst offering to help out for a longer period of time if they can find a use for you.

- **Acknowledge your inexperience and stress your enthusiasm.** Include a sentence in your letter or email that highlights the reason for your application at this early stage of your legal studies. This could be something that indicates your keenness to experience legal practice or a link between the area of practice in question and a subject that you have studied in your first year. Applications have greater success if they appear tailored to a particular work experience opportunity rather than seeming as if you have taken a scattergun approach by targeting any firm that might take you.

- **Suggest tasks that you could carry out.** As you are inexperienced, some firms may wonder how much supervision you will need and what you will be able to do so make some suggestions. You could shadow a solicitor, do some administrative tasks, carry out research, or take notes at court. Make it clear that you are happy to do anything at all but including some specific suggestions may help a firm to think of work they could ask you to do.

- **Make it clear that you do not expect to be paid.** This lets the employer know that you are looking for experience rather than money and that even if you prove to be a nuisance at least it will be for free!

- **Think about the technicalities of writing.** Your letter or email should be relatively short and to-the-point—no more than one side of A4 if typed—and impeccable in terms of its written style, grammar, spelling, and punctuation. Use your application as an advertisement for your writing skills and attention to detail. Write to a specific named person rather than the more general 'to whom it may concern' and provide contact details so that they can get in touch with you.

🔵 You will find some examples of successful applications for work experience written by first year law students on the Online Resource Centre. Have a look at these to see how these have been drafted.

Tell us

Tell us if you followed this advice and were successful in obtaining work experience. Let us know so that we can share your story (using a pseudonym if you wish) to encourage other students. Send us a copy of your application email and we will feature the best ones on the Online Resource

Centre and in the next edition of the book. Contact us at finchandfafinski.com/get-in-touch or @ FinchFafinski on Twitter.

The guiding principle in your first year is that you should be open to any work experience opportunities that are available even if it is not what you had hoped to achieve or if it is not in an area of law that you anticipate that you might like to practise. This is because all work that you do in the legal environment will help you to develop important employability skills and the experience may strengthen your application for other placements that are more in line with your plans and preferences in the future. Besides, it may be that the two days that you have been offered working with, say, an aerospace lawyer actually sparks an interest and influences your future plans. After all, until you have tried various types of legal work, you can only speculate about what it is that you want to do and what you will enjoy so a great many students actually find that work experience expands their ideas of the possible areas of practice available within the legal profession. The final reason that you should seek out many and varied opportunities for work experience as early as possible in your studies is that it will help you to acclimatise to the professional working environment and ensure that you combat any nerves associated with entering into the workplace. By the time that you graduate, you should be confident that you have the skills necessary to survive and thrive in the workplace.

Second year

I felt I gave myself a major advantage in my second year by making sure to get some work experience in my first year. It gave me the chance to get to grips with the basics and the hidden formalities associated with the legal profession, ensuring my second year could be focused on truly assessing the broad range of areas I had the opportunity to experience and seeing what truly suited my tastes.

Ben, law graduate

The second year of your studies is the optimal time to undertake work experience. You have a full year of legal study behind you so you have at least some idea of how the law works and how to undertake legal research but you are not yet facing the pressured final year of your studies. Ideally, you will have undertaken some work experience in your first year and can use this as the basis to make decisions about applications for further placements in your second year. If this is the case, you can make a targeted search for work experience that strengthens and complements that which you have already undertaken. Do this at the beginning of your second year (or as soon as possible thereafter) so that you have time to source suitable work experience and make applications.

Practical advice: reviewing your work experience

Start by listing your work experience thus far using categories such as the area of law practised, the size of the firm, and the duration of your placement and add to that a list of the skills and experience that you gained during the placement.

Can you see any pattern to your placements? Have you achieved sufficient variety in your work experience and are you finding examples of each of the key employability skills? Is there anything that you have not done that other students seem to be doing on work experience: attended court, sat in on a client conference, drafted legal documents etc? Compare your list with your skills audit to check whether there are gaps that need to be filled and then you can target placements that will give the missing skills and experience.

Have a look at the example in Table 7.1. What advice would you give to a student with this work experience about the sorts of placements they should target during their second year? There are three different placements of varying duration in firms of different sizes involving a fair spread of activities but all involve working in family law. This is fine if you are absolutely convinced that your future lies in family law practice but if not, variation would be advisable. After all, how do you know that you would not enjoy criminal law, corporate finance, or personal injury practice if you have not tried it?

Table 7.1 Examples of different types of work experience

Area of Law	Size of Firm	Duration	Skills/Experience
Family	Small firm (four solicitors, no trainees)	2 days	Shadowing a solicitor specialising in care proceedings, attending client meetings, doing general administration, and drafting emails to clients.
Family	Small firm (4 partners, 12 solicitors, one trainee, two branches)	1 week	Assisting the trainee solicitor working in the family department with all aspects of her role. This included two days spent in court for a custody hearing and drawing up some papers relating to financial settlement.
Family	Department in large national firm with over one hundred employees, four trainees, and six offices.	2 weeks	The first week was spent carrying out research for a case on removal from the jurisdiction and preparing a summary of the precedents for the team working on the case. The second week involved shadowing a family solicitor including two days in court dealing with a contentious adoption case and sitting in on four client conferences.

Once you have an idea of the work experience that you wish to obtain in order to strengthen your skills portfolio, you can start to make targeted applications to appropriate firms. Do this as early as possible, preferably before Christmas in your second year, especially if you hope to obtain a summer vacation placement with a large law firm. As a rule of thumb, you should apply for work experience at least two months before you want it to take place. Of course, there is nothing to stop you making approaches at any time—there have been instances of students sending a speculative email of enquiry and being asked 'can you start on Monday?'—but applying well in advance allows you to plan your work experience strategy more effectively. Some law firms and barristers' chambers only accept applications for work experience at particular times of the year. For example, the application period for most summer vacation schemes runs between November and the end of January and applications made outside of this period would not be considered. However, many smaller law firms will consider applications for work experience whenever they are made so do not be afraid to make speculative approaches.

I have a broad range of work experience including two mini pupillages in London and Hull, a week working for the Government chambers in Guernsey, a week marshalling with a Crown Court judge, continued employment as a volunteer with the Youth Justice and Probation Services, and eight weeks in paid employment as a legal researcher for a high street firm assessing the viability of the renewable energy sector as a legal market. I have had the opportunity to experience criminal and civil work, right through to international public and commercial law. Apart from helping me to decide which areas of practice I might be interested in, my circle of contacts has expanded dramatically and my view of the profession has matured significantly.

Ben, law graduate

If you are in your second year but have no work experience, you really must get started. It is unlikely that you will secure a place on a summer vacation scheme without prior work experience and even if you are not interested in this type of work experience, you do need to start gaining some experience to ensure that you are prepared for the business of finding a training contract in the future. Remember, some students will secure training contracts in their second year so if you have still not got any work experience then you are putting yourself at rather a disadvantage. But all is not lost: there is still time to make applications and gain experience, especially if you target smaller firms who are less likely to have rigid timeframes for applications.

Practical advice: make five applications today

If you are in your second year and have no work experience, resolve to try and find at least one placement today. Decide where and when you would like to work and formulate an email based upon the advice given in the previous section of this chapter. Identify five potential employers and email them today.

Tell us

Tell us whether you were successful at finchandfafinski.com/get-in-touch or @FinchFafinski on Twitter. Good luck!

Final year

Your primary focus in your final year should be on your studies and ensuring that you obtain the grades that you need to secure the best possible degree classification. However, unless you are in the fortunate position of having secured a training contract, you should still give some time and thought to the matter of work experience. The level of attention that this requires will depend upon how much work experience you have already acquired.

For students with a solid foundation of work experience gained over the previous two or three years of study, the emphasis in your final year should be on adding value to your portfolio of work experience. This could be targeting work experience that will fill a gap in your employability skills or by adding something unusual that will help to make your application stand out to prospective employers. This does not have to interfere with your study time: you could simply ensure that you find and secure such an opportunity for work during the summer following graduation.

Practical advice: finding unusual opportunities

If you want your application to stand out amongst the many others that employers will receive, try to have at least one piece of work experience on it that is a real conversation point: something above and beyond the usual run of work experience.

- **Law work in another country.** You could seek work experience in a law firm in another jurisdiction during the summer vacation (remember practical considerations, though, such as the cost of travel and accommodation and the possible need for a visa). If it is not an English-speaking country, you should emphasise your proficiency in another language (valuable as some law firms value language skills), or your ability to work in an unfamiliar setting where you are not conversant in the language. There are numerous opportunities for law work experience abroad in countries such as China, Ghana, and South Africa at **www.projects-abroad.co.uk** or you could seek an internship with a capital defence lawyer representing prisoners on death row.

- **A different perspective on the law.** Try not to think of the law only in terms of legal representation. You could seek work experience that allows you to see the law from a different perspective such as working in a local authority legal department, volunteering as a prison visitor, training as a magistrate, or by assisting an MP to draft a Private Members Bill.

Tell us

Tell us about your unusual work experience. What did you do and did it work in making your application-to-interview rate more successful? Contact us at finchandfafinski.com/get-in-touch or @FinchFafinski on Twitter.

For students with little or no work experience, the emphasis in the final year should be on acquiring any work experience that you can manage to fit in provided that this does not interfere with your study commitments. Remember that you have the entirety of the summer holiday after graduation to undertake work experience and that you have the option of taking up employment as a paralegal for a year (or more). Of course, the option of working as a paralegal is not limited to students with insufficient work experience: it is a really great opportunity to experience the day-to-day life in legal practice whilst earning money so many students choose to do this before commencing the LPC.

How much work experience am I expected to have?

This is a difficult question to answer as it requires the quantification of something that is, in reality, unquantifiable, rather like students who expect a straightforward numerical answer to the question 'how many cases should I put in my contract coursework essay?'. The answer, in both cases, is 'it depends' and 'as much/as many as you need'. A more helpful, although equally imprecise, answer is that you should have sufficient work experience to demonstrate to prospective employers that you have a commitment to a career in law and that you have set about gaining a good insight into the working life of a legal professional and the skills involved in legal practice.

> ## Practical example: how much work experience?
>
> We asked practitioners how much work experience they would expect students to have at the end of the degree. As you will see, there is no precise answer to this but their responses do identify a number of factors that you might want to bear in mind when making decisions about work experience.
>
> ....
>
> Ideally, students should have some work experience gained in each year of study. I don't think there is ever too much.
>
> Variety is more important than quantity. Students should not keep returning to the same firm, unless there is a training contract on the horizon, because repeated experience of the same sort of work adds nothing that wasn't demonstrated by their first stint at the firm.
>
> At least one longer period—a month or more—is useful as it means that students will have been exposed to more complex aspects of practice and have become used to the daily rhythm of life in a law firm.
>
> I think that there is an important balance that students need to strike between sampling a variety of different types of legal work and doing too many different things. It is all very well and good to have a range of different work experience but you need to be able to explain why you did the things that you did otherwise you just look aimless.
>
> ....

The extent to which you are able to demonstrate these things from work experience will depend not upon the number of different work placements that you have undertaken but instead upon the extent to which these placements afforded you with an opportunity to expand your knowledge and understanding of legal practice. For example, the duration of a work experience placement varies from a single day to several months. It is obvious that you will gain a far greater insight into the day-to-day work of a solicitor or barrister if you work with them for a month than you will from working for a week. You will be better able to follow the progression of cases and to learn the procedural steps involved if your work experience lasts for a longer period of time. As such, you could say that you gain more experience from a one month placement than you would from four one-week placements. Of course, you could counter-argue, as all good lawyers should, that four one-week placements demonstrates your ability to adapt to new working situations and new colleagues so there is merit in both. The key point really is to try and ensure that you have at least one lengthy period of work experience undertaken over the summer vacation as well as shorter periods of work. The other factor to bear in mind when selecting work experience is to aim for a degree of variability.

In summary, you should measure the extent and adequacy of your work experience on the basis of the range of opportunities that it has afforded for you to gain essential lawyering skills and experience of the legal environment rather than by counting the number of work placements completed. It should be a qualitative, rather than quantitative, exercise. Aim to gain as much work experience as you can manage within the time constraints of your studies and any necessary paid employment but try to make sure that you vary the sort of work placements that you do to ensure that you build up a portfolio of varied experience of different kinds of legal practice.

Types of work experience in law

The majority of students setting out upon a law degree do so with the aim of entering the legal profession as either a solicitor or a barrister. Of course, it may be that you change your mind during the course of the degree and embark on an entirely different career or that you simply chose law out of general interest as a good solid academic degree with no plan to practise law. However, unless you have actively and definitely ruled out any possibility that you will want to work within the legal profession, the most obvious type of work experience that you should gain will come from working with a solicitor or barrister. There are a number of forms that this may take, as you will see in the sections that follow, and you should also consider other forms of legal work experience such as voluntary work and marshalling a judge to build up a varied portfolio of experience that will give you plenty of opportunities to enhance your employability skills and impress prospective employers.

Mini pupillage

A mini pupillage is work experience, usually for one or two weeks, with a barrister although some barristers do offer a single day mini pupillage as a snapshot of life in chambers. This usually involves working with a particular barrister to observe every facet of their work and may also include talks about life as a barrister and social events. A mini pupillage may include a piece of assessed work and may be part of the selection process when recruiting for pupillage.

Practical example: what is it like?

Each chambers will have a different approach to the nature and content of a mini pupillage and much will depend upon what work the supervising barrister is doing at the time.

- **Falcon Chambers, London**. On arrival, you will be given an introductory talk and assigned to your mini pupilmaster who will ensure you see a variety of work. Each afternoon, there will be a talk from one or more members of chambers and clerks on different aspects of life at the Bar (applying for pupillage, life at the Bar, the running of chambers). We aim to give you the opportunity to meet as many members of chambers as possible during the course of your visit and there will usually be an informal gathering with some of our barristers and clerks on the last day. www.falcon-chambers.co.uk

- **Guildhall Chambers, Bristol.** Undertaking a mini pupillage provides an opportunity to experience all elements of life as a barrister including being in court, observing conferences with lay clients and instructing solicitors, and drafting legal documents. Mini pupils will also have the opportunity to talk with members of chambers and ask them questions about their profession and the pupillage application procedure. www.guildhallchambers.co.uk

- **No 1 High Pavement, Nottingham.** A mini pupillage will consist of one week shadowing one or more members of chambers at court, in the Robing Room, and in chambers. The student may be allowed access to counsel's papers but will not be required to prepare any written work. The student may be allowed to sit in on conferences when counsel deems it appropriate and the client consents. www.1highpavement.co.uk

---

Tell us

Tell us about your mini pupillage. How did you secure the mini pupillage and what work did you do? Contact us at finchandfafinski.com/get-in-touch or @FinchFafinski on Twitter.

....

The benefit of mini pupillage varies enormously depending on the set you are with and the supervisor you are given. I had one week at a commercial mega-set where I sat in the office of a leading junior. In effect, it was a week of one-to-one tuition and the work I was involved in was first-class. It was a fantastic experience. I had another mini where my role was to simply spectate from a distance. This was much less beneficial, but still useful—if only to rule out applying to that chambers.

Rupert, law graduate and barrister

....

For students wishing to practise law as a barrister, it really is essential to undertake at least two, preferably more, mini pupillages as it will be extremely difficult to succeed in the competition to secure a pupillage without this experience. Some chambers will not accept a pupillage application from students who have not undertaken a mini pupillage whilst some will not accept applications unless students have undertaken a mini pupillage with them. For students who wish to practise as solicitors or who are undecided about their destination after graduation, there is no reason not to do a mini pupillage: it is an excellent addition to your work experience portfolio and it will give you an insight into the life of a barrister which will help you to make decisions about your career path.

Practical example: good etiquette whilst on a mini pupillage

We asked several barristers to tell us what a student can do to make a good impression during a mini pupillage:

....

If you are given a piece of written work, make sure you give it the time, care, and attention it deserves—it may be filed and re-assessed when the chambers is deciding whether to give you a pupillage interview. And finally, number your paragraphs as barristers do when advising.

Pupillage Committee, 5 Essex Court

....

....

Resist the temptation to fill silences; don't forget the barrister you are shadowing is working, not simply entertaining you for a day. Take notes, remember details, and always offer to help carry papers. A quiet, intelligent mini-pupil who pays attention and asks sensible questions will always make a good impression.

Aiden Briggs, Ely Place Chambers

....

....

First of all, he or she should turn up on time! If we have arranged to meet at court, he should find out in advance where the court is, the name of the case, and which courtroom it is to be held in. Be enthusiastic, be willing, and appear to be interested.

Astra Emir, barrister

....

Minis are difficult because students need to balance being interested and engaged while also taking a step back to allow the barrister they are shadowing to get on with the job. How can students do this?

1. Save all your questions for after the hearing when the barrister will no longer be focused on the case and should be more relaxed.

2. Make sure that you have read all the information available on the website so you don't ask unnecessary questions.

3. Never offer legal advice, particularly in front of a client—unless asked.

4. Look the part. Dress smartly and conservatively. Bring a counsel's notebook, a pen, highlighter. Take a note of evidence/submissions during a court hearing.

Assessed and non-assessed mini pupillages

Many mini pupillages are non-assessed in that they exist to give students an insight into the working life of a barrister without any formal exercises to measure their aptitude for the law and legal practice. Other mini pupillages include some form of written and/or oral assessment that aims to contribute to the selection process by identifying students who are suitable for consideration for a pupillage. For some chambers, this is a crucial part of recruitment.

Practical example: assessed mini pupillage

- Mini pupillages are a vital part of our applications process. Accordingly, no pupillage will be offered at **Blackstone Chambers** unless the applicant has undertaken an assessed mini pupillage.

- At **Brick Court Chambers**, assessment is by a written task that tests the writing skills and analytical ability of students with a view to identifying those who could potentially be offered a pupillage.

- Students undertaking a mini pupillage at **Keating Chambers** are usually asked to complete a written mini pupillage exercise and, if practicable, an advocacy exercise during their time in chambers. This provides students with an opportunity to discuss their work with a member of chambers and identifies promising candidates for pupillage.

In reality, the distinction between an assessed and non-assessed mini pupillage is not great. The work will be the same and all students will be observed with a view to considering whether or not they would be suitable for pupillage at that chambers. So there is an element of assessment to all mini pupillages; the only real difference is whether or not there is a formal written and/or oral exercise that is used for evaluative purposes.

Some [chambers] will set a piece of work, others will run moots or advocacy competitions. Often it will be even more informal and members of chambers will simply send feedback to the Pupillage Committee about how the student performed.

Pupillage Committee, 5 Essex Court

Finding mini pupillages

As with work experience in a firm of solicitors, the opportunities for mini pupillages may or may not be advertised. Advertised vacancies can be found in a number of ways and a speculative application (discussed earlier in relation to work experience with a solicitor) can be made to chambers which do not advertise mini pupillages.

In terms of identifying existing opportunities, you could consult one of a number of online resources that will provide details of chambers with pupillages on offer as these will often also include details of the availability of mini pupillages. For example, the Pupillage Gateway is operated by the Bar Council as the portal through which all pupillage applications are made but the information about each chambers includes details of whether or not mini pupillages are available. Accordingly, a search can be made for chambers that offer mini pupillages in any particular location so, for example, you could search for chambers in the Midlands offering mini pupillages which, at the time of writing, would alert you to only one option with St Mary's Chambers in Nottingham (see Figure 7.1).

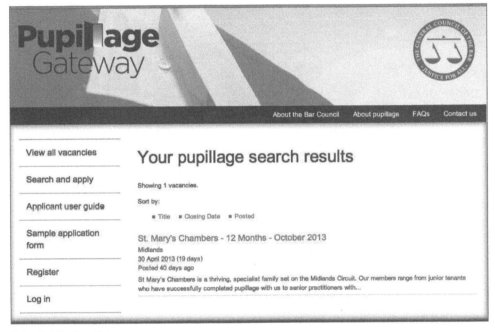

Figure 7.1 Pupillage Gateway

The limitation to this method of finding mini pupillages is that it presents only a partial picture of the opportunities available at any point in time. The Pupillage Gateway is designed to facilitate a search for pupillages, not mini pupillages, so you are using the database to find chambers that offer mini pupillages from amongst those that are currently advertising pupillages. As such, it will not assist you to identify mini pupillages available at chambers that do not have current pupillage vacancies. So it is not a perfect method for identifying mini pupillages but it is at least a starting point.

There are two further alternatives. Firstly, you could take a more methodical approach by compiling a list of all chambers within a particular area and checking their websites one by one to ascertain whether they offer mini pupillages. There are a number of resources that offer listings of barristers and chambers. For example, you could use Legal Hub (**www.legalhub.co.uk**) to list all chambers in a region or narrow your search by reference to the area of law practised to create a list of possible sources of mini pupillages. For example, if you searched for chambers in the Midlands with specialism in crime (see Figure 7.2), you would obtain a list of ten chambers spread across the Midlands (see Figure 7.3).

Figure 7.2 Legal Hub search

5.	No 8 Chambers	Birmingham B4 6DR Tel: 0121 236 5514	Arbitration; Capital tax; Care proceedings; Chancery (land law) ...
6.	Equity Chambers	Birmingham B4 7LR Tel: 0121 236 5007	Common law (general); Corporate fraud; Crime; Employment ...
7.	1 High Pavement	Nottingham NG1 1HF Tel: 0115 941 8218	Corporate fraud; Crime; Licensing
8.	Cornwall Street Chambers	Birmingham B3 3BY Tel: 0121 233 7500	Care proceedings; Children; Commercial law; Common law (general) ...
9.	Regent Chambers	Stoke On Trent ST1 1HP Tel: 01782 286666	Care proceedings; Chancery (general); Common law (general); Corporate fraud ...
10.	KCH Garden Square	Nottingham NG1 5BH Tel: 0115 941 8851	Care proceedings; Chancery (general); Commercial litigation; Commercial property ...

Figure 7.3 Legal Hub search results

Secondly, you could carry out a general search of the Internet using the search term 'mini pupillages' in combination with your preferred geographic location and/or area of legal practice. Although this approach may seem more generic than using a specialist database, it actually offers a couple of advantages. For instance, you can be more specific about the geographic location of where you are looking for work; the searchable databases tend to divide locations to mirror the circuits in which barristers work whereas you can narrow this down to a particular town by carrying out a keyword search on the Internet. Moreover, the professional databases tend to carry details of chambers that subscribe to their services so could return fewer results than a general Internet search as the following example illustrates.

Practical example: internet versus database search

Imagine that you are interested in crime and are looking for a mini pupillage in Nottingham. You would identify two opportunities by using the Legal Hub search:

- KCH Garden Square
- 1 High Pavement.

However, a keyword search of the Internet would identify the following additional possible sources of a mini pupillage at chambers in Nottingham that deal with crime:

- 23 Essex Street
- Trent Chambers.

It is always worth supplementing a database search with a more general Internet search to ensure that you find all the possible opportunities for a mini pupillage in your preferred areas (legal and geographic).

Once you have identified a list of chambers of interest, you can check their website for information about the availability of mini pupillages and the application procedure. In the absence of any specific information, you will need to make a speculative application (see earlier discussion in relation to work experience in a firm of solicitors). As many chambers require that applications are made by the submission of a CV and a covering letter, there is unlikely to be much difference between a response to an advertised mini pupillage and a speculative application.

Practical example: methods of securing mini pupillage

Rebecca Morgan has undertaken three mini pupillages, each of which was obtained in a different way:

St Albans Chambers, St Albans: I contacted the chambers directly. They didn't have a formal application procedure and they were able to accommodate me very quickly.

One Paper Building, London: I sent an online application using the Pupillage Gateway.

4 Breams Buildings, London: I used contacts at the chambers that I had made through taking part in an advocacy course at university.

Bear in mind that barristers can be overwhelmed with applications so you may need to be persistent and make a large number of applications:

I focused on doing mini pupillages because I knew I wanted to train to become a barrister. They can be difficult things to organise as the competition is often fierce, particularly for placements out of term time. I sent out over 30 letters and arranged 5 mini pupillages at chambers that undertook work in different areas.

Rupert, law graduate and barrister

I did get daunted by my lack of success at first but was determined to persevere. It paid off and I eventually obtained three mini pupillages at different chambers but I think that I made about 60 applications to get them.

Suranne, Middlesex University

I got fed up with receiving no response or getting cursory rejection emails so I decided to go and sit in the chambers and talk to barristers in person. I'm quite personable and I was convinced that the direct approach would work and it did. I have to admit that the clerk was quite surprised when I explained what I was doing but I said that I was quite happy to sit in a quiet corner and wait all day if necessary until one of the barristers had time to chat to me. To my surprise, the Head of Chambers came to see me after ten minutes and had a chat. He said he was impressed by my enterprising nature and made me an offer of a two-week pupillage there and then.

Adam, University College London

Pegasus Access Scheme

This is a social mobility initiative launched by the Inner Temple in association with 56 partner chambers that gives students from under-represented groups that may face obstacles in entering the legal profession an opportunity to undertake a mini pupillage. The scheme gives preference to students who have participated on the following programmes:

- Pathways to Law
- Social Mobility Foundation
- Warwick Multicultural Scholars Programme
- Inner Temple Schools Project.

If you are eligible, it is well worth taking part in the scheme as it is a good source of short (two to five days) mini pupillages and reasonable expenses incurred in taking part are also covered. Students who have not taken part in one of the four programmes may still apply if they meet certain criteria and will be considered for any additional places that are available. There is more detail about the scheme and its eligibility requirements on the website: **www.pegasus.me**.

Applications should be made between September and October and involves a short application form and a personal statement of no more than 500 words that sums up why you want to be a barrister and how the scheme will help you achieve this as well as detailing any work experience or extra-curricular activities that demonstrate your interest in the Bar and your academic achievements on your degree.

Vacation placement schemes

Many of the larger law firms offer work experience to second year law students by way of formal vacation scheme placements, generally during the Easter and summer holidays. This is a programme of work experience and other activities—talks about the firm, skills workshops, and social activities—spanning one, two, or three weeks that allows students to experience daily life as a solicitor whilst giving the firm an opportunity to assess the suitability of the students for a future within the legal profession. Indeed, many firms use the vacation scheme as part of the recruitment process.

Practical advice: vacation schemes and training contracts

The vacation schemes run by the larger law firms are regarded as the Holy Grail of work placements both because of the way that they are structured around the needs of the students and because they are so often used as part of the process of recruitment for training contracts.

- At **Nabarro** '[a]lmost all our trainees (95%+) come to us through our multi award-winning vacation schemes'.

- 'Our internships are one of the primary means of selecting candidates for a career at **Simmons & Simmons**. They provide us with the chance to test your suitability for a training contract. They are also a unique opportunity for you to get to know our firm, decide if we are the best firm for you and for you to prove your potential during your time with us.'

- At **Pinsent Masons**, '[a] good 70% of our trainees regularly join us after experiencing the working environment first-hand, through our summer placement programme…If you gain a placement, it's because we're already thinking of you as a potential trainee. And over the course of the placement, we'll do our best to give you every chance to prove us right. That's why placement students don't need to make a separate application for the training programme. If you've already gained a placement, in our eyes you're already in the running'.

Due to the link between the placement and training contract recruitment, the quality of the work experience provided and the reasonable rate of pay (around £250 a week), competition for these places is fierce. Applications are generally made towards the end of the autumn term and into January and the application process often mirrors that used for training contracts so you should expect to complete an application form with some testing questions on it as well as a telephone and/or face-to-face interview plus other recruitment tools such as psychometric tests and assessment centres.

The recruitment process used at Field Fisher Waterhouse is depicted in Figure 7.4.

Do not be deterred by this rigorous recruitment process: It is excellent practice that will stand you in good stead when it comes to making training contract applications. Some firms such as Field Fisher Waterhouse offer detailed feedback to unsuccessful applicants that reach a certain stage of the process so it is also an opportunity to learn how to strengthen future applications.

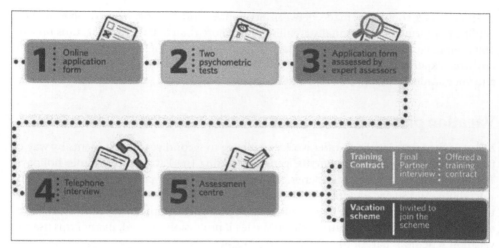

Figure 7.4 Recruitment process at Field Fisher Waterhouse

Practical advice: placement applications

You will find detailed advice on all aspects of the application process in Chapter 11. For now, though, there are some points to bear in mind in relation to your application for a place on a summer vacation scheme.

- **Research**. Set aside an hour or so each week in the autumn term of your second year to carry out research into firms offering vacation schemes so that you can make an informed decision about where to apply.

- **Tailor your application**. A generic application is obvious to recruiters and is rarely welcome. Draw on your research into the firm to tailor your application to its specialisations, ethos, and approach to work experience. List at least three things about the firm and its vacation scheme that attracts you and find a way to work these into your application.

- **Take your time**. Make a list of deadlines for applications in your diary and include a reminder one week before the deadline. Print a copy of the application form as soon as it is available and give yourself time to work out answers to the questions and reflect upon them so that you can make any necessary changes. Most firms require electronic applications either direct by a form completed on their website or via an electronic application system such as Apply 4 Law (**www.apply4law.com**) so check to see if applications can be saved once they have been started.

- **Give full answers supported by evidence**. Some of the questions will be challenging but you must write a complete answer as best you can. You should always substantiate your statements: do not claim to be a good team player unless you can make reference to a specific time that you have worked well with others.

- **Get help**. Show your application to someone from the careers service or your personal tutor and seek their advice on how it can be improved.

- **Check it for errors**. Silly mistakes and grammatical errors condemn your application to the bin so be meticulous in checking the accuracy of your finished application. It can help to get someone else to read it for you—we tend to see what we think we have written so it can be easier for someone else to spot your mistakes. In particular, take care that you have not copied and pasted something from one application into another that is unsuitable: for example, like a section on 'why I want to work for x' without realising that you have not changed the name of the firm.

- **Stick to the deadline**. Late applications will not be accepted even if the reason for lateness is not your fault. Remember that online applications may create a high volume of traffic through the firm's website in the final hours before the deadline so aim to submit your application a few days early, just in case the server goes down under the pressure of applications.

- **Do not be afraid to update the firm on new developments**. If, for example, you win the internal negotiation competition after you have applied for a place on a vacation scheme, there is nothing to be lost by contacting an appropriate person in the firm and asking to update your application with this piece of new information. You should only do this with significant pieces of information.

There are no limits to the number of applications that you can make nor, for that matter, to the number of vacation schemes that you can attend. If you have been offered a place on four, five, six, or however many different schemes then, provided that the dates do not clash, there is nothing to stop you taking up all of the offers. After all, each scheme is with a separate firm and will be structured in a different way with its own approach to work experience so there will always be something new to learn at each firm and you will be building up an excellent portfolio of work experience at some of the biggest law firms.

Practical example: what is it like?

It is difficult to offer a description of what you can expect on a vacation placement scheme as each firm will do things differently but, in general, you can expect to be supervised and given appropriate tasks to do as well as being offered opportunities to take part in social activities, presentations, and workshops as these examples show:

The vacation scheme at **Macfarlanes** aims to provide a two-week snapshot into life as a trainee. You will spend each week in a different department, working with a partner, assistant solicitor or trainee, on real work such as drafting a letter (and working through the draft with the solicitor or trainee) or carrying out research on a live issue for a client.

At **Blandy & Blandy**, you will shadow a different trainee on each day therefore experiencing five departments in the week and, wherever possible, accompany a trainee to court for a hearing or tribunal.

At **Mayer Brown International**, students assist a partner or senior associate on real deals to gain first-hand experience of life in a City law firm. You will sit in two departments and attend presentations on different practice areas to give an insight into the breadth of the firm. There are plenty of social activities including a trip to one of the European offices.

The placement scheme at **Olswang** gives students an insight into the firm's work, culture, and ethos and an opportunity to experience the life of a typical trainee solicitor. You will normally be placed in two different departments during the placement under the supervision of an associate or trainee and given work from a variety of fee-earners within the group. There is a structured timetable of talks, skills workshops, and social events.

The **Simmons & Simmons** three-week summer vacation schemes are designed to make you really feel a part of our firm and get a genuine insight into what it is like to work with us. Working alongside a partner or associate— who will supervise, direct, and coach you—you'll also be matched with a current trainee to help you to settle in. This support will ensure that you get the most out of your time with us and get involved in a host of exciting and challenging projects.

You'll be included in every aspect of working life, from departmental events to firm-wide training sessions, as well as research, drafting, minute taking, and meeting arrangements. You could also work directly with our clients. You and other members of the vacation scheme will also be assigned a project, which will be presented to members of the firm at the end of your stay. In addition, we hold a full programme of lectures, skills sessions, and social events.

Tell us

Tell us about your summer vacation placement. Was it a good insight into life as a solicitor and did it help you to make a decision about working at the firm in the future? Contact us at finchandfafinski.com/get-in-touch or @FinchFafinski on Twitter.

Practical example: on placement at Bircham Dyson Bell

You will spend two weeks with us, gaining valuable experience with two of our legal departments. We aim to give you as much practical experience as possible, plus the opportunity to experience first-hand how our solicitors and partners work.

In each of the departments you will be allocated a supervisor, one of our partners or senior associates, so you have support and guidance during your time with us. You will also have a nominated buddy, one of our current trainees or newly qualified solicitors, so you can hear their experience first-hand.

Additionally, a range of organised activities including a networking event, trainee social and legal research exercises will make your time with us enjoyable as well as insightful. We hope during your time with us you will make friends and we encourage those on the programme to arrange informal activities to build relationships and network further. www.bdb-law.co.uk

Anyone who wants to practise law as a solicitor, particular in the larger City and commercial law firms, should consider applying for a place on at least one vacation scheme. They are designed to provide a good insight into the operation of the firm so will help you to decide whether it is a place that you would like to apply for a training contract as well as strengthening your CV.

Practical advice: researching law placements

It would be unrealistic to think that you will have time to apply for every placement scheme that is available so you will have to find some basis to decide between the different placement providers. You can use the Internet to find details of their placements and to get a feel for what they offer as well as finding reviews written by students who have undertaken placements and who are giving their impressions. Another option would to be to consider firms that have won awards for their placements. There are a number of accolades that could be awarded.

For example, the National Council for Work Experience gives awards on an annual basis to organisations that offer outstanding work experience to students and graduates with particular emphasis on the extent to which the placements offer opportunities for the development of employability skills. For the first time in 2012, a separate award was introduced for the best placement provided by a law firm and this was won by Nabarro.

The law firms short-listed for an award in 2013 are:

- Baker & McKenzie
- Bircham Dyson Bell
- Nabarro (winner)
- Pinsent Masons
- Shearman & Sterling
- Simmons & Simmons (highly commended).

You will find more details of the awards and the judging criteria as well as a wealth of information on work experience in a range of industries on their website **www.work-experience.org**.

Finding vacation schemes

Practical advice: placements and training contracts

Be aware that some firms only consider applications for training contracts from students who have undertaken work experience with them whereas others will offer some shortening of the recruitment process to placement students such as a direct route to interview. Some firms will automatically consider all students who undertake work experience for a training contract and will incorporate an interview into the placement. Even if this is not the case and there seems to be no link between the placement and recruitment for training contracts, it is inevitable that the insight that the firm has gained into you as a prospective solicitor during the placement will be a factor in the recruitment process. As such, you should treat the placement itself as it is one long interview!

Remember that the placement is also a chance for you to get the feel of a firm and to decide if you think that it is a place where you would be comfortable working on a longer term basis. If you dislike the work, your colleagues, or the general atmosphere and find yourself counting the days (or hours) until the end of your placement then it would not be a good idea to apply for a training contract at that particular firm. Try not to worry—law firms differ enormously so there is bound to be a different firm where you feel more at home.

In essence, it is advisable to secure a work placement at any firm where you feel that you would consider applying for a training contract. It will give you an insight into the firm and the firm an insight into you which could work to your advantage in the recruitment process. Of course, you do not have to aspire to work at a firm in order to apply for a place on its vacation scheme: they offer excellent work experience that will strengthen your employability skills and enhance your CV.

Despite these benefits, many students do not even try to secure a placement thus they miss out on one of the best work experience opportunities. This was surprising so we asked students why they did not apply for a place on a vacation scheme. The answers that we received fell into two categories:

1. Lack of awareness about placement schemes and the application process:
   - I didn't realise that there were any formal schemes so I just applied to work with a local solicitor to get work experience
   - I knew that vacation schemes existed but didn't know where to find out about them

- I didn't realise we'd have to apply so early so I didn't start thinking about it until the Easter break and by then I'd missed all the closing dates.

Lack of awareness about vacation schemes, their availability, application process, and the timing of applications is a major factor that causes students to miss out on the opportunity to secure a placement. We have sought to tackle this problem by gathering information on the schemes that exist. Table 7.2 provides an extract from a fuller table that can be found in Appendix A that identifies the vacation schemes available in England and Wales along with information about the number of vacancies, location, and duration of the placement and whether or not it is a paid placement. We have included details about the application process but not the deadline for applications as these can change from year-to-year and it is important that you are not misled by out-of-date information. However, we have included a link to the vacation placement areas of each firm's website so that you can find more information including the closing date for applications.

Table 7.2 Extract from Appendix A

Firm	Placements Available	Application Process	Duration	Location	Pay per Week
Jones Day www.jonesdaycareers. com/offices/office_detail. aspx?office=4&subsection=11	60	Online application plus covering letter	2 weeks	London	£400
K & L Gates LLP www.klgates.com/careers	8	Online application plus interview	2 weeks	London	£300
Kennedys www.kennedys-law.com/ uk/careers/graduates/ summerplacements/	12	Online application plus telephone interview and online ability test	2 weeks	London	£275
Kirkland & Ellis International LLP http://ukgraduate.kirkland. com	20	Online application	2 weeks	London	£250

The application window tends to be open from November to mid- or late-January (although a few deadlines are in February or March) so you should start thinking about vacation schemes and deciding where to apply at the start of your penultimate academic year. The application process can be quite challenging—some firms use the same questions for placements as they do on the training contract application forms— so you should ensure that you have plenty of time to prepare your answers.

Practical advice: plan your applications

Print out the application forms for vacation schemes well before the application deadline and familiarise yourself with the sort of questions that are asked.

Take time to research the firms so that you can tailor your application accordingly: there is usually a question about why you want a placement at that firm and the answer 'I'm not fussy as long as I get work experience' is not a good one (even if it is the truth).

Think about your skills and experience and identify gaps that may jeopardise the success of your application. You will then have time to rectify the situation before you start to complete the application forms.

You will find further information on all aspects of the application process in Chapter 10 and suggestions on the time-management of applications in Chapter 2.

2. **Anxiety or uncertainty about applying for or undertaking a work placement:**

- We were always told how competitive it was to get places and my first year grades were not great so I assumed I'd be unsuccessful

- I had a look at the application forms and they asked really difficult questions that I didn't know how to answer so I gave up and didn't apply

- All the placements are in really big law firms and I found that really daunting plus I don't know how to do any of the things that they would want me to do so I was worried that I'd be really out of my depth.

It is true that competition for places on a vacation scheme can be fierce but you should not let that deter you from making an application; after all, if you do not apply then you will certainly not get a place whereas you are at least in with a chance if you submit an application and your prospects of success increase the more applications that you make.

Practical advice: successful applications

There are over 2000 places available on vacation schemes offered by different law firms each year so there is no reason whatsoever why your application should not be one of the successful ones. There are some things that you can try to improve the chances of success:

- **Start early.** Take time to research each firm and put together a thoughtful and polished application. It is better to make ten good applications than it is to make 50 hurried ones that contain mistakes or lack attention to detail.

- **Target schemes with early closing dates.** The earlier the closing date, the sooner you will find out whether your application has been successful. An unsuccessful application is an indication that something needs to be developed so you will have time to make changes and to strengthen subsequent applications.

- **Spread your applications.** Some firms receive more applications than others so ensure that you target a range of different placement opportunities to maximise your chances of success. For example, work experience at well- known City law firms is highly sought after whereas unpaid placements in smaller firms or in more remote locations may receive fewer applications.

It is also true that the application process can be challenging and time-consuming but it replicates the process used for training contract applications so just putting an application together and discovering whether it was successful is a useful learning experience in itself. You will also see from the table of placement opportunities in Appendix A that the application procedure varies from firm to firm so you can gain experience of different recruitment practices: CVs and covering letters, application forms, telephone and face-to-face interviews and other selection processes such as psychometric tests, verbal reasoning, and aptitude tests.

You will find advice about all aspects of the application and interview process, including how to tackle challenging questions, in Chapters 11 and 12.

Practical advice: overcoming anxiety

It is fair to say that the majority of students feel apprehensive about undertaking a work placement, particularly for the first time. By and large, it is fear of the unknown that is really daunting. What work will I have to do? What shall I wear? What will I do if I don't understand something? Where do I go on the first day? The best way to overcome your fears is to turn the unknown into the known. In other words, make a list of the questions that are bothering you and set about answering them. You will find plenty of information about the vacation scheme on the firm's website or you can contact the person responsible for placement recruitment to ask if you are unsure about anything. Anecdotal accounts from other students may also be reassuring.

Tell us

If you were worried about undertaking a work placement, did your concerns make applying for work experience more difficult? Did you go ahead despite your worries and, if so, how did you deal with your anxieties once you started work? Tell us at finchandfafinski.com/get-in-touch or @ FinchFafinski on Twitter.

It is only natural to feel a degree of nervousness about trying something new in an unfamiliar setting but the only way to overcome this is to take the plunge by undertaking work experience and finding out for yourself what it is like to practise law. After all, unless you abandon your aim of practising law, you are going to have to set foot in a law firm for the first time at some point so it would be a good idea to do it as early as possible as this will help to familiarise you with legal practice and you will soon gain confidence in the professional environment.

Remember that vacation schemes exist to give students at exactly your stage of legal studies some experience of work within the legal profession. In other words, they are designed to be a supportive and informative experience rather than something that puts you off working in law forever. Careful thought is given to the work that you will be given to ensure that it is appropriate and you will have support and supervision at all times. It will be expected that you will need clear instructions and that you may need to ask questions so try not to worry that you will be lost and unable to work out what to do. It is impossible to outline the precise details of what you will be doing during a placement as each firm has its own approach but you could expect to do some or all of the following:

- Office-based work such as undertaking legal research, drafting documents, and completing legal forms
- Work with clients such as attending meetings, taking notes, and drafting correspondence
- Court-based work such as attending hearings, making notes, liaising with counsel, or other professionals such as expert witnesses or social workers
- Presentations on the organisation and work of the firm to give you an insight into its operation on a wider scale

- **Workshops or seminars** to enhance your practical skills such as advocacy, negotiation, client care, or presentation skills
- **Group activities** undertaken with other placement students such as working on a case together, creating a business plan, or putting together a report or presentation
- **Social events** to enable you to meet the various people who work at the firm: trainees, associates, partners, and administrative staff.

You may find an outline of the activities that make up the placement on the firm's website or be sent a schedule of activities once you are accepted on the vacation scheme.

In summary, vacation schemes have a great deal to offer in terms of structured work experience, insight into the operation of the legal profession, the opportunity to network and build up contacts as well as offering the possibility of a head start in training contract applications. Be aware that the application process is time-consuming and often involves answering challenging questions so start early in your second year (or third year if undertaking a four year degree) and give careful thought to the different ways that you can provide evidence of your aptitude for law and employability skills in your application.

Remember that you can take part in more than one vacation scheme: in fact, with careful planning and successful applications, you could fill the entire summer vacation with a series of placements at different law firms. If you aim to do this, it can be a good idea to create a diagram that shows the dates of the various placements that you have applied for so that you can see where gaps exist and to ensure that you do not end up being double booked. If you are going to aim to complete several placements, bear in mind that you need to add variety to your work experience portfolio so, once you have one or two placements confirmed, think about applying for others that differ in some way: size or location of the firm, area of practice, activities offered as part of the scheme etc. Remember also that some firms offer the opportunity to work overseas for some or all of the placement and that this can also add a point of interest to your CV that demonstrates your confidence in working in different environments.

....

I was really determined to get a place on a vacation scheme with one of the big City law firms. I wanted to know what legal practice was like in that sort of firm. and I did think that having an impressive firm on my CV would help me to stand out from other applicants when it came to training contract applications. I did a lot of research on the vacation schemes offered by various firms and created my own 'top twenty' placements to target. I resolved to write one application each day but it turned out to take me a bit longer than that at first as I was determined to get it right and some of the questions were really challenging and I knew that it was important to research the firm and find a way to show that I had done so in my application and that was not always easy. I made a point of finding a way to weave at least two points about the firm that were not taken from its website into my applications. My strategy paid off and I ended up with four offers, two of which unfortunately clashed with each other but, in any case, I did manage to fill my whole summer with work at three top law firms. One of these offered a fast-track into the interview stage of training contract applications for students who had completed the vacation scheme which was a bonus.

Jack, University of Leeds

....

Other work experience in a law firm

Not all law firms operate a vacation placement scheme but that does not mean that it is not possible to secure work experience with them by making a direct approach to the firm. As they do not operate such a structured scheme, smaller law firms can be more flexible in offering work experience at different times of the year for varying durations and may be amenable to an offer of help one day or even one afternoon a week on a regular basis.

If you want to work in a solicitor's firm that does not operate a vacation placement scheme, you will need to make a proactive approach to them requesting work experience. According to the Law Society's annual statistical report, there are 10,202 private practice law firms operating in England and Wales (as of 31 July 2011) which means that there are plenty of sources of work experience in solicitors' offices so, with a little patience and perseverance, you should be able to secure a placement.

Aside from learning more about the day-to-day operation of a law firm, gaining work experience during university gives you a wide range of transferable skills which can be really useful. Helping draft legal documents, learning to deal with clients, and even getting to grips with legal software are all things you will experience if you undertake work experience or summer placements at a law firm. On top of this, the interpersonal skills you pick up from working in this environment and the attention to detail you will develop are really useful in a wider context. Even if you choose to pursue a career in a non-legal sector, all of these skills are universally highly valued by employers.

Adam, Edinburgh University

Finding work in a law firm

The first step in making a speculative application for work experience is to identify a firm to approach. This should not be difficult as every solicitor, with the exception of those that operate a formal placement scheme, is a potential source of work experience. You may have preferences such as the location of the firm (taking into account where you will be living at the time and where you might reasonably travel each day) and the area of legal practice. Having considered these factors, it is a straightforward matter to search the Internet using keywords (for example, solicitors in Bournemouth practising criminal law) or to consult one of the databases of law firms that exist such as:

- www.lawsociety.org.uk/find-a-solicitor/
- www.waterlowlegal.com/directories/solicitors.php
- www.justicedirectory.co.uk.

Take time to make thoughtful and deliberate choices about the firms that you target for work experience rather than simply showering every firm in the local area with copies of your CV. Remember that you should assess the sufficiency of your work experience by its breadth and the extent to which it has enabled you to develop and demonstrate key employability skills rather than by its quantification. In other words, do not accumulate work experience for the sake of it but because it adds strength to your skills and experience portfolio in some way. This means that you should evaluate your work experience, looking for gaps and omissions and then target work experience opportunities that allow you to fill these gaps. For example, you might seek to work in different practice areas, to vary the size of firm in which you have worked, or to expand your skills by working with solicitors who specialise in alternative dispute resolution, asset recovery, or international shipping law. Make every speculative application with a purpose in mind and make this clear in your approach to the law firm as this will highlight the reason for your interest in the firm.

Practical advice: tailor your application

A speculative application should appear to have been written specifically for the firm to which it has been sent. Take the time and effort to research the firm and find out something about it that explains why you want to work with them: an area of law, an approach to practice, a complex or high profile case that they have handed, a particular solicitor that you have seen in action. Look at the firm's website to find out more about what they do and read the solicitor's profiles to see what area of law they practise and what cases they have handled recently and then try and find a link between the firm and your own interests and experience.

- I have undertaken several placements in criminal law firms but would really like to add to this experience by working with your firm due to many cases that you have handled involving witnesses with repressed memory syndrome. I read the article on these cases that was published on your website as part of my extended project in criminal evidence and would really appreciate the opportunity to work in a firm that has so much experience with this issue.

- Having completed work experience placements in City firms, I find myself increasingly disinclined to practise corporate law and drawn to the more personal work of the high street solicitor. In particular, I notice that your firm specialises in contested care proceedings cases and I have a real interest in this area of law due to my experiences last summer doing voluntary work in a children's home.

- I have a passionate interest in technology law and your firm is leading the way in its work with the use of intellectual property as a means of protecting software innovation. I would like to combine my interest in law and technology in my future career so would value the opportunity to work within a leading technology law firm.

Remember, you are more likely to be successful in your search for work experience if your speculative application makes it clear that you want to work for the firm in question for a reason rather than simply wanting any work experience that is available. The message that you should try to communicate is 'I want work experience with your firm' rather than 'I want work experience wherever I can find it'.

Tell us

If you made speculative applications, what did you write and were you successful? How many applications did you make and what was your success rate? Did you write letters or send emails? Tell us at finchandfafinski.com/get-in-touch or @FinchFafinski on Twitter.

Many students are reluctant to make speculative approaches to law firms in their quest for work experience and instead apply only for advertised opportunities, assuming that all firms who offer work experience will publicise information about this and that a formal application process will exist. This is not the case at all and a great many firms that do not operate a formal placement scheme or otherwise advertise that work experience is available are nonetheless happy to oblige if they are contacted with a request for work experience. In fact, it is only a very few law firms who have a blanket policy of refusing requests for work experience: most firms will try to accommodate students seeking work experience although some firms, generally smaller ones, are not able to do so on a regular basis. This is understandable. Law students, however keen and capable, cannot be left to work unsupervised when undertaking work experience and the business of providing supervision, explaining what needs to be done and checking work can be so time-consuming that it cannot be accommodated in a busy office. However, even if a firm does not offer work experience on a regular basis, your speculative application might be so impressive that they decide to make an exception or it may be that they are so busy at the time that your application arrives that they are in need of an extra pair of hands. So, in essence, it is always worth making speculative applications. Law firms that do not advertise work experience may still be prepared to offer some and there may be less competition for the opportunities available than is the case with the formal work placement schemes.

Another factor that deters many students from making speculative applications for work experience is a lack of understanding about various practical matters associated with making an unsolicited application:

- **How do you apply?** Is the best approach by letter, email, telephone call, or just dropping in to the law firm and asking in person? This is a difficult question, in many ways, and the answer depends upon the preferences of the person who you ask for work experience. Some solicitors would say that email is the medium of professional correspondence so should be used whereas others indicate that they are more likely to read and respond to a letter sent in the post. Equally, a telephone call or personal visit can work really well if the timing is right and you make a good impression but could be badly received if you call or arrive at a particularly busy or stressful moment. The sensible approach, then, would be to use a combination of methods. Why not combine postal and email approaches and see which works best for you? You could always make a follow up telephone call if you do not receive a reply after two weeks but mention in your letter or email that you intend to do so. Dropping into the firm on the off-chance that you encounter the right person at the right moment is probably a bit of an unpredictable method: if you really want to take a direct approach, then taking advantage of a chance meeting at court might be preferable (although your ability to produce a copy of your CV at the drop of a hat might raise a few eyebrows).

- **Who should you ask for work experience?** Is it the senior partner, the solicitor who you want to work with, or the person responsible for recruitment at the firm? Again, somewhat unhelpful, the correct answer here is also likely to vary from firm to firm. Some law firms have a dedicated person or team of people who deal with all aspects of recruitment including work experience whereas this function will be fulfilled by the partners in other firms. You want to be sure that your application reaches a person who has the power to make the decision about work experience so you should check the firm's website to see if it specifies a person responsible for recruitment. In the absence of this, telephone the firm's general enquiries number and ask for contact details for the person to whom requests for work experience should be directed. Make sure that you find out the person's name as well as their role within the firm: an application that starts 'Dear Senior Partner' or 'Dear Head of Human Resources' is not impressive because you could quite easily have discovered the name of the person who holds that position. You should also bear in mind that people are more likely to ignore a letter that turns up on their desk if it is addressed to Sir/Madam than they would if the letter was addressed to them by name.

- **What information should go into a speculative letter?** How much detail should you include and what sort of information? How long is too long and how short is too short? Let's deal with length first as that is a straightforward matter. One side of A4—one-and-a-half at most—is sufficient to capture the essential information. A speculative letter is not a summary of your academic achievements or an opportunity to outline career aspirations but a concise and to-the-point advertisement of your suitability for a short period of work experience in the firm. It should start with a statement of purpose, be followed by one paragraph that explains your interest in the firm and another which highlights the skills and experience that will enable you to make a contribution to the firm and conclude with your thanks and with any further details that might be pertinent such as whether or not you expect to be paid, when you are available, and how you can be contacted. An example of a speculative letter is provided in Figure 7.5.

You will find further examples of letters that have been sent successfully by students on the Online Resource Centre.

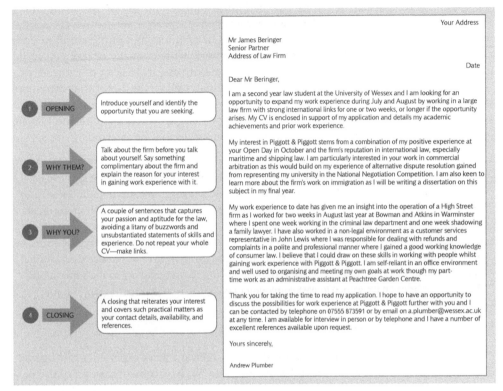

Figure 7.5 Speculative letter

- **What supporting documentation should be included?** Are you going to send a CV along with your speculative letter and, if so, how long should it be? And what about other documents like a transcript of your grades or a reference from previous work experience? The usual approach is to send a short (two to three page) CV that captures your qualifications, experience, and achievements. This should include the grades that you have achieved in your studies thus far obviating the need to include a transcript. Some students feel that the transcript provides substantiating evidence of their grades but most employers state that they prefer speculative applications to be kept short and easy to navigate without any unnecessary additional material. The same arguments apply to sending a reference with your application: many employers are just too busy to wade through pages of different information and will be more receptive to a short and to-the-point application that contains only essential information. However, if there is some defect in your profile that the reference addresses, it might be worth attaching a short open reference from a previous employer: for example, 'My grades so far have been in the 2.2 bracket but I have a far greater aptitude for the law in practice than I do for its academic study as the attached reference from Law Firm & Co indicates'. It can also be a way to strengthen your application if your previous speculative approaches have been unsuccessful. You will find further guidance on overcoming unsuccessful applications later in the chapter.

Hopefully, by addressing these common questions, you will feel more able to grasp the nettle and start to make some speculative approaches to law firms with the aim of securing work experience.

Treat your speculative application as a piece of marketing literature aimed at marketing you to a law firm as a potential employee. With this in mind, you need to ensure that your letter and the accompanying CV are polished, professional, and wholly free from errors. Remember that the ability to use language in an effective and accurate manner is essential for a solicitor so the misuse of language and errors in grammar and punctuation in your application suggest that either you do not know how to write correctly or that you could not be bothered to check your application before submitting it. Neither of these gives a positive impression to a prospective employer and may well be the factor that convinces the firm to discard your application. The employer's perspective on a poorly constructed application can be seen in the thoughts expressed by John Redwood MP in relation to the quality of applications for work experience and internships that he received:

> I have been sifting through CVs and application letters…Many of the ones I have been reading about have degrees. They send in CVs which start with similar paragraphs that they have been taught to write. They usually claim to be excellent at team working, brilliant communicators, and to offer good leadership. They are all highly motivated, enthusiastic, pro-active with strong organ-isational and problem solving skills. The rest of the CV sometimes belies the standard phrases of the opening. Some are unable to write a sentence. There are usually spelling and typing errors—understandable in the rush of everyday communication but glaring in a considered and formal document like a CV. One example produced the following second sentence to the application: 'I fill the experience I have gained in past employment will put me in good persian for this role'.

Sandwich placements

One way to ensure that you are guaranteed to gain relevant work experience during your degree is to select a course that includes one or more work placements as part of the pro-gramme of study.

- A thick sandwich course is one in which the student spends an entire year, usually the third, away from university in one or more work placements.
- A thin sandwich course involves two six-month placements with each placement taken in a separate year of study.

There are a number of advantages to undertaking a sandwich degree. Firstly, as already noted, it guarantees that you will have work experience at the end of your degree. Moreover, this is of a prolonged nature as you will work for at least six months, if not a year, in a single work environment thus getting a far greater insight into ordinary life in legal practice than is possible in a two-week placement. In fact, many students find it strange to return to university after their placement year as they are so used to working that they feel as if they are already qualified. A longer placement will ensure that you are given more responsibility and get far more experience at doing the job of a lawyer than would otherwise be possible. A further advantage is that universities offering a sandwich degree tend to find the placements for you thus removing the pressure on you to find your own work experience opportunities. Finally, this period of work in the law environ-ment offers wonderful networking opportunities as you meet other solicitors and barris-ters so you should build up some good contacts. You will get to know the people at your placement very well so should obtain a good reference that will support your application for training contracts and may even put yourself in the running for a training contract with your placement firm.

I spent a year working at Minter Ellison, one of the 'Big Six' law firms in Australia and it was the most amazing experience. I am actually quite a shy person so I really tried to challenge myself by applying to do my placement year halfway around the world in a country where I knew nobody and had no knowledge of the law. I can remember landing in Australia and thinking 'I must be mad' and there was just a little part of me that wanted to find the first flight back to England. But everyone was really friendly and I soon got in the swing of the work. The legal system is not dissimilar to our own and the law itself often works on similar principles so I was not as out-of-my-depth as I feared. It has done wonders for my confidence and it was always something that I was asked about at interview and I have no doubt at all that it was instrumental in me receiving offers of not just one but two training contracts!

Jenny, University of Leicester

Practical example: Work experience case study

The biggest dilemma for students is how to stand out. Employers want evidence that you can enter a job role and hit the ground running; good grades are not enough and this is particularly pertinent within law. I chose what is known as a sandwich course at Brunel University; a law degree that specifically incorporates work experience within a law firm, over two six-month periods, so that when I finished my degree I obtained an LLB with professional development.

Brunel has fostered a number of close links with the legal community in London, so finding a placement in London is relatively easy. You perfect your CV with the help of the careers team and then you register your interest with whatever firms take your fancy. Brunel has a list of employers ranging from high street solicitors to chambers willing to provide six-month placements, practising everything from criminal law to commercial law with some firms offering a generous salary and others seeking passionate students willing to work for free. As I was unable to secure a paid placement in London, I went in search of my own placement in Birmingham.

I already had links with the Birmingham legal community through work experience so I approached the criminal defence firm who had taken me on previously and pitched the following: A law student, who already knew the firm, had a good grasp of criminal law and better still was willing to work free of charge. With legal aid as it is free labour is welcome labour but a general willingness to pitch in where needed and contacts within a firm will go a long way too.

I spent six months at this firm working closely with the solicitors and with a set of chambers that the firm instructed exclusively. As an aspiring criminal barrister I had hit the jackpot; I attended everything from conferences with clients to week long trials with the offences ranging from theft to attempted murder. This placement gave me a unique insight into various types of advocacy at an early stage of my legal career.

The greatest benefit of this scheme? If you prove yourself, you will be given real responsibility which is something you will not gain whilst on a mini pupillage or vacation scheme. Brunel University ensure that any placement they authorise will include quality legal work; making a good cup of coffee is not included in the job descriptions. I represented the firm whilst in court meeting defendants and barristers and that sort of experience is invaluable. I drafted witness statements, proofs of evidence, submitted legal aid forms, took notes during trials to be used during closing speeches by counsel, and was responsible for my own caseload.

The experience I gained made studying criminal practice and litigation on the BPTC a lot more understandable as I had real experiences I could relate the material to. When it came to legal scholarship and pupillage interviews, the panels always wanted to know about my work placement and it made for a good talking point, gave me the opportunity to emphasise my practical experience in conjunction with my academic knowledge, and enabled me to demonstrate that I knew yet more hard work lay ahead.

My time at the criminal defence firm continues to be a focus in interviews and employers are often intrigued by the addition of 'with professional development' on my CV. Many of the skills that I have gained you simply cannot gain whilst on conventional work experience but are necessary for fee earning positions within legal firms. Firstly managing your own caseload: prospective employers will always want to know how many files you handled and this experience will make you incredibly employable. Following that is file management, working to strict court deadlines and procedure and working on files from inception to completion is something employers want to avoid having to train you in if possible.

Even basic skills such as already knowing how office telephones work, how to make a photocopier hole punch and staple documents, and being comfortable dealing with all manner of people in a professional setting enables an employer to sleep easy and have confidence in the fact that not only do you have experience of the more complex processes but you also have the basics down to a fine art.

Most of all this type of experience shows your dedication to law and will make entering the legal market a little less formidable.

Lyndsay, Brunel University

Voluntary work

Any work undertaken without remuneration falls under the heading of voluntary work but the focus in this chapter is on voluntary work with a legal emphasis. There is a section further on in the chapter on pro bono work. This is a particular form of voluntary work in which legal advice and/or representation by a solicitor or barrister is provided free of charge to individuals and organisations that cannot afford it but there is other voluntary work that touches base with law and the legal system that you might also like to consider as a means of gaining valuable work experience and strengthening your employability skills. In the sections that follow, there will be a consideration of work of various kinds within the legal system or involving legal advice or issues. This is a guide only and you should remember that there are many other opportunities available. If you undertake other kinds of voluntary work with no hint of law about them, you will find a discussion of how to use this to strengthen your skills portfolio in Chapter 5.

Practical advice: voluntary work

Volunteering can be a good way to gain law-based work experience and strengthen key employability skills so it would be a useful addition to your CV. It also indicates that you are the sort of person who will expend time and effort on an activity that does not carry a financial reward: something that is of particular importance given the emphasis on corporate social responsibility. You might want to check what activities a particular law firm or chambers is involved with prior to applying to them and see if you can tie your own voluntary work in with their corporate social responsibility agenda.

I believe work experience provides the opportunity to develop a multitude of transferable skills such as communication, time management, professionalism, and learning to adapt to a goal centred environment. For me, with my work in a children's charity, not only have I developed the above skills (particularly strong non-verbal communication skills) but I have also developed the skill of understanding my own personal approach to goals and how I individually manage situations. This is important as it means I can structure my work accordingly (as far as I am able) to ensure quality and efficiency on all my tasks.

Catie, Southampton University

Citizens Advice Bureau

The Citizens Advice Bureau (CAB) is a charitable organisation that provides free advice on legal and financial matters to members of the public. Some of the issues that it encounters on a regular basis involve giving advice about managing debt, accessing benefits, and dealing with disputes with landlords and employers. It also advises on consumer complaints and problems associated with immigration and asylum. As you can see from this, a great deal of the work of that CAB is legal in nature so it is an excellent opportunity for you to gain experience in dealing with legal disputes thus strengthening many of the professional skills that are important in legal practice. For example, you may be involved in drafting a letter or court documents for a client or need to engage in legal research to inform the advice given to a client. You might negotiate with a landlord on behalf of a client or use your advocacy skills to represent the client's interests at a hearing to determine their entitlement to benefit. As you will be dealing with members of the public who have come to the CAB for help, this will also give you experience in customer service: a very important skill that students often struggle to demonstrate to prospective employers. There may also be opportunities to develop numeracy skills as many of the cases involve debt management.

- Have a look at the Citizens Advice Bureau website for further information and details of the training programme for volunteers: **www.citizensadvice.org.uk/index/join-us.htm**.

Appropriate adult service

The role of an appropriate adult was created by the Police and Criminal Evidence Act 1984 as an additional means of safeguarding the rights of children and vulnerable adults in police custody. It is not a substitute for legal advice and you would not be expected or permitted to give legal advice but instead to assist the person who has been arrested to understand what is happening and to support them during the period of their detention and questioning. It will be important that you are familiar with the rights of a detained person (these are set out in the Codes of Practice attached to the Police and Criminal Evidence Act 1984) and that you understand the duty of the police to treat the suspect in a fair manner. You may also need to facilitate communication between the police and the person who has been arrested, be present whilst the suspect is searched, fingerprinted, or during any identification procedure as well as when the police review decisions about detention or charge the suspect.

- Have a look at the National Appropriate Adult Network website for further details including a map that will show whether opportunities are available in your area: **www.appropriateadult.org.uk**.

Youth offender panels

People under the age of 17 who commit offences that will not justify the imposition of a custodial sentence are referred by the courts to youth offender panels as part of the restorative justice initiative. This consists of a member of the youth offending team and two volunteers from the local community. The panel acts as a neutral party and discusses the offence with the offender, their parents and, wherever possible, the victim with a view to formulating a suitable remedy that becomes part of a contract to ensure that the offender makes reparation to the victim or the wider community and addresses the causes of their offending behaviour.

The Youth Justice Board offers training for volunteers which consists of a three-day foundation programme focusing on young people and crime followed by four days of training that explains the work of youth offender panels and the role of panel members. The role will give you a good insight into the operation of restorative justice as well as a sound knowledge of issues surrounding young offenders. You will need to be an objective and balanced listener and have the ability to formulate a solution to the problem that suits both the offender and the victim.

- You will find more details of the work of youth offenders panels and the training programme on the Youth Justice Board website: **www.justice.gov.uk/youth-justice/ workforce-development/working-with-volunteers/training-for-volunteers**.

Victim support

Victim support is a national charity that provides free confidential support and advice for victims of crime and their families as well as running a witness service at every criminal court to support those who are called to give evidence in criminal cases. There are a number of roles available for volunteers and there is a good general training package for volunteers plus the opportunity to undergo further specialist training in areas such as sexual offences, hate crimes, and homicide. There is no requirement that volunteers have any legal knowledge but the role involves knowledge of the operation of the criminal justice system. The opportunity to work at a court as part of the witness service might be particularly useful for law students and give rise to some useful networking opportunities.

- Details of the work of victim support volunteers and the application process are available on their website: **www.victimsupport.org.uk/Get-involved/Volunteering/ Being-a-volunteer**.

Prisoner advice service

There are over 80,000 people in prison in England and Wales. The prisoner advice service is a charity committed to ensuring that these prisoners have access to legal advice and are kept informed as to their rights whilst they are in prison. Volunteers support the work of employed caseworkers and solicitors in communicating with prisoners and advising on penal law, criminal law, and human rights issues. This work provides a good insight into the operation of the custodial system as well as an opportunity to see the law in action.

- You will find further details of the work of the Prisoners Advice Service and volunteering opportunities on their website: **www.prisonersadvice.org.uk/volunteer.html**.

Magistracy

You may have been to a magistrates' court to watch a case or whilst undertaking work experience with a criminal solicitor and so seen magistrates in action but did you realise that there is no reason why you, as a law student, should not sit as a magistrate? Magistrates are ordinary members of the community with no legal knowledge who are trained to adjudicate in criminal cases that are not sufficiently serious to be heard in the Crown Court. Anyone aged 18 to 65 can apply to be a magistrate but they are particularly keen to appoint younger people. Magistrates sit in panels of three so the decision-making responsibility is shared and there is a good programme of training and preparation for new members plus the support of a more experienced mentor for the first two years. This is a great opportunity for law students to gain familiarity with the workings of the criminal justice system and to observe the work undertaken by solicitors in a magistrates' court.

- There is further information about the work of magistrates and the qualities required in volunteers plus details of the application process on the government website: **www.gov. uk/become-magistrate/what-magistrates-do**.

Finding voluntary work

If you are interested in voluntary work, you may already have a type of work or particular voluntary organisation in mind in which case it is likely that you have sufficient information to investigate whether opportunities exist. If, however, you have no prior interests or associations with particular work or organisations then you can use one of the voluntary work resources that will enable you to explore what volunteering opportunities are available.

There are a number of organisations that exist to allow organisations looking for volunteers and people interested in voluntary work to find each other. Do-It is one of the leading volunteering websites that has details of over one million different voluntary work opportunities both in this country and overseas (**www.do-it.org.uk**).

Do-It has a searchable database that will help you find opportunities based upon a combination of the location, the nature of the work, and your availability as well as a wealth of informative resources to help you to understand more about the types of voluntary work available.

Practical example: finding voluntary work

One of the categories of voluntary work available through Do-It is law and legal support. This would always be worth investigating as it might turn up some interesting law-based opportunities that you had not previously considered. For example, if you were looking for law-related voluntary work in the Reading area, you would have the following options:

- Working as a mentor to support sex offenders in the community on a one-to-one in partnership with the police and probation service

- Sitting as a panel member on the Thames Valley local security improvement panel that meets quarterly and examines cases relating to racially aggravated and religious crime, homophobic, and disability hate crime

- Working on the front counter of a police station where you would deal with enquiries over the phone or face-to-face, receive and record documents, and undertake a range of administrative activities

- Acting as a trustee of the Citizen's Advice Bureau therefore undertaking a legal responsibility for the organisation and running of a local branch, ensuring its objectives are met and its financial position is sound.

Any of these would make a useful addition to your portfolio of work experience.

⚫ Think about how you would use each of these four opportunities to demonstrate key employability skills to prospective employers. You will see our thoughts on this on the Online Resource Centre.

Do not feel that you have to find voluntary work of a legal nature in order to enhance your skills portfolio. Remember that almost every activity that you can think of is regulated by the law one way or another so there will be an opportunity to find a legal perspective in most forms of voluntary work if you look for one. Alternatively, you might find a way to carry out non-law work in a legal setting or simply undertake work that has no link with the law whatsoever and instead highlight the skills involved, especially those which you have had little opportunity to develop during your studies. The quotations that follow give you an insight into how students have used their voluntary work to impress employers:

- **Finding a legal perspective.** I volunteered at an animal rescue centre. It was quite a small local charity and I really enjoyed the work. One day, knowing that I was a law student, one of the trustees asked me some questions about charity law and the way that it worked that led to me preparing a paper for the board of trustees about their legal duties. It was strange because I hadn't enjoyed trust law when I studied it but putting together a paper for the trustees really brought the subject alive and made me realise its real-world significance. So I had an unexpected opportunity to use the law and I was able to emphasise this on my CV.

- **Non-law work in a legal setting.** I was looking for voluntary work that would give me a break from law and my studies and would make use of my skills as a musician but then I found something that combined the two and I ended up doing music therapy and song writing workshops in an immigration detention centre. Not only was it an amazing experience, it was something that I got asked about a lot at interviews, including the one for my Bar scholarship, which was successful, so I think it really caught the interest of people reading my applications.

- **Emphasising the skills involved in non-law work.** I am passionate about old buildings and worked as a heritage volunteer for a week each summer when I was at university. I still had plenty of time left for legal work experience and I felt that it gave me an opportunity to show that I was a well-rounded person with plenty of interests besides the law. On my CV, I emphasised how I learned to work well with others and lead a small team on a restoration project as well as the importance of being methodical and able to work without supervision so that my interest had some resonance to working life.

Tell us

Did you undertake any voluntary work? Did it involve the law or was it an unrelated area of work? How did you use it on your CV and in job applications? Were employers interested? Tell us at finchandfafinski.com/get-in-touch or @FinchFafinski on Twitter.

Pro bono work

The phrase 'pro bono' refers to work undertaken by professionals who do not charge a fee for their services. It originates from the Latin phrase pro bono *publico* which means 'for the public good' as the public is benefitted by the availability of free services that they need but could not otherwise afford. In relation to lawyers, pro bono refers to legal advice and representation undertaken free of charge. Much of the pro bono legal work in England and Wales is coordinated by the National Pro Bono Centre which is a 'hub' for pro bono charities such as LawWorks and the Bar Pro Bono Unit.

- **www.nationalprobonocentre.org.uk/**
- **www.lawworks.org.uk/**

- www.barprobono.org.uk/
- www.thefru.org.uk/.

The work of each of these organisations and the volunteering opportunities that they offer to law students will be considered in the sections that follow. There will also be a discussion of other pro bono opportunities such as those arranged through your university.

LawWorks

LawWorks is a charitable organisation that provides free legal advice to individuals and community groups who cannot afford to pay but who do not qualify for Legal Aid. It is the leading pro bono organisation for solicitors and has links with over 100 law firms and organisations with a significant in-house legal department such as Aviva and Tesco. By and large, LawWorks coordinates pro bono opportunities for qualified solicitors but there is a section on the website that lists volunteering opportunities that are open to students:

- **www.lawworks.org.uk/current-student-volunteering-vacancies**.

LawWorks is keen to encourage law students to get involved with pro bono work and has a separate branch devoted to this: **www.studentprobono.net**. This provides help and support for student pro bono projects within universities. You can use the Student Pro Bono website to find out what is happening in your own university or to get inspiration from schemes in operation at other institutions if you wanted to set up your own pro bono project.

Bar Pro Bono Unit

The Bar Pro Bono Unit provides legal advice from barristers by acting as a clearing house that matches individuals and groups in need of legal advice but unable to afford it with a barrister with appropriate expertise. Although it does not offer opportunities for student volunteers to get involved with case work, there are a number of ways that you can participate in the work of the Bar Pro Bono Unit thus gaining valuable experience and demonstrating your commitment to working within the legal profession.

- **Administrative work.** The unit has some limited volunteering opportunities for students in an administrative capacity. This would enable you to demonstrate your skills in organisation and planning and give you a valuable insight into the 'behind the scenes' workings of the legal profession. These roles are based in the London office and requires volunteers who can commit time during working hours. You can register your interest for this role on the Bar Pro Bono Unit website.

- **Fund raising.** The unit organises the Law School Challenge in which teams of five students compete to raise the most money for the unit. The winner is the team that raises the most money and the prize is an audience with a judge, lunch at one of the Inns of Court, and visits to a city law firm and the pro bono centre. There is also a prize for the most creative approach to fund-raising. There are some great networking opportunities for the winning team but all participants could use this as a way of demonstrating their entrepreneurial spirit and to highlight skills in team working, organisation, leadership, verbal communication, and decision-making.

- **Bar in the community.** This is a match-making service that brings together solicitors, barristers, and law students wishing to undertake voluntary work with organisations that are in need of help. It is organised by region and covers a wide range of organisations seeking assistance of various kinds so you can be sure to find something that suits your expertise, skills, and interests. Not all of the work is legal in nature but remember that you are seeking to develop your transferable skills so do not be deterred from a volunteering opportunity that has no legal content provided that it offers an opportunity to strengthen your skills portfolio.

Free Representation Unit

The Free Representation Unit (FRU) provides legal advice and representation for individuals at tribunals and in appeals against a tribunal decision, mainly in the areas of employment law and in relation to decisions involving social security. Volunteers are given training and, under supervision, undertake responsibility for the entire management of a case from initial interview to tribunal representation and all the stages in between thus offering a really great opportunity to develop a full range of professional skills.

Students are accepted as volunteers provided they are able to travel to London regularly and are at an appropriate stage of their legal education, which varies according to whether you wish to train to deal with employment or social security cases:

* Social security volunteers must either be in the third year of an LLB, have reached May in the penultimate year of an LLB, or be a GDL student
* Employment volunteers must either be an LLB graduate, have reached May in the final year of an LLB, or be an LLM or GDL student.

FRU operates a four-stage recruitment process involving attendance at a training day, a test based upon interpretation of a statute and its application to a factual scenario, observation of a tribunal, and an office induction session. There are examples of the test on the FRU website: **www.thefru.org.uk/volunteers/tests**.

Once accepted as a volunteer, you would be allocated a client and take responsibility for the entire conduct of the case so you would interview the client, take instruction, liaise with the other party or their representative, negotiate settlements, draft witness statements and other documents, and represent the client at tribunal. In essence, this would give you hands-on experience of work within the legal profession and an opportunity to develop skills in customer service as well as a whole host of professional skills such as drafting, negotiation, and advocacy that can be quite hard to demonstrate within the confines of academic study.

In-house schemes

A number of universities have established their own pro bono schemes or law clinics, often working in conjunction with local solicitors and barristers, so make sure you find out what is available at your own institution and get involved if such a scheme exists. If there is no in-house pro bono scheme, perhaps you could think about exploring the possibility of establishing one as this could be used to demonstrate any number of employability skills—leadership, organisation, decision-making, planning, and problem solving—as well as giving you access to the benefits of taking part once the scheme was up-and-running.

Practical example: Cardiff University pro bono centre

There is an excellent pro bono scheme at Cardiff University that works with local law firms to offer a range of volunteering opportunities to its students that includes working at an asylum centre in Cardiff, providing advice on healthcare issues as part of the NHS Continuing Healthcare Scheme, and working with the Welsh Rugby Union to provide free legal advice to Welsh rugby clubs.

Marshalling

Marshalling (sometimes called shadowing) describes the process of following a member of the legal profession as they go about their working life and is usually used to refer to sitting with a judge in court. This will be in the county court, Crown Court, or the High Court: it is not usually possible to shadow Court of Appeal or Supreme Court judges. Most judges who are prepared to be marshalled by students will be quite keen to explain things to you and will try to involve you with as much of their work as is possible in the context of the case. You may read skeleton arguments and case summaries, hear submissions being made in court, and discuss proceedings with the judge. Some judges will comment on litigation techniques that you have observed, explain the procedural intricacies of the case, and outline what they expect to happen to the case in the future. All-in-all, it is a very informative experience.

Practical advice: marshalling a judge

Try to ensure that your work experience includes at least one example of marshalling as this gives you a view of the operation of the legal system from a different perspective. Do not forget that you are not limited to marshalling in this jurisdiction: why not try to sit with a judge in a court in a different country if, for example, you have a work placement abroad or even if you visit another country on holiday.

Tell us

Tell us about your marshalling experience. How did you go about getting it and how did it enhance your employability skills? Contact us at finchandfafinski.com/get-in-touch or @FinchFafinski on Twitter.

....

I undertook some judicial marshalling at both Chester Civil Justice Centre and also at Nottingham Crown Court. I was able, during the work experience, to view a number of very different civil and criminal hearings from full trials to interlocutory applications. I found that sitting with experienced Circuit Judges allowed me to become familiar with the processes involved in a number of different hearings. I also found that sitting with the Judge gives the opportunity to hear a professional, unbiased, and knowledgeable opinion from somebody in possession of all the facts. I also found it useful as Judges can give their opinion on the future of the legal professions and also give you hints and tips as to the best way to put forward an argument in Court, they were particularly good after a hearing at pointing out the techniques of advocates which they found most convincing. Some of the best career advice I got was from Judges.

Josh, law graduate

....

Once you are on the BPTC, you should find it relatively easy to get some shadowing experience as the Inns of Court tend to make arrangements for this and, in any case, you will have many opportunities to meet judges at events at your Inn so could make your own arrangements with them directly. You may also find that your BPTC provider organises marshalling opportunities for its students so keep a look out for information about this.

If you want to experience the legal proceedings from a judicial perspective whilst still undertaking your undergraduate studies, you will probably have to make your own arrangements to do so. There are a number of ways that you could do this:

- **Contact the court.** Write a letter or email to the clerk of the court or the court manager at the court you wish to attend (one that is not in a university town is less likely to be overwhelmed by requests) and ask if there are any marshalling opportunities available. You could also go to the court and ask about this in person.

- **Make use of any contacts.** Many lecturers are also practitioners or have been in the past so ask if they know any judges who might be amenable to offering you some marshalling experience. Equally, think about whether any of your family or friends has a connection with a judge that you can use to ask for experience. If you happen to encounter a judge at a work placement or, for example, if they come to judge a moot, you can ask them directly. Never be afraid to ask: the worst that can happen is that they will say 'no' and they might say 'yes'.

- **Attend court and watch a case.** Make a note of the name of the judge and write directly to them (care of the court) explaining why you found the case interesting and what it was about their comments that grabbed your attention and asking if you might be able to sit with them for a day (or two) in the future.

Obviously, any written contact with a judge, their clerk, or other court personnel must be meticulously polite and scrupulously well written, grammatical, and free from errors. Remember that this letter is marketing you to the recipient so make sure that it does a good job. Equally, if you are fortunate in securing some marshalling experience, remember that the court is a professional environment and dress (and behave) accordingly. This includes addressing the judge as Your Honour (or other appropriate title according to the judge's status) unless you are explicitly invited to address them otherwise.

Making the most of work experience

If you have been able to obtain work experience, make sure you make the most of the opportunity that it offers. Even if it is not the sort of work experience that you really wanted, remember that it will still be an opportunity to develop your skills, network, and see the legal profession in action. The experience that you gain on this placement may help you to secure the one that you really want next time.

Create a favourable impression

It is important that you leave your work placement having made a positive impression on everyone that you have encountered. You want to leave the firm having made people think that you are exactly the sort of person that they want to work for them in the future, either on a further work placement, as a trainee, or far in the future once you are qualified. Moreover, you should leave the placement with at least one person who will act as a referee for you to support your future applications. Having a good reference from a work placement will help you to get future work placements as employers can see from the get go that you are not going to be a nuisance and might actually make a positive contribution.

Practical example: making an impression

We asked solicitors and barristers for examples of things that students had done during a work placement that created a particularly favourable impression. They also provided some good examples of things that students on work experience should not do:

- I like students who show a genuine enthusiasm for the work we do. Some of them set about even the most mundane tasks with excitement whereas others act as if you are putting upon them if you ask them to send a fax.

- If I ever see a student checking their watch, I send them home so that they can do whatever it is that they would rather be doing than being at work. If they come back the next day with a better attitude then that is fine otherwise I end their placement early. I am too busy to waste time with people who are not committed to making the most of their placement with us.

- Students should be presentable, polite, and prepared to work. A good level of initiative is handy as there isn't the time to guide them through every step of the work that we give them.

- The most impressive students are the ones who have got into the mind-set of a lawyer and do more than they are asked. Delivering good work is a given, but the most impressive will be thinking about clients, communicating, meeting deadlines, and going out of their way to get to know people around the firm.

- I remember a student who would email me every evening with a short summary of what he had done that day and any questions he had about the day's work. It always ended with an invitation for me to point out anything that he had done wrong or could have done better and asked if there was anything that I'd like him to prepare or read up on for the next day. I was hugely impressed by his methodical approach to work and his determination to really learn and improve his performance.

- I was most impressed by a student who turned up on the first day to find us in the midst of a crisis. I managed to point him towards a desk, show him the facilities and give him a two sentence summary of what the problem was before dashing off to a meeting. He joined us shortly afterwards bringing a tray of coffee and a notepad. He stayed unobtrusively for an hour or so before disappearing. I found him two hours later glued to his computer screen and expected him to be fiddling with email or something but he was actually reading up on the area of law that prompted our crisis as it was unfamiliar to him and he wanted to be able to understand our discussions.

- My most overwhelming memory of a student on work experience was not a good one. A young lady who scowled a lot and inexplicably refused to take her coat off at all on the first day and refused to photocopy a document on the basis that she was 'here to learn how to be a solicitor not to do secretarial work'. I am a patient man but I eventually gave up on the third day when we were in court and I had to collect her at the end of the day from the coffee shop where she'd been reading a magazine because there was nothing for her to do while I was in action in the courtroom.

Be proactive in finding tasks

It is likely that you will be assigned to work with one particular person who will supervise your work and allocate tasks to you but do not sit around doing nothing if you complete your work and your supervisor is not available to give you more work to do. Ask other people to see if there is anything that you can do to help them with their work. It can help if you are specific about the timeframe that you have available so that they understand what sort of work you could undertake. For example, you might say 'Mr X has been held up in court for the rest of the day and I've finished drafting the document that he wanted so is there anything that I could do for you for the rest of the afternoon?'.

Practical advice: finishing tasks

One of the things that students often say worries them about work experience is knowing what to do when they finish a particular task. Tackle the problem before it occurs by asking your supervisor how they would like you to fill any spare time:

- What would you like me to do when I've finished this?
- Are there any general tasks such as filing or copying that I can do if I am at a loose end?
- Should I offer to help anyone else in particular if I complete my work and you are not available?
- Are there any areas of law that I should research for you if I find myself with spare time?
- How would you like me to occupy my time if I finish the work you have given me and you are not around to ask?

If nobody has any work for you, find some for yourself. Check through what you have already done and make sure it is perfect and then do some further research on the law relevant to a case that you are working on or read the previous day's judgments from the Court of Appeal, perhaps preparing a case note on any that seem relevant to the work of your supervisor or others working in the firm. Do something so that your time is occupied with relevant work. Under no circumstances should you start sending personal emails, surfing the net, or updating your Facebook page!

Keep your skills portfolio in mind

All work experience is useful but try to ensure that you maximise its value to you by keeping an eye on the skills that you possess and have already demonstrated and the skills that you still need to develop. Make sure that you have a clear idea of areas where you need to focus your attention and try to target work experience opportunities that will enable you to build on hitherto undemonstrated skills.

- If you have not had an opportunity to demonstrate numeracy skills, try to obtain work experience in a financial or associated environment. Perhaps you could target insolvency practitioners or apply to HM Revenue & Customs for a work placement.
- If you have not yet had much experience of litigation, target work placements in areas of practice that involve a high degree of court work such as criminal law and family law. Alternatively, see if there is any work experience available that will enable you to attend tribunal hearings: employment law, immigration, and social security law are good areas here.

Practical advice: list your skills

Check to see which of the employability skills you can demonstrate by means of work experience. Make a list of your work experience and think carefully about the extent to which each placement gave you an opportunity to develop each of the employability skills that you need to be able to demonstrate to employers. Remember that you need to be able to point to specific examples of the skills in operation so jot down particular activities that provide supporting evidence. This will help you to see which skills you still need to be able to demonstrate so that you can target work experience accordingly.

Ask for feedback

It can be difficult for you to know whether or not you are doing a good job because you have so little experience of the workplace so be sure to ask your supervisor, or anyone else who gives you a task, for feedback. Always check that you have completed every task to their satisfaction, asking them to give you an opportunity to rectify it if it is not satisfactory or requesting that they show you how to improve it.

Employers do have fairly high expectations of law students so you should also ask for general feedback on your performance from your supervisor at regular intervals: is the speed of your work satisfactory, are you making too many mistakes, is there anything that you need to improve or do differently? It is important that you find out what is wrong and that you try to put it right. This may mean that you need to accept criticism. Try not to get defensive or upset if the feedback that you receive is negative. Nobody is trying to hurt your feelings: they are trying to help you to understand how you could improve your performance and develop the skills that you need to practise the law. Of course, they may do this in a way that is a bit blunt or tactless but remember that they have nonetheless still taken the time to try and help you to improve. The best way to deal with negative feedback is to thank the person giving it to you and assure them that you will address their concerns. You should then check again in a few days' time to see if they have noticed an improvement.

It is very easy to say 'thank you for pointing that out. I didn't realise that I was working so slowly but I'll certainly try and speed up now that I know what you expect'—you can always cry at home later or rant to your friends over a drink!

Practical advice: references

Ask for a reference after every piece of work experience to build up a selection of different referees. You can then select the ones that are most suited to subsequent vacancies. If you are struggling to get more work experience, ask for an open reference from a previous placement and attach it to your applications.

Get involved

Work experience is a networking opportunity as well as a chance for you to gain an insight into the workings of the legal profession. Make sure that you talk to as many people as possible and that you leave them with a good impression: ask questions about their work and seek their advice whilst being careful not to make too many demands on their time. By and large, people like it when others are interested in them so asking questions, particularly work-related ones, can be a good way of getting to know people working at the firm. One of the skills that employers want prospective employees to possess is the ability to get on with others and to integrate smoothly within an existing team so use your work experience as an opportunity to develop and demonstrate this skill.

Talk to people at all levels—partners, salaried lawyers, trainees, and paralegals—and find out what goes on in different departments so that you can build up a picture of the firm that goes beyond your own direct experience. Remember, just as the firm is evaluating you to see if you would be a good investment as a trainee, so you are assessing whether the firm would be a supportive and challenging place to undergo your training. With this in mind, you should get involved with any social activities that are going on as it will give you the chance to get to know people on a less formal basis and it is a further opportunity for them to get to know you.

Keep a record of your work

Remember that you are undertaking work experience to help you to secure a training contract or pupillage in the future so it would be a good idea to keep a detailed record of the work that you do so that you can have this to hand when completing applications. It will be useful to get into the habit of doing this every day so that there is less chance that you will forget details of your work. Take particular care to record specific tasks undertaken and areas of law that you have encountered.

In terms of your future employability, it would be useful to tie your work experience in with your skills audit so look on a regular basis to see what links you can make between the work you are doing and the skills that are valued by prospective employers. This can also help to remind you of the need to ensure that you maximise the benefit of your work experience: if you see that you are not gaining any experience of a particular skill that you had hoped to strengthen, you could make a specific enquiry about whether there is any work available that would give you an opportunity to do so. If no such opportunities exist, you can try to target work experience in the future that will enable you to fill this gap in your skills portfolio.

WHERE NEXT?

You cannot have failed to have noticed that this chapter is rather long. However, the justification for its length is that work experience is a very important topic and there was a lot of advice that we wanted to impart about it, particular as it is something that is a cause for concern for many students. Hopefully you will now have a much clearer idea of the different sorts of work experience that you could undertake, what they are likely to involve, and where you would go about finding opportunities to do them. If we were to distil the entire chapter down into three pieces of advice, it would be these:

- Do not let your understandable anxiety about going into a strange environment hold you back from applying for work experience. It is the best way to find out what solicitors and barristers actually do on a daily basis and your skills and confidence will grow as a result. But you do have to take that first step. Why not follow Jenny's example (see earlier) and apply to do something that frightens you? Jumping in at the deepest possible end can be a really good way to overcome your nerves because everything that you do thereafter seems easy by comparison. Alternatively, make it easy for yourself by thinking of the least threatening type of work experience possible and using that as a starting point to build up to more challenging things.

- It is never too late to start looking for work experience but make a decision not to delay any longer. We were serious when we said that you should start today—that advice applies whether today is the first day of your degree or you are reading this chapter on the morning of your graduation. So make a plan and start putting it into action.
- Be persistent. There are a lot of law students looking for work experience so be prepared to stick with it in the face of fierce competition. You might find it useful to look at some of the other chapters in this book for more advice on ways that you can strengthen your skills portfolio and make your application for work experience the one that really stands out.

Negotiation skills

19

INTRODUCTION

The focus of this chapter is negotiation which is a method of alternative dispute resolution that seeks to resolve the dispute without the need for litigation. This chapter will provide an introduction to the skills needed to prepare for and conduct an effective negotiation including the research process and different negotiation styles. It will also cover the sorts of problem that can arise during negotiation and outline a range of strategies that can be used to overcome them. In essence, it is a step-by-step introduction for those with no previous negotiation experience as well as a source of advice for the more experienced negotiator. The chapter will make use of a range of examples to demonstrate the skills involved in negotiation.

The role of alternative dispute resolution has increased dramatically in recent years with approximately 90 per cent of civil and family disputes settled by negotiation or mediation rather than in the courtroom. It plays a role in the lives of most legal professionals and the ability to conduct an effective negotiation that reaches a settlement which is acceptable to both parties is an important legal skill. It is increasingly common for negotiation to feature in the lives of undergraduate law students, as well as those on the LPC and BPTC, either as an extra-curricular activity or as part of the skills programme that is embedded within the curriculum. Participation in negotiation will give you a feel of how the law operates in practice as opposed to limiting your experience to 'law on paper' and it demonstrates a commitment to the development of legal skills that should strengthen your curriculum vitae.

LEARNING OUTCOMES

After studying this chapter, you will be able to:

- Appreciate the role of negotiation in professional practice and have some insight into skills necessary to conduct an effective negotiation

- Analyze a negotiation scenario and extrapolate information that provides insight into the aims and interests of the client

- Engage in preparation and planning for the negotiation which includes detailed research into the legal and factual issues

- Open the negotiation in a professional manner and establish a workable agenda of issues that need to be addressed during the negotiation

- Deal with each of the issues in an effective and ethical manner, eliciting information from the other team and asking questions to clarify areas of uncertainty

- Engage in critical reflection of the success of the negotiation and your performance in a way that enables you to use the experience as an opportunity for skills development

19.1 About negotiation

The courts are keen to encourage parties to a dispute to seek alternative means of resolution without using the ordinary civil court system wherever possible. In addition to the courts and tribunals system, there are a number of other less formal mechanisms that may be employed: arbitration, mediation, and conciliation.

In November 2008 the Master of the Rolls, Sir Anthony Clarke, commissioned a report to review the costs of civil litigation. Jackson LJ was appointed to lead the review and to examine in detail the rules and principles governing costs in civil litigation. The final report was published in January 2010 and contained a number of wide-ranging recommendations. Amongst these is the recommendation that a 'serious campaign' should be undertaken to ensure that both lawyers and judges fully understand how all forms of alternative dispute resolution (ADR) work and the benefits it can bring. Jackson suggests that a 'handbook for ADR' should be prepared for use by clients and as a training guide for lawyers and the judiciary, along with a simple and clear brochure to educate the public and small businesses about ADR.

At the heart of ADR is the desire to reach a negotiated settlement: negotiation, therefore, is the process by which (usually) two parties with an interest in the same issue seek to reach an agreement that is acceptable to both sides. This may be done directly but is frequently done via lawyers. It can take place by telephone, in writing, or by email but is usually conducted face-to-face. Distance negotiations give less opportunity to interpret and respond to visual cues but that distance can be preferable when dealing with complex or emotional issues. Many negotiations use combined methods; for example, an initial meeting at which the issues are introduced and explored, followed by an exchange of written communications and a final face-to-face negotiation to finalize the details of the agreement.

Agreement between the parties is the essence of negotiation. Without agreement, there is not settlement, unlike arbitration where a third party is able to impose an outcome on the parties, making it more akin to litigation. Mediation is more similar to negotiation except that, rather than the face-to-face oppositional process that characterizes negotiation, proceedings are controlled by a mediator who coordinates and facilitates the discussion. Although mediators are objective, they are able to introduce issues for discussion whereas parties to negotiation have direct control over which issues are discussed.

Negotiations can occur at any stage in the proceedings and can feature in most types of dispute. Even in criminal law, there is scope for negotiation prior to court proceedings as representatives of the defendant can explore the possibilities for withdrawing or altering the charges for the CPS.

In recognition of the importance of negotiation as a legal skill, there is a national negotiation competition each year which is open to teams of undergraduate and postgraduate students and is organized by the Centre for Effective Dispute Resolution.[1]

---

1. You can find out more about the negotiation competition and the work of CEDR more generally by visiting their website at <http://www.cedr.com>.

19.1.1 Types of negotiation

It is generally accepted that there are two main types of negotiation (although the terminology used to describe these categories varies) (see Figure 19.1).

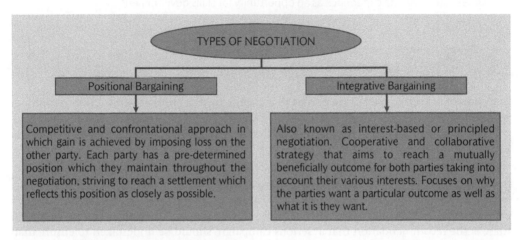

Figure 19.1 Positional and integrative bargaining

19.1.1.1 Positional bargaining

This approach is best deployed in situations where the issue is purely financial, there are no other issues to take into account, and no need to preserve amicable relations between the parties.

For Example:

Mark damaged two panels of his neighbour's fence beyond repair and agrees to pay for replacements. Dawn, his neighbour, maintains that Mark should pay for the entire fence (ten panels) to be replaced as two new panels would stand out and spoil the look of the garden. She also demands top quality panels (£50 each) whilst Mark proposes to provide average quality panels (£30 each). Dawn can fit the panels herself and there are no delivery costs.

The sum payable could be calculated four different ways:

- Two panels of average quality £60
- Two panels of high quality £100
- Ten panels of average quality £300
- Ten panels of high quality £1000

This gives a range of possible negotiated outcomes as shown in Figure 19.2.

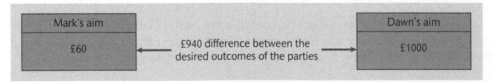

Figure 19.2 Positional bargaining

From a positional bargaining perspective, every pound gained for Dawn leaves Mark one pound worse off. This is described as a zero-sum game.

Zero-sum game describes a situation in which one party's gain is equivalent to the other party's loss. In the example above, if you calculate one party's gain and deduct the other party's loss, the total would be zero. It is useful to think of this in terms of sharing out a pie: the larger the slice taken by **A**, the smaller the piece remaining for **B**.

Positional bargaining is criticized for its inability to deal with non-pecuniary issues and its ineffectiveness in tackling complex negotiations involving multiple issues. Not everything can be reduced to monetary value: imagine using financial incentives to settle a dispute about access to children following marital breakdown.

It can be useful in negotiations involving a strong financial element or one in which there is a narrow issue to be resolved and where reference to broader issues would emphasize the differences between the parties.

19.1.1.2 Integrative bargaining

Integrative bargaining focuses on the interests of the parties. It focuses on the client's needs, fears, desires, and emotions in order to reach a negotiated outcome that is compatible with their goals. If you focus exclusively on *what* the client wants without any understanding of *why* they want it, you could reach an objectively reasonable settlement that wholly fails to satisfy your client's subjective interests, as this simple example illustrates:

> Tom and Jonathan are arguing over one remaining orange. Their mother, Jenny, cuts the orange in half and gives half to each child, seeing this as a perfect compromise. However, if she had asked *why* each child wanted the orange, Jenny would have discovered that each had a different assignment at school the following day that involved part of an orange: Tom needed the juice for home economics whilst Jonathan needed the peel for an art class. As such, Jenny's objectively fair solution failed to meet the subjective needs of either child whereas asking *why* they wanted the orange would have led to a different basis for division that would have given each child exactly what they wanted.

As this example shows, it is not useful to make assumptions about a client's goals or to impose your interpretation of a good outcome on the client. With knowledge of the client's goals, you will be able to negotiate more flexibly to achieve these in the face of unexpected offers from the other side.

 Self-test questions

Make a note of the sorts of interests that could be at stake in the following situations for each party. Remember, you need to move beyond an identification of *what* each party might want in order to discover *why* they want it.

1. A husband and wife engaged in negotiations for his access to their children following the breakdown of the marriage.

2. Negotiations for the sale of a house between the vendor and purchaser.

3. Contract negotiations undertaken on behalf of a professional golfer and a new sponsor.

4. The owner of a hotel and a carpet fitter concerning the supply and installation of new carpets.

 Answers to the self-test questions can be found on the Online Resource Centre.

Even in cases which appear to be limited to negotiations of a financial nature, integrative bargaining can be a more effective approach to adopt than positional bargaining. A client whose instruction is to obtain the highest financial settlement possible may actually want money for a number of reasons. Asking *why* should provide insight into the issues motivating the client and therefore give you greater flexibility in achieving a favourable settlement.

Asking *why* may be useful even in situations that appear to be exclusively financial and may give greater flexibility and creativity in reaching a favourable settlement that fulfils the client's needs.

> David agreed to renovate Lydia's classic car by the end of March but fell behind schedule and is in breach of contract. David has completed most of the work and has purchased some expensive parts but Lydia wants her money refunded in full.

This seems straightforward but further insight is provided by enquiring into Lydia's goals. She needs the money to pay Shane who has agreed to fix the car within a week. Lydia needs the car within this time so that it can be used at her sister's wedding. Awareness of this goal gives more flexibility to negotiate with David on non-financial terms as David is able to offer Lydia a choice of three classic cars to use for her sister's wedding if she agrees to allow him to complete work on her car and keep the payment that has been made.

This should go some way to demonstrating the benefits of looking beyond the seemingly straightforward financial aspects of a dispute in order to find a more creative solution.

19.2 Negotiation skills

It is likely that you have a great many of the skills needed to negotiate already. Most people do as we learn how to make bargains from a very early age. Think of the sorts of deal that are struck between parents and children such as those shown in Figure 19.3.

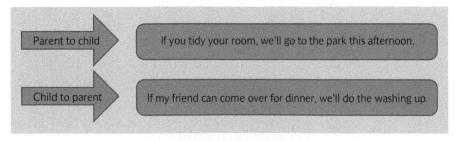

Figure 19.3 Deals between parent and child

Various factors will influence the success of the negotiation. For example, the child may think that a trip to the park does not justify the effort of tidying his room whilst the parent may feel that the responsibility of feeding and entertaining another child is too onerous to be repaid by washing-up.

Experience teaches us to deal with more complex negotiations in which more accurate predictions are made about factors that will act as an incentive to the other party (see Figure 19.4).

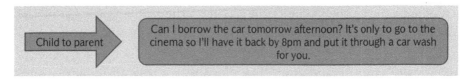

Figure 19.4 A more complex deal between parent and child

The child attempts to predict factors that might deter the parent from accepting the bargain and negate them in order to gain agreement (a venue not associated with alcohol consumption and an early return time). This is supported with an incentive (washing the car) that involves little effort or loss to the child but which is consistent with the notion of taking care of another's property.

We also learn the value of allowing room for manoeuvre and of asking questions to elicit information about the concerns of the other party (see Figure 19.5).

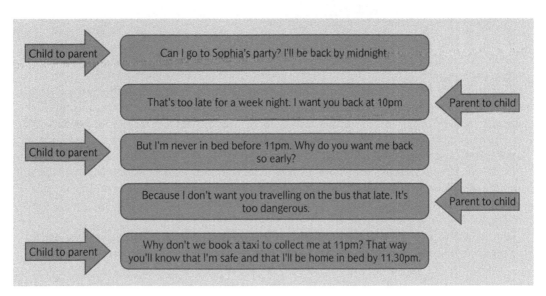

Figure 19.5 Room to manoeuvre

The child starts with a later return time so that she can be seen to make concessions but still stay until the desired time of 11 p.m. This gives room for movement and prevents an appearance of stubbornness. By asking questions about the parent's concerns, the child is able to make a suggestion that overcomes these fears and contributes to achieving her own objective.

From these simple examples of negotiation that have resonance with the everyday experience of many people, we can identify some key negotiation strategies:

- The deal needs to be attractive to the other party so you need to offer them something of value
- Find out (by asking questions) or predict (on the basis of your knowledge of the other party) what will hold value for them
- Enhance your offer by 'throwing in' things of little value to you (this illustrates the variable nature of 'value': what holds value for one person may be of little significance to another)
- Keep the tone of negotiation amicable by making reasonable offers that leave you room to manoeuvre

You may wonder why you need this chapter if negotiation skills are learned in childhood. The answer is that you need to be able to use the principles of negotiation in a structured and methodical way in relation to multifaceted and complex issues. Everyday negotiations between parents and children may give you some skills but do little to prepare you to negotiate access arrangements for children following divorce or multimillion pound commercial negotiations.

Overall, although it is fair to say that most individuals have some experience of the basic tools of negotiation, they are not sufficiently developed or sophisticated to deal with the complexities of conducting legal negotiations on behalf of a client. They do, however, provide a basis upon which we can build.

19.3 Preparing to negotiate

Simulated negotiations involve two teams (usually with two students in each team) who each represent one party to a legal dispute. It is usual for each team to be given a set of written facts that outline the facts of the dispute from the perspective of their client, although some negotiations may also involve a set of common facts which are distributed to both teams. In more sophisticated negotiations, the parties may have the opportunity to ask questions of their client, usually by email to a member of staff responsible for the negotiation who formulates an appropriate response. It is more usual for the facts to be limited to a written outline.

It is sometimes the case that students negotiate, having done nothing more than read though their instructions. This tends to lead to a weak performance as the team is not sufficiently familiar with the facts and has not undertaken the necessary research and preparation to reach a favourable settlement.

Rather than thinking of 'the negotiation' as solely concerned with the face-to-face discussion between the teams, it is preferable to think of it as a two-stage process (see Figure 19.6).

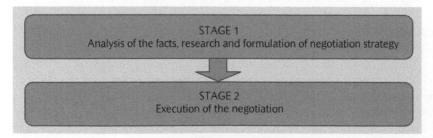

Figure 19.6 Negotiation as a two-stage process

Although settlement is reached at the second stage, the preparatory process should be viewed as the essential foundation to conducting a negotiation and should be undertaken with diligence. The second stage simply cannot be completed with success if the first has not been undertaken thoroughly.

19.3.1 Analysis of the scenario

As the scenario is the only information that the team has as the basis of the negotiation (plus common facts if they are available), it is essential that it is subjected to careful analysis to identify the client's interests and priorities, whether explicit or implicit, and to determine what, if any, instructions limit the scope of the settlement.

Working as a team has advantages in terms of the execution of the negotiation but it is useful during the preparation too as two pairs of eyes minimize the risk that a key fact will be overlooked. It may also draw attention to ambiguities in the scenario if the team members have drawn different inferences from the same facts or reached divergent conclusions about the client's priorities.

When analyzing the scenario, make a note of the key points:

- What does the claim concern? In other words, identify the relevant area of law, e.g. contract, family law, negligence, personal injury

- What does the client want? Make a list of things that you need to achieve for your client during the negotiation, taking note of implied as well as express aims such as a quick resolution, a desire for an amicable resolution, or reluctance to litigate

- What are the client's interests? Again, these might be stated explicitly in the scenario or you may need to read between the lines. Exercise caution in doing this; remember the pitfalls of making false assumptions about the client's interest noted earlier. Identify the client's interests by working down the list of 'wants' and asking the question 'why'. For example, the client may want to avoid court action but do you know why? It may be because it is expensive or in order to avoid any negative publicity and maintain an undamaged reputation. The underlying issue is likely to have an impact on the way in which the negotiation is handled

- What, if any, limitations are there? For example, are you instructed to prioritize a particular aspect of the negotiation? Are you told that a particular outcome is unacceptable?

- What, if anything, does the scenario suggest about the issues that are important to the other party? Are there any clues that provide insight into their priorities?

- What are your strengths and weaknesses and how do you plan to deal with them in the negotiation?

This is an example of a scenario that might be given to one team. This negotiation will be used as the basis for many of the practical exercises in the remainder of this chapter. The facts that would be given to the opposing team can be found on the Online Resource Centre.

Access Negotiation Scenario A:
Rhys has been married to Angharad for twelve years and they have three children: Tomas (ten), Gethin (seven) and Bethan (five). Rhys has felt that the marriage was unfulfilling for several years but stayed with Angharad because he had always had very strong Christian views and believed that marriage was a lifelong union of man and woman. Three months ago, he went on a 'Discover Yourself' course organized by his local church and, unfortunately, returned from this course with

an insight into his own personality that has made it difficult for him to continue with his marriage as he realized that he would like to live life as a woman. He tried to discuss his views with Angharad but she refused to listen and Rhys became increasingly depressed. He feels that he will suffer irreparable harm if he remains married to Angharad but he wants to have an ongoing relationship with his children. Unfortunately, Angharad has told him that she will only tolerate him having any contact with the children if he 'behaves like a normal husband and father'. Rhys tried to carry on but became very depressed and was hospitalized after a suicide attempt. He realized that he cannot deny his true feelings and has investigated the possibility of gender reassignment surgery. In pursuit of this, he has started to dress as a woman and has changed his name to Rhiannon.

Rhys/Rhiannon has purchased a small house near to Angharad and the children. He says that he has been accepted by his friends and neighbours and that he has not encountered any hostility for his choice to live as a woman except from Angharad and her family. He wants this to stop. To make matters worse, Angharad has discussed matters with the children that Rhys/Rhiannon had assumed would remain personal between himself and his wife and now his older son, Tomas, has declared that he never wants to speak to his father again and his younger son, Gethin, is afraid to be in his company. Angharad says that Gethin has a panic attack if his father's name is mentioned and that she is afraid to allow him to see his father.

Rhys/Rhiannon wants regular access to his children that commences immediately. He would like them to stay with him in his new house every other weekend and for them to visit two afternoons a week after school. Rhys/Rhiannon is a freelance writer so he has no difficulty in being able to find time to care for his children. He is prepared to agree to any financial demands that Angharad makes provided he obtains an access agreement that gives him regular contact with his children. He wants Angharad to agree to stop turning the children against him and not to make any adverse comments about transgendered people in general in front of the children. Angharad has also started to attend a very traditional church that preaches that alternative lifestyles are wrong and that transgendered people will go straight to hell. He is afraid that this will alienate his children even further so he wants Angharad to stop going to this church and to return to the church that they attended together as it has more moderate views—the priest has already made it clear to Rhys/Rhiannon that he will be welcome to rejoin the congregation as a woman.

Self-test questions

Analyze the negotiation scenario provided, remembering to take into account the six points noted above:

1. What is the legal framework for the negotiation?
2. What does your client want?
3. What are your client's interests?
4. What boundaries are placed upon the negotiation?
5. What are the other side likely to want?
6. What are your strengths and weaknesses?

You will find answers to these questions and guidance on how they were reached on the Online Resource Centre. There is also an analysis of the other side of the negotiation but it might be useful if you do not look at it yet as it will be harder for your work on this side if you have already seen what the other party wants and how it plans to tackle the negotiation.

19.3.2 Research

Once you have a good grasp of the facts of the scenario and have identified the general area of law raised, you will be ready to engage in research.

19.3.2.1 Researching the law

Researching the legal issue should be straightforward as it should be apparent what area of law is raised by the scenario. The emphasis in negotiation is on use of the facts, so it should not be necessary to do any more than read the relevant sections in one or two textbooks to gain an appropriate grasp of the law.

It may be that your scenario raises issues that you have not covered in mainstream textbooks; for instance, there may be legal limitations on the rights of pre-operative transgendered people. If you do identify any uncommon legal issues, you will need to use some of the methods outlined in chapter 2 and chapter 5 for finding the relevant legal provision.

You must be focused in your legal research. Try to isolate particular questions that need to be answered. One of your key tasks should be to work out how the case would be decided if it went to court. This gives rise to two questions, the answers to which should help you to formulate a negotiation strategy:

1. **If this case was heard in court, would I win?** Unless the answer is an unequivocal 'yes', you have every incentive to work towards a negotiated settlement, even if this means achieving an outcome that is less than your client hoped; remember, part of something is better than all of nothing. Even if you are confident that your case would succeed in court, there are still incentives to negotiate. Litigation is costly and time-consuming and it may be that your client is unwilling to go to court. Moreover, there is more flexibility in negotiation for your client to determine the shape of the settlement that is reached to suit his or her requirements.

2. **If this case succeeded in court, what would I receive?** This should be your bottom line as there are few advantages to reaching a negotiated settlement that leaves your client with a worse outcome than that which would have been imposed by the court. You will need to take into account factors such as the cost of litigation and the likely time frame of events, so be sure to work this into your calculation. Where the dispute may involve a financial settlement, remember to take advantage of tables for calculating damages,[2] for example, in working out the likely position of your client following court action or looking for decided cases with analogous facts as a basis for comparison. You can refer to these in your negotiation, to give support to your arguments.

BATNA (best alternative to a negotiated agreement) is an acronym used to describe the best possible outcome that will result for your client if you do not negotiate or if the negotiation fails. This will be explored in more detail in relation to negotiation strategy but needs to be taken into account at this stage because you need to know whether your case would win or lose at court and what the outcome would be if you won in order to work out your BATNA.

These two questions may not be relevant if the scenario involves preliminary steps to enter into an agreement as illustrated by the example negotiation used in this chapter where the parties are hoping to seek resolution to a family dispute. If this is the case, you should research

---

2. W Norris and others, *Kemp & Kemp: Quantum of Damages* (Sweet & Maxwell 2012). Updated quarterly; also available online via Lawtel.

the relevant law on access to children to ensure that you cover all the necessary requirements to agree an access agreement during your negotiation.

Remember that negotiation is an agreed settlement and is not binding. This is important, whether the negotiation is aimed at resolving a dispute or if it is a facilitative negotiation, i.e. agreeing the terms of a contract. The lack of enforceability should give you cause to consider one further question that is pertinent to your legal research:

3. **What will happen if the agreement is breached?** If the negotiation is aimed at dispute resolution, the answer is usually that the injured party will either give up or the case will end up in court. Therefore, there is a real need to ensure that the settlement is genuinely acceptable to both parties as this minimizes the chances of breach. If the negotiation is aimed at agreeing terms of a contract, for example, do not forget to consider the consequences of breach. Think about all the possible things that could go wrong and try to ensure that you find a way to write ways of dealing with these problems into the contract.

19.3.2.2 Researching the facts

Conducting research into other issues is less straightforward as the scenario will often involve factual issues about which you have no prior knowledge. This is a fair approximation of what will happen in legal practice. However, in simulated negotiations, unlike practice, you cannot simply ask the client for that information. In any case, you should never place too great a reliance on the facts presented by a client if they can be objectively ascertained. A client may be misguided or simply have chosen the facts that most suit their expected outcome. For example, imagine conducting a negotiation for the sale of a property based exclusively on the client's estimation of the value of the property! You would not place reliance on this and you should always ensure that facts which are objectively determinable are objectively determined. In other words, if it is possible for you to find something out for yourself, you should do so as only then will be you be confident that you are basing your negotiations on accurate and unbiased information.

It is impossible to cover all the sorts of questions that you would want to research given the infinite range of scenarios that you might encounter, so this aspect of research will be demonstrated in relation to the access negotiation.

 Practical exercise

Think about the facts you would need to know in preparation for the access negotiation.

 You will find some suggestions on the Online Resource Centre along with explanations of the reasoning behind them.

It is important to research the facts as well as the law as this may disclose all manner of negotiation points that you would not have considered otherwise, particularly if you keep your client's interests in mind.

Take the facts at face value and research accordingly. For example, you know that Rhys wants Angharad to stop going to her traditional church and return to the church that they attended together before he started living as a woman. Could you suggest an alternative which proposed a different church for Angharad that she could attend without Rhys? This might temper her 'extreme' views without requiring her to be seen out with Rhys dressed as a woman. Try to be flexible and creative—what alternative ways could you suggest to achieve the client's goals without departing from the instructions given?

It is worth emphasizing that your research into factual issues must be conducted in an honest manner. For instance, please do not call a surgery and make enquiries about gender reassignment surgery; that would be simply unethical. The Internet is a wonderful repository of all sorts of information that is readily available to researchers prepared to exercise a little effort and ingenuity.[3]

19.3.3 Strategy

Formulating a research strategy is not a straightforward matter as there are a multitude of factors to take into account. Foremost amongst these is the need to evaluate the strength of your case and the various potential outcomes of the negotiation.

19.3.3.1 Identifying potential outcomes

In light of your analysis of the scenario and your research, you should be able to establish four things (see Figure 19.7).

It is essential that you establish each of these as this will enable you to calculate a strategy designed to achieve the most favourable outcome for your client.

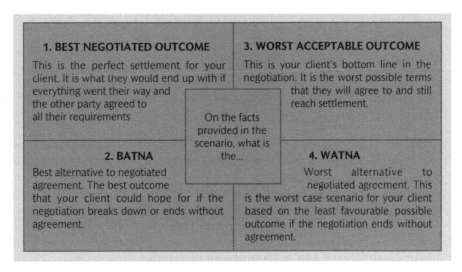

Figure 19.7 Identifying potential outcomes

3. See, for example, the Chartered Institute of Personnel and development introductory guidance on sex discrimination, sexual orientation, gender reassignment and employment at <http://www.cipd.co.uk/hr-resources/factsheets/sex-discrimination-sexual-orientation-gender-reassignment-employment.aspx>.

3. Worst acceptable outcome.

4. WATNA.

Having done this, consider the strength of the client's position to negotiate? What do you consider to be the characteristics of a strong bargaining position?

 Answers to the self-test questions can be found on the Online Resource Centre.

19.3.3.2 Formulating the issues

Once you have identified the most beneficial negotiated outcome for your client, you can break this down into a series of issues that can be dealt with individually within the negotiation.

For example, in relation to the access negotiation, you may have decided that the best negotiated outcome for the client is:

- for Rhys to have immediate regular access to his children every other weekend and for two afternoons each week
- for Angharad to stop making derogatory comments about transgendered people in general and Rhys in particular
- for Angharad to stop attending her new church and return to the former marital church with Rhys.

This can be broken down into three separate issues:

1. Access: how frequently and where will the access visits take place?
2. Comments: how can Rhys enforce the agreement even if Angharad concedes?
3. Church: which church will Angharad and Rhys attend?

Once you have identified the issues, you might want to decide in what order you would like to take them. There is no right or wrong answer to this but be prepared to justify your decision. For example, given that access to the children is at the heart of the negotiation, it could be beneficial to deal with it first as there is no point in agreeing the other issues if this point cannot be settled. Alternatively, given that the client needs to reach an agreement (because the BATNA is not particularly advantageous), it might be preferable to start with an issue such as financial arrangements (with which Rhys has no real issue), so the negotiation starts with the client offering something potentially advantageous to the other party.

Practical exercise

1. Do you agree with the division of the negotiation into these three issues? Are there other issues that could be included? Could any of these issues be (a) combined or (b) divided and what are the advantages of taking this action?
2. What order would you take the points in and why? What other order did you consider and why did you reject it?

It is important that you reflect upon the reasons for your decisions. In a negotiation competition, the judge(s) will ask you why you chose a particular course of action and expect you to have a reasoned explanation for this, so it is useful to form the habit of scrutinizing your own decision-making process.

 Answers to these questions can be found on the Online Resource Centre.

19.3.3.3 Balancing the issues

Negotiations involving multiple issues can be difficult because you cannot expect to achieve your desired outcome on every issue. You need to be able to see the relationship between the issues so that you can exercise flexibility on one issue in order to gain ground on another.

There are two aspects to this process:

1. Establishing a top and bottom line of each of the issues

2. Ranking them in order of importance to the client.

When you can see the boundaries of each issue and their relative importance to the client, you can start to think about trading them off against each other. You may have to make concessions on one issue in order to gain ground on another issue. This is an effective negotiation strategy, provided you always keep the 'big picture' of the client's goals in mind and you do not act contrary to any explicit instructions.

For example, the most pressing need for the client in the access negotiation is to gain regular access to his children. Therefore, although they might like to do this with twice weekly and alternate weekend visits to his home, provided a solution can be found that facilitates access, the client is likely to be satisfied. As such, you may be able to make concessions on the location of the access or the way in which Rhys dresses when he sees his children so long as Rhys actually manages to find a way to spend time with his children. This would not be a possibility if, for example, the instructions said that it was essential for the client always to be dressed as a woman when the children pay a visit.

Self-test questions

1. Rank the issues in the access negotiation in order of importance to the client. Note that this may well differ from the order in which you decided to negotiate the issues.

2. Calculate the boundaries of each of the issues, i.e. work out the best and worst outcome on each issue to determine how much bargaining scope there is on each point.

3. Consider ways in which you could offer concessions on one issue in order to gain something beneficial for the client on one of the other issues.

 Answers to the self-test questions can be found on the Online Resource Centre.

19.3.3.4 Generating more options

The negotiation scenario does not provide detailed instructions of all the potential outcomes that are agreeable to your client. You are provided with some indication of their aims and also of their broader interests and you should have tried to anticipate what the other party will want from your client. Working within this framework, try to generate some creative ways in which the aims of both parties could be satisfied.

For example, if the issue of surgery becomes contentious, i.e. both parties are insistent that they want incompatible outcomes (Rhys wants to undergo gender reassignment surgery and Angharad wants him to remain as he is), it could be a useful way of breaking a potential deadlock to offer a delay in the date for surgery in return for supervised child access for your client, whilst agreeing that surgery can take place at a later date once the parties are more used to the unusual arrangements.

This is just one example of a creative use of the facts that could help you to reach an agreement. Remember that you are not permitted to make up facts that are not included in your scenario (and in competition will be heavily penalized for doing so) but you can make reasonable inferences from the facts provided that you are acting within the spirit of your instructions.

Self-test questions

Go back to the access negotiation scenario and review your analysis of it. Can you think of any other creative ways in which the needs of the parties can be fulfilled that are not immediately obvious? Try to focus in particular on what your client has identified as a potential difficulty: regular contact with his children. Your client is prepared to agree to any financial demands to achieve this but will that be acceptable to the other party (remember that cutting the orange in half did not work in the example given above)? Assuming that both parties would ideally like incompatible outcomes, are there any other ways that this could be achieved? Think about the interests of your client and think of potential interests that could be motivating the other party; does this help to formulate creative solutions to this Solomon-esque dilemma?

 Answers to the self-test questions can be found on the Online Resource Centre.

19.3.3.5 Negotiation plan

Once all the analysis and planning is complete, you might find it useful to prepare yourself a schedule of negotiation that notes the issues that you need to discuss, the order in which you would like to address them and your best and worst outcome on each issue so that you can see quite clearly how much scope for negotiation there is on each point. This can serve as a particularly useful reminder not to move outside your instructions. This need be no more than one side of A4 and should be used as a reminder of your key issues rather than a strict schedule (you will be expected to demonstrate flexibility, so must be prepared to depart from your plan) or a crib sheet (good negotiations involve personal contact, not paper shuffling).

19.4 Conducting the negotiation

Negotiation is an inherently reflexive activity. The ability to listen and to ask appropriate questions are essential skills that contribute to a successful negotiation as they will help you to piece together a complete picture of events. A good negotiator will be able to elicit information from the other parties and incorporate this into their understanding of the situation in order to make appropriate proposals for resolution based upon the information received. It is essential that you do take the other party's interests into account as a negotiated settlement is one that suits both sides rather than one in which the stronger party forces an outcome on the weaker party.

This final section of the chapter covers some of the key components of an effective negotiation.

19.4.1 Preliminary matters

It will be tempting, particularly in a competition that involves completing the negotiation within a tight time frame, to jump straight into a discussion of the first issue but there are certain preliminary matters that will need to be completed before the negotiation proper commences. Not the least of these is reaching an agreement with the other parties as to what the first issue for consideration should be.

19.4.1.1 Introductions

It is a matter of good practice to introduce yourself and identify the party that you are representing. This need not be a lengthy business and involves little more than a handshake and a brief sentence. More important than the words themselves can be the manner in which the introductions are undertaken. First impressions are important, so think carefully about what image you want to present, both individually and as a team.

19.4.1.2 Establishing the framework for negotiation

It is useful to outline, in a couple of sentences, the factual basis of the negotiation. This should be a very basic statement of the facts that are likely to be agreed between both sides. For example:

> We have been instructed by Angharad Evans to seek to reach an agreement regarding access to her children.

In this negotiation, the name of one of the parties is actually a sensitive matter and should be treated as such in the introduction:

> We have been instructed by Ms Rhiannon Evans, who you will know as Mr Rhys Evans, in order to make arrangements for child access.

19.4.1.3 Setting an agenda

As part of your preparation, you will have decided the order in which you want to negotiate the various issues. As outlined earlier in this chapter, there are various factors that might influence how you prioritize the order of your issues and decide what issue to deal with first:

- The issue that is of primary importance to the client as settlement may not be possible unless a core objective of the client is achieved
- The most complicated issue to get it out of the way, or
- The most straightforward issue so that the negotiation starts with an issue on which agreement is reached easily, as this sets a positive tone for the remainder of the negotiation.

It is possible that the other side will disagree either about the issues for negotiation or about the order in which they should be addressed. This can lead to a 'negotiation within a negotiation' as the agenda itself becomes a contentious issue. This process might set the tone for the negotiation, so treat it with importance but do not fall into the trap of spending too much valuable time determining the agenda. Ultimately, provided all your issues are on the agenda, the order in which they are discussed should not make too much difference to the overall outcome. This stage can be important, however, in setting the tone of the negotiation, so it is important that you do not become too insistent about following your own agenda or allow the other party wholly to override your wishes.

The overall objective at this stage is to establish an agreed agenda.

19.4.2 Fact-finding

Eliciting information from the other team is an important aspect of negotiation. It should not be confined to the start of the negotiation but should take place throughout the discussions.

It can be a useful starting point if one of the parties commences by providing a brief summary of their client's position. Some students are reluctant to do this as they feel that it 'gives away' important information to the opposing team; try to remember that a negotiated outcome is one that suits both sides, so there is little to be gained by being reticent with information. However, that does not mean that you have to be wholly forthcoming at this stage, particularly with information that weakens your client's position.

If you decide to offer an outline, select your facts carefully. Do not overwhelm the opposing side with detail. Try to contain your outline to the material facts that provide the framework for the negotiation. If the opposing team offers an outline of their facts, try not to interrupt even if you disagree with them; after all, they are giving you information that you need to know in order to understand their position, so it is important to listen carefully and make notes of any key points.

Good negotiation involves interactive, not unidirectional, communication. This means that it is important that each side has the chance to ask questions, to seek clarification, and to add information. Ending the summary of the facts with an invitation to comment will facilitate interactive communication:

- Is there anything that you would like to add?
- Do you have any questions?

19.4.2.1 Ask questions

The most effective means of eliciting information is to ask questions. If you are unclear about something or are struggling to grasp the other party's position, you should ask questions to help you gain a better understanding. These fall into two general categories (see Figure 19.8).

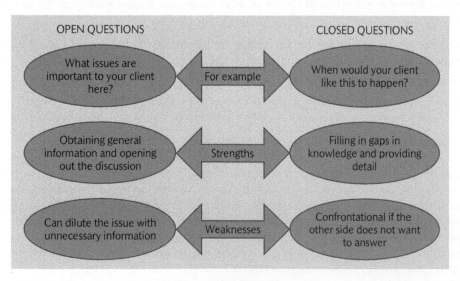

Figure 19.8 Open and closed questioning

Remember the importance of 'why' questions that provide insight into the motivation of the client and shed light on the 'big' aims that the client wishes to achieve. If you can elicit information about the overall objective of the other client, you will be better placed to make creative solutions which might achieve that objective.

It can be helpful if you prepare a list of information that you feel you need to know prior to the start of the negotiation and then think of the most effective types of question to ask to elicit this information. If you prepare this as a grid, you can tick off the questions that have been answered (to avoid repetition) and make a quick note of the answer as seen in Figure 19.9:

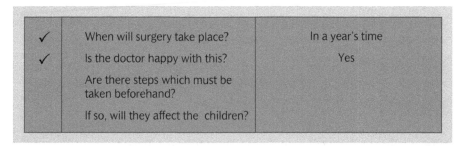

Figure 19.9 Question checklist

19.4.2.2 Give reasons

If you tell the other team that you do not understand or provide some other explanation of why you want to know a particular piece of information, it makes it harder for the other team to refuse to provide it.

- I don't understand why your client wants access to the children to commence immediately. Are there other factors that are important here that I need to take into account?

- You don't seem receptive to my suggestion of a significant financial payment in return for access. I thought this would be an attractive proposition so is there some reason why you feel this would not be welcomed by your client?

19.4.3 Breaking deadlock

Deadlock occurs when the parties cannot reach agreement on a particular issue and are no longer prepared to make any movement towards each other. This can occur all too easily. Imagine the following situation in Figure 19.10:

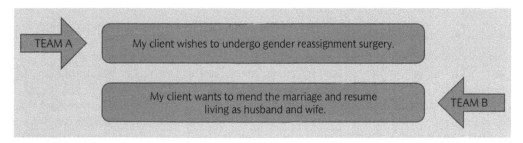

Figure 19.10 Deadlock

19.4.3.1 Avoiding deadlock

The most effective strategy is to avoid deadlock occurring in the first place. Try to avoid making 'make or break' demands in absolute terms. If you allow yourself no room for movement, there is nowhere for you to go if the other side refuses to agree with your requirements. Moreover, backing the other side into a corner in which they either have to stand against you or give in entirely is confrontational and aggressive, so is viewed as bad negotiation practice. You are supposed to be reaching mutual agreement, not imposing your will on others.

19.4.3.2 Keep the negotiation moving

If you cannot settle a particular issue, it can be a good idea to move away from it and find an issue where agreement can be reached:

> It seems that we're struggling to find common ground in relation to the way in which my client dresses. Would it help to move on to consider the other arrangements for access to the children to see if this helps us to resolve the perceived gender issue?

Even if this does not resolve the disputed issue, at least it keeps the negotiation in progress and demonstrates your commitment to finding a way around deadlock.

19.4.3.3 Ask questions and offer solutions

As mentioned previously, if you can gain insight into why the other team is adopting a particular position, you may be able to find an alternative way to help them to achieve their objectives:

* Why is the choice of church so important to your client?

If the other team is not forthcoming with explanations, it might help to posit potential explanations:

* Is your client unwilling to return to the church she previously attended because she is concerned about being seen with her husband dressed as a woman? If so, perhaps we could agree that they both attend a different church in which they were not previously known?

The other team will either have to agree and confirm that your speculation was correct, in which case you can work towards resolving the problems or they will deny that this is the reason, in which case you can at least rule it out as a possibility. Whichever of these applies, you will have demonstrated your willingness to explore all the options and an inclination to reach agreement, both of which are key negotiation skills.

Be creative in the solutions that you offer but do ensure that they are within the overall spirit of your instructions. There is no point in finding a solution to the problem that your client finds unacceptable.

19.4.3.4 Highlight concessions

This is an assertive way of applying reasonable pressure to the other team to demonstrate flexibility. Although negotiation should not be aggressive, undue passivity could allow you to be pressured into accepting an agreement that is not on particularly favourable terms for your client, so do not be afraid to apply a little pressure if it seems appropriate. It is important that you do not seem unreasonable, so identifying areas where you have already made concessions can underline the facts that you have been reasonable and flexible whilst the opposing team has been inflexible:

- I understand that the issue of church attendance is important to your client but it would help us to reach agreement if you could be a little flexible here. After all, the issue of immediate access to the children was important to our client and yet we moved towards you considerably on this point by agreeing to a timetable of supervised visits.

It is for this reason that it can be useful to move away from a contentious issue into more straightforward areas as settlement reached elsewhere can be a useful lever to prompt settlement once the difficult issue is revisited.

19.4.3.5 Take a break

There is provision within most negotiation competition rules for both teams to take a short break during the negotiation. This can be used effectively in a number of ways but can be a particularly useful strategy for breaking deadlock, especially if relations between the teams have become strained. It will give you the opportunity to have a private discussion with your team mate in which you can discuss how to deal with the situation. Remember to do your best to cast off any negative emotions during this period and come back into the negotiation room in an objective and professional frame of mind.

19.4.3.6 Walk away

There is no point in reaching an agreement that is unacceptable to your client, so if none of the other strategies succeeds in breaking the deadlock and the other team's requirements are outside your instructions, there is no option other than to end the negotiation without reaching agreement. If you contemplate doing this, you should cast your mind back to your BATNA and WATNA as these were the possible outcomes if no agreement could be reached. However, if you make it clear that you are contemplating ending the negotiation without agreement, the other team will also reflect about their BATNA and WATNA which might make them realize that there is room for movement after all.

19.4.4 Teamwork

One of the criteria upon which your negotiation will be judged is your ability to work effectively with the other member of your team. It would be useful to give this some thought during the planning period and consider how you are going to relate to each other in the most effective way. Factors that you might like to take into account are as follows:

- Your relative skills as communicators (assertive, conciliatory, patient, forceful, etc.) and how these can be used to best effect in the negotiation
- Distribution of workload such as allocation of issues, responsibility for note-taking, strategies for intervention if the other person is struggling, and dealing with opening and closing the negotiation
- Dealing with conflict within the negotiation. It can be useful to decide how you will respond if the other team introduces an option that you had not considered if you disagree about its value to your client. **Never** argue with each other

19.4.5 Ethical considerations

It is important that your negotiation is conducted within the parameters of professional practice, which means that you must act in an ethical manner. It is of the utmost importance that you do not misrepresent your position or otherwise mislead the other team. Not only must you not do this deliberately, you must be cautious in your choice of language to avoid any possibility that you will mislead the other team inadvertently.

It can be particularly tempting to misrepresent the upper and lower limits in relation to a financial issue, for example, in order to obtain a more favourable deal for your client. You must not do this.

Imagine that you are trying to negotiate a settlement for personal injury following an accident that the other team concedes was the fault of their client. Your client has instructed you to get 'as much as possible and certainly not less than £5,000'. If the other team suggests £6,500, you are not compelled to accept it but you cannot say 'my client would not agree to that, he would rather go to court' as this is simply not true. You need to find alternative ways of seeking to persuade the other team to increase their offer without making false representations of your instructions:

- That is towards the lower end of the usual award of damages for this type of injury. Let's not forget that your client was wholly responsible for the accident and my client has suffered a great deal of pain since this happened.

19.4.6 Closing the negotiation

It is important to close the negotiation in an effective way so that everybody is clear about the terms of the agreement that has been reached. It can be useful to refer back to the agreed agenda and make a note of the outcome of each point that was listed, drawing particular reference to any issues that might require further consultation. Remember that the agreement that you have reached is subject to your client's agreement, so be sure to reflect this in your closing comments.

19.5 Post-negotiation reflection

Most negotiation competitions allocate a period of time at the end of the negotiation in which each team deliberates on their performance in the presence of the judges. This is not done in the presence of the opposing team. This stage of the negotiation gives the judges insight into the success of the negotiation from the perspective of the teams. This should include:

- Did the negotiation go according to plan? If not, what aspect of it was unexpected and could a different approach to planning and preparation prevent such an occurrence in subsequent negotiations?

- How well did the team work with each other and how well did they relate to the other team? If there were problems, what was the cause of these and were they resolved in an effective and professional manner?

- Was the outcome of the negotiation acceptable? Did the team gain a better deal for their client than they had anticipated or is the agreement that is reached disappointing? What factors might account for this?

- What were the strengths and weaknesses of the negotiation? Do not be afraid to identify weaknesses as this demonstrates to the judges that you are aware of the shortcomings of your own performance. If you are able to suggest ways that you would improve upon these areas in the future, this will satisfy the judge that you have gained something of value from participation in the negotiation

- If you conducted the negotiation again, what would you do differently and why?

 It can be difficult to reach an understanding of such a practical activity from reading a chapter such as this, so you might find it useful to look at some of the examples of negotiation on the Online Resource Centre and think about the commentary that accompanies the clips.

CHAPTER SUMMARY

Planning and preparation

- Analyze the negotiation scenario to ensure that you have a clear grasp of the issues that need to be resolved

- Use the strategies outlined in this chapter to assess the strength of your position. Work out the scope of movement in relation to each issue and consider how the issues can be used in conjunction to strengthen your bargaining power

- Research the relevant law and the facts to ensure that you have a thorough grasp of the key information

- Take a holistic view of your client's aims and think of creative ways to achieve these objectives within the spirit of your instructions

Conducting the negotiation

- Make a firm professional start with clear introductions, a summary of the factual situation, and a suggested agenda. Be prepared to amend your proposed agenda to reflect the requirements of the other team

- Remember that you only know half the story, so take time to find out about the issues that concern the other team and fill in the gaps of your factual knowledge

- Elicit information by asking questions. Remember that 'why' questions give insight into the aims of the other team's client and this may enable you to propose creative solutions that facilitate agreement

- A skilled negotiator will try and work around obstacles rather than stopping when confronted with them to try to use a range of different strategies to avoid or break deadlock

- It is important to evolve a strategy that enables you to work as a team and to form an effective working relationship with the other team, irrespective of their approach to negotiation

- Ensure that you are always ethical in your dealings with the other team, taking care not to mislead them or misrepresent your position

- Conclude by outlining the proposed agreement to ensure that everyone is clear on its terms

- Critical reflection will help you to improve your negotiation skills and enable you to improve upon your performance

Tell us

If you are trying to organise your own moot feel free to ask us for help. Who knows, we might offer to run a mooting skills workshop for you or to judge your competition. Alternatively, we might feature a film of your moot on our website: a great advertisement for your mooting skills! Or simply tell us how you got on. Get in contact at finchandfafinski.com/get-in-touch or @ FinchFafinski on Twitter.

Negotiation

All legal disputes that are resolved in court have a winner and a loser. One party gets everything that they want and the other party gets nothing. Negotiation is a method of alternative dispute resolution in which the parties, or their representatives, engage in a process of bargaining in order to reach an agreement that gives each of the parties something of what they want thus avoiding the need to litigate. Negotiation is based upon cooperation between seemingly opposed parties: although both sides want different things, agreement is only possible if they are prepared to compromise. Negotiation competitions offer an excellent opportunity to strengthen communication skills and to develop a flexible approach to fact management and problem resolution. These skills are central to legal practice but will be valued by employers in a wide range of professions as they enhance your ability to create consensus out of conflict and demonstrate a flexible approach to problem solving as well as showcasing excellent verbal communication skills. Participation in negotiation competitions will also help you to appreciate the way in which the law works in the real world which will help you to prepare for legal practice.

What is negotiation?

Everyone can negotiate. We negotiate all the time as we strike bargains with other people and make concessions that will ultimately gain us something that we want. For example, if you want to borrow your mother's car to go to the shops, you might promise to drive carefully and to pick up her dry cleaning for her. By giving another person something they want, we can persuade them to give us what we want. That is the essence of negotiation. Negotiation as a legal activity is not so very different. It is about mastering a set of facts that encapsulate your client's circumstances and managing these facts to obtain their desired outcome by ensuring that the other party also received something that is important to them. It is an excellent activity that encourages quick thinking and a flexible approach to problem solving as well as providing a valuable opportunity to develop communication skills in a professional setting.

In legal practice, negotiation is a method of alternative dispute resolution that seeks to resolve the dispute without the need for litigation. The role of alternative dispute resolution has increased dramatically in recent years with over 90% of civil and family disputes settled by negotiation or mediation rather than in the courtroom. It plays a role in the lives of most legal professionals and the ability to conduct an effective negotiation that reaches a settlement which is acceptable to both parties is an important legal skill. In recognition of the importance of negotiation as a skill in legal practice, it has become increasingly common for negotiation to be encountered by undergraduate law students, either as an extra-curricular activity or as part of a skills programme embedded within the curriculum. There is a national negotiation competition each year which is open to teams of undergraduate and postgraduate students and is organised by the Centre for Effective Dispute Resolution.

A typical negotiation scenario involves a set of common facts that are shared with both teams. Each side will also receive a set of confidential instructions that lays out the details of the problem from the perspective of their client and explains what it is that the client wants to achieve from the settlement. An extract from a negotiation scenario is given in Figure 4.4.

⚫ You will find a more detailed scenario on the Online Resource Centre.

COMMON FACTS

Alice was injured when she was struck by a car driven by Jemima as she was crossing the road by the train station in Swindon. The police attended the accident and administered a breathalyser test to Jemima which was negative. There were no witnesses to the accident and the police do not intend to charge Jemima with any driving offence. Alice is seeking compensation for her injuries and both parties have instructed solicitors to reach an agreement on their behalf.

CONFIDENTIAL FACTS: ALICE

Alice knows that she had not checked for oncoming traffic when she stepped into the road as the only thing on her mind was getting across as quickly as possible as she was afraid she was going to miss her train to Leeds. However, Alice believes that the driver of the car was speeding and may have been using a mobile phone as she certainly had one in her hand when she got out of the car following the accident. Presumably the police would be able to check the driver's phone for recent calls if the matter progressed further. However, Alice does not really want the police to become involved as they would check her medical records and discover that a great many of her injuries had been sustained in the fight with her boyfriend the following day. She does, however, feel that she is entitled to compensation as she was hurt in the accident, albeit not as badly as she claimed at the outset, and instructs you to obtain as much money as possible from the driver of the car. At the very least, she would like £150 because this will enable her to repay the money she owes her boyfriend and she thinks that the driver of the car should pay for her train ticket as she was in too much pain to make the journey. When Alice was receiving medical treatment at the side of the road, her bag was stolen and she would like Jemima to cover the cost of replacing the bag and its contents which she values at £500.

CONFIDENTIAL FACTS: JEMIMA

Jemima absolutely refutes the allegation that she was using her mobile telephone at the time of the accident: she simply grabbed it as she jumped out of the car in case she needed to call an ambulance for the injured pedestrian. However, she does not want to take the risk that the police will become involved with the accident investigation as she had been taken prescription medication on the day in question and had been advised that she should not drive as it might make her drowsy or affect her judgement. Although she feels that she is not in any way to blame for the accident as Alice walked out in front of her car without looking, she is prepared to pay a sufficient sum of money to Alice simply to stop the matter from progressing any further but would prefer not to pay more than £2000 (this is half of the money in her savings account).

Figure 4.4 Extract from a negotiation scenario

⚫ You may also want to look at the video clip of a negotiation competition on the Online Resource Centre to give you an idea of what is involved and how negotiation works in practice.

How does negotiation work?

Simulated negotiations usually involve two teams of two students with each team representing one party to a legal dispute. The four participants will sit around a table together and try to find a resolution to the dispute that suits both clients. It is usual for the negotiation to start with each side identifying the issues that they want to discuss during the course of the negotiation. This may take the form of a written agenda or the participants may simply list the points for discussion. There will usually be a fair degree of correspondence between the two sides about the issues to be discussed even though they will be coming at it from different angles: for example, the team representing Alice in the negotiation scenario in Figure 4.4 will want to discuss how much compensation she will receive whilst the team representing Jemima in that scenario will want to cover how much compensation she will have to pay. So there is a single issue here—the level of compensation payable—viewed from two different perspectives. Of course, there may be an issue that is raised by one side which will come as a surprise to the other side as it is not contained in their facts but this should not prove too much of a problem provided that it is revealed at this early stage of the negotiation. As part of this initial stage of the negotiation, the two sides will agree not only what points will be addressed but what order these will be taken in and this creates a structure for the negotiation.

Once discussion of the first issue has commenced, the negotiation will involve a combination of questioning and bargaining. Questioning is an important part of negotiation as both sides have only a partial knowledge of the facts having heard the story from the perspective of their client only. The more facts that you have, the easier it will be to bargain effectively so you should never be afraid to ask questions: if you are wondering why the other side want something, ask them. When you know why somebody wants something, you can exercise more flexibility and creativity in finding a way for them to have it that does not damage the interests of your own client.

As the negotiation progresses, the teams work through each of the issues and try to find a compromise position on each that is agreeable to their client. This can be difficult: some negotiations contain issues that simply cannot be resolved in which case you have to agree as much as possible and seek further instructions from your client on the outstanding matters. When agreement is reached, it is important to keep a note of the terms of the agreement so that you have an accurate record of the terms of the negotiated settlement. It is also worth checking and double checking with the other team to make sure that you have the same understanding of what has been agreed as each point is settled. It is most unfortunate to reach the end of a negotiation thinking that there is an agreement only to find out that the other side has a different understanding of what has been agreed, particularly if there is insufficient time remaining to revisit the issue.

By the end of the negotiation, you should have reached a provisional agreement to take back to your client. Remember that you cannot agree to settle on your client's behalf—you must achieve the best deal that you can and then put this to your client to see if they will accept it.

The stages of a negotiation

Negotiation training provided me with a crucial insight into the practical aspects of the commercial world. I was introduced to the importance of several skills in such a context including the ability to empathise with the other party whilst maintaining a strong grasp on my position through calm and coherent reasoning.

Ray-Shio, King's College London

The easiest way to explain how a negotiation works is to consider the stages of a negotiation that are used by the judges in the National Negotiation Competition. These cover the extent of preparation, the proficiency of the negotiation, the professionalism of the negotiators, and their insight into their own performance. Each of the judging criteria shown in the competition scoresheet in Figure 4.5 and the skills involved will be explored in detail in the sections that follow.

Negotiation competition scoresheet

Judge

Room

Name of Negotiation Scenario

Team letter

This team's overall ranking

1 = Most effective team   3 = Third most effective team
2 = Next most effective team   4 = Least effective team

Tie-break score

Total score based on the seven judging criteria below

I - Negotiation planning

Judging from their overall performance and apparent strategy, how would you describe how well-prepared for the negotiation this team was?

1	2	3	4	5	6	7
Flawless	Outstanding	Excellent	Very good	Good	Adequate	Weak

II - Concession management

How would you describe how effective this team was in managing the time and the nature of any concessions made; holding a position or being flexible as appropriate?

1	2	3	4	5	6	7
Flawless	Outstanding	Excellent	Very good	Good	Adequate	Weak

III - Teamwork

How would you describe how effective these negotiators were in working together as a team; sharing responsibility and providing mutual backup?

1	2	3	4	5	6	7
Flawless	Outstanding	Excellent	Very good	Good	Adequate	Weak

IV - Relationship between the negotiating teams

How would you describe the way in which this team managed its relationship with the other team, either contributing or detracting from achieving the client's best interests?

1	2	3	4	5	6	7
Flawless	Outstanding	Excellent	Very good	Good	Adequate	Weak

V - Outcome of session

In light of both the negotiation and the self-analysis, **and regardless of whether agreement was reached,** how would you describe the outcome of the session in respect of it having served the client's goals and interests?

1	2	3	4	5	6	7
Flawless	Outstanding	Excellent	Very good	Good	Adequate	Weak

VI - Negotiation ethics

To what extent did this negotiating team observe or violate the ethical requirements of a professional relationship?

1	2	5	6	7
Observed		Violated somewhat	Violated	Strongly violated

VII - Self-analysis

Teams should begin this 10-minute period by addressing the following questions:

(a) "In reflecting on the entire negotiation, if you faced a similar situation tomorrow, what would you do the same and what would you do differently?"

(b) "How well did your strategy work in relation to the outcome?"

Based on this team's self-analysis, how would you describe how well the team learned from this negotiation and how adequate was their process of self-analysis?"

1	2	3	4	5	6	7
Flawless	Outstanding	Excellent	Very good	Good	Adequate	Weak

Figure 4.5 Negotiation competition scoresheet

Negotiation planning

There is a fair amount of work to do prior to the negotiation. You must start with a careful analysis of the facts in order to identify the client's issues and to formulate a strategy that will enable you to use the facts to achieve your client's objectives. Start by creating a list of the objectives and work out what your best and worst positions are on each of these. In other words, identify your best case scenario outcome and your least-good-but-still-acceptable outcome as this identifies the parameters within which you will need to negotiate. For example, Alice in the earlier scenario has stated that she wants at least £150 compensation for her injuries so this is your bottom line on this issue—anything less is not acceptable to her. What you do not know is the other end of the spectrum as she has only said that she wants 'as much money as possible'. Elsewhere in the negotiation, information was provided about the nature of Alice's injuries so you would be able to conduct research into the level of compensation that would usually be payable to give you some guidance as to what you can expect to achieve on this issue. It is always important to have some idea of the parameters of negotiation on each issue. You can plot these on a scale so that you have a visible reminder of your scope to negotiate on each point. An example of this can be seen in Figure 4.6.

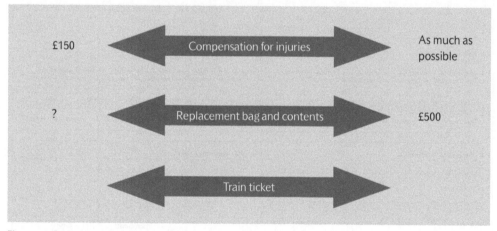

Figure 4.6 Room to negotiate on various issues

The benefit of listing the issues in this way is that you can see at a glance how they relate to each other, particularly if you plot what you have already agreed and try to offset any shortfall by aiming for a better deal on other issues. For example, if the negotiators representing Jemima refused to go higher than £175 in relation to compensation for injuries, you could see that this was towards the lower end of what you had hoped to achieve (although still acceptable to Alice). As such, you might want to try to achieve something closer to Alice's desired figure in relation to the handbag as a means of increasing the overall financial package. There are ethical issues in relation to this that will be discussed later in this section.

Research is an important part of negotiation planning as it is inevitable that there will be facts that you need to know that are not included in your instructions. This may involve the law—such as the quantum of damages for personal injury—or it may relate to other matters raised by the facts. For example, you would need to find out the cost of a train ticket from Swindon to Leeds in order to recover its cost for Alice.

The essence of the planning stage of the negotiation is the extrapolation of key information and its reorganisation into a series of inter-related goals, each of which could be satisfied by a range of outcomes. Essentially, it is a process of analysis and information management combined with an ability to distinguish between facts that are relevant and those of little or no significance. These are essential legal skills that will be important for students wishing to enter the legal profession as a solicitor or barrister. However, this ability to manage data and to sift through facts is one which will also be useful outside of the legal profession.

Concession management

Negotiation involves finding a mutually agreeable position that is some point between the desired outcome of the two parties. As such, an effective negotiation involves the timely and appropriate making of concessions—it is all about knowing what to give to the other side in order to gain something of greater importance to your client. Despite the planning that has taken place prior to the negotiation, concession management usually involves the need to think quickly and to work out how any particular concession affects the overall profile of the negotiation and whether it serves the client's interests. What will you give to get what you want and will that make your client happy? This requires that you are able to stand your ground to resist making unsuitable concessions and that you use the facts effectively to explain your position to the other team. Equally, it is important that you are flexible in suggesting ways that meet the needs of both clients: if both parties want the same thing and this is not possible, you need to be able to think of creative suggestions within the scope of your instructions that might resolve this potential deadlock. If it is not possible to divide up the pie, you will need to make the pie bigger!

There is a great skill in recognising objectives and identifying a creative way to achieve these objectives. Given the emphasis on alternative dispute resolution, this is an essential skill for those aiming to work within the legal profession. However, most forms of employment involve problem solving and the ability to respond in a timely and positive way to tricky situations with a creative and flexible solution is one that is of almost universal value.

Working in social work has made good use of the negotiation skills that I gained on my law degree. My work often involves conflict between different factions within a family and I am able to guide them towards agreement and help them to find consensus.

Kate, Southampton University

I decided not to practise law and instead took a graduate diploma in nursing and I now work as a psychiatric nurse. The ability to work through conflict in a calm way and to suggest alternative ways of resolving conflict is a key part of my role.

Dave, Southampton University

Team work

Negotiation usually involves teams of two students working together. Preparation is generally undertaken collaboratively and it is usual for students to allocate responsibility for particular aspects of the negotiation as part of the planning process. For example, you might agree that you will deal with the first issue about compensation for Alice's injuries and your partner will tackle the matter of recompense for the stolen bag. This helps to ensure that each person gets fully involved in the discussion once the negotiation gets under way and should go some way to ensuring that you are not talking over each other during the negotiation.

This may sound straightforward but it can be rather more tricky in practice. Imagine that you are listening to your partner trying to deal with an issue that you had both agreed would be their responsibility but you can see that they are struggling. Perhaps the other team has introduced factors that you did not foresee during your planning or maybe your partner has encountered a particularly hostile or argumentative opponent. Whatever the cause, you can see that they are struggling. Do you intervene? If you do, it may look like you are overriding your partner and not allowing them to play a full role in the negotiation. This would not be good team work. However, leaving them to struggle without providing assistance is also poor team work as there is an expectation of mutual backup and support. There is a fine line between interfering with your partner and abandoning them! Many students find it useful to think about how they will (tactfully) signal to their partner that they would like them to intervene and think about a form of words that can be used to precede an intervention that makes it less like a usurpation of their partner's role.

Managing communication is a central part of a successful negotiation. You will need to speak to both members of the opposing team and your partner at different points of the negotiation (see Figure 4.7) and it can be difficult, particularly if the discussion becomes heated, not to interrupt or talk over other people. However, a negotiation can become chaotic very quickly if people start talking over each other. Give some careful thought to how you will manage communications with your partner and the other team and consider what you will do to resolve the situation if the other participants become heated and start interrupting each other.

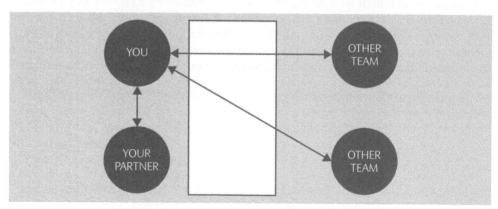

Figure 4.7 Managing communication in a negotiation

Finally, it is important to remember that team work in negotiation involves more than the distribution of responsibility for dealing with particular issues: it also necessitates the division of labour in terms of other matters such as keeping a record of what has been agreed—someone has to keep notes but it would not be professional if you were both writing at the same time—or making calculations if the negotiation involves finances.

The ability to work with colleagues in a cooperative and supportive manner that allows people to play to their strengths and bolsters their weaknesses is a highly valuable skill.

People who work well in a team are more attractive to employers as they can be used more flexibly and efficiently to achieve the objectives of the organisation. If you can work well with others, your skills can be used in a wider range of settings because they can be combined with the skills of many other employees. By working with others in a work setting, you will also be learning from them and enhancing your value to your employer. It is also a sign of professionalism to be able to work with others to achieve a common goal irrespective of your personal feelings for them.

Relationship between the negotiating teams

Negotiation is an unusual activity as it requires not only that you work in collaboration with a partner, who wants the same things that you want, but also that you form an effective working relationship with your opponents who, after all, seem to be trying to achieve the exact opposite of your client's goals. Despite this seeming opposition, it is important to remember that both sides share a common objective which is to reach an agreement that will give both parties something of what they want thus avoiding the need for litigation. A cooperative relationship that acknowledges the tension between the clients' objectives but which seeks to resolve this without acrimony between the negotiators is the best way to achieve this shared goal. This may be difficult to achieve if the other side take a hostile or aggressive approach to the negotiation but the ability to diffuse such an atmosphere is a valuable skill that can be developed through negotiation.

This aspect of negotiation will also help you to develop the ability to resist pressure as it will not always be possible to give the other party what they want without an adverse impact on your own client's interests. Any seeming lack of agreement has to be managed firmly and fairly without damaging the professional relationship between the negotiating teams.

Any number of workplace situations will involve differences of opinion or bring together people with competing goals. The ability to reconcile differences emphasises commonality and to achieve consensus out of conflict is a skill that will be valued by employers. The element of dispute management that is inherent in negotiation will enable you to experience the different strategies that can be used to manage conflict and to break deadlock.

Outcome of the session

There are a number of skills tied up with bringing the negotiation to a successful conclusion that achieves an outcome that is compatible with the client's goals and interests. It requires a good level of insight into the client's objectives and creativity in finding ways to serve these interests that are consistent with your instructions. You will need to ensure that you have covered all the points that were important to your client so you must manage your time carefully, particularly bearing in mind that the other side may raise points on behalf of their client that were not part of your instructions. You must be clear about what has been agreed during the session so you will need to summarise the points that have been concluded and draw attention to anything that is yet to be resolved. Remember that it is essential that the final outcome of the session is one that is likely to be acceptable to both clients as an unhappy client will not accept the terms of the negotiation and it will have been a pointless exercise. For this reason, it is always a good idea to check that the other team have covered all their points and have reached a provisional agreement that is acceptable to their client.

Negotiation makes great demands on your organisational skills as you have to balance all the facets of your client's case with the requirement of the other team's clients in order to find a mutually acceptable resolution within a tight time limit. As such, negotiation gives you the opportunity to demonstrate your ability to manage a complex situation and take account of a range of competing interests whilst still achieving your overall objective.

Negotiation ethics

Participation in negotiation will give you an insight into the professional framework of ethical behaviour in which lawyers operate. This is an important aspect of professional practice as it is incumbent upon all solicitors and barristers to act in an ethical way to uphold the standards and reputation of the legal profession. There is great scope for unethical behaviour within a negotiation as one way to achieve a better deal for your client is to misrepresent what it is that they would accept.

For example, if you had obtained a low sum for Alice in relation to her injuries, you might want to push for a higher sum in relation to her bag to compensate for this. However, if you said 'the value of the bag and its contents was £750' then this would be unethical as it is deliberate misstatement of the facts. Even a careless turn of phrase can give rise to ethical problems. If the other side offered you £150 as compensation for injuries and you replied 'that wouldn't be acceptable to my client' then this would also be a misrepresentation. Of course, if you simply said 'ideally, my client would be looking for more money than that' then this would be true so sometimes it is simply a matter of choosing your words carefully. Any deliberate or inadvertent falsehood is unethical and unprofessional and would be penalised by the judge in a negotiation competition.

....

I was asked a question about ethics at a pupillage interview and was able to draw on my experience in the National Negotiation Competition to demonstrate not just that I could comment on the problem that the panel posed but that I had some experience, albeit it in a competition rather than in real life, of recognising and resolving ethical issues.

Nick, University of Sussex

....

Practical exercise: ethical considerations

There are often ethical dilemmas hidden within the instructions from your client in a negotiation competition so you will need to ensure that you are able to spot these and be prepared to formulate a strategy to deal with them. For example:

- Alice has a medical report that outlines her injuries, some of which were quite serious. However, she tells you that some of these were sustained the previous day when she was beaten by her boyfriend during a drunken argument.

- Jemima tells you that she was driving whilst under the influence of prescription medication and had been told not to drive. During the negotiation, the other side ask if there was any factor that affected the quality of Jemima's driving.

- The other side ask 'what is the lowest sum that your client will accept?' You know that this is £150 but do not want to come away with such a poor settlement so you say that your client is ideally looking for a sum over £1000.

Think about the ethical consideration raised by these situations and ponder how you would deal with them.

⚫ You will find some comment upon this on the Online Resource Centre.

Most industries operate within some regulatory framework and have expectations of standards of ethical behaviour. Participation in negotiation gives you an opportunity to get a feel for how such ethical requirements operate in practice and to understand the constraints that they place upon your professional practice. If you plan to work within the legal profession, you will have gained useful experience of the ethical issues that arise within law that will enable you to demonstrate to potential employers your awareness of the ethical considerations within the legal profession. If you are seeking employment in other industries, you could use your experience from negotiation to demonstrate your ability to adapt to an ethical framework and you may be able to draw parallels between the legal environment and the industry in question.

Self analysis

The national negotiation competition concludes with a period for reflection after which each team reflects on their performance in the presence of the judges. This centres around two questions:

- How well did your strategy work in relation to the outcome of the negotiation?
- In reflecting on the entire negotiation, if you faced a similar situation tomorrow, what would you do the same and what would you do differently?

The purpose of this is to ensure that students learn from their experience in the competition with a view to enabling them to improve on their performance in subsequent negotiations.

The ability to reflect on your own performance and evaluate it in a frank and honest way that picks up on areas of weakness and considers ways in which these could be strengthened is an important personal skill that is essential to self-improvement. This process of self-analysis can be exercised in a number of settings beyond the negotiation competition and will enable you to continually build upon your skills set and ensure that you are always seeking to enhance your performance.

What employability skills does negotiation develop?

Although negotiation is a common extra-curricular activity for law students and the alternative dispute resolution has a central role in legal practice, there is nothing essentially legalistic about negotiation. There will be a need to engage in formal negotiations in a range of professional settings but, more than this, the skills involved in negotiation in mustering facts and presenting these in a way that achieves your desired outcome are of wide application. This section highlights the ways in which negotiation skills are relevant to employability by using the categories outlined in Chapter 1 that have already been discussed earlier in this chapter in the context of mooting.

Practical skills

- **Problem solving.** Negotiation often involves factual situations that are outside the experience of the students taking part in the competition. For example, one recent scenario involved a dispute arising from an international space treaty and another concerned the breeding arrangements of a rare breed of donkey. Students often find it useful to investigate the factual setting to ensure that they have a grasp of the background within which the negotiation takes place but this can be complicated particularly when the subject matter is so far removed from existing knowledge.

- **Numeracy.** Negotiation scenarios often involve money and finances. It is often the case that part of a dispute involves money owed by one party to the other and these figures are sometimes complex, involving percentage profits/losses or predictions about costs. In such negotiations, the students who are able to manage the figures are always at an advantage. Remember also that finances might be at issue in negotiations involving contract formations and business arrangements as well as those involving disputes.

Personal skills

- **Time management.** As with any extra-curricular activity, you will have to manage your time carefully to ensure that your participation in negotiation competitions does not interfere with your other study commitments and deadlines. There is also a need to manage your time very carefully in the negotiation itself. You will have a limited period of time within which to try and reach a conclusion and it is up to you to ensure that all the points at issue are discussed and, hopefully, an agreement reached during that time.

- **Professional and ethical behaviour.** Professional ethics are a crucial aspect of negotiation. As the other side have no way of knowing details of the confidential facts that sets out details of your client's situation, it would be easy to misrepresent or mislead in order to obtain a more favourable outcome for your client. As such, negotiation provides an excellent opportunity to experience working within the parameters of an ethical framework and understanding how these influence professional behaviour.

- **Flexibility.** Negotiation will develop your ability to move beyond an initial strategy and to respond in a flexible manner to propositions put to you by the other side. As you only know half of the scenario, you will have to be prepared to incorporate the other party's goals into your approach to negotiation which will often mean a wide-ranging rethink of your planned strategy.

- **Planning.** Although flexibility is the key to successful negotiation, a good negotiation is based upon meticulous planning during the preparation stages. It is important that you muster all your facts and decide how to deal with them with as many alternative strategies as possible to help you to accommodate the interests that are likely to be raised by the other side.

- **Decision-making.** There are many decisions to be made during the planning stages of negotiation: what points need to be addressed, what is the range of acceptable outcomes on each point, what order will the points be taken in, and who will be responsible for doing what during the negotiation. However, by far the most difficult decisions will need to be made during the negotiation as you decide at what point to stop pushing for more and to accept the other side's suggested settlement on each issue.

- **Team working.** Negotiation is a highly collaborative activity. You should expect to analyse the scenario with your partner and to plan a strategy for the negotiation. This includes a planned division of labour in terms of which of you is to take the lead on particular points. However, the execution of negotiation is likely to involve a far more fluid approach to team working as you will need to be alert for problems encountered by your partner and to be willing and able to intervene to support them if they are struggling.

- **Verbal communication.** Negotiation requires that you are able to communicate the nature of your client's case to the other side in a clear and concise manner. You will need to be able to ask questions, using a variety of open and closed questions, in order to elicit information about their client's claim and to provide succinct summaries of what has been agreed to ensure that everyone is clear on the terms of the agreement reached.

Negotiation also depends upon your ability to listen to the other team as it is crucial that you have an awareness of what they want so that you can take it into account when formulating suggestions for a settlement.

Professional skills

- **Legal research.** The level of legal research needed to negotiate varies according to the nature of the problem scenario. Some negotiations require no legal knowledge whatsoever whereas others are based in a particular legal framework so that you will need to know, for example, the level of damages for personal injury so that you can work out what sort of figure to seek on behalf of an injured client. Remember, however, not to get too tied up with what would happen if the case went to court: a negotiation is an alternative to the strict application of the law in a courtroom setting so your legal research should guide your negotiation, not rule it.

- **Legal problem solving.** There is an element of problem solving inherent in negotiation in that you are interested in finding a resolution to a legal dispute but, as mentioned earlier, negotiation is not concerned with what the outcome of a case would be if it were heard in court. Nonetheless, it still involves the application of the law to a set of facts even if the likely legal outcome is disregarded in favour of a negotiated settlement. In essence, it is important background knowledge against which the negotiation takes place.

- **Negotiation.** It is difficult to think of any activity that will do more to develop your negotiation skills than taking part in a negotiation competition!

In conclusion, negotiation involves a range of skills that are of relevance to a career in the legal profession and which will enhance your employability in other non-law settings. Negotiation provides excellent experience in dispute management as a successful outcome is one that satisfies your client's objectives whilst still accommodating the needs of the other party to a dispute. It requires that you juggle facts with dexterity and present these in a clear manner to the other party whilst persuading them to agree to things that fulfil your client's objectives. It is a highly skilful activity that will develop your ability to manage facts and, more crucially, other people in a potentially acrimonious setting. It is invaluable for students wishing to practise law as it gives you first-hand experience of a common means of dispute resolution but it is also a fantastic (and fun) way of developing and demonstrating a wide range of the skills that will be useful in any number of professional settings and which will be valued by prospective employers.

I work as an estate agent and the skills that I learned by taking part in negotiation are one of the most valuable parts of the law degree for me. I often find myself marooned in the middle of the vendor and the purchasers as I try to persuade each of them to give the other just a little bit more of what they want to make a deal. Negotiation taught me to manage the facts, to look at them from the perspective of more than one party and to think about ways to present them that make them palatable to my clients.

David, Nottingham Trent University

Finding opportunities to negotiate

Whilst most students are aware of the importance attached to mooting as a method of developing skills and demonstrating commitment to a career in law, the benefits of taking part in negotiation competitions tend to be less well known. This is probably because negotiation competitions have only gained popularity in law schools in relatively recent years whereas mooting has a long-standing history as a method of inculcating key legal skills.

Opportunities to get involved in negotiation competitions tends to be more limited than opportunities to moot as many law schools have no internal negotiation competition at all and there is only one national competition. In the following sections, you will find guidance on how to get involved with these competitions and how to gain negotiation skills if your university does not run a negotiation competition.

Internal negotiation competitions

If there is an internal negotiation competition at your university or a training course or workshops available, be sure to take part in them. Remember that you will gain skills through participation in the training but will put these into practice in the competition so try to do both if you can find the time: it does not take long to prepare for a negotiation competition (far less than preparing for a moot) so concerns about distracting from your study time should not prevent you from taking part. Moreover, you should remember that building skills is an investment in your future career so you should try to make the time to take part in any negotiation activities that are available. In an ideal world, you should do this as soon as the opportunity arises so this could mean that you take part in negotiation activities in all three years of your studies.

If there is no negotiation competition at your university, then you could always start such a competition, either alone or in conjunction with other students to share the workload (remember that working with others demonstrates skills in team work).

Practical advice: organising a negotiation competition

If you want to start a negotiation competition from scratch, there are certain things that you will need:

- **At least one negotiation scenario.** The negotiation scenario is comprised of sets of confidential instructions, one from each fictitious client, and may be accompanied by a set of common facts that are made known to both teams. It is possible to have a negotiation involving three or more parties but the dynamic of the negotiating relationship is trickier so it is advisable to start with a two-way negotiation if everyone is new to negotiation. The scenario will need to be distributed to the teams at least one day before the negotiation is due to take place. The organiser will need to ensure that teams are divided into two groups (one representing each party) and that the correct scenario is sent to each team.

- **A schedule of negotiations.** How many negotiations need to take place? This depends upon three factors: how many teams enter the competition, how many judges are available, and how you plan to organise the competition (a knock-out competition is likely to involve more rounds than using a points system to put the four highest scoring teams straight into the semi-final). If students are working in teams of two then four students may up a single negotiation and you can hold these simultaneously if you have more than one judge. Think about how long the negotiation will last (20 minutes should be ample for the first round provided you pick a relatively straightforward negotiation scenario) and be sure to give the judge(s) a break between sessions to gather their thoughts and work out the scores. It is a good idea to publish the schedule of negotiations in advance so that all students taking part are clear about the time commitment involved in the competition.

- **A set of rules that govern the competition.** It helps enormously if you can work out the rules in advance and publicise them rather than trying to deal with problems as they arise. As a minimum, your rules should specify the duration of each negotiation, the method of scoring, the timing of the rounds, whether teams can take a break, the degree of feedback provided to competitors, and the way that progression through the competition will be determined.

- **A score sheet that specifies the judging criteria.** The teams will need to understand in advance what skills are being tested and the judge will need to know how to allocate scores to the negotiations. It would be sensible (and easiest) to use the criteria that are used in the national competition but you could always create your own.

- **Facilities and equipment.** You will need to book suitable rooms for an appropriate amount of time, remembering that teams may need somewhere to wait before the competition and whilst waiting for feedback from the judges. You may want to arrange a video camera if you decide to record the negotiations and the judge will need a pen, paper, method of timing the negotiation, and water. The final should be held in a large venue and students invited to attend as this is likely to encourage participation in subsequent years.

⬤ You will find some negotiation scenarios on the Online Resource Centre with an indication of an appropriate timeframe for the negotiation and its level of complexity. There are also some suggestions for rules and a sample of a score sheet.

Although it will be a wonderful opportunity to show your entrepreneurial spirit and organisational skills, there is a disadvantage to setting up a negotiation competition as it makes it harder for you to take part. Harder but not impossible. The essence of the problem is that other students might perceive that you have an advantage in that you would be able to see both sides of the negotiation in advance and you could 'fix' the draw to give yourself an advantage against a less proficient team of negotiators. The best way to deal with these problems if you do want to take part is to tackle them head on. When you first publicise the competition, make it clear that you are prepared to put the work into organising it because you want to take part and that you will deal with the issues surrounding the confidentiality of the scenarios by asking a lecturer to select and distribute them and the objectivity of the competition draw by putting names of teams into a hat and making the draw in public. Give students the opportunity to object to either of these suggestions or invite alternative solutions. In this way, you have been open about the possible problems of you taking the roles of organiser and competitor and publicised your proposed solutions so that all students who take part do so with the full knowledge of how these issues will be addressed.

Practical advice: getting negotiation experience

If all else fails and you are really keen to get some negotiation experience, you can do so provided you can find one other student who wants to get involved. You can negotiate against each other as individuals rather than in a team of two and you can use some of the sample scenarios that you will find on the Online Resource Centre. You would need to ensure that you did not give in to the temptation to peek at the other student's scenario (it will spoil your ability to negotiate if you know their side of the story) and give yourselves a set amount of time (half an hour should be fine) to reach a conclusion. To make the experience really worthwhile, you could film the negotiation and watch it back with your opponent afterwards and, having exchanged scenarios, discuss what you could have done differently.

If you use the scenarios on the Online Resource Centre, we would be interested to hear what deal you reached and whether you think it was one that would please your client. Tell us at finchandfafinski.com/get-in-touch or @FinchFafinski on Twitter.

National negotiation competition

The national negotiation competition sponsored by the Centre for Effective Dispute Resolution (CEDR) takes place every year in the spring term, with the regional heats being held in February at four venues around England and Wales and the final taking place in April.

The competition is open to two teams of two students from each institution irrespective of whether they are studying at undergraduate or graduate level. This includes students on the CPE/GDL as well as LPC and BPTC students. The only restriction upon entry is that students may not compete more than once so you will need to think carefully about whether you want to take part whilst undertaking your undergraduate degree or to wait until you progress to the professional stage of your training.

Practical advice: when to take part

Very few universities teach negotiation skills to undergraduates although some may run extra-curricular workshops or training courses. This means that undergraduates could feel at a competitive disadvantage compared to LPC or BPTC students who will have taken a module on negotiation skills. However, as entry is limited to four students from each institution, there may be greater competition to take part at these later stages of study so it may be that you have more opportunity of being selected to take part in the national competition whilst you are an undergraduate. It is important to remember that, despite the lack of formal training, many undergraduate teams have won the competition so it is no bar to achieving success.

Progression from the regional heats to the national final is based upon the points awarded to each team over the course of two negotiations. In this competition, the lowest scoring teams are the most successful. Three teams from each of the four regional heats will progress to the final. The 12 qualifying teams receive a one-day training course at CEDR to help them to prepare for the final. The ultimate winner of the competition goes on to represent England and Wales in the international negotiation competition so it really is a prize worth having in terms of enhancing your CV and helping you stand out to prospective employers.

- National Negotiation Competition website: **www.cedr.com/skills/competition/**.
- International Negotiation Competition website: **www.chapman.edu/law/competitions/ dispute-resolution/international-negotiation-competition/index.aspx**.

Client interviewing

All legal disputes are initiated by people—either acting as individuals or as representatives of an organisation—thus dealing with clients is a central part of life within the legal

Alternative dispute resolution

 Key issues

- Most lawyers spend far more time negotiating than they do in court.
- Increasingly, parties are encouraged to use alternative ways of resolving their disagreements rather than going to court.
- Much controversy surrounds whether alternative dispute resolution (ADR) is preferable to litigation.

Introduction

Anyone who thinks, after watching television crime shows, that a lawyer's day is typically spent in court is very much mistaken. Very few cases go to court. Most are resolved by negotiation, mediation, or other forms of **alternative dispute resolution (ADR)**. We will explore all of these in this chapter.

Definition

Alternative dispute resolution (ADR) refers to the various ways of settling a dispute that avoid the parties going to court. It typically involves the parties negotiating a resolution themselves or through their lawyers. Sometimes, a third party, such as a mediator, can be brought in to resolve the disagreement.

The ethical issues raised by ADR are complex. First, there is the question of whether mediation and negotiation are to be encouraged. Many people assume that ending up in court is the worst possible outcome and that the more cases in which the parties reach agreement on their own, the better. There is said to be a sign in a US magistrate's office that reads: 'To sue is human; to settle, divine.' This is echoed by two leading American academics, who have written:

A trial is a failure. Although we celebrate it as the centerpiece of our system of justice, we know that trial is not only an uncommon method of resolving disputes, but a disfavored one. With some notable exceptions, lawyers, judges, and commentators agree that pretrial settlement is almost always cheaper, faster, and better than trial.[1]

But not everyone agrees. Some see grave dangers in ADR. Certainly, there are serious concerns about it, as well as undoubted benefits. We will explore these concerns later.

Second, there is an issue about the ethical standards that lawyers should use while negotiating. Lawyers acting in court are open to public scrutiny and assessment. There are reasonably clear rules that govern how they should behave. Judges will quickly spot whether or not lawyers have done their preparation properly, or if they are employing unethical tactics. By contrast, negotiation and mediation are undertaken in private, and thus are not subject to overt scrutiny. There are few clear ethical guidelines that apply to negotiation. Indeed, it perhaps not too cynical to suggest that one reason why lawyers are keen on settlement may be that it means they avoid public scrutiny and regulation.

The forms of ADR

The following are some of the ways in which a case might be resolved without going to court.

1. *Negotiation between lawyers* This refers to situations in which lawyers reach a settlement between themselves by discussing the issues. The clients are normally involved only when asked to approve the agreement that the lawyers have reached. The client will normally trust the lawyer to get the best deal possible.

2. *Negotiation between the parties* This refers to situations in which the discussions take place between the parties, in which instance the lawyers have relatively little to do. They may advise the clients on the legal position at the start of discussions or they may be asked to comment on the proposed settlement that the parties have reached. Of course, in some cases, clients will reach agreement without seeking the advice of lawyers at all.

3. *Mediation* The clients may seek the help of a mediator—that is, someone trained in helping parties to reach an agreement. The precise role of a mediator is somewhat controversial and will be discussed in detail later in this chapter. In England, the most popular model is to use a neutral mediator, whose primary role is to help the parties to reach an agreement, irrespective of the content of the bargain. In other words, the mediator should not express a view on whether the agreement is fair and should not seek to usher the parties towards the agreement that he or she thinks is best; rather, the role of the neutral mediator is simply to facilitate the parties' discussions and in doing so help them to reach an agreement. Other models

---

[1] S. Gross and K. Syverud, 'Getting to no: A study of settlement negotiations and the selection of cases for trial' (1991) 90 Michigan Law Review 319, 320.

give mediators a more interventionist role, encouraging the parties to reach a fair agreement. Sometimes, lawyers can act as mediators and can then give neutral legal advice while also facilitating consensus.

4. *Alternative adjudication* Alternative adjudication, or arbitration as it is sometimes known, is in some ways similar to court procedure. The parties ask an arbitrator to hear their arguments and to determine the best solution. Usually, such a hearing will be less formal than that which would take place in court. Arbitrators are sometimes preferred to courts because they are cheaper and less formal. Depending on the nature of the matter, the parties might ask lawyers to represent them at the arbitration.

The main variations between these four methods can be summarised as follows.

1. *The role of the third party* As already indicated, at one extreme is arbitration, in which the arbitrator determines the outcome much as a judge rules on a case. By contrast, in mediation, the mediator usually is not meant to impose, or even influence, a decision; the mediator is merely meant to help the parties to reach an agreement.

2. *The effect of the decision* Different processes will create results that are more or less binding. In arbitration, the parties typically agree that they will comply with the decision of the arbitrator, whereas mediated agreements are binding only in so far as the parties are happy to comply with them. Indeed, one of the aims of a mediated settlement is that the parties are equipped to review the agreement over time.

3. *The role of lawyers* The extent to which lawyers are involved may vary. In some systems, such as arbitration, solicitors may play a major role. In some forms of mediation, the use of lawyers is positively discouraged.

4. *The role of law* In some systems, the aim is to produce the result that best reflects the legal principles. Arbitrators will typically determine the result that reflects the law. When lawyers negotiate, they normally seek to agree on a solution similar to that which a court might reach. In mediation, by contrast, the mediator will expect to help the parties to reach the conclusion that they think is fair, which may or may not be what a judge would think appropriate.

Digging deeper

Although the different forms of ADR are offered as alternatives to litigation, the contrast is not that straightforward. Marc Galanter is critical of the description of negotiation as 'alternative dispute resolution', arguing that:

> [T]he negotiation of disputes is not an alternative to litigation. It is only a slight exaggeration to say that it *is* litigation. There are not two distinct processes, negotiation and litigation; there is a single process of disputing in the vicinity of

official tribunals that we might call *litigotiation*, that is, the strategic pursuit of a settlement through mobilizing the court process.[2]

As we shall see, predictions about litigation impact on negotiations, and what has happened in negotiations can impact on how the court resolves a dispute. Where it is very clear what a judge would order if a case were to go to court, this can be a powerful incentive on the parties to settle with an agreement along those lines, but without incurring the expense of going to court.

There is much pressure in the legal system to discourage the parties going to court. Court proceedings are expensive to the parties, and take up judicial and court time. Most lawyers will attest that finding a negotiated settlement with which both parties can live is preferable to fighting it out in the courtroom.

Even if the case is not settled and litigation is instigated, studies suggest between 60 and 80 per cent of cases settle.[3] Of course, many more settle even before litigation is started. The Civil Procedure Rules (CPR) encourage the parties to make sensible offers and to reach agreement. A study of the new CPR found that all involved agreed that the Rules now strongly encourage settlement.[4] In particular, the new rules governing costs (see Chapter 7) and single-expert reports created a strong incentive to settle.

This chapter will start by looking at the process of negotiation, which is the way in which lawyers resolve most disputes. We will then look at other forms of ADR, including mediation and, briefly, arbitration.

Negotiation

Negotiation is at the heart of a lawyer's job. Whether it is finding a mutually acceptable set of terms for a contract or determining what damages should be paid following injuries caused by a road traffic accident, negotiation is key. There are some areas of work in which standard forms make matters easier. In conveyancing, for example, there is standard documentation for buying a house that can be used with relatively little need for negotiation, other than over the price. Similarly, there are standard levels of award available for certain injuries and so there will be little to discuss about

---

[2] M. Galanter, 'Worlds of deals: Using negotiation to teach about legal process' (1984) 34 Journal of Legal Education 368, 398.

[3] J. Peysner and M. Seneviratne, *The Management of Civil Cases: The Courts and the Post-Woolf Landscape* (Department for Constitutional Affairs, 2005).

[4] S. Gibbons, 'Group litigation, class actions and collective redress: An anniversary reappraisal of Lord Woolf's three objectives', in D. Dwyer, *Civil Procedure: Ten Years On* (Oxford University Press, 2009).

those. But in other areas there will be plenty to debate. In commercial work, the lawyers will be involved in negotiating a contract tailored to the case, designed to meet the needs of the parties. In a family case, the lawyers will seek to negotiate the set of arrangements that will work best for the particular family.

Although negotiating is probably the most important part of a lawyer's job, the area is largely unregulated. There are the general duties in the professional codes to be honest and to treat third parties fairly, discussed in Chapter 11, but these are not specific to negotiation. Indeed, neither professional code offers any specific guidance on negotiation at all. The contrast between the extensive regulation of litigation and the lack of guidance on negotiation is stark. A client claiming that his or her lawyer had negotiated negligently or in breach of ethical principles would face a huge battle.

One explanation for this is that there are a wide range of theories about the best way in which to negotiate: there may be few standards because there is little agreement over what good mediation involves. We will now look at some of the different theories on how to negotiate.

Theories of negotiation

There are a number of issues that will impact on how the parties go about negotiating.

The approach to negotiation

There is a vast literature on negotiation strategy and it would not be possible to set out all of the issues here. There are, however, two basic theories: win–lose approaches; and problem-solving approaches.

The *win–lose approach* assumes that there is a finite asset that must be divided between the couple. For example, if a divorcing couple has assets of £100,000, the lawyers may need to negotiate how that sum is to be divided. In a commercial transaction, one company will be trying to get as large a sum in payment as possible in payment for a product and the other, to pay as small a price as possible. In such a negotiation, a gain for one side must be matched by a loss to the other. Obviously, in the divorce case, the more the wife gets, the less the husband will get; the same applies to the parties in the commercial transaction. It is a little like a game of tug of war, with each side pulling as hard as it can and hoping to get as much as possible. This approach, well captured in the book *Start with No*,[5] encourages a forceful, even aggressive, style of negotiating, regarding the other side as an enemy to be exploited for gain. That may sound harsh, but remember that a lawyer must strive to do his or her best for the client. A lawyer who is kind to the other party and agrees a 'reasonable' settlement may not be doing his or her job. If you were choosing a lawyer, would

---

[5] J. Camp, *Start with No* (Crown Publishing, 2002).

you not rather have a negotiator striving to get the best possible settlement for you, rather than a negotiator who was trying to be fair to each side?

The *problem-solving approach* is somewhat different in that it focuses on the needs of the parties. In particular, this explores ways of meeting the needs or interests of *both* parties. In relation to our divorcing couple, it may be that the central wish of the wife is to be able to stay in the family house, while that of the husband is to be able to buy a flat of his own. The negotiators must then find a way of achieving both parties' goal. Exploring ways of meeting these needs may be more productive than looking at the dispute from a 'win–lose' perspective. The aim is to move away from seeing the matter in terms of a 'winner' and 'loser', towards seeing both parties finding a way in which to meet both of their needs. To consider another example, in a commercial transaction, if a suitable price cannot be found, it may help to explore what the parties really need. It may be that one company is suffering a cash flow problem and needs money quickly. That company may be happier with a smaller sum, if it is paid quickly. It may be willing to agree to that smaller sum if the other company were to introduce it to other clients. In such a case, both sides may feel that they have had a successful outcome.

Carrie Menkel-Meadow explains:

This problem-solving model seeks to demonstrate how negotiators, on behalf of litigators or planners, can more effectively accomplish their goals by focusing on the parties' actual objectives and creatively attempting to satisfy the needs of both parties, rather than by focusing exclusively on the assumed objectives of maximizing individual gain.[6]

Supporters of the problem-solving approach often claim that the win–lose approach pitches the parties against each other as adversaries. This creates a competitiveness that can disguise from the parties the solution that may be apparent to an outside observer. The parties become so fixed on winning or losing that they lose sight of what they really want from the negotiations. In the literature, an example is commonly used of two children disputing the right to the last orange in a fruit bowl. Both are adamant that they want the orange and will not share it. When the parent intervenes, it transpires that one wants the skin for a recipe for orange cake and the other, the segments to eat. There is an easy way in which both of them can have their desires met.

There is a danger of idealising the problem-solving approach, however. The example of the orange is homely, but reality is rarely that easy: usually, both children want to eat all of the orange! Going back to the divorcing couple, it is easy to pretend that finding the solution that gives the husband the flat and the wife the house is the answer, but in reality, the bigger the flat the husband gets, the less money there will be for maintenance payments to the wife. In a case involving money, a gain for one nearly always means a loss for another. We cannot skin money like we can an orange.

---

[6] C. Menkel-Meadow, 'Toward another view of legal negotiation: The structure of problem solving' (1984) 31 UCLA Law Review 754, 767.

Nevertheless, there is no doubt that encouraging parties to think about what they really want from the solution can help them to get around some seemingly impassable problem. In particular, persuading the parties to think about whether they have each reached their goals can be more helpful than thinking about who has won or lost.

Imaginative solutions are often essential to successful negotiations. Sometimes, it is not the sum of money that is the central issue, but the packaging of it: if payments were to be made in advance, would a lower sum be acceptable? Would offering a childcare subsidy encourage the applicant to take the job? Would delaying the start of the contract by six months ease matters? Sometimes, it is not the content of the agreement, but how it will appear to others that lies behind the dispute. Perhaps the job applicant is willing to agree to take the new job even if there is a lower salary, but does not want others to know that he or she has done so. Giving the role a fancy job title might be the key to making the offer acceptable. These are just a few examples of the kind of imaginative thinking that a good lawyer negotiating a dispute needs to employ.

It is also important to realise that *people* are at the heart of any negotiations and that we cannot abstract the people from the problem. Indeed, there are dangers in negotiation of treating everything in a logical way and overlooking the emotional values that may be at play.[7] That is why much of recent writing on good negotiation has emphasised the importance of the value of empathy—that is, of being able to imagine yourself in the other party's shoes. Only then can you begin to imagine the kind of offer that the other party may find acceptable.

Some commentators draw a distinction between competitive and cooperative negotiators.

- *Competitive* negotiators will try to get the very best deal for their clients (or themselves). They will squeeze the other party for every last concession and reach agreement only when no more concessions can be made.

- *Cooperative* negotiators will seek to find an agreement that is reasonably fair to both parties. They will not push for every last penny if they feel that both parties can agree on a price that is reasonable.

A good example of a more cooperative approach is given in a leading work on negotiation theory written by Roger Fisher and William Ury, *Getting to Yes*.[8] This promotes a principled negotiation that seeks a result that fulfils three goals:

- a fair and reasonable agreement;

- an agreement that is sufficient in expression and operation; and

- an agreement that improves, or at least does not harm, the relationship between the parties.

[7] C. Menkel-Meadow, 'Negotiating with lawyers, men, and things: The contextual approach still matters' (2001) 17 Negotiation Journal 257.

[8] R. Fisher and W. Ury, *Getting to Yes: Negotiation Agreement without Giving In* (Random House, 2008).

It is also notable that the goal of a lawyer under this approach is not to get the largest amount of money for the client, but rather a fair and reasonable amount. But is that ethically supportable if lawyers are meant to do the best for their clients?

Boon and Levin have made an ethical case for problem-solving negotiation, which they call 'principled negotiation':

> Principled negotiation also promotes core ethical principles, such as promoting individual autonomy, beneficence, non-maleficence and justice. By seeking to meet people's needs, principled negotiation respects individual autonomy; by attempting the [sic] expand the 'negotiating pie', it supports beneficence; by not taking advantage of the other side, it respects the principle of non-maleficence; by identifying positive criteria for resolving distributional ideas, it seeks to do justice.[9]

This depends very much on what you regard the role of the lawyer to be (see Chapter 2). It is one thing to put fairness above self-interest if you are negotiating for yourself, but if you are acting for someone else, should you do so? Perhaps the answer is that the lawyer should discuss negotiation tactics with the client, or choose what will be best for the client, regardless of what is fair for the other side.

 What would you do?

You are a family law solicitor. You represent a husband who is divorcing his wife. The wife is looking after the couple's four young children. The husband instructs you to make sure that he pays as little as possible in maintenance, and to use every trick and pressurising tactic that you can. What do you do?

What would you do if you were acting for the wife and she were to ask you to get every last penny that you could for her and the children by using every trick and pressurising tactic that you could?

Would it be justifiable to have different tactics whether acting for the wife or the husband in this case?

What would they do?

This 'What would you do?' scenario is accompanied by a podcast in which current law students debate the issues and articulate their own responses to the ethical questions that it raises. The podcast is available online at www.oxfordtextbooks.co.uk/orc/herringethics/

[9] A. Boon and J. Levin, *The Ethics and Conduct of Lawyers in England and Wales* (Hart, 2008), 368, citing T. Beauchamp and J. Childress, *Principles of Biomedical Ethics* (Oxford University Press, 2001).

Empirical studies suggest that solicitors and barristers normally negotiate by means of a win–lose approach.[10] Each party sets out its 'maximum offer' and then there is an attempt to reach an agreement that falls somewhere between the two figures. The studies suggest that this is done with a low-level intensity.[11] Andrew Boon and Jennifer Levin argue that this is partly because this positional approach is familiar and recognised. Perhaps such an approach assists with reaching a solution rapidly? After each side posits its opening offer, all that is left to do is to find a suitable figure somewhere between the two. But it may be that as teaching on negotiation techniques and books on the issue proliferate, styles of negotiation may change. Indeed, there is some evidence that the style adopted depends on the kind of work on offer. Studies of family lawyers in particular found little evidence of confrontational negotiation techniques; many operate instead in ways that promote the well-being of children and seek not to exacerbate conflict.[12] The problem-solving approach seems to be used more often by family lawyers.

Digging deeper

You might think that the competitive style will lead to the best results for the client, but that is not necessarily so. Competitive negotiators more often find that negotiations simply break down: they push so hard for the best deal that the other party walks away. Competitive negotiators may not mind that result: they want a deal only if it is a bargain. That works well for the client only if it is not important for him or her to get a contract. Perhaps more to the point is that competitive negotiation can backfire, especially in cases involving long-term relationships. Where the matter under negotiation is part of an ongoing relationship between the parties, then it is in both parties' interests that they leave the negotiations feeling reasonably happy with the settlement. If one party feels hard done-by, then it is unlikely to return to the other party next time it wants to transact that type of business. In family cases, if the parents are going to have to cooperate and communicate in the future, that is most likely if neither party feels taken advantage of. In short, the maintenance of goodwill between the parties may be of greater value than obtaining every last penny.

One final and very important point is that many theories on negotiation assume that the parties are rational. It is, however, crucial in some cases to be aware of the psychological and relational issues involved.[13] If we go back to the two children arguing over the orange, the truth may be that neither of them even wants the orange,

[10] Menkel-Meadow (n. 7).

[11] Boon and Levin (n. 9), 372, referring to M. Murch, 'The role of solicitors in divorce proceedings' (1977) 40 Modern Law Review 625 and J. Morison and P. Leith, *The Barristers' World and the Nature of Law* (Open University Press, 1992).

[12] J. Eekelaar, M. McLean, and J. Beinart, *Family Lawyers* (Hart, 2000).

[13] D. Kolb and J. Williams, *The Shadow Negotiation: How Women Can Master the Hidden Agendas that Determine Bargaining Success* (Simon & Schuster, 2000).

but that they have fallen out over something else and the orange is simply a symbol of the disagreement.[14] Again, family lawyers will be familiar with bitter disputes over apparently trivial matters being masks for a deeper anguish between the parties. Good negotiators will exercise high levels of empathy and insight to see what is really at the heart of the dispute. Emotion may be more important than logic in such a case.

The importance of bargaining power

A key issue in negotiations is bargaining power. The person in the stronger position at the start of the negotiations is in a better position to get a good deal. This involves a consideration of his or her current position. What will be lost if he or she does not get a deal? What might be gained if he or she wins? An example would be a small manufacturer trying to persuade a large supermarket to stock its product. If the supermarket is making good profits and is happy with its current suppliers, it will feel that it is in a good position and so has little to gain from entering into a contract with the small manufacturer. The manufacturer will need to provide the supermarket with a really good reason to enter into the deal—perhaps an exceptionally low price. However, if the supermarket is in desperate need of a refreshing new look and the small manufacturer's product is very popular, then the supermarket may have much to gain from entering into the contract. It may well be willing to pay a higher price than it would otherwise.

So, at the start of the negotiation, a key issue is always what position the parties will be in should a deal not be reached and what position they will be in if it is. Where the party is currently in a good position and the deal will not put him or her in an obviously better position, there is little incentive for him or her to reach agreement. Where the party is in a bad position and the agreement will put him or her in a good one, he or she will be keen to reach an agreement. The party with the stronger bargaining power, with less incentive to get a deal, can normally get away with making extreme demands and need to make few concessions. A key job for lawyers is to be honest with clients about their bargaining strength, so that they can be realistic about what outcome to expect.

It should not be assumed that the bargaining position of the parties is the only relevant factor; the two lawyers may also have positions of power in relation to each other. They may well need to negotiate with each other on further matters in the future; there may be rivalry between the firms or the lawyers: these matters may affect the outcome of the negotiations.

The 'shadow of the law'

There is one way in which negotiation using lawyers can differ from other negotiations: the legal dimension. Imagine, for example, that you are negotiating with a builder over the price of a job. At the end of the day, if the negotiations break down,

---

[14] Menkel-Meadow (n. 7).

the builder will walk away and that will be that. But with negotiations involving law-yers, if those break down, the parties will not necessarily walk away because of the spectre of litigation. This has led to what is called 'negotiation in the shadow of the law'. In other words, the order that a court is likely to make will influence the parties' discussion. So if an offer of £3.2 million to settle a dispute is on the table, a client is likely to refuse it if the lawyer says: 'We can reject this offer and go to court, and I predict the court will order that we be given £6 million.' However, if the lawyer were to say 'We can reject this offer and go to court, but I can't see the court giving us more than £3.5 million—and that's only if we win and there will be around £300,000 in costs if we proceed to court', then the client will be tempted to accept the offer. We might therefore expect the results reached in lawyer negotiations to be similar to those that would emerge in court.

It is not only the predicted results that impact on the negotiations. The lawyers will typically conduct their negotiations on the basis of legal principles and language. They will focus on the factors that a court would take into account. This all means that lawyers have considerable power in negotiations because they will set the tone and scope of the discussions.

Rebecca Hollander-Blumoff explains further how predictions over what the court will order can influence the outcome of the negotiations:

> Economic theories of negotiation in the civil justice system share a premise: legal actors in the civil system will settle a case if the value of the settlement is greater than the expected value at trial, minus transaction costs. If the parties agree on the expected value at trial, all cases will settle. However, parties will not always agree, because they do not have perfect information, the law is uncertain, or both. If parties had complete information and the law was entirely predictable, so that litigants could calculate perfectly accurate figures for the expected value at trial, then all cases would settle because transaction costs could be saved for both sides by avoiding trial.[15]

It would be wrong to suggest that, inevitably, a negotiated settlement will match what a court would award. Some people may have strong incentives not to go to court, owing to the publicity or time involved. Others may find legal proceedings stressful. In such cases, the parties may be willing to agree to settle for much less than a court would award. In other cases, the law may be unclear, in which case it can provide little guidance.

The role of the lawyer

As already noted, in a case involving negotiation through lawyers, the lawyer will have a key role to play. One important job of a lawyer in negotiations can be to manage cli-ents' expectations. A client may be convinced that he or she is bound to win the case and be awarded millions of pounds in damages. If the client believes this, he or she is unlikely to settle for anything less than what he or she thinks the court will award. If

---

[15] R. Hollander-Blumoff, 'Just negotiation' (2010) 88 Washington University Law Review 381, 398.

that belief is based on an overinflated view of what a court is likely to award or of his or her chances of success, then it is crucial that the lawyer is realistic with the client about what to expect.

Much has been written about the barriers that prevent people from reaching sensible agreements. These range from overconfidence to risk aversion and even prejudice.[16] People tend to place an irrational weight on avoiding risks. For example, if offered a £100 prize or a 50 per cent chance of winning £200, studies suggest that most people take the £100, even though, in economic terms, they are equivalent. Interestingly, when faced with a definite £100 fine or a 50 per cent chance of a £200 fine, however, they will prefer to take the chance, hoping to avoid any loss.[17] Lawyers should be alert to these barriers, so that they can give clients good advice. This all means that although studies of negotiations often focus on the communications between the lawyers, the discussions between the lawyers and their clients can be just as important.[18]

One ethical issue is the extent to which the lawyer should encourage the client to agree to a proposed settlement. This reflects the broader discussions over the role of a lawyer at which we looked in Chapter 3. For those who see the role of the lawyer as being simply to follow the instructions of the client, the job of the lawyer may be to advise and inform, but to respect the decision of the client. Those who see a more interventionist role for a lawyer may see his or her job as being to put pressure on the client to accept a reasonable compromise.

Lying and negotiation

Perhaps the major ethical issue in relation to this topic is whether it is acceptable to lie during negotiations. Most people, at first thought, believe it clearly to be wrong to be deceptive in negotiations. However, lying is regarded by some to be an inevitable part of the process. Typically, in negotiations, one side will start with its 'best deal' and say that it 'could not possibly accept less', even if in fact it *would* be willing to do so. Is that very common practice unethical? One of the 'tricks' of negotiating is trying to find out the other party's real 'bottom line'. If lying is unethical, there are many unethical negotiators out there.[19]

Professor Welaufer is blunt: '[E]ffectiveness in negotiations is central to the business of lawyering and a willingness to lie is central of one's effectiveness in negotiations.'[20] Niccolò Machiavelli, as is well known, was positively enthusiastic about the

[16] B. Spangler, 'Heads I win, tails you lose: The psychological barriers to economically efficient civil settlement and a case for third-party mediation' [2012] Wisconsin Law Review 1435.

[17] Spangler (n. 16).

[18] R. Mnookin, S. Peppet, and A. Tulumello, *Beyond Winning: Negotiating to Create Value in Deals and Disputes* (Harvard University Press, 2000).

[19] A. Hinshaw and J. Alberts, 'Doing the right thing: An empirical study of attorney negotiation ethics' (2011) 16 Harvard Negotiation Law Review 95.

[20] G. Wetlaufer, 'The ethics of lying in negotiation' (1990) 76 Iowa Law Review 1219, 1221.

benefits of lying: '[Y]ou must be a great liar.... [A] deceitful man will always find plenty who are ready to be deceived.'[21]

That conclusion—that, to be a good negotiator, you must be a good liar—is uncomfortable for many lawyers. Indeed, the Bar Council Code of Conduct (the Bar Code) seems to forbid it.

Follow the Code

The Bar Code, para 708.1, requires that:

> A barrister instructed in a mediation must not knowingly or recklessly mislead the mediator or any party or their representative.

As the Bar Code indicates, lying is seen by many as a clear moral wrong. Sissela Bok, in her influential book *Lying: Moral Choice in Public and Private Life*, sets out the wrongs of lying.[22] Lying, she argues, undermines the trust that is essential for human interaction; it interferes in the freedom of others to make informed choices about how to live their lives and it undermines the integrity of the liar.

So is there any way in which lying in negotiations can be justified? It may be said that to describe negotiation 'bluffing' as lying is unfair because there is no real deception involved. Both parties know that what is being said is not literally true.[23] When one side presents its 'best offer', all those involved realise that it may not literally be the best offer that the party can make.

An analogy might be drawn with a fruit seller in a market shouting out that her oranges are the tastiest in the world. No one really believes such a statement; rather, they interpret it in the context within which it is made. Because of the context of the comment, the statement is not a lie, because it is understood to be a deliberate exaggeration. Similarly, when advertisers tell us that a particular beer 'reaches the parts other beers cannot reach', we know that they are not being serious and that it is an advertising 'puff'. It may be that we can say the same of negotiation. Some statements are not to be taken seriously as literally true. This argument is particularly convincing if we accept that parties to negotiation share the same understanding about bluffing strategies.[24]

If we accept that argument, then it may be necessary for us to draw a distinction between different kinds of 'lie'. We may readily agree that 'I could not accept anything

---

[21] N. Machiavelli, *The Prince* (trans. Robert M. Adams, W.W. Norton & Co, 1977), ch. XVIII.

[22] S. Bok, *Lying: Moral Choice in Public and Private Life* (Vintage, 1999).

[23] C. Provis, 'Ethics, deception and labor negotiation' (2000) 28 Journal of Business Ethics 145.

[24] A. Carr, 'Is business bluffing ethical?'(1968) 46 Harvard Business Review 143.

less than £100,000' is not to be taken as literally true—but other statements of fact during the negotiations might be. We might need to explore the 'rules of the negotiating game' to see which kinds of statement were generally understood to be puffs and which were generally understood to be taken as true.[25]

This still leaves a degree of uncertainty over quite where the line is on what is or is not proper. John Cooley notes that 'white lies' in fact permeate our social interactions.[26] From 'How nice to see you' to 'I love your new haircut', we use phrases that are not literally true in order to avoid hurting our friends' feelings and to ease social interactions. And this is not limited to chit chat: employment references inflate the qualities of the applicant; politicians seek to sell policies to a doubting public; and doctors try to paint a positive picture to seriously ill patients. With that in mind, if the lies in negotiations are only 'white lies' intended to oil the cogs of negotiation, perhaps we should not be too worried about them. Indeed, Cooley argues that negotiation and mediation nearly always involve deception.

 Alternative view

Not everyone agrees that deception is expected or required as part of negotiation.[27] An understanding based on complete honesty might lead to the best results. Indeed, there is some evidence that being very honest in negotiations produces better results for you than being dishonest.[28] Notably, if, during negotiation, an overt deception is uncovered, then that deceitful behaviour is regarded as unacceptable and negotiations often break down.[29] Similarly, if a party later finds out that it was deceived into accepting a settlement, this may impact on the long-term relationship between the parties, which, in some contexts, will harm the deceitful party. Perhaps the truth depends on context.[30] Is there a difference expected in negotiations between, say, divorcing spouses and business rivals? If so, who would you expect to be more honest?!

[25] D. Schmedemann, 'Navigating the murky waters of untruth in negotiation: Lessons for ethical lawyers' (2010) 12 Cardozo Journal of Conflict Resolution 83.

[26] J. Cooley, 'Defining the ethical limits of acceptable deception in mediation' (2004) 4 Pepperdine Dispute Resolution Law Journal 263.

[27] C. Provis, 'Ethics, deception, and labor negotiation' (2000) 28 Journal of Business Ethics 145.

[28] J. Banas and J. McLean Parks, 'Lambs among lions? The impact of ethical ideology on negotiation behaviors and outcomes' (2002) 7 International Negotiation 235.

[29] R. Croson, T. Boles, and J. Murnighan, 'Cheap talk in bargaining experiments: Lying and threats in ultimatum games' (2003) 51 Journal of Economic Behavior & Organization 143.

[30] For a review of the evidence, see R. Lewicki and R. Robinson, 'Ethical and unethical bargaining tactics: An empirical study' (1998) 17 Journal of Business Ethics 665.

Peter Reilly suggests a different response to the prevalence of lying:

> Good negotiators must therefore learn how to conduct extensive background research, to engage aggressively and relentlessly in asking questions and digging for answers, and to take other proactive steps to unearth or extract the most (and most accurate) information possible from all parties at the table.[31]

His approach starts with the assumption that people will lie and that we need to try to ensure that people minimise the risk of their being exploited. Our focus should be on training negotiators to find out the truth, rather than on combating lying.

Another ethical question arises where one party to the negotiations realises that the other is under a mistake. Unusually, the issue came before the courts in the following case.

 ## Key case

Thames Trains v Adams [2006] EWHC 3291

Mr Adams was an American citizen who had suffered serious injuries in a train crash in England, for which Thames Trains Ltd was liable. The solicitors for Thames Trains (TT) paid £9.3 million into court. Negotiations were ongoing over the final amount that should be paid. A solicitor for Adams, Ms C, told TT's solicitors that Adams sought a total of £10 million. TT's solicitors told Ms C that no further money was available. Ms C then told another solicitor in her firm to send a fax accepting the £9.3 million paid into court as a final sum. The fax was sent, but owing to an internal error at TT's solicitors, the fax was not received properly. TT's solicitors discussed the case with TT and decided to offer a further £500,000, bringing the total to £9.8 million. Ms C then accepted that offer and a consent order was prepared on those terms. TT's solicitors later found the fax and sought to set the consent order aside.

Nelson J heard the case. Under the terms of contract law, the fax was an offer, but one that had not been accepted. Instead, TT had made an alternative offer (for £9.8 million), which had been accepted and which thus created a contract. The question Nelson J held, however, was whether Ms C had behaved unconscionably in accepting the offer for £9.8 million, knowing that TT's solicitors must not have received, or had forgotten, her offer to settle for £9.3 million. In the end, he concluded that she had not. He noted that, when Ms C accepted the higher offer, she did not know for sure whether her colleague had sent the fax. She did not know for sure that she was taking advantage of a mistake. Further, she was not under a general duty to correct her opponent's misunderstanding.

---

[31] P. Reilly, 'Was Machiavelli right? Lying in negotiation and the art of defensive self-help' (2008) 24 Ohio State Journal on Dispute Resolution 481, 484.

Perhaps the most helpful test in the judgment was given when Nelson J asked whether the reasonable person would have expected Ms C, acting honestly and responsibly, to tell TT of her earlier offer. He asked whether the conduct was 'deceitful' or 'sharp practice'. He thought not. He relied on three particular points. The first was that Ms C had not lied; she had simply remained silent. A second was that TT had not been entirely open in saying that no further money was available when, in fact, it was. Neither side was seeking to be entirely open with the other. The third factor was that the difference between the two figures was not vast, so it was not as if one party was gaining a huge sum of money by means of an obvious mistake.

There is clearly no general obligation on a lawyer to be completely open with the other side.[32] In *Ernst & Young v Butte Mining plc*,[33] Mr Justice Walker said:

Heavy, hostile commercial litigation is a serious business. It is not a form of indoor sport and litigation solicitors do not owe each other duties to be friendly (so far as that goes beyond politeness) or to be chivalrous or sportsmanlike (so far as that goes beyond being fair). Nevertheless, even in the most hostile litigation (indeed, especially in the most hostile litigation) solicitors must be scrupulously fair and not take unfair advantage of obvious mistakes.... The duty not to take unfair advantage of an obvious mistake is intensified if the solicitor in question has been a major contributing cause of the mistake.

In that case, there was a crucial difference between misleading conduct, which would be seen as improper, and a failure to notify the other person of a fact about which he or she was mistaken, which would not.

Regulatory possibilities

There has been some discussion over whether we need a code of ethics for negotiation.[34] There is a real difficulty inherent to developing a regulatory regime for negotiations, however. First, there needs to be a consensus over the appropriate bargaining model and, as we have seen, that does not exist. Boon and Levin, for example, are critical of the current system:

Trust is vital to cooperation and generally benefits markets by facilitating agreement and reducing transaction costs. The current situation, where there are no definitive rules of bargaining for lawyers, is inimical to an environment of trust. In each interaction, the protagonists are unsure what to expect, and this breeds excessive caution and results in poor solutions for clients in the long term.[35]

[32] *Thompson v Arnold* [2007] EWHC 1875 (QB).   [33] [1996] 1 WLR 1605, 1612.
[34] W. Steel, 'Deceptive negotiating and high-toned morality' (1986) 39 Vanderbilt Law Review 1387.
[35] Boon and Levin (n. 9), 384.

They suggest that we could apply the principle that the parties will be honest in relation to material facts and add to this the following three principles:

- to explore with clients their perceptions of their interests;
- to seek a settlement where that is in the client's best interests; and
- to seek a settlement which satisfied the client's interests as far as possible and which is fair and reasonable to both sides.[36]

The difficulty is probably the last factor. The line between an unfair deal and one that is good for one side is hard to draw. If a lawyer is instructed to get the best possible price, is he or she doing anything wrong? Imagine that someone is reluctant to sell a house, but will do so if the purchaser offers an extravagant price. Is he or she doing anything wrong? These questions show how hard it can be to determine what is 'fair' or 'reasonable'.

At the root of the problem is the difficulty in defining what is 'good' negotiation. Carrie Menkel-Meadow, supporting the problem-solving approach to negotiations, helpfully suggests the following questions that could be asked to determine the answer:

1. Does the solution reflect the client's total set of 'real' needs, goals and objectives, in both the short and the long term?

2. Does the solution reflect the other party's full set of 'real' needs, goals and objectives, in both the short and long term?

3. Does the solution promote the relationship the client desires with the other party?

4. Have the parties explored all the possible solutions that might either make each better off or one party better off with no adverse consequences to the other party?'

5. Has the solution been achieved at the lowest possible transaction costs relative to the desirability of the result?

6. Is the solution achievable, or has it only raised more problems that need to be solved? Are the parties committed to the solution so it can be enforced without regret?

7. Has the solution been achieved in a manner congruent with the client's desire to participate in and affect the negotiation?

8. Is the solution 'fair' or 'just'? Have the parties considered the legitimacy of each other's claims and made any adjustments they feel are humanely or morally indicated?[37]

These questions are helpful ones for negotiating lawyers to think about. Whether they could be formulated into clear rules that provide ethical guidance is less clear. It may be, however, that posing the guidance in the form of such questions is more helpful in this context than offering a vaguely defined set of rules.[38]

---

[36] Boon and Levin (n. 9), 383.   [37] Menkel-Meadow (n. 6), 755.
[38] See Hollander-Blumoff (n. 15).

Mediation

In mediation, the clients seek to resolve the dispute themselves, with the help of a third party, a mediator. This can be done without the involvement of lawyers at all. Sometimes, lawyers advise the parties before they enter into mediation; sometimes, they do so at the end. Mediation has become a popular form of resolving disputes, particularly in family cases.[39]

There are undoubtedly a wide range of reasons why there has been an increase in the use of mediation, including the following.

- *Cost* Mediation is sometimes regarded as a cheaper alternative than litigation. The government, in the area of family law especially, has been keen to cut back the legal aid bill and mediation may offer a cheaper way of dealing with such cases.

- *Lack of confidence in the court* The appeal of mediation is that the parties can resolve the dilemma themselves and that the state is not required to take a particular line on a controversial issue. Indeed, there may be more generally a feeling that, in hotly disputed cases, a mediated resolution is as likely to be a good outcome as one produced by a judge. This has been a particularly influential argument in family law, in which cases the courts have been criticised as being anti-men or anti-women. In the government's *Family Justice Review*, it was stated:

> Generally it seems better that parents resolve things for themselves if they can. They are then more likely to come to an understanding that will allow arrangements to change as they and their children change. Most people could do with better information to help this happen. Others need to be helped to find routes to resolve their disputes short of court proceedings.[40]

- *Long-term benefits* Where the parties are likely to have an ongoing relationship, mediation offers to give the parties the tools with which they can pursue a continued relationship in an amicable way.

Much support for mediation has come from the government, in the form of the cutbacks in legal aid, which were explored further in Chapter 7. However, the judiciary too has encouraged mediation. In *Day v Cook*,[41] Ward LJ concluded his judgment thus:

> Finally, I ask in utter despair, and probably in vain, is it too much to expect of these parties that they seek to avail of this court's free ADR service so that a legally qualified mediator can guide them to a long overdue resolution of this dispute which reflects little credit to the legal profession?

---

[39] J. Lande, 'The revolution in family law dispute resolution' (2012) 24 Family Law Dispute Resolution 411.

[40] D. Norgrave, *Family Justice Review* (Department of Education, 2012), para. 104.

[41] [2002] 1 BCLC 1, [188].

The Civil Procedure Rules (CPR) allow judges to manage cases, and this includes 'encouraging the parties to co-operate with each other in the conduct of…proceedings'[42] and alternative dispute resolution (ADR) when 'appropriate'. This is backed up by the power of a judge to award costs for unreasonable conduct, which can include refusing to mediate.[43] In *Dunnett v Railtrack*,[44] the Court of Appeal took into account the fact that Railtrack had refused to attempt mediation to resolve the dispute when it decided not to award it costs, even though it had won the litigated case.[45]

What is mediation?

The government White Paper on divorce reform defines mediation as 'a process in which an impartial third person, the mediator, assists couples considering separation or divorce to meet together to deal with the arrangements which need to be made for the future'.[46] The core goal in mediation is:

> …to help separating and divorcing couples to reach their own agreed joint decisions about future arrangements; to improve communications between them; and to help couples work together on the practical consequences of divorce with particular emphasis on their joint responsibilities to co-operate as parents in bringing up their children.[47]

While these comments were made in the context of divorce, they can be applied generally to the idea of mediation.

While there is agreement that the basic idea of mediation is that a mediator helps the parties to reach an agreement, however, there is disagreement over exactly what role the mediator is to play.

The role of the mediator

It is striking how little control there is over mediation. There is no state regulation of mediators' training, accreditation, or performance.[48] There are the College of Mediators and the Family Mediation Council, but these neither regulate the profession nor control who can act as a mediator.[49] They provide general guidance and

---

[42] CPR 1.4(a).

[43] CPR 44.4(a). See also *Burchell v Bullard* [2005] EWCA Civ 358; *Rolf v De Guerin* [2011] EWCA Civ 78.   [44] [2002] EWCA Civ 302.

[45] J. Mason, 'How might the adversarial imperative be effectively tempered in mediation?' (2012) 15 Legal Ethics 111.

[46] Lord Chancellor's Department, *Looking to the Future: Mediation and the Ground for Divorce* (HM Stationery Office, 1995), para. 5.4.

[47] Lord Chancellor's Department (n. 46), para. 6.7.

[48] A. Boon, R. Earle, and A. Whyte, 'Regulating mediators?' (2007) 10 Legal Ethics 26.

[49] L. Webley, 'Gate-keeper, supervisor or mentor? The role of professional bodies in the regulation and professional development of solicitors and family mediators undertaking divorce matters in England and Wales' (2010) 32 Journal of Social Welfare and Family Law 119.

support for mediators, but no official regulation. One consequence of this is that there is little formal guidance on precisely what role the mediator should play. This has enabled a broad range of styles of mediation to develop. As Andrew Boon, Richard Early, and Avis Whyte note:

> As to approaches to the process of mediation, there are, as currently conceived, a range of perspectives on how mediation can or should be practised. Mediation practices can be seen as involving open or closed processes; a variety of models—facilitative, evaluative (including elements of arbitration), transformative (seeking education and empowerment), activist (substantial mediator involvement, including elements of conciliation), pragmatic (agreement orientated), bureaucratic (institutional setting), therapeutic, and narrative; and involving specific areas of expertise such as international, commercial, family oriented, and community based.[50]

The following are some of the main models that a mediator could choose to adopt.[51]

1. *Minimal intervention* This model requires the mediator to ensure that there is effective communication between the parties, but it is not the job of the mediator to influence the content of the agreement.[52] So even if the mediator believes that the parties are reaching an agreement that is wholly unfair to one side, the mediator should not try to correct the balance. At the heart of this model is the notion that the agreement should be the parties' own decision. If the agreement seems fair to them, then it is not for anyone else to declare it unfair.

2. *Directive intervention* Under this model, the mediator might provide additional information and seek to influence the content of the agreement if the proposed agreement is clearly unfair to one side or the other. He or she may try to persuade one or both parties to change their views, and may attempt to persuade the parties to agree to the arrangements that the mediator believes are most suitable. The mediator may seek to change the way in which the parties view each other or their dispute.[53] It is still the parties who find the solution, but the mediator helps the parties to see the problems in a way that facilitates their resolution.

3. *Therapeutic intervention* This model sees the mediator focusing on the relationship between the parties. It promotes the belief that the dispute is merely a symptom of a broken relationship. The time spent in mediation may not therefore focus on the actual issues in dispute, but rather on trying to improve the parties' relationship

---

[50] Boon et al. (n. 48), 27.

[51] C. Menkel-Meadow, 'The many ways of mediation: The transformation of traditions, ideologies, paradigms, and practices' (1995) 11 Negotiation Journal 217; S. Imperati, 'Mediator practice models: The intersection of ethics and stylistic practices in mediation' (1997) 33 Willamette Law Review 703.

[52] K. Stylianou, 'Challenges for family mediation' (2011) 31 Family Law 874.

[53] J. Bush and R. Folger, 'Transformative mediation and third-party intervention: Ten hallmarks of a transformative approach to practice' (1996) 13 Mediation Quarterly 26.

generally. This view is influenced especially by the perception that the issue of dispute is often a symptom of an underlying relationship problem, rather than the real problem itself. This kind of approach is most useful in cases involving people in a close relationship, such as neighbours, family, or co-workers.

4. *Bureaucratic mediation* This is a highly formalised style of mediation, with strict rules about the kind of information that can be used and the style of discussion. This might be used in a school setting or in the workplace, for example. It is hoped that the formality will keep the parties calm and will encourage settlement. It keeps the discussions bounded and focused on the issue at hand. Some court-based settlements may operate in this way, with the judge guiding the parties towards a solution and playing the role of mediator.

5. *Activist mediation* In this model, the mediator comes to the case with a clear agenda and a degree of expertise. The parties expect the mediator to find the solution with them, with the agenda in mind. A good example will be a religious couple who ask a religious leader to resolve their dispute. They hope that the religious leader will use religious principles to work through the issues to find a solution. Clearly, this is only acceptable when the parties know that this is happening, because it blurs the line between mediation and arbitration.

6. *Community mediation* Community-controlled mediation typically involves quite a number of community members. It will appear more like a meeting than a private mediation. This is normally used when the dispute is seen as harming the community and there are communal interests involved. There are concerns about who takes a leading role in this approach, with self-appointed community leaders often seen to be exercising power over vulnerable members.

7. *Pragmatic mediation* This type of mediation tends to be 'on-the-spot peacemaking', and occurs when someone steps in to help parties to resolve an immediate situation and to find a resolution.

In England and Wales, the model of minimalist intervention is the most often used.[54] Resolution, the solicitors' organisation promoting non-contentious approaches to family law, explains this standard model to the public in the following way:

> Mediators are trained to help resolve disputes over all issues faced by separating couples, or specific issues such as arrangements for any children. A mediator will meet with you and your partner together and will identify those issues you can't agree on and help you to try and reach agreement.
>
> Mediators are neutral and will not take sides, so they cannot give advice to either of you. They will usually recommend that you obtain legal advice alongside the mediation process and will guide you as to when this should happen.[55]

---

[54] UK College of Family Mediators, *Mediation* (UK College of Family Mediators, 2000), para. 42.

[55] Resolution, *Alternatives to Court* (Resolution, 2013), 1.

It is important to realise that, under this model, the mediator is not powerless to prevent an unfair agreement being reached.[56] Commonly, before commencing mediation, a mediator will hold a 'screening meeting' to ascertain whether or not mediation is suitable. If the mediator decides that the parties were not in a fair bargaining position (for example one had been violent to the other in the past), then he or she may refuse to go ahead with the mediation. Similarly, if during the mediation the mediator is concerned that one party is taking advantage of the other, the mediator is free to stop the mediation and to encourage the parties to seek legal advice.

Although this minimalist model is still the standard one, it has been questioned. There is some evidence that the goal of non-intervention is rarely achieved in practice.[57] We will discuss this issue shortly. Some commentators believe that there is gradual change in attitudes over the role of mediators and that they are becoming increasingly interventionist, at least on key principles.[58] So a mediator in a family case might encourage the parties to put the interests of the child first and to decrease the bitterness of the family dispute.[59] There may therefore be some basic cultural norms of which it is legitimate for the mediator to remind the parties.[60] What is not permissible is for the mediator to seek to impose his or her own norms on the couple.[61] However, this view is based on our being able to draw a reasonably clear line between which norms are social and which are personal. One suggestion is that as long as the mediator is open about what norms he or she is bringing to the discussion and the couple accept this, the mediator is acting appropriately.[62]

One important aspect of mediation is that it is designed to be forward-looking.[63] In other words, the focus is on how the parties can move forward and find a solution to their problems. Hence, in the family law context, the mediator does not encourage the parties to look back at which of them were to blame for the breakdown of the relationship, but rather to look to the future and work out who is going to care for the children. A similar attitude is found in employment disputes, in which the focus

[56] E. Waldman, 'Identifying the role of social norms in mediation: A multiple model approach' (1997) 48 Hastings Law Journal 703.

[57] R. Bush and J. Folger, *The Promise of Mediation: Responding to Conflict through Empowerment and Recognition* (Jossey-Bass Publishers, 1994); D. Kolb, *When Talk Works: Profiles of Mediators* (Jossey-Bass Publishers, 1994); S. Engle Merry and N. Milner (eds) *The Possibility of Popular Justice: A Case Study of American Community Justice* (University of Michigan Press, 1993).

[58] B. Wilson, 'Do mediators care?' (2009) 39 Family Law 201.

[59] M. Stepan, 'Mediation is moving on' (2010) 40 Family Law 545.

[60] S. Belhorn, 'Settling beyond the shadow of the law: How mediation can make the most of social norms' (2005) 20 Ohio State Journal on Dispute Resolution 981.

[61] See the discussion in Stepan (n. 59).

[62] S, Imperati, D. Brownmiller, and D. Marshall, 'If Freud, Jung, Rogers, and Beck were mediators, who would the parties pick and what are the mediator's obligations?' (2007) 43 Idaho Law Review 645.

[63] J. Poitras, 'The paradox of accepting one's share of responsibility in mediation' (2007) 23 Negotiation Journal 267.

is on how the employer and employee can work together in the future rather than on getting too tied up with who said what to whom. Indeed, some mediators claim that focusing on the past prevents the couple from moving on to the future.[64] This can provide a clear distinction between mediation and legal proceedings, in which typically the primary role of the court is to establish the facts of the case before it can determine how the parties should move on.

We can now consider the arguments over the benefits and disadvantages of mediation.

The case in favour of mediation

The following are some of the arguments used to support mediation.

1. A key argument in favour of mediation is that there is no 'right answer' to a particular dispute. If the parties reach a solution that is right for them, no one else should be able to regard their agreement as the wrong one. It could be said to be none of the state's business to seek to interfere in the arrangement that the parties have reached. Supporters of litigation might think that courts can ascertain the facts and provide the correct answer. But that is rather old-fashioned, as Carrie Menkel-Meadow argues:

   If late-twentieth century learning has taught us anything, it is that truth is illusive, partial, interpretable, dependent on the characteristics of the knowers as well as the known, and, most importantly, complex. In short, there may be more than just two sides to every story.[65]

   Alex Wellington argues that ADR is consistent with the basic tenets of liberalism—in particular, the importance of state neutrality over concepts of the good life, the respect for autonomy, and the importance of tolerating different ways of life and values.[66] We should prefer the parties using their own values and understandings of fairness to a privileged judge using his. Indeed, in the context of family law, the House of Lords itself has accepted that, in many cases, a variety of solutions could be appropriate and that there is not necessarily a right or wrong one.[67] If that is so, should not the solution to which the parties agree be preferred over one imposed on them? Indeed, Menkel-Meadow goes further and questions whether courts are a good way in which to ascertain facts: 'Binary, oppositional presentations of facts in dispute are not the best way for us to learn the truth; polarized debate distorts the truth, leaves out important information, simplifies complexity, and obfuscates rather than clarifies.'[68]

---

[64] Poitras (n. 63).

[65] C. Menkel-Meadow, 'The trouble with the adversary system in a postmodern, multicultural world' (1996) 38 William and Mary Law Review 5, 23.

[66] A. Wellington, 'Taking codes of ethics seriously: Alternative dispute resolution and reconstitutive liberalism' (1999) 12 Canadian Journal of Law and Jurisprudence 297.

[67] *Piglowska v Piglowski* [1999] 2 FLR 763, HL.   [68] Menkel-Meadow (n. 65).

There are three key issues here. The first is whether it is correct that there is no right answer for a court to declare. If there is not, then the solution reached by the parties is likely to be as good as the solution that would be reached by anyone else.

If, however, you do not accept this and believe that it is possible to state that some solutions are better than others, then the second key issue is whether there is a good reason to believe that the court is more likely to find a better solution than the parties in mediation.

Third, even if you accept that some solutions are better than others and that the court is more likely than the parties to find a better solution, there is still the issue of whether the state, through the courts, should be able to impose the right answer (or *a* right answer) on the parties. The law might want to impose a right answer on the parties because there are interests either of third parties, or of the state itself, which justify its doing so.[69] So, for example, many argue that mediation is not acceptable in family cases because it does not adequately protect the interests of the child: there is nothing to prevent the parents from reaching an agreement in mediation that does not promote the interests of the child. However, such an argument would need to demonstrate that allowing judges to resolve disputes over children has a better chance of promoting children's interests than letting parents reach their own decisions.

2. Supporters of mediation claim that the solutions agreed by the parties are more effective than court orders in the long term.[70] There are three aspects to the argument that mediation produces more effective results. The first is that, because the parties have reached the agreement themselves, they will more easily be able to renegotiate it together if difficulties with the agreement subsequently arise.

Second, the solution reached through mediation will be one that the parties can tailor to their particular lifestyles rather than a formula applied by lawyers or judges to deal with 'these kinds of cases'.

Third, it is argued that, because mediation can be hard work and emotionally exhausting, the parties will therefore feel more committed to the agreement than if it had been given to them by a judge. In fact, there is some dispute over whether mediated settlements do last well, with one study finding that only half of all mediated agreements were intact six months after they were reached.[71]

---

[69] Or even that there are rights that the divorcing couple have themselves, which they should not be permitted to negotiate away during the process of mediation.

[70] HM Government, *Parental Separation: Children's Needs and Parents' Responsibilities* (HM Stationery Office, 2004), para. 2. For a discussion of the evidence against this proposition, see Eekelaar et al. (n. 12).

[71] G. Mantle, *Helping Families in Dispute* (Ashgate, 2001). For other studies finding no evidence that mediated agreements were longer-lasting than court orders, see, e.g., J. Walker, *Picking up the Pieces: Marriage and Divorce Two Years after Information Provision* (Department for Constitutional Affairs, 2004).

3. Mediation enables the parties to communicate more effectively. The mediators can take the parties in dispute and give them the tools with which to communicate with each other, which may be essential if they are in an ongoing relationship. Opponents of mediation argue that lawyers can filter out particularly offensive communications and so, in fact, reduce bitterness, while mediation, by contrast, can increase bitterness, especially where it fails. The questions are: are parties helped by mediation or does the process of mediation exacerbate bitterness; and does litigation make the parties enemies of each other?[72] The answer to both questions is: in some cases, it does, and in some cases, it does not. We simply do not yet know which outcome is the commonest.

4. Mediation gives time for all issues that are important to the parties to be discussed. It has been a complaint of the legal process that it 'transforms' the parties' disputes: their arguments are put into legal terminology and some issues that might be of concern to them are ignored.[73] This argument can include a claim that mediation can tackle the emotional issues involved in divorce. The mediation process can not only help to resolve the dispute, but perhaps also help the parties to come to terms with their feelings about one another and begin the post-breakdown healing process.[74] This might be why, in successful mediation, parties report high levels of satisfaction with the result.[75]

5. Mediation saves costs—or at least the government certainly hoped that mediation would save costs. By using only one mediator rather than two lawyers, and with the hourly rate for mediators being generally less than that for lawyers, savings could be made. In fact, whether or not mediation saves money depends on the success rate of mediation. The present research indicates that, in the context of family law, if all couples were required to attend state-subsidised mediation, it would be likely to lead to increased, not reduced, costs.[76] This is because of the extra costs involved where mediation fails. The Newcastle study (based on people volunteering for mediation) suggested that only about 39 per cent of mediations were wholly successful; 41 per cent were partially successful and 20 per cent failed.[77] For the 20 per cent of totally failed mediations,[78] there are inevitably greater costs than if the parties had gone to lawyers to begin with, without using mediation. If mediation is partly successful, the parties still need to consult lawyers to resolve the remaining issues. But asking a lawyer to resolve 50 per cent of a dispute does not mean incurring only 50 per cent

---

[72] Mason (n. 45).

[73] A. Sarat and W. Felstiner, *Divorce Lawyers and their Clients* (Oxford University Press, Oxford University Press).

[74] C. Richards, 'Allowing blame and revenge into mediation' (2001) 31 Family Law 775.

[75] L. Teitelbaum and L. Dupaix, 'Alternative dispute resolution and divorce: Natural experimentation in family law', in J. Eekelaar and M. MacLean (eds) *A Reader on Family Law* (Oxford University Press, 1994).

[76] Walker (n. 71), 134.   [77] Walker (n. 71), 134.

[78] The success rate would be likely to be significantly lower if mediation were forced on all divorcing couples, because the survey covered those who had volunteered to participate in mediation.

of what the costs would have been had he or she been asked to resolve the whole of the dispute. This is because it is the gathering together of all of the facts and information that takes up most of a lawyer's time, and this will need to be done whether the lawyer is resolving all or only a part of a dispute. So resolving 50 per cent of a dispute may cost 75 per cent of what the fee would have been for resolving all of a dispute, in which case it is not clear that mediation actually saves costs.[79] Even if the mediation is completely successful, there are some who believe the costs will be greater.[80]

An important study looking at the comparative costs of mediation and solicitor-based negotiation found that mediation could cost between 65 per cent and 115 per cent of the solicitor-based negotiation.[81] The study suggested that if the success rate for mediation were to fall below 60 per cent (which the evidence suggests it is very likely to do), there would be no savings. A more recent study found that 59 per cent of cases were wholly or partially successful for mediation.[82] A study looking at the outcomes for non-family cases found the settlement rate among small claims cases that proceeded through mediation to be 82 per cent. This is impressively high, but in fact that represented only 34 per cent of cases that were referred to mediation at one venue and 10 per cent at another. In other words, while many cases were referred to mediation, only a small number were able to be taken on, although where they were there, there was a good success rate.[83] Although a definitive answer is not yet available, it seems that there are some categories of case in which mediation offers a cheaper solution, but that this cannot be assumed to be true in all kinds of case.

The case against mediation

The following are some of the arguments against mediation.

1. Some opponents of mediation argue that it is, in fact, impossible for a mediator to be purely impartial.[84] A mediator can influence the content of the agreement, through explicit as well as indirect means, such as body language or the way in which he or she responds to one party's proposal.[85] For example, one party might make a proposal and whether the mediator immediately asks the other party what

[79] G. Davis, S. Clisby, and Z. Cumming, *Monitoring Publicly Funded Family Mediation* (Legal Services Commission, 2003) found that 57 per cent of their sample stated that their partner was not keen to resolve the legal disputes and compromise.

[80] Davis et al. (n. 79), 5.

[81] G. Bevan and G. Davis, 'A preliminary exploration of the impact of family mediation on legal aid costs' (1999) 11 Child and Family Law Quarterly 411.

[82] House of Commons Public Accounts Committee, *Legal Services Commission: Legal Aid and Mediation for People Involved in Family Breakdown* (HM Stationery Office, 2007).

[83] Advice Services Alliance, *Small Claims Mediation: Does It Work?* (Advice Services Alliance, 2006).

[84] C. Piper, 'Norms and negotiation in mediation and divorce', in M. Freeman (ed.) *Divorce: Where Next?* (Dartmouth, 1996).

[85] R. Dingwall, 'Divorce mediation: Should we change our mind?' (2010) 32 Journal of Social Welfare and Family Law 107.

he or she thinks about the proposal or asks the first party to expand on the proposal might have a profound effect on the course of the negotiation. Piper, in her study of mediation, notes that a mediator would not repeat what one party had said and would move on if that party were to be introducing what the mediator believed to be 'non-relevant matters'.[86] Scott Jacobs found three ways in which a mediator, often unintentionally, can influence the course of the discussion: by asking questions (for example asking a party 'Do you think that's fair?'); in summarising the discussions that the parties have (inevitably, highlighting some points and glossing over others); and in the provision of information.[87] He accepts that mediators may be unaware that subtly, but significantly, these can influence the course of the discussions.

If the mediator does directly or indirectly affect the content of the agreement, then there are concerns that mediation will become, in effect, adjudication in secret.[88] The mediator will act like a judge, but without having to give any reasons for a decision or to be publicly accountable for the outcome.

2. One powerful criticism of mediation is that mediation can work against the interests of the weaker party. Weakness in the bargaining position may stem from three sources, the first among which is a lack of information, coupled with the inability to verify presented information. Because mediators have less effective methods of checking facts compared with the disclosure mechanisms used by lawyers,[89] it is likely to work against the interests of the more honest party. A party's lack of personal expert knowledge may also impede its bargaining position. For example, if one party is a trained accountant and the other has an aversion to figures, then, when the parties discuss financial issues, there might be an inequality of power.

The second weakness in the bargaining process may result from a lack of negotiation skills. One party may regularly take part in negotiations in the course of his or her work and may be trained to push for an agreement, while the other may not.

The third weakness can be psychological. Women, it is argued by some, are generally naturally conflict-averse.[90] They may more readily agree to a settlement rather than argue, partly as a result of being socially conditioned to avoid conflict.[91] There is also an argument that women generally may put greater value on things that are not material in value and/or that they may have lower self-esteem.[92] One survey of

[86] Piper (n. 84).

[87] S. Jacobs, 'Maintaining neutrality in dispute mediation: Managing disagreement while managing not to disagree' (2002) 34 Journal of Pragmatics 1403.

[88] C. Izumi, 'Implicit bias and the illusion of mediator neutrality' (2010) 34 Washington University Journal of Law and Policy 71.

[89] P. Parkinson, *Family Law and the Indissolubility of Parenthood* (Cambridge University Press, 2011).

[90] J. Doughty, 'Identity crisis in the family courts? Different approaches in England and Wales and Australia' (2009) 31 Journal of Social Welfare and Family Law 231.

[91] Walker (n. 71) argues that women are more concerned than men with keeping the relationship amicable.

[92] P. Bryan, 'Killing us softly: Divorce mediation and the politics of power' (1992) 40 Buffalo Law Review 441.

the research concluded that, generally, women were not putting their own interests first in mediation and therefore were losing out to men, who were.[93] However, these points are controversial and there is, in fact, much debate over whether women do better or worse when using mediation.[94]

There are particular concerns about using mediation in family law cases in which the relationship has been characterised by violence.[95] In such cases, mediators themselves accept that mediation is unsuitable because cooperation and proper negotiations can take place only where there is no abuse or fear of abuse.[96] The concern is whether the mediators can always ascertain those cases in which there has been domestic violence.[97] Particularly difficult are cases in which the parties do not regard themselves as victims of domestic violence.[98] In a recent study of mediation, it was found that mediators used a variety of techniques to put domestic violence issues to one side.[99] It may be that increased awareness of domestic violence issues and improved training can improve the response to violence among mediators.[100] These are powerful points, but we may need to consider whether litigation offers a better protection for victims of domestic abuse.[101]

3. Perhaps most fundamentally there is an issue about whether, if you believe that people have legal rights, we should have a system that does not guarantee their enforcement. Lord Dyson, a Supreme Court judge, has asked:

> Can it be right that parties who have exercised their right to go to court can be forced to sit down with the individual they believe to have wronged them to try to find a compromise which would probably leave them worse off than had they had their day in court? Leaving aside any human rights issues then, in my view, this simply cannot be right… [102]

When discussing the benefits of mediation, supporters emphasise the benefits of allowing the parties to bring their own values to the dispute. But that can be seen

---

[93] S. Tilley, 'Recognising gender differences in all issues mediation' (2007) 37 Family Law 352.

[94] Menkel-Meadow (n. 65).

[95] F. Kaganas and C. Piper, 'Domestic violence and divorce mediation' (1994) 16 Journal of Social Welfare and Family Law 265.

[96] Where mediators detect a clear imbalance of power that they cannot counter, they should terminate the mediation.

[97] R. Ballard, A. Holtzworth-Munroe, A. Applegate, C. Beck, and J. Connie, 'Detecting intimate partner violence in family and divorce mediation: A randomized trial of intimate partner violence screening' (2011) 17 Psychology, Public Policy, and Law 241.

[98] Davis et al. (n. 79), 5, found that 41 per cent of women and 21 per cent of men in their sample stated that fear of violence made it difficult to resolve issues in their case.

[99] T. Trinder, A. Firth, and C. Jenks, '"So presumably things have moved on since then?" The management of risk allegations in child contact dispute resolution' (2010) 24 International Journal of Law, Policy and the Family 29.   [100] Parkinson (n. 89).

[101] M. Moffitt, 'Three things to be against ("settlement" not included)' (2009) 78 Fordham Law Review 1203.

[102] Lord Dyson, *Mediation in the English Legal Order Six Years after Halsey* (Ministry of Justice, 2010), 11.

as undermining the importance of law and legal rights. If the law has decided that a consumer should have a right to a certain remedy in a particular case, should we not insist on the law's values being upheld? This is a particular concern if the prejudices of the parties or their ignorance are used as ways of denying one of the parties his or her rights.

4. There are concerns over whether mediation affects the interests of third parties. Mediation allows the couple to find a solution that works for them; in a court, however, the judge can consider the interests of other people involved and even the interests of the wider community. A particularly telling point on this concerns children's interests on separation. In mediation, the parents might agree on the solution that they think is best, but that is no guarantee that the solution will work well for the children. As Martin Richards explains:

> [W]hile mediation may do much to help parents reach agreements and set up work-able arrangements for children, it cannot protect children's interests. It must rely on the information about children that the parties bring to the sessions. Necessarily this information will be presented in the light of parental perceptions, hopes, fears, anxieties, and guilt. In most cases this will serve children's interests well enough, but it cannot be termed protection as it is not based on an independent view.[103]

Certainly, there seems little in mediation that will ensure that the rights of children are protected. The argument applies not only to children; a court can also take into account the interests of the environment or the general good, which will be over-looked in mediation.[104]

5. There are doubts whether mediators have the expertise to consider the complex tax and financial issues that may have to be dealt with in some cases.[105] For example, even experienced solicitors struggle with the valuation and sharing of pensions on divorce, and most seek expert advice. To expect mediators and the couple to deal with such issues themselves is to expect too much.

 What would you do?

Do you think that there are some kinds of case that are better suited to mediation than others? Do you think that you would like to mediate if you were in dispute? Why? If you were a mediator, what approach would you take to mediation?

---

[103] M. Richards, 'But what about the children? Some reflections on the divorce White Paper' (1995) 4 Child and Family Law Quarterly 223, 224.

[104] R. Baruch Bush and J. Folger, 'Mediation and social justice: Risks and opportunities' (2012) 27 Ohio Journal of Dispute Resolution 1.

[105] R. Dingwall and D. Greatbatch, 'Family mediators: What are they doing?' (2001) 31 Family Law 379.

Lawyers and mediation

Lawyers can interact with mediation in many ways. They can, of course, recommend that their clients use mediation if they are in an intractable dispute, although it seems rare that lawyers choose to do so.[106] Lawyers may be asked by clients either before or during mediation for some general advice as to their legal rights. Alternatively, a lawyer might be consulted after mediation and be asked to put the agreement reached into the form of a court order.

Lawyers may feel uncomfortable advising clients in this way. Without fully ascertaining the facts and receiving all of the documentation, a lawyer may feel that he or she cannot give adequate advice. Yet that will involve the kind of detailed investigations that mediation is, in part, designed to avoid. Lawyers advising in these contexts will want to be very careful in explaining what kind of advice they are giving.

Occasionally, lawyers can be involved by sitting in on mediation, or at least by being regularly consulted during its course. Mediators complain that this decreases the chance of a settlement and there is some evidence in support of that argument.[107] Lawyers may respond that their involvement saved the client from accepting an unfair mediated agreement.

In an interesting analysis, John Lande suggests that mediation will play an increasing role in lawyers' practice.[108] He foresees 'liti-mediation' under which mediation becomes 'the normal way of ending litigation'. He foresees that a broad range of styles of mediation will be available, often specialised for particular kinds of cases, and that lawyers will need to assist their clients in selecting and being involved in the mediation.

Mediation and confidentiality

Mediation is based on trust. Each side is expected to be fully open with the other. To assist this, the content of the discussions and all information disclosed in mediation is protected by the rules of confidentiality, and cannot be disclosed without the consent of both parties.[109] There is, of course, an exception where the mediation discussions reveal a risk to children, in which case the potential harm to a child can justify interference with confidentiality.[110]

---

[106] L. Mulcahy, ' Can leopards change their spots? An evaluation of the role of lawyers in medical negligence mediation' (2001) 8 International Journal of the Legal Profession 203.

[107] J. Poitras, A. Stimec, and J.-F. Roberge, 'The negative impact of attorneys on mediation outcomes: A myth or a reality?' (2010) 26 Negotiation Journal 9.

[108] J. Lande, 'How will lawyering and mediation practices transform each other?' (1997) 24 Florida Law Review 839.

[109] *Practice Direction (Family Division: Conciliation)* [1992] 1 WLR 147.

[110] *Re D (Minors)* [1993] Fam 231.

 **Application**

> It is especially important, if mediation breaks down and the matter then becomes subject to litigation, that you remember the importance of confidentiality. You cannot rely in the litigation on matters that have been spoken about in mediation. This can be very frustrating, especially if you know that the other side is lying, because of what was said in mediation.

Collaborative law

Collaborative law is an approach that has been adopted and developed by quite a number of firms of solicitors. It is growing in popularity. It is perhaps best seen as a middle path between mediation and negotiation through lawyers. At its heart is a rejection of litigation as a helpful way of resolving financial disputes and the development of the following four principles.

- There is to be an open, but privileged, sharing of advice and information with the other participants.

- There is to be a face-to-face four-way meeting (two clients, each with their lawyer) designed to reach an agreement.[111] The parties may also be assisted by other professionals, such as an accountant.

- The negotiations are interest-based. This means that the process begins by identifying the interests of the parties and then negotiations seek to find a solution to meet those interests. This differs from the orthodox approach in which each party sets out what it wants.

- The clients and lawyers commit to resolving issues without going to court. Participants sign a formal participation agreement, including that the lawyers will not represent the parties in any litigation if the negotiations break down.

Users of the collaborative approach claim a success rate of over 85 per cent and increased rates of satisfaction from clients, although there is not yet sufficient data to confirm this.[112] There is much that is attractive about this model, which in a way formalises what was common practice in the past. It has received support from the judiciary, being described in *S v P (Settlement by Collaborative Law Process)*[113] as designed 'to provide as much encouragement as possible to people to resolve their difficulties in this civilized and sensible way'.[114] Unsurprisingly, it is family law that has led the way in the use of collaborative law.

---

[111] K. Wright, 'The evolving role of the family lawyer: The impact of collaborative law on family law practice' (2011) 23 Child and Family Law Quarterly 370; G. Bishop, S. Kingston, S. Max, and P. Pressdee, 'Collab lite: No substitute for the real thing' (2011) 41 Family Law 1556.

[112] Bishop et al. (n. 111).   [113] [2008] 2 FLR 2040.

[114] For further discussion, see P. Tesler, *Collaborative Family Law* (William Morrow, 2011).

The focus of collaborative law is on the objectives of each of the parties and seeking to find a solution that meets as many of these objectives as possible.[115] Where helpful, other professionals can be brought in to give specialist advice. A divorcing couple, for example, might bring in a pensions expert to advise on that issue.

Collaborative law is not without its critics. There have been concerns that people feel under considerable pressure to reach an agreement. The process is about putting the client in charge of the settlement, with the lawyer being a facilitator of that. If a party is particularly meek, or attaches great significance to one issue and is willing to sacrifice anything for that issue, his or her interests may not be adequately protected. Katherine Wright's study found cases in which agreements were reached that the lawyers agreed they would have urged their clients not to agree to in a traditional negotiation approach.[116] Solicitors using collaborative law can be put in a difficult position if they feel that their clients are not negotiating effectively or are agreeing to a settlement that is to their disadvantage.

Resolution defines collaborative law in the following way:

> Under the collaborative law process, each person appoints their own collaboratively trained lawyer and you and your respective lawyers all meet together to work things out face to face. Both of you will have your lawyer by your side throughout the process and so you will have their support and legal advice as you go.
>
> You and your lawyers sign an agreement that commits you to trying to resolve the issues without going to court and prevents them from representing you in court if the collaborative process breaks down. That means all are absolutely committed to finding the best solutions by agreement, rather than through court proceedings.[117]

Collaborative law shares many of the advantages of mediation, without some of its disadvantages. By being outside the court system, it can progress at the speed that the parties wish and focus on the issues closest to their hearts. It is private. The parties can tailor solutions that work for their lives. It has the benefits of legal advice, ensuring that the parties know their legal positions. Further, with a lawyer representing each party, there is perhaps less chance of one party taking advantage of the other. A major disadvantage, of course, is costs: with both parties receiving and paying for legal advice, collaborative law is currently available only to wealthier clients.

Arbitration

Arbitration has been increasing in popularity in recent years, especially in commercial cases. Essentially, it involves the parties reaching a contract under which they agree to take their dispute to a third party (an arbitrator) and to be bound by his or her

---

[115] G. Voegele, L. Wray, and R. Ouskytt, 'Collaborative law: A useful tool for the family law practitioner to promote better outcomes' (2007) 33 William Mitchell Law Review 971.

[116] Wright (n. 111).   [117] Resolution, *Collaborative Law* (Resolution, 2013), 1.

decision. Often, the parties, when entering a contract, will agree in advance that if a dispute arises, the issue will be resolved by arbitration. London has been increasingly recognised as one of the world's leading centres for arbitration.

The attraction to companies of this approach is that it offers a cheaper form of dispute resolution. It also enables the parties to determine their own rules for the arbitration. The arbitrator could apply English law to determine the resolution, but often the parties will use their own, or internationally developed, principles. This can be particularly helpful in international disputes, in which the worry may be that litigation in a range of countries may be recommended if there is a dispute, creating considerable expense.

An added benefit of arbitration is that the dispute can be kept private and confidentiality can be preserved. The parties can also select as an arbitrator an expert in their field. This may be particularly beneficial in a highly specialised area (such as intellectual property). The parties may believe that an expert, familiar with the commercial realities, will be better equipped to find an appropriate resolution than a judge. A further benefit is that the parties can limit rights to appeal and therefore that arbitrated settlements may be more final than litigated ones.

Despite these advantages, there are some disadvantages. The arbitrator has no power to compel third parties to disclose documents or to attend the arbitration; a judge's powers in relation to a third party are far more extensive. Specialist arbitrators can become very busy and so delays can result from that. Further, the lack of coercive powers of an arbitrator can mean that a party to arbitration who is determined to be uncooperative can cause severe delays and costs. There are fewer sanctions available to an arbitrator than there are to a judge in such a situation.

Arbitration is governed by the Arbitration Act 1996. This is a complex piece of legislation and we cannot go into the detail of it here. The key points to note are that section 9 makes it clear that if a party seeks to bring court proceedings over breach of the arbitration agreement, the court can stay the proceedings and require the parties to arbitrate. Under section 24, the court does have the power to remove an arbitrator who has abused his or her position or in the event of his or her incapacity. There is also a general duty under section 33 that the arbitration tribunal acts fairly and impartially.

Conclusion

The cost, publicity, stress, and time involved in litigation have all meant that clients are often keen to avoid going to court. It is not surprising therefore that the vast majority of cases are resolved by negotiation through lawyers. In some areas, lawyers are being avoided altogether and the parties are seeking to use mediation to resolve their disputes. These forms of alternative dispute resolution (ADR) are marked by the lack of clear regulation governing them. As we have seen, there is little agreement over the ethical principles that govern those negotiating or mediating. One thing is clear, however: the issues covered in this chapter are perhaps the most important in this book. We need to get better at negotiating and mediating in an ethical and successful way.

Further reading

On mediation:

R. Baruch Bush and J. Folger, 'Mediation and social justice: Risks and opportunities' (2012) 27 Ohio Journal of Dispute Resolution 1.

S. Belhorn, 'Settling beyond the shadow of the law: How mediation can make the most of social norms' (2005) 20 Ohio State Journal on Dispute Resolution 981.

A. Boon, R. Earle, and A. Whyte, 'Regulating mediators?' (2007) 10 Legal Ethics 26.

J. Bush and R. Folger, 'Transformative mediation and third-party intervention: Ten hallmarks of a transformative approach to practice' (1996) 13 Mediation Quarterly 26.

R. Field, 'Exploring the potential of contextual ethics in mediation', in F. Bartlett, R. Mortensen, and K. Tranter (eds) *Alternative Perspectives on Lawyers and Legal Ethics* (Routledge, 2011).

S. Imperati, 'Mediator practice models:T intersection of ethics and stylistic practices in mediation' (1997) 33 Willamette Law Review 703.

C. Izumi, 'Implicit bias and the illusion of mediator neutrality' (2010) 34 Washington University Journal of Law and Policy 71.

J. Lande, 'How will lawyering and mediation practices transform each other?' (1997) 24 Florida Law Review 839.

T. Trinder, A. Firth, and C. Jenks, '"So presumably things have moved on since then?" The management of risk allegations in child contact dispute resolution' (2010) 24 International Journal of Law, Policy and the Family 29.

On negotiation:

A. Hinshaw and J. Alberts, 'Doing the right thing: An empirical study of attorney negotiation ethics' (2011) 16 Harvard Negotiation Law Review 95.

R. Hollander-Blumoff, 'Just negotiation' (2010) 88 Washington University Law Review 381.

C. Menkel-Meadow, 'Toward another view of legal negotiation: The structure of problem solving' (1984) 31 UCLA Law Review 754.

C. Menkel-Meadow, 'The trouble with the adversary system in a postmodern, multicultural world' (1996) 38 William and Mary Law Review 5.

M. Moffitt, 'Three things to be against ("settlement" not included)' (2009) 78 Fordham Law Review 1203.

B. Spangler, 'Heads I win, tails you lose: The psychological barriers to economically efficient civil settlement and a case for third-party mediation' [2012] Wisconsin Law Review 1435.

W. Steel, 'Deceptive negotiating and high-toned morality' (1986) 39 Vanderbilt Law Review 1387.

On collaborative law:

G. Voegele, L. Wray, and R. Ouskytt, 'Collaborative law: A useful tool for the family law practitioner to promote better outcomes' (2007) 33 William Mitchell Law Review 971.

K. Wright, 'The evolving role of the family lawyer: The impact of collaborative law on family law practice' (2011) 23 Child and Family Law Quarterly 370.

22

PROCEDURE BEFORE SENTENCING

This Chapter, and the three which follow, summarize the sentencing process, placing empha- **22.01**
sis upon its procedural aspects. For more detail, reference should be made to *Blackstone's
Criminal Practice 2012*, Part E.

Once the accused has pleaded guilty or been found guilty by the jury or magistrates, the **22.02**
court's task is to sentence him. Before it does so, the procedures described in this Chapter
must be gone through. The court may either embark on them immediately after conviction,
or it may adjourn (e.g., to obtain reports on the offender, or to await the outcome of a co-
accused's trial so that, in the event of his being convicted as well, they can both be sentenced
together). During the period of any adjournment the offender may be remanded in custody
or on bail at the court's discretion. The description that follows is mainly of procedure preparatory to sentencing in the Crown Court. Although the same basic principles apply in the
magistrates' courts, what happens there tends to be less elaborate and less formal than the
Crown Court equivalent. Paragraphs 22.75 to 22.76 deal with the differences.

In the magistrates' courts the decision on what sentence to impose, like the decision as to **22.03**
verdict, may be taken by a majority of the magistrates. In the Crown Court, the responsibility
for sentencing rests solely upon the judge (and any magistrates with whom he may be sitting

where the case is an appeal from the magistrates' court). The only way a jury may try to influence sentence is by adding a rider to their verdict recommending leniency. They very rarely
do so. Since advocates in their speeches and the judge in his summing-up do not refer to the
possibility of recommending leniency, the jurors probably do not even know that they could
make such a recommendation. Moreover, in *Sahota* [1980] Crim LR 678, where the jury asked
if they could recommend leniency and the judge answered 'yes', the Court of Appeal stated
that he should have told them that matters of sentencing were not for their consideration.

22.04   If the jury indicate on their own initiative a view of the facts which is relevant to sentence,
the judge is not bound by that view when he decides upon sentence. In *Mills* [2003] Crim
LR 896, the defendant was convicted of being knowingly concerned in fraudulently evading
the prohibition on the importation of cocaine and other drugs. The judge stated he would
sentence on the basis that the defendant knew he was importing drugs with a high value, and
sentenced him to 16 years' imprisonment. The jury submitted a note signed by 11 of them
stating that their verdict of guilty was based on a view that the accused genuinely believed
that the goods he was importing were not drugs but were prohibited. The sentencing judge
concluded that he was not bound by the note, and refused to vary the sentence. The Court of
Appeal agreed that he was not bound by the jury's finding, and dismissed the appeal.

22.05   The procedure before sentencing is divided into the presentation of the facts of the offence by
the prosecution; the reading of any reports on the offender; and mitigation by the defence.

A   THE FACTS OF THE OFFENCE

22.06   Where the offender has pleaded not guilty and has been convicted by the jury, the Crown
Court judge, having heard the evidence, knows full well the facts of the offence, and does not
need to be reminded of them. If the offender pleads guilty, on the other hand, it is prosecuting
counsel's duty to summarize the facts of the offence. He does this partly to assist the judge,
partly to establish the prosecution version of how the offence was committed, and partly so
that the public may know what occurred and form their own views on the justice of the sentence passed. The Attorney-General has issued guidance (*Guidelines on Acceptance of Pleas and
the Prosecutor's Role in the Sentencing Exercise*) which lays down that the prosecution must set
out in advance, and in writing:

* the aggravating and mitigating features of the offence which will form the opening of its
  case;
* any statutory provisions or guidelines on sentencing applicable to the offence or the
  offender;
* evidence of impact on the victim and community; and
* any ancillary orders which the prosecution intends to apply for.

The intention is that this statement will be notified in advance to the court and the defence.
The guidelines apply to all cases before the Crown Court, and cases in the magistrates' court
where the issues are complex or there is scope for misunderstanding.

22.07   In summarizing the facts, counsel makes use of copies, given to him in his brief, of the statements made by the prosecution witnesses for purposes of the committal proceedings. He

explains how the offence was committed, mentioning facts especially relevant to its gravity—e.g., if it was an offence of theft, he tells the judge the value of the property stolen and the amount which has been recovered; if it was an offence of violence, he recites the injuries suffered by the victim. He goes on to describe the arrest of the offender, and his reaction when asked about the offence. If the offender was immediately cooperative, admitting his guilt to the police, it is a point in his favour which may result in the sentence being lighter than it would otherwise have been. Therefore, prosecuting counsel should acknowledge, if it be the case, that the offender did frankly confess to the crime. If there was a formal interview with the offender at the police station, counsel could either read out the record of it in full, or, more usually, summarize its contents and leave the defence to refer to it in more detail if they so wish.

At the sentencing stage, the prosecution take a neutral attitude towards the case. They do not **22.08** suggest any particular sentence, nor do they advocate a severe sentence. Prosecuting counsel is still to regard himself as a minister of justice (see 20.06), conceding to the defence those points which can fairly be made on the offender's behalf. This general statement is subject to some qualifications. For example:

(a) Prosecuting counsel should apply for compensation, confiscation, or forfeiture, backing up the application with evidence and argument if necessary (see 25.72 to 25.94 for details).

(b) Counsel should assist the judge by drawing attention to any limits on the court's sentencing powers, so that no unlawful sentence is passed. This duty applies also to defence counsel (*Komsta* (1990) 12 Cr App R(S) 63). Prosecuting counsel should also draw the judge's attention to guidelines cases (*Panayioutou* (1989) 11 Cr App R(S) 535; see 23.23 to 23.27 for the role of guideline cases).

Rather more controversial is the question of the extent to which the prosecution should make **22.09** reference to the impact of the offence on the victim. In *Attorney-General's Reference (No 2 of 1995)* [1996] 1 Cr App R(S) 274, the Court of Appeal said it was appropriate that a judge should receive factual information as to the impact of offending on the victim. Any such information should, however, be put in proper form, e.g., a witness statement, served on the defence in advance and forming part of the judge's papers (see *Hobstaff* (1993) 14 Cr App R(S) 632, where the point was also made that the prosecution should avoid colourful and emotive language in dealing with the impact on the victim). In *H* (1999) *The Times*, 18 March 1999, the Court of Appeal emphasized that where the prosecution does provide a statement from the victim, then the sentencer should approach it with some care. Since it was generally inappropriate for the defence to investigate such a statement, it would necessarily reflect one side of the case only.

In *Perks* [2001] 1 Cr App R (S) 66, the following guidelines were laid down for courts when **22.10** taking into account what have become known as 'victim impact statements':

(a) a sentencer should not make assumptions unsupported by the evidence about the effect of an offence on the victim;

(b) if the offence had a particularly distressing or disturbing effect upon the victim, the court should be so informed and account should be taken of this fact in passing sentence;

(c) evidence of an offence on the victim should be in the proper form as a witness statement or expert report, and be properly served on the defence prior to sentence;

(d) evidence of the victim should be approached with care, particularly if it dealt with matters which the defence could not be expected to investigate; and

(e) opinions of the victim's close relatives on the appropriate level of sentence should not be taken into account.

(See also *Consolidated Criminal Practice Direction* III.28)

22.11   In any event, the prosecution should not accept the defence version of the offence if it does not accord with the account given by the prosecution witnesses. Hence, there is the possibility of a dispute arising about the facts of the offence, even after the offender has quite properly entered a plea of guilty. If the dispute is on a minor point, it can be glossed over because the sentence the judge passes will be the same irrespective of which of the opposing contentions he believes. But, where there is a 'substantial conflict between the two sides' involving a 'sharp divergence on questions of fact', the judge, having heard submissions from counsel, must *either*:

(a) obtain the answer to the problem from a jury; or

(b) accept the defence account 'as far as that is possible', *or*

(c) give both parties the opportunity to call evidence about the disputed matters,

and then decide himself what happened 'acting so to speak as his own jury on the issue which is the root of the problem'.

What he must *not* do is to come down in favour of the prosecution version of events without hearing evidence. The benefit of any reasonable doubt should be given to the offender. The above statement of the law is based on Lord Lane CJ's judgment in the leading case of *Newton* (1982) 77 Cr App R 13, the facts of which illustrate the importance which can attach to disputes about the facts after a guilty plea. N pleaded guilty to buggery of his wife. Buggery of a female was at that time an offence punishable with life imprisonment, regardless of whether the 'victim' consented. The wife, in a complaint she made to the police, said that she had not consented, but N claimed that she had. On his own admission, he was guilty as charged, but the appropriate sentence would be significantly more severe if he acted against his wife's will. Without hearing evidence from N or from the wife, the judge announced that he was sentencing on the basis that she had not consented, and he imprisoned N for seven years. The Court of Appeal (in reducing the term of imprisonment so as to allow for N's immediate release) said that the judge should not have decided such an important issue against the defence without hearing evidence. (The substantive law has been amended. Buggery of a man or woman now constitutes rape where the victim did not consent and the accused knew of that lack of consent or was reckless as to whether there was consent or not. If N was to be dealt with today, the indictment would no doubt include a count of rape, and the procedural problem would be resolved in that way.)

22.12   Uncertainty about the facts of the offence can also occur where the offender pleaded not guilty and was found guilty by the jury. For example, in *Stosiek* (1982) 4 Cr App R(S) 205, S, who had punched a plain-clothes police officer and broken his nose, was found guilty of assault occasioning actual bodily harm. Prior to the assault, the officer had touched S lightly on the arm, shown him his warrant card, and said 'I want a word with you'. The evidence was consistent either with S having realized that a policeman was trying to arrest him and committing the assault to resist arrest, or with his not noticing the warrant-card and over-reacting to what he took to be a minor assault on him by a member of the public. On either hypothesis, the jury would have to convict, but on the first-mentioned hypothesis a sentence of imprisonment was almost inevitable, whereas on the second (given that S was of previous good character) non-custodial sanctions were appropriate. The Court of Appeal held that in such cases it is for the judge to assess the evidence led before the jury, and decide on the basis thereof what the facts of the offence were. He is not obliged to accept the least serious construction of the evidence consistent with the jury's verdict (*Solomon* [1984] Crim LR 433), but he should be 'extremely astute' to give the benefit of any doubt to the offender (*Stosiek*). In passing sentence, the judge must always respect the jury's verdict, so that if the offender was found guilty merely of a lesser offence the sentence must be appropriate to that lesser offence, even if the judge thinks that the evidence showed beyond doubt that the offender was guilty as charged: *Hazelwood* [1984] Crim LR 375.

A judge must not, under guise of hearing evidence about the facts of what occurred, in effect find the accused guilty of an offence more serious than that to which he has pleaded guilty (*Courtie* [1984] AC 463). **22.13**

The decision in *Nottingham Crown Court ex parte Director of Public Prosecutions* [1995] Crim LR 902 would appear to run counter to the well-established principle outlined in the preceding paragraph. In that case, the prosecution charged assault by beating contrary to s 39 of the Criminal Justice Act 1988 (which requires no proof of injury), rather than assault contrary to s 47 of the Offences Against the Person Act 1861 (which does). The Divisional Court held that the sentencer should have taken into account, in passing sentence, injuries caused to the victim. It is submitted that the decision is best viewed as confined to the offence of assault by beating, and should not be extended to other offences. **22.14**

A judge must also not use an inquiry into the facts of the offence as a means of deciding that the offender has committed similar offences on other occasions. This principle is important to bear in mind should the prosecution, in their summary of the facts following a guilty plea, suggest that the counts on the indictment merely represent a sample of a continuing course of conduct by the offender. If this is accepted by the defence, the judge may pass sentence on that basis. There is also the possibility that the prosecution may make formal application under s 25 of the Domestic Violence, Crime and Victims Act 2004 for some of the counts to be treated as a sample, with the remainder being tried by the judge alone (see 15.15 for details of this procedure). However, if neither of these events occur, then the judge must ignore the allegations about a continuing course of conduct, and sentence on the basis of the offences to which the defendant has pleaded guilty. Thus, in *Huchison* [1972] 1 All ER 936, the Court of Appeal halved a four-year sentence passed on H for incest with his daughter. The indictment contained one count to which H pleaded guilty. The prosecution alleged that there had been regular intercourse over a long period, whereas the defence said it had only happened the once. Having heard evidence from both the daughter and H, the judge believed the daughter, and sentenced on the basis that the count represented but a small part of a continuing course of conduct. Their Lordships held that the judge had adopted the wrong procedure. Instead of hearing evidence himself, he should have sentenced H strictly for the one offence to which he had pleaded guilty, leaving the prosecution to commence further proceedings for the other alleged acts of incest if they so wished. In *Canavan* [1998] 1 Cr App R 79, the Court of Appeal said that the court below could not base its decision as to sentence on the commission **22.15** of offences not forming part of the offence for which the offender was to be sentenced. This seems to resolve the matter authoritatively.

22.16 Since the Court of Appeal's decision in *Newton* (above) there has been a plethora of decisions refining and expanding upon Lord Lane CJ's basic dictum that, if the prosecution and defence disagree about the facts of the offence, the judge must either proceed on the basis most favourable to the defence or himself hear evidence on the disputed issues. Among the points dealt with in the post-*Newton* cases are those set out in the following Paragraphs.

22.17 The Court of Appeal has stated that counsel are under a duty to make it clear when a *Newton* hearing is appropriate. In *Gardener* (1994) 15 Cr App R(S) 667, the court said that where there is a dispute about relevant facts which might affect sentence, defence counsel should make that clear to the prosecution. The court should be informed at the outset of the hearing, if not by the prosecution then by the defence. If for any reason this did not happen, defence counsel should ensure during mitigation that the judge was aware, not merely that there was a dispute, but that the defence wished to have it resolved in a *Newton* hearing. The Court of Appeal would not normally consider an argument that the sentencer had failed to order a hearing unless the possibility of such a hearing was raised unequivocally and expressly in the Crown Court (see also *Attorney-General's References (Nos 3 and 4 of 1996)* [1996] Crim LR 607). In *Tolera* [1998] Crim LR 425, the Court of Appeal said that the initiative rested with the defence to make it clear that it was asking the court to pass sentence on any basis other than that disclosed by the prosecution case. The mere fact that the defendant put forward an alternative version to the probation service, which was reflected in the pre-sentence report, was not sufficient to alert the judge to the need for a *Newton* hearing. If the defendant wanted that account to be used as the basis of sentence, he should expressly draw the relevant paragraphs of the report to the attention of the court, and ask that he be sentenced on that basis.

22.18 Some difficulty arises where the defendant changes his plea to guilty after some evidence has been given by prosecution witnesses. In *Mottram* (1981) 3 Cr App R(S) 123, it was held that the judge should then hear evidence from the defendant (and, presumably from any witnesses the defence wished to call), before deciding on the version of the facts which will form the basis for sentence. The totality of the evidence received on the point relevant to sentence can then be treated as a *Newton* hearing (see also *Archer* [1994] Crim LR 80).

22.19 Sometimes an agreement is reached between prosecution and defence as to the basis on which a plea of guilty will be given and accepted, e.g., the accused agrees to plead guilty to assault occasioning actual bodily harm, but only on the basis of recklessness, and the prosecution are willing to accept this. In *Beswick* [1996] 1 Cr App R(S) 343, the Court of Appeal set out principles to guide the court in such cases. It stressed that the court should sentence an offender on a basis which was true, and that the prosecution should not lend itself to any agreement with the defence based upon an unreal set of facts. If that had happened, then the judge was entitled to call for a *Newton* hearing to determine the true factual basis for sentence. The judge's decision to do so did not of itself entitle the defendant to change his plea from guilty to not guilty. Once the judge had decided to hold a *Newton* hearing, then the prosecution should no longer regard themselves as bound by the original agreement which they had made with the defence, which was conditional on the sentencer's approval. They should therefore assist the court in the conduct of the *Newton* hearing by presenting evidence and testing any evidence called by the defence.

In *Underwood* [2005] 1 Cr App R 178, the Court of Appeal stressed that, where the Crown agreed **22.20** the defendant's account of facts, which were originally disputed, the agreement should be set out in writing and signed by both advocates. It should then be made available to the judge before he was invited to approve acceptance of the plea. Crucially, the Crown's acceptance of the proposed basis of the plea of guilty must be conditional upon the judge's acceptance of it. Where, on the other hand, the defendant's version was rejected by the Crown, the precise facts in dispute should be identified in a document for the attention of the court. In any event, it was for the judge to determine whether there should be a *Newton* hearing to ascertain the truth about those facts.

In *Oudkerk* [1994] Crim LR 700, it was held that where the imposition of a longer than normal **22.21** sentence is contemplated, the sentencing court must resolve by a *Newton* hearing any important issue relevant to the application of that provision (see 24.34 to 24.42 for longer than normal sentences).

If the court decides to have a '*Newton* hearing', the same rules apply regarding burden and **22.22** standard of proof as apply at the trial of a not guilty plea. In other words, the court may sentence on the prosecution version of what occurred only if satisfied beyond reasonable doubt that the defence version is wrong (see dicta in *Ahmed* (1984) 6 Cr App R(S) 391 and *Stosiek* (above)). In *Ahmed*, the Court of Appeal also intimated that they will not interfere with the Crown Court's decision as to the facts established at a *Newton* hearing unless the appellant can show that it was totally unreasonable or arrived at by applying incorrect principles (e.g., not giving him the benefit of any doubt). *Gandy* (1989) 11 Cr App R(S) 564 makes it clear that, where there is a *Newton* hearing:

(i)   the rules of evidence should be strictly followed; and
(ii) the judge should direct himself appropriately as the trier of fact, e.g., in accordance with the guidance in *Turnbull* [1977] QB 224 on identification evidence.

Where the differences between the prosecution and defence as to what occurred are too slight **22.23** to affect sentence, the Crown Court may sentence on the basis of the facts alleged by the prosecution without hearing evidence. (In such a case, the judge will frequently indicate that he is accepting the defence version purely for the purpose of sentence. Since it will not make any difference to the outcome, there is no point giving the offender a sense of grievance by openly disbelieving what is put forward on his behalf.) Thus, in *Bent* (1986) 8 Cr App R(S) 19, the Court of Appeal dismissed B's appeal against a sentence of six months' youth custody for assaulting a store detective who tried to arrest him for shoplifting since, although the judge in passing sentence clearly accepted the prosecution case that B had used a stick in attacking the detective (whereas defence counsel had said in mitigation that his client merely *threatened* to use a stick), the gravamen of the charge was that the appellant had resisted arrest. As there was no suggestion even from the prosecution that the store detective had suffered actual harm through the assault, the question of whether the stick had lightly come into contact with his face or had merely been waved threateningly was peripheral to sentence.

Sometimes it is possible to avoid a *Newton* hearing by inviting the prosecution to add a sub- **22.24** sidiary count to the indictment which will enable a jury, in effect, to decide how the offence alleged in the primary count was committed. Thus, if the accused pleads guilty to robbery but denies the prosecution allegation that he used a firearm to commit the offence, the correct procedure is to have a second count for carrying a firearm with intent to commit an indict-able offence. The accused will presumably deny that charge, and, if the jury acquit him, the sentence for robbery will have to be passed on the basis that it was committed unarmed.

22.25 The principles explained in *Newton* do not apply when the facts advanced by the defence in mitigation are peculiarly within the knowledge of the accused himself, so that the prosecution cannot realistically be expected either to accept or to challenge what is put forward on his behalf, for example, where the accused pleads guilty to importing cocaine but says that he thought the drug was cannabis, or where he claims to have committed an offence as a result of threats that fell short of actual duress. In such cases, which have been usefully described as 'reverse *Newton*' situations, the onus would seem to be on the defence to establish the mitigation. Whether they do so simply by counsel making assertions of fact in his speech in mitigation (see 22.53 to 22.59) or by calling evidence, is a matter for their judgment. In *Guppy* (1994) 16 Cr App R(S) 25, the Court of Appeal held that where the defendant raised extraneous matters of mitigation, a burden of proof rested upon the defence, i.e., on the balance of probabilities to the civil standard. The court did state, however, that in the general run of cases the sentencer would readily accept the accuracy of defence counsel's statements. In *Tolera* [1998] Crim LR 425, however, the defendant pleaded guilty to the possession of heroin with intent to supply, and claimed that he had been threatened with violence if he did not assist in the drug dealing. The Court of Appeal held that there was an onus on the prosecution to rebut an explanation of this kind, and reduced the sentence from five to four years because they had not done so. In *Underwood* [2005] 1 Cr App R 178, the Court of Appeal stated that neither the prosecution nor the judge is bound to agree facts merely because the prosecution was unable to disprove the defendant's account. In these cases where an issue raised by the defence is outside the knowledge of the prosecution, both prosecution and defence should call any relevant evidence. Where the issue arises from facts which are within the exclusive knowledge of the defendant, he should be called as a witness and, if he is not, the judge may draw such inferences as he sees fit, subject to any explanation put forward.

22.26 The judge is entitled to decide that the defence version is not capable of belief and thus does not warrant the holding of a *Newton* hearing (see, e.g., *Kerr* (1980) 2 Cr App R(S) 54, *Gandhi* (1986) 8 Cr App R(S) 391). The judge's view that the defence version is manifestly absurd must, however, be in accordance with the facts. In *Costley* (1989) 11 Cr App R(S) 357, C pleaded guilty to inflicting grievous bodily harm. The prosecution alleged that C hit V about the head and body with a piece of wood, causing a fractured rib, a broken arm and extensive bruises. C claimed he struck V with his fists only, after V had made a homosexual approach and dripped blood on him, claiming that he was suffering from AIDS and would pass the condition on to C. The judge sentenced C solely on the basis of the prosecution opening and the defence speech in mitigation. He said:

> I find as a fact that the attack was totally unprovoked by anything [V] said or did…I reject your explanation for the use of violence as being wholly incredible.

The Court of Appeal held that it was not open to the judge to come to these conclusions, and upheld the appeal against sentence. In a case where the judge is faced with a substantial conflict on issues such as this, a *Newton* hearing should be held. In *Tolera* [1998] Crim LR 425, the Court of Appeal stressed that, while the judge was not bound to hold a *Newton* hearing where the defence version was manifestly implausible, he should indicate his view to the defendant. The defendant would then have the opportunity to convince the judge of the truth of his story.

When one accused pleads guilty and a co-accused pleads not guilty, two principles for deter- **22.27** mining the factual basis of sentence come into conflict. Should the judge hold a *Newton* hearing (which would normally be done in respect of a guilty plea)? Or should he rely on the evidence heard in the trial (as would be the usual procedure for the accused who pleaded not guilty)? In *Smith* (1988) 87 Cr App R 393, S pleaded guilty to conspiracy to obtain property by deception, the prosecution case being that he had supplied stolen credit cards to his co-accused (cashiers at a petrol filling-station), who used them to create receipts for non-existent transactions. Two of his co-accused pleaded not guilty, and ran the defence that they acted under duress from S. They were convicted. When the judge came to sentence both S and the co-accused, he said that he was taking the preliminary view that S was the ringleader, but offered S an opportunity to testify that he was not. The invitation was declined, and S was sentenced to 21 months' imprisonment, while his co-accused were given community service. The Court of Appeal held that the judge was entitled, in sentencing S, to take into account evidence at the trial of his co-accused. There was no need to recall the witnesses for cross-examination on S's behalf, notwithstanding the fact that his counsel had had no opportunity to cross-examine them during the trial. As the judge had given S a chance to give evidence himself, he had handled the procedure impeccably, and the appeal was dismissed. The approach in *Smith*, while understandable as a pragmatic solution to a difficult problem, may lead to a sense of unfairness being felt by an offender who is sentenced on a view of the facts which he disputes and which his counsel has not been able to test in the usual way by cross-examination of the witnesses who support the prosecution case. It is worth noting that the Court of Appeal in *Smith* did stress that the sentencing judge should bear in mind that evidence at the trial had not been tested by cross-examination on behalf of the offender who had pleaded guilty (see also *Winter* [1997] Crim LR 66 and *Taylor* [2007] Crim LR 491).

A further anomaly appears when one compares the approach outlined in *Smith* with that **22.28** adopted in a case such as *Gandy* (see 22.22). In *Gandy*, G pleaded guilty to violent disorder. His co-accused were then tried. Once their trial was completed, the judge held a *Newton* hearing to determine whether G had thrown a glass, causing the loss of V's eye. The Court of Appeal held that the judge should, in the *Newton* hearing, have followed the rules which would govern the use of evidence in a jury trial. Clearly, there is no equivalent protection for the accused where the *Smith* procedure is concerned. The resultant distinction seems arbitrary and exacerbates the sense of unfairness already referred to. In *Dudley* [2012] Crim LR 230, the appellant pleaded guilty to conspiracy to supply cocaine on the basis that he had acted as a driver for his co-defendants and had transported drugs which he believed to be cannabis. His co-defendants pleaded not guilty and were convicted. The prosecution case during the trial was that the appellant was more than a courier, and was in fact one of the organizers of the conspiracy. The judge then sentenced the appellant on the basis that he was the right-hand man of the principal conspirator, and that his responsibilities extended well beyond those of a conspirator. The Court of Appeal upheld his appeal, stating that the judge should have accepted the basis of his plea, or offered him the chance of a *Newton* hearing. It is submitted that this approach is preferable, and avoids the unfairness perceived if *Smith* is followed.

22.29 In *Underwood* [2005] 1 Cr App R 178, the Court of Appeal considered the application of the principle that credit should be given for a guilty plea (see 23.39 to 23.46) to a case where a *Newton* hearing had been necessary. Clearly, if the issues on the hearing were resolved in the defendant's favour, the credit due to him should not be reduced. On the other hand, if he was disbelieved or obliged the prosecution to call a witness causing unnecessary distress, and conveyed to the judge a lack of remorse for his offence, the judge might reduce the discount, particularly if the plea was tendered at a very late stage. In an exceptional case, the entitlement to credit might be completely dissipated by the *Newton* hearing, but if that was the case, the judge should explain his reasons.

22.30 In appropriate cases, the Court of Appeal can itself hold a *Newton* hearing: *Guppy* (1995) 16 Cr App R(S) 25. As to the situation where the magistrates court has held a *Newton* hearing and the defendant requests a further such hearing upon committal to the Crown Court, see 22.76.

B   ANTECEDENTS

22.31 Immediately following the committal of the case to the Crown Court, the police should prepare a document containing what are known as the Crown Court antecedents. These should be provided to the CPS, the defence, and the Crown Court within 21 days of committal or transfer, and checked and updated seven days before the hearing: *Practice Direction* (*Criminal Proceedings: Consolidation*) [2002] 1 WLR 2870, para III.27.6 and 7.

22.32 The antecedents should contain details of the offender's age, education, past and present employment, his domestic circumstances and income, the date of his arrest, whether he has been remanded in custody or on bail, and the date of his last release from prison or other custodial institution. There should also be a summary of his previous convictions and findings of guilt. This may include findings of guilt made when the offender was under 14, despite the Children and Young Persons Act 1963, s 16(2), which provides that in proceedings against a person who has attained the age of 21 findings of guilt when under 14 shall be disregarded for the purposes of evidence relating to previous convictions. Attached to the antecedents is a form giving full details of the offender's criminal record, save that, unlike the summary, it omits mention of s 16(2) findings of guilt. As regards each conviction or finding of guilt on it, the form states the name of the convicting court, the offence dealt with, the sentence passed, and the date of release if the sentence was a custodial one. Convictions which are spent (see 22.39 to 22.43) are included in both the summary of convictions and the previous convictions form, but they should be marked as such on the latter. The defence are entitled before or at any stage during the trial to be supplied with details of the accused's previous convictions. The judge also knows about them, in contrast to magistrates trying a case summarily who, if possible, are kept in ignorance of the accused's criminal record until after conviction. In the Crown Court, the police are expected to provide brief details of the circumstances of the last three similar convictions, and also of any offence leading to a community order still in force. This information is provided separately, and attached to the antecedents. Formal cautions (see 5.06 to 5.11) may be cited in court, although they should appear on a separate sheet from previous convictions.

In the great majority of cases where the contents of the antecedents are not challenged, prosecuting counsel will summarize the information which they contain. The judge has the full list and may not want to hear the details of all of them, and so may say, for example, 'last three only', or 'starting from 2009'. Counsel will then read out the last three convictions, or those dating from 2007, as the case may be.   **22.33**

Consolidated Criminal Practice Direction, III.27 deals with the contents of the antecedents.   **22.34**

After these matters have been dealt with, the prosecution case is closed.   **22.35**

Challenges to the antecedents

Where the defence challenge the prosecution version of the antecedents, it would be usual for the prosecution to call the police officer in the case. If the prosecution assertions remain in dispute, the onus remains upon them to satisfy the judge of the truth of the assertion by calling evidence of a type which would be admissible during the trial of a not guilty plea—not, for example, inadmissible hearsay or opinion. If the prosecution fail so to satisfy the judge, he should ignore the challenged assertion in passing sentence, and state that he is ignoring it: *Campbell* (1911) 6 Cr App R 131.   **22.36**

The prosecution should, in any event, be restrained from making generalized allegations, prejudicial to the offender, which are incapable of strict proof or disproof. In *Van Pelz* (1942) 29 Cr App R 10, where VP had been convicted of an offence of larceny, the Court of Criminal Appeal criticized the prosecution for allowing the officer giving the antecedents to say that VP had led a loose and immoral life, was very well known as a prostitute, had associated constantly with thieves, and was regarded as a very dangerous woman indeed. Even where a prejudicial allegation is specific, it should be made by an officer with first-hand knowledge of the matter, not by an officer relying upon what others have told him. In *Wilkins* (1978) 66 Cr App R 49, the Court of Appeal reduced W's sentence for living on the earnings of prostitution from three years to two years because the officer giving the antecedents evidence testified that some 82 women, who had worked for an escort agency run by W, had stated that they used the agency as a medium for prostitution. The evidence at W's trial, while satisfying the jury that he had lived on the earnings of prostitution, had not suggested that he was involved in the organization of prostitution on such a substantial scale. Clearly, the officer in making his allegations was not speaking of matters within his first-hand knowledge—he was repeating what the prostitutes had said.   **22.37**

If the defence challenge the correctness of the prosecution evidence about any of the previous convictions, the principles described above apply, so the prosecution must provide strict proof of the conviction. They can do this by (a) producing a certificate of conviction, signed by the clerk of the convicting court, and (b) adducing evidence that the offender who is to be sentenced is the person named in the certificate: Police and Criminal Evidence Act 1984, s 73. The evidence of identity could come from someone who was present in court on the occasion of the previous conviction. Alternatively, s 39 of the Criminal Justice Act 1948 enables the prosecution to produce further certificates, establishing that the fingerprints of the person named in the certificate of conviction are identical to the fingerprints of the offender.   **22.38**

Spent convictions

22.39 The Rehabilitation of Offenders Act 1974 is meant to enable offenders to 'live down' their past. Broadly speaking, the scheme of the Act is that after the elapsing from the date of conviction of a certain period of time (known as the 'rehabilitation period'), the offender becomes a rehabilitated person and his conviction is spent. A rehabilitated person is treated 'for all purposes in law as a person who has not committed...or been convicted of or sentenced for the offence or offences' of which he was convicted (s 4(1) of the Act). This means, e.g., that when a rehabilitated person applies for a job he does not, generally speaking, have to disclose his spent convictions, and any questions on the job application form about the applicant's criminal record are deemed not to relate to such convictions. Similarly, in most civil proceedings questions about spent convictions and evidence of the offences to which they related are inadmissible.

22.40 Section 4(1) is subject to the remainder of the Act, which contains provisions restricting the circumstances in which the subsection is to apply. Thus, a person wishing to follow certain professions or occupations designated by the Home Secretary may be asked about spent convictions by a person assessing his suitability for the profession or occupation. Not surprisingly, any would-be barristers, solicitors or judges must declare their spent convictions. More to the point as far as criminal procedure is concerned, s 7(2) provides that s 4(1) is not to apply at all to criminal proceedings—i.e., there is no statutory restriction on the evidence which may be given of, and questions which may be asked about, spent convictions that does not apply equally to convictions which are not spent. However, the *Consolidated Criminal Practice Direction* I.6 states that both courts and counsel should give effect to the general intention of Parliament expressed in the debates leading up to the passing of the Act, and should not refer to a spent conviction when that can reasonably be avoided. Indeed, counsel must always obtain the judge's authority before mentioning a spent conviction, that authority only being given where the interests of justice so require. At the sentencing stage of proceedings, the record supplied to the court of the offender's convictions should mark those which are spent. In passing sentence, the judge may disclose the existence of a spent conviction only if that is necessary to explain the sentence he is passing (e.g., because it would seem unreasonably severe were it not revealed that in the relatively recent past the offender had committed an offence similar to that for which he is now being sentenced).

22.41 The period after which a conviction becomes spent (the rehabilitation period) depends upon the sentence passed for the offence. The periods for the most common sentences are as follows:

(a) If the offender was sentenced to imprisonment for life or for a term exceeding 30 months (or to equivalent sentences of detention in a young offender institution or detention under Powers of Criminal Courts (Sentencing) Act (PCC(S)A) 2000, s 91) then the conviction never becomes spent.

(b) If the sentence was one of more than six but not more than 30 months' imprisonment, detention in a young offender institution or youth custody, the period is ten years for an adult, five years for a juvenile.

(c) If the sentence is one of imprisonment, detention in a young offender institution or youth custody for six months or less, the period is seven years for an adult, three and a half years for a juvenile.

(d) Where the offender was given a detention and training order and was aged 15 or over at the date of conviction, the period is five years if the order exceeded six months, and three and a half years if it did not.

(e) Where the offender received a detention and training order and was aged under 15 at the date of conviction, the period is one year after the order expired.

(f) For most community sentences, the period is five years for an adult, two and a half years for a juvenile.

(g) For bindovers and conditional discharges, the period is one year or the date on which the order ceases, whichever is the longer.

(h) For supervision orders the period ends on the date when the order ceases or after one year, whichever is the longer.

(i) For attendance centre orders and secure training orders, the period ends one year after the order expires.

(j) For disqualification from driving, the period is that for which the offender remains disqualified.

(k) If discharged absolutely the period ends after six months.

Where a custodial sentence is suspended, the period is the same as if it had been immediate. When the LASPO Act 2012, s 131 comes into effect, the above rehabilitation periods will be significantly reduced, i.e., the conviction will generally be spent at an earlier point in time.

22.42 Where more than one sentence is imposed for a conviction (e.g., for a drink/driving offence the offender is sentenced to six months' imprisonment suspended for two years; is fined £100, and disqualified from driving for three years), the rehabilitation period is the longest of the relevant periods (i.e., in the example given above, seven years for the suspended prison sentence, not five years for the fine or three years for the disqualification).

22.43 A convicted person can be rehabilitated only if not reconvicted during the rehabilitation period (s 6(4)). If an offender is reconvicted of anything other than a summary offence, the rehabilitation period for the first offence continues to run until the expiry of the rehabilitation period for the second offence. This is very important in practice, since it means that persistent offenders are unlikely to have any spent convictions. The rehabilitation periods for their early convictions are extended by their later convictions. This subsequent-offence rule does not, however, apply to orders of disqualification (s 6(5)).

Suspended sentence etc.

22.44 If the offence of which the offender has been convicted was committed during the operational period of a suspended sentence, the Crown Court or, in certain circumstances, a magistrates' court can bring the suspended sentence into effect (see 24.61 to 24.63). Also, if the offence was committed during the currency of a conditional discharge the court may sentence the offender for the original offence (see 25.42). When it becomes apparent during the evidence of previous convictions that the offender is in breach of a suspended sentence or conditional discharge, he should be asked whether he admits the breach. If he does, the court may deal with him for that matter when it sentences him for the present offence. If he does not, strict proof must be provided of the previous conviction and sentence (see 22.36 to 22.38). Upon such proof, the court may deal with the breach.

C   REPORTS ON THE OFFENDER

22.45   After the prosecution opening, the judge reads any reports which have been prepared on the offender. The defence are given copies of the reports. Counsel may refer to their contents in mitigation, but it is not normal practice to read them out in full. Where medical or psychiatric reports are concerned, it is obviously necessary to use them with discretion.

22.46   Pre-sentence reports are prepared by probation officers if the offender is an adult. In the cases of offenders under 18 the report is prepared by a probation officer, a social worker, or a member of a youth offending team. Typically, the report should address the offender's explanation for the offence, acceptance of responsibility, feelings of remorse, motivations, character, criminal history, relationships, personal problems such as alcohol or drug misuse, difficulties with finance, housing or employment, and any medical or psychiatric information available.

22.47   It is customary for reports to make proposals, particularly as to any community sentence which might be suitable. If the pre-sentence report proposes a community sentence (see Chapter 25 for details), then it must state whether it is available. By the CJA 2003, s 156, the court must obtain a pre-sentence report when it is considering passing a custodial sentence or community sentence. Where the offender is aged 18 or over, however, the court need not have a pre-sentence report if it is of the opinion that it is unnecessary to have one. Where the offender is aged 17 or under, the court must obtain a pre-sentence report, unless there is a pre-existing report and the court has considered its content.

22.48   Even if there is no statutory requirement to have a report, the court may well regard it as good sentencing practice to have one, particularly if it is firmly requested by the defence. Nevertheless, even where the obtaining of a pre-sentence report is 'mandatory', the court's failure to obtain one will not of itself invalidate the sentence. If the case is appealed, however, the appellate court must obtain and consider a pre-sentence report unless that is thought to be unnecessary. Should the court want a report but one is not available when an offender initially appears to be sentenced, there will have to be an adjournment. To avoid such unnecessary delays, the probation service often prepare reports in advance of conviction. They are generally reluctant to prepare pre-trial reports on defendants who plead not guilty, because the accused obviously cannot be asked about his or her attitude to the offence. Practice as to pre-trial reports in the adult magistrates' courts and youth courts varies too much for any helpful generalizations to be made. A copy of the report must be given to counsel or solicitor for the offender, or, if he is unrepresented, to the offender himself. If the offender is a juvenile and unrepresented, the report may be given to his parent or guardian: PCC(S)A 2000, s 156. The prosecution are also given a copy of the pre-sentence report. The defence may ask for the probation officer who prepared the report to give evidence, so that for instance they can challenge unfavourable comment about the offender contained in the report. In *S* [2006] Crim LR 459, however, the Court of Appeal stated that it would only be in very rare cases that the judge would be obliged to permit the author of a pre-sentence report to be cross-examined in relation to an assessment of seriousness (that is, in respect of whether an offender was to be categorized as dangerous—see 24.39 to 24.42).

22.49   Medical and psychiatric reports may also be required. As already explained at 10.72, a magistrates' court has power to remand a person (in custody or on bail) for the preparation of medical reports. Following conviction on indictment or prior to sentencing on a committal for sentence, the Crown Court also may adjourn with a view to the preparation of medical reports. Again, the offender may be remanded in custody or on bail as the court sees fit. A further option—namely to remand an accused person/offender to hospital for the preparation of reports on his mental condition—has been given to the courts by s 35 of the Mental Health Act 1983 (see 25.108).

Medical and psychiatric reports are essential if the court is to make an order under s 37 of **22.50** the Mental Health Act 1983 (detention in a mental hospital), or under PCC(S)A 2000, s 42 (community rehabilitation) with a requirement that the probationer receive treatment for a mental condition). In addition the court must order a medical report to be prepared on any offender who appears to be mentally disordered before a custodial sentence (other than for murder) is passed (Criminal Justice Act 1991, s 4(1)). The court need not obtain one if it thinks it unnecessary (s 4(2)). Failure to comply does not render the sentence invalid, but places a duty to obtain one on the appellate court where the matter is appealed (s 4(4)). Where the offender is legally represented, a copy of the report must be given to his counsel or solicitor, but if he is unrepresented he is not entitled to look at the report himself although the gist of it should be disclosed to him: Mental Health Act 1983, s 54(3). The practitioner who prepared the report may be required to attend to give oral evidence, and evidence may be called on behalf of the offender to rebut that contained in the report. In practice, it is often difficult to obtain psychiatric reports through the court, and it may be necessary for defence solicitors to take the initiative and ask a consultant who has been treating their client for a mental condition to prepare a report on him. It appears to be open to the defence to choose whether to put that report in front of the sentencer. The psychiatrist, on the other hand, if he discovers that his evidence is not to be put before the judge, is free to make it available through other channels, e.g., via the prosecution (*Crozier* [1991] Crim LR 138).

In the case of a juvenile, there may be reports from social workers involved with the juvenile **22.51** and his family. Where the juvenile, prior to being dealt with for the offence, is remanded in the care of a local authority, detailed reports may be prepared on him covering matters such as his intelligence, behaviour in care, reaction to persons in authority, and relationships with his peers. There may also be a report from his school.

The mere act of adjourning for a pre-sentence report can raise in the offender's mind an expec- **22.52** tation that, should the report be favourable in the sense of recommending a non-custodial disposition, the court will follow the recommendation. If, notwithstanding a favourable report, he is then given a custodial sentence, he will have an understandable sense of grievance, and the Court of Appeal will feel obliged to quash the custodial sentence, even if it was perfectly justifiable in the light of the gravity of the offence and the offender's record (see *Gillam* (1980) 2 Cr App R(S) 267). To avoid such an outcome, a court adjourning for reports but wishing to leave all options open should tell the offender that there is no implied promise of a lenient sentence, and, whatever the reports say, the eventual outcome may well be imprisonment or detention. Provided the above was made clear at the time of the adjournment, there can be no objection to the court rejecting a non-custodial recommendation in a report: *Horton and Alexander* (1985) 7 Cr App R(S) 299. Moreover, the mere fact that the judge, on adjourning for reports, remains silent as to the prospect of a custodial sentence, should not be taken as an indication that a non-custodial sentence will eventually be passed (*Renan* [1994] Crim LR 379).

D   MITIGATION

22.53   Once the reports have been read and, if necessary, the makers of the reports called to give
evidence, defence counsel presents the mitigation on behalf of the offender. Much of it may
be foreshadowed in the reports, and counsel can refer the judge to passages in them which
are of especial assistance to his argument. Usually, counsel deals with the immediate circumstances of the offence, stressing any factor which may lessen its gravity. If it is an offence of
dishonesty, he may be able to say that it was committed on the impulse of the moment, when
temptation was suddenly and unexpectedly placed in the offender's way. If it is an offence of
violence, he could point to extreme provocation which led the offender to lose his temper.
Counsel must be careful, however, not to put forward in mitigation anything which in fact
amounts to a defence to the charge—e.g., he should not assert that an assault was committed in self-defence. Where there is nothing that can sensibly be said with a view to making
the offence appear less serious, it is best to turn rapidly to the circumstances of the offender.
If the offence was committed when the offender was going through a period of difficulty,
financial or otherwise, that may provide some explanation for what occurred. Looking to
the future, there may have been a change in the offender's circumstances which offers hope
for him staying out of trouble—he may have found a good job, or been reconciled with his
wife, or accepted treatment for a drink problem which contributed to his offending. Finally,
a cooperative attitude with the police when arrested, and a plea of guilty in court are both
good points in mitigation.

22.54   In addition to his speech in mitigation counsel may call character witnesses on behalf of the
offender to say, e.g., that the offence was completely out of character and that they are convinced nothing like it will ever happen again. Such character witnesses can be called at the
beginning or end of mitigation, or in the middle. If the offender has no previous convictions
it is, of course, a very strong argument in mitigation whether or not any character witnesses
are called. (For further details see 23.49 to 23.53.)

22.55   The Criminal Procedure and Investigations Act 1996, s 58 gives a court power to impose
reporting restrictions on false or irrelevant assertions made during a speech in mitigation,
where they are derogatory to a person's character. No such order can be made if the assertion
has been made at an earlier stage of proceedings, e.g., at trial. Orders may be revoked at any
time by the court, and if not revoked expire after a year. It is an offence to publish or broadcast
in breach of such an order.

22.56   The offender may decline legal representation and put forward his mitigation in person if
he so wishes. Generally speaking, however, it is of assistance to the court to have counsel or
solicitor emphasize those matters which genuinely argue for a light sentence—an offender in
person, through ignorance, may concentrate upon points which if anything exacerbate the
offence and ignore some which are good mitigation. Legal representation for the offender
is especially important where he is in danger of a first sentence of imprisonment. Except as
a last resort when it is really unavoidable, the courts should try to avoid sending to prison
an offender who has not previously been there, if only because having experienced prison
he may become hardened to it, and not deterred by the risk of it as he was before serving his
sentence. So that all possible alternatives to imprisonment can be explored, it is desirable to

have a lawyer mitigate for the offender. As Lord Bridge of Harwich put it in *Re McC (A Minor)*, [1985] AC 528:

> No one should be liable to a first sentence of imprisonment . . . unless he has had the opportunity of having his case in mitigation presented to the court in the best possible light. For an inarticulate defendant, such presentation may be crucial to his liberty.

Therefore, the PCC(S)A 2000, s 83 provides that a court shall not pass a sentence of imprisonment on an offender who is not legally represented, and who has not previously been so sentenced unless he has been informed of his right to apply for representation by the Criminal Defence Service and has had the opportunity to do so but has failed to make any application. Broadly speaking, the effect of s 83 is that a court considering a first sentence of imprisonment must tell an unrepresented offender that he can apply for free legal representation, and grant, say, a week's adjournment to allow him to make the application. If he makes the application and is represented at the resumed hearing, the object of the section has been achieved. If he fails to make any application and is still unrepresented, the court has done all it reasonably could to persuade him to be represented, and is at liberty to pass whatever sentence it thinks fit. **22.57**

Legal representation is also important whenever a court is considering depriving a young offender of his liberty. Therefore, identical provisions apply to the passing of a sentence of a detention and training order or detention under s 91 of the PCC(S)A 2000. In the above cases, no distinction is drawn between an offender who has, and an offender who has not, previously been dealt with by means of the sentence or order in question. **22.58**

A sentence of imprisonment which is suspended (see 24.48 to 24.63) is nonetheless a prison sentence, and so s 83 of the PCC(S)A 2000 will apply when a court is considering suspended imprisonment just as it applies when it is considering immediate imprisonment. But the statute provides that, for purposes of deciding whether or not an offender has previously been sentenced to imprisonment, a suspended sentence which has not been brought into force shall be disregarded. Thus, before passing even a suspended sentence on an unrepresented offender whose only previous prison sentence is an unactivated suspended one, the court is obliged by s 83 to adjourn to let him apply for free legal representation. **22.59**

E   TAKING OTHER OFFENCES INTO CONSIDERATION

A suspect who is questioned by the police about an offence and admits that he committed it may be further questioned about other crimes, as yet unsolved, which bear some similarity to the crime to which he has confessed. If the suspect is responsible for some or all of these other crimes, he might nevertheless be unwilling to acknowledge responsibility should each crime appear as a separate count on an indictment against him. A system has therefore developed which allows an offender to admit to other offences without actually being convicted of them. It is known as taking other offences into consideration when passing sentence. The procedure can be used in both the magistrates' courts and Crown Court. **22.60**

The police prepare a list of the other offences which they believe or suspect the offender has also committed. The offender studies the list, and, if he so wishes, indicates that he did **22.61** commit at least some of the offences. He then signs the list, those offences which he denies having been deleted. At the trial, the offender pleads guilty to the counts in the indictment. During his summary of the facts, prosecuting counsel tells the judge that he understands that the offender wishes to have other offences taken into consideration. The judge, who is given the list of offences which the offender has signed, asks him whether he admits committing each of the offences and whether he wants them taken into consideration when sentence is passed. Upon the offender answering 'yes' the judge will nearly always comply with his request. Prosecuting counsel will not give full details of the way the other offences were committed, but he may tell the judge for instance the total value of the property stolen in the other offences and the amount recovered.

22.62   In passing sentence, the maximum sentence the court may impose is the maximum for the offences of which the offender has been convicted. This, in practice, is not a significant limitation on the court's powers, since maximum penalties are usually far in excess of that which the court would want to impose even for a serious instance of the offence in question. To take a typical example, an offender might plead guilty to an indictment containing two counts of theft from cars and a burglary from a dwelling-house. He might also ask for three further counts of thefts from cars to be taken into consideration. Theft carries a maximum penalty of seven years' imprisonment and burglary from a dwelling-house 14 years. He would therefore face a total of 28 years' imprisonment for the counts on the indictment. Even with the additional offences taken into consideration, it is most unlikely that he would face a sentence of more than a fraction of the maximum.

22.63   The judge should not automatically take other offences into consideration merely because the prosecution and defence wish him to do so. Where the other offences are of a different type from those charged in the indictment, it may not be right to agree to the request to take them into consideration. Certainly, an offence which is punishable with endorsement of the driving licence and discretionary or obligatory disqualification from driving should not be taken into consideration when none of the offences on the indictment are so punishable: *Collins* [1947] KB 560. The reason is that, since the court's powers of sentencing are limited to those it possesses in respect of the counts in the indictment, an offender who was allowed to 't.i.c.' an endorsable offence when none of the offences on the indictment carried endorsement, would unfairly escape endorsement of his licence and possible disqualification. In addition, the court may be reluctant to take an offence into consideration where it is more serious than the offence charged: *Lavery* [2008] EWCA Crim 2495. Further, it is wrong for magistrates to take into consideration offences which they have no jurisdiction to try—i.e., they should not 't.i.c.' offences triable only on indictment.

22.64   Where an offence is taken into consideration, the offender is not convicted of it and accordingly could not successfully raise the plea of autrefois convict if subsequently prosecuted for the offence: *Nicholson* [1947] 2 All ER 535. In practice, the police would never consider instituting proceedings for an offence which was taken into consideration. The 't.i.c.' system helps them to reduce the list of unsolved crimes by encouraging offenders who have little option but to admit to one offence, to admit, at the same time, to other offences which, in the absence of such admission, it would be difficult or impossible to prove against them. The obvious question is—why should an offender admit to and ask to have taken into consideration other offences when, if the police had had sufficient evidence against him, they would have arrested him for those other offences? The answer is that, although the judge may increase his sentence somewhat because of the 't.i.c.' offences, the increase is unlikely to be significant, and the offender has the advantage of having his 'slate wiped clean'. When he has served his sentence, he can lead an honest life without worrying about the police uncovering evidence which would enable them to prosecute him for one of his past crimes.

The above discussion of taking offences into consideration has proceeded on the assump- **22.65** tion that the offender is pleading guilty to the counts in the indictment or the informations preferred against him. However, there is nothing to stop the police asking an accused who is pleading not guilty whether, in the event of a conviction, he would like to have other offences considered, or there may be an opportunity between conviction and sentence to raise the matter with him. In general, though, the 't.i.c.' system is geared to the offender who is plead-ing guilty. Most of the points dealt with in the preceding discussion are contained in the 'Offences Taken Into Consideration Guideline' issued by the Sentencing Council. In addition, the Guideline states that the sentencer should go through the following steps in deciding on sentence where offences are taken into consideration:

(a) determine the sentencing starting point for the conviction offence based on the relevant guidelines;
(b) consider any aggravating or mitigating factors to justify an upward or downward adjust-ment from the starting point. The presence of 't.i.c' offences should generally be regarded as an aggravating feature so as to require an upward adjustment. The court is limited to the statutory maximum for the offence of which the defendant has been convicted or pleaded guilty;
(c) consider whether the frank admission of a number of offences is a sign of genuine remorse and/or a determination to take steps to address addiction or offending behaviour;
(d) reduce the overall sentence to reflect a guilty plea;
(e) consider the totality of the sentence.

F   VARIATION OF SENTENCE

The sentence imposed or other order made by the Crown Court when dealing with an **22.66** offender may be varied or rescinded within a period of 56 days beginning with the date of sentence: PCC(S)A 2000, s 155 (it was increased from 28 days in 2008). The obvious use of s 155 is to correct some technical error in the original sentence, or to alter it substantially to the offender's advantage if the judge after sentencing thinks he might have been too severe. The section may, however, be used to add to a sentence (e.g., *Reilly* [1982] QB 1208 in which the Court of Appeal held that the Crown Court judge had power to add to his original sen-tence of three years' imprisonment a criminal bankruptcy order in the sum of £178,000). Only in exceptional circumstances, however, would it be right to increase the length of a cus-todial sentence or to replace an original non-custodial sentence with a custodial one. Thus, in *Grice* (1978) 66 Cr App R 167, where the judge had passed a suspended sentence for an offence of unlawful sexual intercourse, the Court of Appeal reversed his subsequent decision to make the sentence immediate. The reason for the variation was that the judge had suspended the sentence in return for G promising that he would not go near his adopted daughter, with whom he had committed the offence. G's breaking his promise within the period for variation was not a sufficient reason for 'unsuspending' his sentence. There is one group of cases where the power to increase sentence is likely to be held to be properly exercised. That is where the trial judge has failed to implement the 'dangerous offender' provisions, e.g. by failing to impose an extended sentence (see 24.34 to 24.42). In such a case, the increase upon variation will be seen as the court seeking to comply with its statutory obligations: *Reynolds* [2007] Crim LR 493.

22.67   Once the period specified in s 155 has elapsed the Crown Court has no power to vary or rescind its sentence. Thus, an order made outside the relevant period that the offender should forfeit money which he had been carrying in order to facilitate the commission of drugs offences, was quashed by the House of Lords because the addition of a forfeiture order amounted to a variation of sentence, and so had to be made within the statutory time limits (*Menocal* [1980] AC 598). In *Reynolds* [2007] Crim LR 493, it was held that the Crown Court had power, after rescinding its original order in whole or in part, to adjourn the final sentence until a later date. In effect, this will result in an extension of the period for variation beyond 56 days. (In so deciding, the Court of Appeal refused to follow *Stilwell* (1991) 94 Cr App R 65.)

22.68   A magistrates' court can also vary or rescind a sentence or other order made when dealing with an offender: Magistrates' Courts Act 1980, s 142(1), which does not set down a time limit for variation. Similar provisions apply when a magistrates' court has convicted an accused, and the magistrates who made up the court have doubts about the correctness of their decision (see 10.64).

G   DEFERRING SENTENCE

22.69   Counsel mitigating for an offender often makes optimistic or even extravagant claims on his behalf. If given a chance by the court (i.e., not sent to prison) his client will cease to commit crime; settle down in society; hold a steady job; marry his girlfriend; and make full reparation to the victims of his past offences. The court, having perhaps heard such claims on many previous occasions and not always found them borne out by subsequent events, may not be convinced by counsel's argument, but nevertheless may feel that the offender deserves a chance to prove himself. Time will show whether he can live up to the promises made on his behalf. To give him that time, the court may defer sentencing him.

22.70   Sections 1 to 1D of the PCC(S)A 2000 empower both the Crown Court and magistrates' courts to defer passing sentence on an offender for up to *six months* so that, when the court does come to determine what the sentence shall be, it may have regard to (a) the offender's conduct after conviction; and (b) any change in his circumstances. Conduct after conviction is expressly stated to include making reparation for the offence where that is appropriate. Deferment under s 1 is always conditional upon the offender consenting to it and, subject to an exception explained below, is not allowed more than once per case. Moreover, it is desirable that sentence should actually be passed on the date specified by the court when it deferred sentencing. However, the court does not lose jurisdiction to sentence if it cannot deal with the offender on that date (e.g., because the judge reserved the case to himself and then is unavailable on the relevant day, or because the offender fails to appear, or because necessary reports have not been prepared)—see *Anderson* (1983) 78 Cr App R 251.

The approach to and procedure for deferring sentence was summarized by Lord Lane CJ in his **22.71** judgment in *George* [1984] 1 WLR 1082. It is the responsibility of the deferring court to make it clear to the offender why sentence is being deferred, and what conduct is expected of him during the deferment. Obviously, he will be expected not to commit further offences, but he might also be told that he should stay in and/or make genuine efforts to find employment, or that he should accept help and advice from a probation officer, or that he should save money with a view to making reparation for the offence, or that he should cut down on his consumption of alcohol. It is not appropriate, however, to tell the offender that he must go to hospital to receive treatment for a mental condition, for such restrictions on an offender's freedom of action should be imposed by virtue of a hospital order or probation order with a requirement for treatment, not as a side wind of a deferment of sentence: *Skelton* [1983] Crim LR 686. In general, the courts should not defer sentence when the desired improvements in the offender's conduct are sufficiently precise to be included in requirements attached to a community sentence (see 25.04 and 25.14). The court should make a note of the reasons for deferment and give a copy to the offender and to his probation officer or other person appointed to supervise him (PCC(S)A 2000, s 1(5)). When the offender appears to be sentenced, the sentencing court may then easily ascertain, with the help of up-to-date reports, whether he has 'substantially conformed or attempted to conform with the proper expectations of the deferring court'. If he has, an immediate custodial sentence should not be imposed; if he has not, the sentencing court should state precisely in what respects there has been failure (see Lord Lane CJ's judgment in *George* at p. 1085). Commission of further offences during the deferment period is likely to result in a custodial sentence both for the subsequent offence and the deferred-sentence offence. But, merely staying out of trouble will not necessarily guarantee the offender a non-custodial sentence. Thus, in *Smith* (1977) 64 Cr App R 116 the Court of Appeal upheld a sentence of 18 months' immediate imprisonment for several burglaries, the facts being that S (with a bad record for dishonesty) had had sentence deferred to see if he would (a) work regularly and (b) cut down on his drinking. He had done neither, and his not having committed further offences was not sufficient to save him from prison. Conversely, if the offender has both 'gone straight' and done at least most of what the deferring court required of him, an immediate custodial sentence will be wrong in principle (see *Smith* (1979) 1 Cr App R(S) 339 for an example). *Aquilina* (1990) 11 Cr App R(S) 431 deals with the situation where it is alleged that the offender has committed offences during the period of deferment, but the allegations remain unresolved. It was held that they should not influence sentence in any way unless and until he has been convicted of the later alleged offences.

One of the reasons for asking courts to make a note of why they defer sentence is that the **22.72** sentencing court may well not comprise the same judge or magistrates who deferred sentence. Wherever possible, though, the deferring judge or magistrates should make themselves available to pass sentence (*Gurney* [1974] Crim LR 472), and counsel who represented the offender at deferment should also do his utmost to be there for sentencing (*Ryan* [1976] Crim LR 508).

When sentence is deferred, the offender is not bailed, but is simply told that he must come **22.73** to court on the appropriate day. If he fails to do so, a summons or warrant for his arrest may be issued. Conviction for a further offence during the deferment period entitles the deferring court to sentence the offender immediately upon securing his attendance before it. Alternatively, the court convicting of the subsequent offence may also sentence for the deferred-sentence offence, save that a magistrates' court may not deal with a matter in respect of which the Crown Court deferred sentence. Also, the Crown Court, when dealing with a matter in respect of which magistrates deferred, is limited to the sentencing powers which a magistrates' court dealing with the offender would have.

22.74 It was stated above that sentence may only be deferred once. There is one exception to this rule, which arises as follows. The exercise by magistrates of their power to defer sentence does not preclude them, when the offender appears to be sentenced, from committing him to the Crown Court to be dealt with. The Crown Court may then, if it chooses, also defer sentence.

H   SENTENCING IN MAGISTRATES' COURTS

22.75 The pre-sentencing procedure described in this Chapter is essentially applicable in both the Crown Court and magistrates' courts. Thus, Crown Court judges and justices alike must be told the facts of the offence and be informed about the offender's antecedents, after which they read reports and listen to mitigation. Similarly, specific procedures such as taking other offences into consideration and deferring sentence are the same in both the higher and lower tribunals. However, in the magistrates' courts, the whole sequence of events is swifter and less formalized than in the Crown Court. In particular, the antecedents are given simply by the prosecutor handing to the court a list of previous convictions. Furthermore, where the court is merely dealing with a road traffic matter, the practice is not to obtain a full list of previous convictions but to sentence on the basis of the endorsements shown on the motorist's licence. If there is no licence, a print out of the offender's driving record is obtained from the Drivers and Vehicles Licensing Centre in Swansea.

22.76 The justices are required to hold a *Newton* hearing in the same circumstances as a Crown Court judge. What if an offender is committed to the Crown Court for sentence (see Chapter 12) and there is a dispute about the facts of the case upon which he has been committed? Which court ought to hold the *Newton* hearing: the Crown Court or the magistrates court? In *Munroe v Crown Prosecution Service* [1988] Crim LR 823, the Divisional Court held that:

(a) Where the matter arises before the magistrates, they should conduct the *Newton* hearing, and, if they decide to commit, ensure that the Crown Court is informed of their findings of fact. The Crown Court should sentence on that basis.

(b) If the issue arises for the first time in the Crown Court, then it should conduct the *Newton* hearing.

(c) Where there was doubt whether the issue had been raised before the magistrates, then the Crown Court could either resolve the matter itself, or remit it to the magistrates, at its discretion.

What was said in *Munroe* should now be read subject to *Warley Magistrates' Court ex parte DPP* [1998] 2 Cr App R 307 (see 12.16). If it appears to the magistrates that they will be committing the case to the Crown Court for sentence in any event, then they should not conduct the *Newton* hearing, but should leave it for the Crown Court to do so. If the outcome of the *Newton* hearing is crucial to their decision whether to commit for sentence, however, then the magistrates must conduct it. It may therefore still happen that the magistrates conduct a *Newton* hearing where the matter ends up in the Crown Court. In *Gillan* [2007] EWHC 380, it was held that, where the magistrates have held a *Newton* hearing and found against the defendant, the Crown Court has power to hold a second *Newton* hearing, but is not obliged to do so.

23

DETERMINING THE SENTENCE

23.01 Chapter 22 dealt with the procedure which the court follows prior to passing sentence. The sentencer should therefore have the information upon which to decide sentence. That decision involves a choice between a series of options. In any particular case, the range of options will be in part determined by the circumstances of the offence (e.g., whether it is imprisonable and the maximum punishment which the law lays down) and of the offender (e.g., his age). Usually, however, the sentencer has a fairly wide range of possibilities for disposing of the case. The various options for sentence are considered in detail in Chapters 24 and 25. Without any attempt to be exhaustive, such options include (in roughly increasing order of gravity):

(a) an absolute or conditional discharge,
(b) a fine,
(c) a community sentence,
(d) a suspended sentence,
(e) an immediate custodial sentence.

23.02 As already mentioned, the nature of the offence and the characteristics of the offender impose certain limitations upon the freedom which the sentencer has to choose between the available options. In addition, a legislative framework is laid down in the Criminal Justice Act 2003 (CJA) which imposes criteria for determining whether the sentencer may pass a custodial sentence, for example. This legislative framework is detailed in 23.07 to 23.13.

Within that framework, the decisions of the courts provide further guidance in determining **23.03** the sentence which a court is likely to impose (as distinct from the question of the sentence which it is empowered to impose). Certain points need to be borne in mind in considering the guidance available from the courts, however.

On passing sentence, judges need to keep the reasons short and simple so that the offender **23.04** can readily understand what is being said to him. The principles governing the sentencing process therefore have to be deduced from sources other than the words of the sentencing judges themselves.

In addition, it should be emphasized that precedent plays a relatively small part in sentencing. **23.05** This is for three reasons. First, the truism that every case turns upon its own facts is never truer than in the context of sentencing. No two offenders and no two offences are ever precisely the same, whatever the similarities between them. Therefore, if told about a Court of Appeal decision in a comparable case, a judge can always find a reason for distinguishing it if he so chooses. Second, the Court of Appeal does not attempt to prescribe the one right sentence for a particular case. Instead, their lordships allow Crown Court judges a broad discretion, and, in general, only interfere to reduce a sentence if it is outside the range of sentences appropriate to the gravity of the offence when taken in conjunction with any mitigating factors. Third, until the passing of ss 35 and 36 of the Criminal Justice Act 1988 (see 26.80 to 26.87) there was no procedure that was apt to allow the Court of Appeal to pronounce a sentence too light. It remains the case that, if the defence appeal, the Court of Appeal has no power to increase sentence, although their lordships do on occasion state that, if they had been sitting in the Crown Court, they would have imposed a harsher penalty.

Despite these limitations, and the growth in importance of the statutory dimension, reports of **23.06** Court of Appeal decisions provide a useful guide to the way in which judges arrive, or should arrive, at their sentencing decisions. A number of sources are available to assist the court, and counsel appearing before it. There is a series of reports consisting entirely of sentencing appeals: *Criminal Appeal Reports (Sentencing)* cited as Cr App R(S). The *Criminal Law Review* publishes reports of sentencing decisions on a monthly basis. *Blackstone's Criminal Practice 2012* contains a substantial section on sentencing (Part E), and deals with the guideline cases, which encapsulate the Court of Appeal's views on sentencing for particular offences, under the offences in question (Parts B and C). A great number of decisions of the Court of Appeal are collected together and organized according to subject matter in the encyclopaedia, *Current Sentencing Practice*. Even more important in providing a framework for the sentencer are the guidelines issued by the Sentencing Guidelines Council, which are described in greater detail in 23.17 to 23.27 and 23.41 to 23.46.

A THRESHOLDS AND PURPOSES

The CJA 2003 lays down the criteria which the sentencer must consider in deciding: **23.07**

(a) whether to impose a community sentence; and
(b) whether to impose a custodial sentence.

23.08   These provisions are perhaps best seen as thresholds. In other words, the sentencer must consider whether the offender has crossed the threshold for a community sentence, or, as the case may be, a custodial sentence.

23.09   Under s 148 of the CJA 2003, a court shall not pass a community sentence 'unless it is of the opinion that the offence, or the combination of the offence and one or more offences associated with it, was serious enough to warrant such a sentence'.

23.10   The position as far as custodial sentences is concerned is slightly more complex, in that the court must find one of three alternative justifications for such a sentence. By s 152 of the CJA 2003 such a sentence may be imposed if either:

(a)   the offence (in combination if necessary with one or more offences associated with it) was so serious that only a custodial sentence is justified; or

(b)   the offender fails to express his willingness to comply with a requirement which the court proposes to include in a community order, where the requirement requires an expression of such willingness; or

(c)   he fails to comply with an order for pre-sentence drug testing.

23.11   The concept of seriousness is examined in rather more detail below (see 23.14 to 23.22), together with the related concept of offence combination (23.28 to 23.33). The overall effect of these provisions is to create a hierarchy of sentencing bands. In the bottom band are the discharges (whether absolute or conditional). In the next band comes the fine. No specific conditions have to be met for the imposition of these relatively less severe penalties, although there are, of course, considerations which the court must bear in mind in deciding, for example, the size of the fine (see Chapter 25). The next band upward is occupied by community sentences. Before imposing such a sentence, the court must have formed the view that the offence is sufficiently serious to warrant it. In the top band come the various forms of custodial sentence. Again, the court must decide whether the offender has passed over the custodial threshold, applying this time the alternative criteria set out above.

23.12   Section 142 of the CJA 2003 sets out in legislation for the first time the purposes of sentencing. Those aged under 18 at the time of conviction are excluded from its ambit, as are those convicted of murder, those subject to mandatory minimum sentences (see 24.43 to 24.47), those who come within the provisions for dangerous offenders (see 24.34 to 24.42), and those where the sentencer makes a disposal of the offender which is directed towards his treatment for a mental disorder (e.g., a hospital order). For the remainder of offenders, the 'purposes of sentencing' specified in s 142(1) apply. They are listed as follows:

(a)   the punishment of offenders;

(b)   the reduction of crime (including its reduction by deterrence);

(c)   the reform and rehabilitation of offenders;

(d)   the protection of the public; and

(e)   the making of reparation by offenders to persons affected by their offences.

Whilst it is helpful to have these purposes set out, what is notably absent is any sort of priority as between them. Some of the purposes may conflict, e.g., punishment and reparation, or deterrence and rehabilitation, and no guidance is given to the sentencer (or the advocate) on how such conflict might be resolved.

The CJA 2003 has made a noteworthy change to the way in which the thresholds described in **23.13** this section will operate. The change is contained in s 151(2). The subsection states that 'the court may make a community order in respect of the current offence instead of imposing a fine if it considers that, having regard to all the circumstances including [where relevant, the offender's previous convictions], it would be in the interests of justice to do so'. This provision serves to emphasize that a community sentence may be imposed on an offender with limited financial means, rather than a fine, provided that the offence is of sufficient seriousness to justify a community penalty. Conversely, a substantial fine can properly be imposed for a case which is above the community sentence threshold. The change appears to be a reflection of the current approach of the courts, and is not likely to result in any major change in practice.

B   OFFENCE SERIOUSNESS

It is the seriousness of the offence which is the sole criterion in determining whether a com- **23.14** munity sentence or a custodial sentence may be passed. Offence seriousness is, again, the crucial factor in determining the length of a custodial sentence. It also looms large in fixing the amount of a fine.

The question of whether an offence is a serious one is clearly, then, a vital one for the sen- **23.15** tencer. There are really two issues at stake:

(a) What is the test to apply in determining whether an offence is serious?
(b) What *material* ought the court to take into account in deciding whether an offence is serious?

As far as (a) is concerned, some statutory assistance is provided by s 143(1) of the CJA 2003, **23.16** which states:

> In considering the seriousness of any offence, the court must consider the offender's culpability in committing the offence and any harm which the offence may have caused, was intended to cause or might foreseeably have caused.

It follows that the distinct but related concepts of harm and culpability have been selected as determinative of the seriousness of the offence. As a result, they are central to the way in which the sentencer must deal with the offence.

The newly created Sentencing Guidelines Council chose 'seriousness' as one of the first topics **23.17** on which it issued guidelines in December 2004. (The guidelines can be accessed at <http://www.sentencingcouncil.org.uk>, and more information about the way in which the guidelines system operates is set out in 23.23 to 23.27). Following the scheme of the statute, the Guidelines on Seriousness deal with two main parameters: the culpability of the offender and the harm caused or risked by the offence.

The Guidelines (in para 1.7) identify four levels of criminal culpability for sentencing pur- **23.18** poses:

(a) The offender has the *intention* to cause harm, with the highest culpability where the offence is planned. The worse the harm intended, the greater the seriousness.

(b) The offender is *reckless* as to whether harm is caused, i.e., he appreciates at least some harm would be caused but proceeds giving no thought to the consequences despite a risk which would be obvious to most people.

(c) The offender has *knowledge* of the specific risks entailed by his actions but does not intend to cause the harm that results.

(d) The offender is guilty of *negligence*.

This analysis is, of course, quite separate from the requirement for a particular mental state as the *mens rea* for an offence, e.g., intention or recklessness. In dealing with the sentencing aspect, the focus is upon intention to cause harm, recklessness as to whether harm is caused etc. The Guidelines (para 1.22) set out a list of some 21 'factors indicating higher culpability' which includes some statutory factors (e.g., offence committed on bail, racial or religious aggravation) and others based upon common law (e.g., planning, professional offending, abuse of a position of trust). It is also emphasized (para 1.17) that culpability will be greater if an offender:

(a) deliberately causes more harm than is necessary for the commission of the offence; or

(b) targets a vulnerable victim (because of their old age, youth, disability, or by virtue of the job they do).

23.19 The Guidelines also distinguish between different types of harm. In some cases, what will be crucial will be the impact upon an individual victim. Such harm may take the form of physical injury, sexual violation, financial loss, damage to health, or psychological distress. Other offences may cause harm to the community at large, as well as or instead of an individual victim, e.g., economic loss, harm to public health, or interference with the administration of justice. The Guidelines (para 1.23) set out factors indicating a more than usually serious degree of harm, such as multiple victims, an offence committed against those providing a service to the public, high value in property offences.

23.20 The Guidelines (para 1.25) make brief reference to mitigating factors, stating that the following factors indicate significantly lower culpability:

(a) a greater degree of provocation than normally expected;

(b) mental illness or disability;

(c) youth or age, where it affects the responsibility of the individual defendant; or

(d) the fact that the offender played only a minor role in the offence.

In addition, mention is made of the statutory provisions in relation to mitigation, and the separate set of Guidelines issued on reduction for a guilty plea (see 23.41 to 23.46).

23.21 The guidelines on seriousness also deal with the issue of prevalence and its relationship to offence seriousness (para 1.39). What is said, in effect, is that the sentences laid down as general guidance by the Court of Appeal already take into account the need to deter offences which are prevalent nationally. It is therefore 'wrong to further penalise individual offenders by increasing sentence length for committing an individual offence of that type'. If a sentencer is minded to increase a sentence on the basis that a particular crime is prevalent in the locality, he must have supporting evidence from an external source (e.g., the local Criminal Justice Board) to show that the crime is in fact more prevalent than it is nationally (see *Oosthuizen* [2005] Crim LR 979 and *Lanham* [2009] Crim LR 125 for the application of this principle).

When we come to the material which the court should consider in deciding whether an **23.22** offence is serious then the statute is directly helpful in the following respects:

(i)   In certain circumstances, the court must obtain and consider a pre-sentence report (CJA 2003, s 156 and see 22.47).
(ii) The court must take into account any matters that, in its opinion, 'are relevant in mitigation of sentence' (CJA 2003, s 166(1) and see 23.34 to 23.48).
(iii) By virtue of CJA 2003, s 143(1), the court may have regard to previous convictions and the failure to respond to previous sentences in considering the seriousness of the current offence. This provision is considered further at 23.49 to 23.53.
(iv) CJA 2003, s 143(3), states that the court must treat the fact that an offence was committed on bail as an aggravating factor—hence increasing its seriousness. The reason would seem to be that an offender committing an offence while on bail is in breach of the trust reposed in him by the court.

C   GUIDELINES

During the 1980s, the Court of Appeal developed the practice of issuing sentencing guide- **23.23** lines when dealing with an appeal (or linked appeals) against sentence. It would consider the existing practice in sentencing for the offence in question, identify mitigating and aggravating features, and set out a starting point for judges passing sentence at first instance. It would then deal with the appeal before it in accordance with the guidelines suggested. By and large, these judgments concentrated upon relatively serious cases emanating from the Crown Court, e.g., *Billam* (1986) 8 Cr App R(S) on rape, *Aramah* (1982) 4 Cr App R(S) on drugs offences and *Barrick* (1985) 7 Cr App R(S) on theft in breach of trust. In addition, the Magistrates' Association developed, with the approval of the senior judges, their own *Sentencing Guidelines*.

The CDA 1998, ss 80 to 81 charged the Court of Appeal with the responsibility for produc- **23.24** ing guidelines for criminal offences, and established the Sentencing Advisory Panel to act as an independent body to assist it in this function. The machinery for setting guidelines was further amended by the CJA 2003 which established the Sentencing Guidelines Council, chaired by the Lord Chief Justice. There was a further change with the implementation of the Coroners and Justice Act 2009. This set up the Sentencing Council, with a chair appointed by the Lord Chief Justice (Leveson LJ was the first appointee), seven other judicial members, and six non-judicial members. The judicial members must include at least one circuit judge, a district judge and a lay magistrate. The non-judicial members are drawn from various backgrounds related to the criminal justice system e.g., defence, prosecution, victims, academics.

By s 120 of the CJA 2009, the Council is to issue guidelines on both sentencing and 'alloca- **23.25** tion', or the decision on whether magistrates should send a triable-either-way case to be tried in the Crown Court (see 8.20). Section 125(1) of the CJA 2009 requires that 'every court must, in sentencing an offender, follow any guidelines which are relevant to the offender's case'. These guidelines include both those issued by the Sentencing Council and those of its predecessor body, the Sentencing Guidelines Council. The Court of Appeal retains its power to 'provide guidance relating to the sentencing of offenders in the judgment of the court'. There is an apparent difference, however, between the 'guidance' of the Court of Appeal, which relies upon the authority of precedent, and the definitive guidelines issued by the Sentencing Council, which have statutory binding force. In any event, the Court of Appeal will continue to amplify and explain the guidelines. As Lord Judge CJ put it in *AG's References Nos 73, 75 and 03 of 2010* [2011] Crim LR 580, the jurisdiction of the Court of Appeal (Criminal Division) to amplify, to explain, or to offer a definitive sentencing guideline if it thinks fit, is undiminished. It follows that a guideline produced by the Sentencing Council cannot be applied without having regard to later decisions of the Court of Appeal on its interpretation and application (*Thornley* [2011] Crim LR 415).

23.26   It follows that the Guidelines form the most important source material for those who wish to ascertain the likely sentence which a court will impose in respect of a particular offence. To a lesser extent, Draft Guidelines may be regarded by the court as persuasive, even though it is under no obligation to follow them. Where an offence committed before the introduction of a relevant set of Guidelines is dealt, it should be dealt with under the Guidelines in force at the time of the offence, rather than those at the time of sentencing (see *Moon* [2011] 1 Cr App R(S) 34 and *AG's Reference No 78 of 2010* [2011] Crim LR 665). The Guidelines, together with consultation material, are available on the website of the Sentencing Guidelines Council (for the address, see Key Documents at the end of this Chapter).

23.27   At the time of writing, the Sentencing Council and its predecessor, the Sentencing Guidelines Council, had produced a substantial number of sets of guidelines. Some of them deal with general principles, while others focus upon specific offences. They include:

(a) *Overarching Principles: Seriousness* (see 23.14 to 23.22).

(b) *New Sentences: Criminal Justice Act 2003* (see Chapters 24 and 25).

(c) *Reduction in Sentence for a Guilty Plea* (see 23.39 to 23.46).

(d) *Breach of a Protective Order*. This deals with sentencing for breach of restraining orders and non-molestation orders.

(e) *Breach of an Anti-Social Behaviour Order*.

(f) *Overarching Principles: Domestic Violence*. This sets out the approach to sentencing for the variety of offences which can form part of this increasingly important area of practice. Domestic violence is defined to include 'any incident of threatening behaviour, violence or abuse [psychological, physical, sexual, financial or emotional] between adults who are or have been intimate partners or family members, regardless of gender or sexuality'.

(g) *Overarching Principles: Sentencing Youths*.

(h) *Failure to Surrender to Bail*.

(i) *Attempted Murder*.

(j) *Manslaughter by Reason of Provocation*.

(k) *Corporate Manslaughter and Health and Safety Offences Causing Death*.

(l) *Causing Death by Driving*.

(m) *Robbery*.

(n) *Fraud*.

(o) *Theft and Burglary of a Building other than a Dwelling*.

(p) *Sexual Offences*. The very wide range of offences in the Sexual Offences Act 2003 is covered in a substantial and comprehensive document.

(q) *Assault and other offences against the person*—again, a detailed and comprehensive document.

(r) *Assaults on children and cruelty to a child*.

Perhaps the most important set of Guidelines, having regard to frequency of use, is the *Magistrates' Court Sentencing Guidelines*, which consists of some 221 pages of material, including an explanation of the steps in the sentencing process and detailed guidance on individual offences.

D COMBINATION OF OFFENCES

How should the courts deal with cases where the offender has to be sentenced for two or more offences? The court may consider 'the offence, or the combination of the offence and one or more other offences associated with it' when determining whether the case crosses over the seriousness threshold so as to justify custody (CJA 2003, s 152(1)) or a community sentence (s 148). **23.28**

As a result, the sentencer can lump together a series of minor offences and decide that they merit custody (or a community sentence) once viewed together. In order to do so, however, the offences must be 'associated'. Section 161 of the Powers of Criminal Courts (Sentencing) Act (PAC(S)A) 2000 lays down that offences are associated if: **23.29**

(i)   the offender is convicted of the offences in the same proceedings (a plea of guilty being equivalent to a conviction);
(ii) the offender is sentenced for the offences at the same time; or
(iii) the offender is convicted of one offence and asks for the other or others to be taken into consideration.

If the court has decided on a custodial sentence, can it aggregate a number of offences for the purpose of deciding on the proper length of the sentence? This time, the answer is contained in CJA 2003, s 152(2), which states that the court may have regard to 'the combination of the offence and one or more offences associated with it' in determining the duration of the sentence. Again, the meaning of 'associated' offences is to be found in s 161 of the PCC(S)A 2000. **23.30**

There are some offences which do not fall within the scope of 'associated offences', however, e.g., an earlier offence for which a suspended sentence was imposed, of which the offender is now in breach: *Crawford* (1993) 98 Cr App R 297. Similarly, where an offender has been convicted of a number of charges described as 'sample counts', offences not on the indictment or formally taken into consideration are not associated offences: *Canaan* [1998] 1 Cr App R(S) 79. **23.31**

The way in which the principle operates is illustrated by *Claxton* (1992) 13 Cr App R(S) 165. The approach in this case is consistent with the current statutory rules, although it predates them. C obtained £5,000 by deception in 100 transactions worth £50 each. The court aggregated the offences and imposed a sentence of three years' imprisonment, which was upheld on appeal. The severity of the sentence could be justified only by the process of aggregating the various offences. **23.32**

Where an offender is being sentenced for several offences, there is a danger that the total sentence might be disproportionate to the overall seriousness of what the offender has done. In order to avoid such a result, the 'totality principle' has evolved. This requires a court to con- **23.33** sider the overall sentence in relation to the totality of the offending, and in relation to sentence levels for other crimes. Hence it would be wrong just to perform the arithmetic and pass a sentence for a number of offences of theft which exceeded that for a single offence of, say, rape. This sentencing principle now finds statutory expression in the CJA 2003, s 166(3)(b), which states that 'nothing shall prevent a court . . . in the case of an offender who is convicted of one or more other offences, from mitigating his sentence by applying any rule of law as to the totality of sentences'. In addition, the Sentencing Council has issued a 'Totality Guideline', which gives guidance on sentencing for a combination of offences, and includes examples of when concurrent and consecutive sentences are appropriate.

E   MITIGATING AND AGGRAVATING FACTORS

23.34   Some of the potential effect of mitigation both in relation to the offence, and personal to the offender has already been indicated in this Chapter. The paragraphs which follow deal first with the statutory considerations which affect the court's consideration of mitigation (and its converse, aggravation), and then discuss some of the factors taken into account.

The statutory framework

23.35   The CJA 2003 makes specific mention of mitigating factors, usually in conjunction with aggravating factors, as follows:

(a) Before imposing a discretionary custodial sentence, the 'court must take into account all such information as is available to it about the circumstances of the offence or (as the case may be) of the offence and the offence or offences associated with it, including any aggravating or mitigating factors' (s 156(1)).

(b) There is a similar requirement in relation to any decision to impose a community sentence.

(c) The same obligations attach to the consideration of the *length* of any custodial sentence.

(d) The above points need to be considered alongside s 166(1), which makes provision for the sentencer to take account of any matters which 'in the opinion of the court are relevant in mitigation of sentence'.

23.36   It seems that there is a distinction between the provisions summarized in (a), (b), and (c), on the one hand, and the way in which (d) is meant to operate. In considering the matters under (a), (b), and (c), the court is looking at the factors which affect the seriousness of the offence. It is under an obligation to consider those factors. The scope of its duty includes both mitigation (e.g., provocation, acting on impulse rather than with premeditation, peripheral role in the enterprise), and aggravation (e.g., abuse of trust, gratuitous violence, the high value of unrecovered property stolen).

23.37   Section 166(1), however, is rather different (see (d) above). It encompasses matters other than the seriousness of the offence which the court might wish to take into account in deciding whether to impose a custodial sentence, and its length, or, for that matter, a community sentence. It permits consideration of *mitigating* factors only. It gives the court a *discretion* to consider such factors if it wishes to take them into account. Notwithstanding this discretionary form, it is submitted that the courts will continue to take into account the variety of factors relating to the offender's personal circumstances which they have considered in the past. Further, failure to do so will no doubt provide good grounds of appeal in appropriate cases. The following paragraphs deal with four of the grounds most commonly relied on by the defence as good mitigation.

One general point which should be borne in mind is that, even if the offence is such that it **23.38** passes the custody threshold, personal mitigation such as that set out below may pull the offender back from the threshold, so that he receives a non-custodial sentence: *Cox* [1993] 1 WLR 188. This principle receives statutory confirmation in the CJA 2003, s 166(2).

Plea of guilty

A judge must not increase the sentence he passes because the accused pleaded not guilty, even **23.39** if he considers that the accused, in giving evidence in his own defence, committed perjury (*Quinn* (1932) 23 Cr App R 196). Nor must he increase sentence because the nature of the defence involved grave allegations against the police officers in the case (*Scone* (1967) 51 Cr App R 165), or because, by pleading not guilty, the accused forced the prosecution to call witnesses who might well have found giving evidence particularly distressing or even harmful (e.g., child witnesses to a sexual offence). The principle is, however, slightly unreal because it is a well-established common law principle (now set out in statute) that a guilty plea attracts a lighter sentence than a conviction following a not guilty plea (*Cain* [1976] QB 496), and, if the accused does not know this before he decides on his plea, he should be told it by advocate. In other words, a guilty plea is an excellent reason for reducing sentence, but a not guilty plea is no justification for increasing sentence.

The common law principle that a discount should be given for a guilty plea is given statutory **23.40** backing by the CJA 2003, s 144. This section deals with the determination of sentence where the offender has pleaded guilty. It states that the court must take into account—

(a) the stage in the proceedings for the offence at which the offender indicated his intention to plead guilty, and
(b) the circumstances in which this indication was given.

In 2004, the Sentencing Guidelines Council produced guidelines on *Reduction in Sentence for a* **23.41** *Guilty Plea*, and they were amended after consultation in 2007. The purposes of the reduction are set out in para 2.2. A guilty plea avoids the need for trial, enabling other cases to be disposed of more expeditiously. It shortens the gap between charge and sentence. It saves considerable cost. Finally, in the case of an early plea, it saves the victim and witnesses from concern about having to give evidence. The statement constitutes a frank summary of what are (in the main and with the important exception in relation to sparing victims and witnesses) advantages to the criminal justice system. There is a clear recognition that an incentive is desirable in order to deal with cases more efficiently and cheaply. This is rather different from the historical justification put forward for the reduction: that the plea reflected remorse on the part of the offender which ought to be rewarded with some credit. In fact, the guidelines go on to spell out that 'the sentencer should address separately the issue of remorse, together with any other mitigating features, *before* calculating the reduction for the guilty plea' (para 2.4).

23.42 The guidelines make it clear (para 2.3) that the reduction principle can result in a sentence which is different in *type*, e.g., where the sentencer is in doubt as to whether a custodial sentence is appropriate, in appropriate circumstances a fine or discharge can be imposed rather than a community sentence, or a community sentence rather than a custodial one, as a result of the offender's plea of guilty.

23.43 More usually, however, the reduction will be a proportion of the total sentence imposed, depending on the stage of the proceedings at which the guilty plea was entered. Generally, it will operate as follows:

    (a) a maximum of one-third where the guilty plea was entered at the first reasonable opportunity in relation to the offence for which the sentence is being imposed (para 4.2). The first reasonable opportunity may be the first time that a defendant appears before the court and has the opportunity to plead guilty, although the court may consider that an indication of willingness to plead guilty could have been given earlier, perhaps in interview. In any event, the court will need to be satisfied that the defendant and any legal adviser had sufficient information about the allegations (annex 1);

    (b) in the region of 30 per cent where an offence triable either way is committed to the Crown Court for trial and the defendant pleads guilty at the first opportunity in that court (annex 1, para 3(c));

    (c) a maximum of one-quarter where a trial date has been set (para 4.2);

    (d) a maximum of one-tenth for a guilty plea entered at the door of the court, or after the trial has begun (para 4.2);

    (e) in murder cases, the process of determining the level of reduction is different (paras 6.1 to 6.6). In brief, any reduction should not exceed one sixth, and will never exceed five years.

23.44 Where a court has decided to sentence on the basis of dangerousness (see 24.34 to 24.42) for the protection of the public, the minimum custodial term (but *not* the protection of the public element of the sentence) should be reduced to reflect the plea.

23.45 One of the issues which led to the consultation about the revision of these guidelines was the extent to which credit should be withheld or reduced because the offender was caught 'red-handed'. The version of the guidelines issued in 2004 stated that the normal sliding scale should apply. That position is modified in the 2007 version, which states:

> Where the prosecution case is overwhelming, it may not be appropriate to give the full reduction that would otherwise be given. Whilst there is a presumption in favor of the full reduction being given where a plea has been indicated at the first reasonable opportunity, the fact that the prosecution case is overwhelming without relying on admissions from the defendant may be a reason justifying departure from the guideline.... Where a court is satisfied that a lower reduction should be given for this reason, a recommended reduction of 20% is likely to be appropriate where the guilty plea was indicated at the first reasonable opportunity (paras 5.3 and 5.4).

23.46 In a case where the offender enters a guilty plea in the magistrates' court, with the result that the bench decides to deal with the matter themselves, rather than commit to the

Crown Court, they may impose the maximum sentence available, e.g., a sentence of six months' imprisonment for a single either-way offence, where the offence would have attracted a sentence in the region of nine months if it had been committed to the Crown Court (para 5.5). Similarly, a detention and training order of 24 months might be imposed on an offender aged under 18 if the offence was one which, but for the plea, would have attracted a sentence of long-term detention in excess of 24 months under the PCC(S)A 2000, s 91.

Cooperation with the authorities

Cooperation with the police, in the sense of not resisting arrest and confessing frankly to   **23.47**
the offence at the police station, is good mitigation, although it may not add much to the effect of an early guilty plea. Cooperation in the sense of giving 'Queen's evidence' (evidence for the prosecution against one's accomplices) may lead to a substantial reduction in sentence. Even greater reductions are available for the handful of offenders who give information and/or evidence which leads to the conviction of large numbers of their criminal associates: *Lowe* (1977) 66 Cr App R 122. In *King* (1985) 7 Cr App R(S) 227, the Court of Appeal indicated that an offender who has given really substantial help to the police in relation to serious crime, including naming names and either confronting the persons named or giving evidence against them, is entitled to as much as a half to two-thirds off the normal 'tariff' sentence. Other cases have shown that a proportionate reduction should also be made in more trivial cases where neither the crimes for which the offender is sentenced nor those about which he gives evidence or information are in the first rank of gravity (see *Thomas* (1985) 7 Cr App R(S) 95). In *Wood* [1997] 1 Cr App R(S) 347, the amount of discount was said to depend on the quality, quantity, accuracy, and timeliness of the information.

Credit for giving Queen's evidence was given statutory form in Serious Organised Crime   **23.48**
and Police Act (SOCPA) 2005. It provides (s 73) for the court to give a reduction to reflect assistance given or offered to the authorities, and to this extent reflects the common law. It lays down that the statutory scheme is conditional upon a guilty plea, and a written agreement with a designated prosecutor (the CPS and the usual public prosecuting authorities are designated). The statute says that the judge must state in open court that a lesser sentence has been given because of the assistance, unless it is not in the public interest to do so. The discount can later be reviewed if the assistance is not forthcoming, or if further assistance is given (resulting presumably in an upward or downward movement in sentence accordingly). Even if the offender is not given a discount at the time of sentence and later gives assistance, his (non-discounted) sentence can be reviewed. The provisions were subject to analysis by the Court of Appeal in *P* [2007] EWCA Crim 2290. Their lordships made it clear that the provisions relating to review of sentences could apply even if the crime was committed and sentence passed before the provisions came into operation. The discount for assistance should be assessed first, and the notional sentence calculated should then be further discounted for the guilty plea. Where an agreement was reached under s 73, sentences should usually be concurrent. This was likely to be of importance, as the offender would be disclosing criminal activities of his own which would probably not have come to light without an agreement being reached. In deciding on the sentence to be imposed, the normal

level of reduction for substantial assistance in relation to serious crimes should continue to be between one half and two thirds of the total sentence which would otherwise be passed. Only in the most exceptional case would the appropriate level of reduction exceed three quarters of the total sentence which would otherwise be passed. In *D* [2010] Crim LR 725, a discount of 25 per cent was upheld. The Court of Appeal considered that the sentencing judge had been right to consider that the agreement into which the appellant had entered was much less comprehensive than it might have been—he did not agree or offer to give evidence against anyone, nor describe his own full criminality, and hence could not expect the 'normal' discount of 50 to 66 per cent indicated in *P* (see also *Bevels* [2010] 2 Cr App R(S) 31). In *Cadbury* [2010] Crim LR 246, it was made clear that SOCPA did not abolish the common law system, which could still be used where a defendant had provided assistance which did not fall within the statutory scheme, and in particular where there had been no written agreement. However, the reduction would usually be less for those who relied upon the old system rather than the statutory scheme, since the latter offered greater potential public benefit.

Good and bad character

23.49 Traditionally, the courts have regarded the previous good character of the offender as excellent mitigation. The long-standing sentencing policy of the courts, underpinned by the decisions of the Court of Appeal, is to treat first offenders with leniency.

23.50 A variation on the argument that the offender has no previous convictions whatsoever is that he has no previous convictions for the kind of offence of which he has been convicted. For example, counsel in mitigation might say that, although his client has a record for petty dishonesty, he has no history of violence so that *vis-à-vis* the assault for which he is to be sentenced he should be treated as a person of good character. Yet another argument is that there has been a substantial gap between the present offence and the last one, indicating that the offender has made a genuine effort to 'go straight'. Thus, in *Canfield* (1982) 4 Cr App R(S) 94, a nine-month prison sentence for a clumsy attempted burglary from a social club was replaced with community service. C (aged 32) had had an appalling record for burglary during the period 1967 to 1976 but, after his release from prison in 1977, he had changed his way of life, found a job and married. Apart from some road traffic matters (which had led to loss of his job), this was the first time he had been in trouble since 1977. The five years of good behaviour saved him from going to prison again.

23.51 The common law principles set out above have been characterized as 'progressive loss of mitigation'. The offender may be thought of as starting with substantial credit for good character. That credit is progressively diminished by each offence of which he or she is convicted. If there is a break in offending, some credit accumulates again, only to be diminished with a subsequent offence.

23.52 The principles are reinforced by the CJA 2003, s 143(2), which states:

> In considering the seriousness of an offence ('the current offence') committed by an offender who has one or more previous convictions, the court must treat each previous conviction as an

aggravating factor if (in the case of that conviction) the court considers that it can reasonably be so treated, having regard, in particular, to—

(a) the nature of the offence to which the conviction relates and its relevance to the current offence, and

(b) the time that has elapsed since the conviction.

In *Howells* [1998] Crim LR 836, Lord Bingham CJ said that leniency would ordinarily be **23.53** extended to offenders of previous good character, the more so if there was evidence of positive good character (such as a solid employment record or faithful discharge of family duties) as opposed to a mere absence of previous convictions. Such 'positive good character' was given weight, for example, in *Clark* (1999) *The Times*, 27 January 1999. The Court of Appeal were dealing with an offender who had brought up her four nephews and nieces in difficult circumstances when their mother died, and who was involved in a number of local community and charitable activities. Although she had pleaded guilty to two offences of false accounting and one of obtaining property by deception, amounting to fraud of £18,000 in total, her sentence of six months' imprisonment was reduced to seven days.

Youth

The youth of the offender can be a most important mitigating factor. If a young offender is **23.54** given a custodial sentence, its length is likely to be shorter than the corresponding sentence of imprisonment which an offender over 21 would receive. For example, in *Storey* [1984] Crim LR 438, sentences of five years' detention passed on three 16-year-olds who had burnt down part of their school, causing £370,000-worth of damage, were reduced to three years. The Court of Appeal's reason was that, although severe sentences were called for because of the exceptional nature of the case, the term chosen should not be so long that 'to young men like this [the end would] seem completely out of sight'. More generally, youth is accepted as an important mitigating factor in the various sets of guidelines issued by the Sentencing Guidelines Council. For example, the *Guidelines on Sexual Offences* state that 'youth and immaturity must always be potential mitigating factors' unless the offence is 'particularly serious'.

There is also some authority for the view that youth can be crucial, not just in reducing sen- **23.55** tence length, but in determining the type of sentence (see, e.g., *Seymour* (1983) 5 Cr App R(S) 85, where the Court of Appeal urged the use of community sentences rather than custody in dealing with certain categories of burglary committed by young offenders).

Racial or religious aggravation

The Court of Appeal has made it clear for a number of years that racial motivation for an **23.56** offence is 'gravely aggravating' (*Attorney-General's References (Nos 29, 30 and 31 of 1994)* (1994) 16 Cr App R(S) 698). This principle was given statutory backing by the CJA 2003, s 145 which states that, if an offence is racially aggravated, the court must treat it as a factor which increases the seriousness of the offence.

Section 145 applies to sentencing generally, except where the court is imposing a sentence **23.57** for one of the racially or religiously aggravated offences set out in the CDA 1998, ss 29 to 32 (certain aggravated assaults, aggravated criminal damage, certain aggravated public order offences, and aggravated harassment). As far as those offences are concerned, they carry higher maximum penalties than their non-aggravated equivalents, and would be expected to attract enhanced sentences in any event.

Aggravation related to disability or sexual orientation

23.58   By s 146 of the CJA 2003, sentencers are compelled by statute to take two further factors into account—aggravation related to disability or sexual orientation.

KEY DOCUMENTS

Powers of Criminal Courts (Sentencing) Act 2000, as amended.

Criminal Justice Act 2003, as amended.

The guidelines produced by the Sentencing Council are available on: <http://sentencing-council.judiciary.gov.uk>.

Tell us

If you use the scenarios on the Online Resource Centre, we would be interested to hear what deal you reached and whether you think it was one that would please your client. Tell us at finchandfafinski.com/get-in-touch or @FinchFafinski on Twitter.

National negotiation competition

The national negotiation competition sponsored by the Centre for Effective Dispute Resolution (CEDR) takes place every year in the spring term, with the regional heats being held in February at four venues around England and Wales and the final taking place in April.

The competition is open to two teams of two students from each institution irrespective of whether they are studying at undergraduate or graduate level. This includes students on the CPE/GDL as well as LPC and BPTC students. The only restriction upon entry is that students may not compete more than once so you will need to think carefully about whether you want to take part whilst undertaking your undergraduate degree or to wait until you progress to the professional stage of your training.

Practical advice: when to take part

Very few universities teach negotiation skills to undergraduates although some may run extra-curricular workshops or training courses. This means that undergraduates could feel at a competitive disadvantage compared to LPC or BPTC students who will have taken a module on negotiation skills. However, as entry is limited to four students from each institution, there may be greater competition to take part at these later stages of study so it may be that you have more opportunity of being selected to take part in the national competition whilst you are an undergraduate. It is important to remember that, despite the lack of formal training, many undergraduate teams have won the competition so it is no bar to achieving success.

Progression from the regional heats to the national final is based upon the points awarded to each team over the course of two negotiations. In this competition, the lowest scoring teams are the most successful. Three teams from each of the four regional heats will progress to the final. The 12 qualifying teams receive a one-day training course at CEDR to help them to prepare for the final. The ultimate winner of the competition goes on to represent England and Wales in the international negotiation competition so it really is a prize worth having in terms of enhancing your CV and helping you stand out to prospective employers.

- National Negotiation Competition website: **www.cedr.com/skills/competition/**.
- International Negotiation Competition website: **www.chapman.edu/law/competitions/ dispute-resolution/international-negotiation-competition/index.aspx**.

Client interviewing

All legal disputes are initiated by people—either acting as individuals or as representatives of an organisation—thus dealing with clients is a central part of life within the legal profession. Clients are the legal equivalent of a doctor's patients but, unlike medical students who are taught how to deal with patients from the outset of their medical training, law students do not encounter clients during the academic stages of their legal education. Indeed, law is taught as an academic discipline in an abstract way so that students learn about legal principles and precedents rather than about the people whose lives are affected by the law and who are at the heart of every legal dispute. Client interviewing competitions seek to remedy this situation by providing some insight into the way that each case is started: with a person who arrives in a solicitor's office in the hope that their problem can be resolved. Admittedly, such competitions provided quite a limited insight into the true complexities of dealing with clients because there are no emotions involved in a simulation and nothing at stake for either the client or the solicitors but it is nonetheless an approximation of a real life situation that allows students to understand part of the day-to-day business of legal practice.

What is client interviewing?

As its name suggests, client interviewing is a practical legal skills exercise that involves a simulation of an interview with a client. The idea is that students, again working in a team of two, take on the role of solicitors to conduct a preliminary interview with a new client (played by an academic or another student) to elicit details of their problem and to formulate a course of action based upon the information disclosed during the interview. The students are given very little information about the client's problem in advance of the interview—just a few lines that capture the general nature of the issue as illustrated in Figure 4.8.

I have made an appointment for Mrs Geraldine Baker to see you tomorrow at 2pm. Mrs Baker is a new client and she has a problem with her neighbours.

Figure 4.8 A client interviewing memo

This may seem like a very small amount of information but it mirrors the situation in practice when solicitors conduct a first meeting with a new client knowing little or nothing about them other than the general nature of their problem. The person playing the role of the client will have been given a detailed account of their situation to enable them to present their problem to the solicitors and this may include instructions about their demeanour as illustrated in Figure 4.9.

The challenge involved in client interviewing is for the solicitors to find out as much of the information from the client scenario as possible so that they can propose a course of action for the client. This involves assessing whether the client has the basis for a legal claim and, if so, evaluating the strength of this claim. There is also a need to recognise non-legal aspects of the case, such as the client's distress and anxiety, and suggest avenues for dealing with these issues. All of this must be done within the time constraints of the competition and in accordance with the rules of ethical and professional practice.

⊙ You will find a video clip of client interviewing in operation on the Online Resource Centre.

Your name is Geraldine Baker. You are 45 years old and have lived at 81 Station Road in New Milton for two years since the breakdown of your marriage to your husband, Arthur. This is a terraced house in a much less desirable area than you were used to living in and you have not settled in well. You find it hard to get on with your neighbours, most of whom seem to think that you are snobbish and unfriendly. You are very much preoccupied by the unfairness of your accommodation situation and will explain this to the solicitors at length if they give you an opportunity to do so. You used to live in 'a nice house in a nice neighbourhood' until your husband left you for a much younger woman. He gave you a fair sum of money that represented half the value of the marital home which enabled you to purchase your current house but you resent the fact that he still lives there with his girlfriend whilst your standard of living had fallen dramatically. You live alone as your children, Jennifer (13) and James (12), attend boarding school paid for by their father and prefer to spend most of the school holidays in the family home with their father, his girlfriend, and their new baby. All of this causes you a great deal of anguish.

It is fair to say that you have never been on good terms with any of your neighbours and have rebuffed any overtures of friendship. The neighbours are aware that you think that they are 'beneath you' and 'common' so tend to avoid you but a problem has arisen with the people living next door that has escalated into a really nasty situation that has included damage to property and threats of personal violence. It all started six months ago when a new family, the Bells, moved into the semi-detached house adjoining your property. The Bells have three children (aged 6, 10, and 12) who like to play noisily in the garden which disturbs you whether you are outside or in the house. You complained about this about two weeks after the family moved in but were met with a very hostile reaction from the mother, Kate, who told you that she had no intention of modifying the way that her children play as it is important that they are able to express themselves and let off energy in their garden. Since then, the family have introduced more and more play equipment into the garden—a climbing frame, a trampoline and a water slide—which has increased the boisterousness of the children and the noise levels. The Bells have also had several parties to which all the neighbours and their children have been invited and these have been very noisy and lasted all day and into the early hours of the morning. Their garden is also overrun with animals: they have two dogs (that always seem to be outside and bark frequently), two cats (that dig up your flowerbeds), and numerous rabbits and guinea pigs (that are kept in hutches next to your fence and often smell). Last month, they installed a chicken run into the garden and have introduced eight chickens and a cockerel that crows at daybreak every day. You think that there must be laws that control what type and number of animals that can live in a residential garden but you do not know how to find out about this. You have complained a number of times in person but the Bells do not listen and are very rude to you.

Last week, your children came to stay and there was some hostility between them and the Bell children that involved bullying and threats of violence to the extent that your children would not go into the garden. You went round to speak to Kate Bell but she became very angry and, after an exchange of words, pushed you bodily down her front path and onto the pavement where you fell and hurt your back. You reported this to the police who called at the Bell's house but have since told you that Kate denied that this happened and they could not proceed without witnesses. Since then, you have been subjected to a hate campaign by the Bells. You have had paint stripper poured on the bonnet of your car, your tyres have been slashed, and excrement smeared on your front door. Your children were so upset that they asked to go home to their father two days early and have since said that they do not want to visit the house again. The Bell children have shouted abuse at you in the street and when you bumped into the family in the supermarket. Basically, they are making your life an absolute misery and you want it to stop. You are at the end of your tether.

Figure 4.9 A client interviewing role

How does client interviewing work?

In a client interviewing competition, a pair of students have a set period of time— usually 20 minutes—to conduct an interview that elicits details of the client's problems so that they can offer some preliminary legal advice and formulate a plan for achieving the client's objectives. In many respects, the success of the interview rests upon the effectiveness of the approach to questioning taken by the interviewers as this is the key to obtaining all the necessary information from the client. However, it can be difficult to work out what questions to ask the client as only scant information about the nature of the client's problem is provided prior to the interview. Part of the process of preparing to interview should involve speculation about what the problem might be as this will enable you to formulate questions and to consider what area of law might be involved.

The interview will generally start with a series of questions aimed at eliciting factual details about the client—contact details, occupation, and other such necessary information. This gives you an opportunity to assess the demeanour of the client: perhaps they are relaxed and chatty or nervous and uncomfortable. You should use this stage of the interview to think about your interviewing style and ensure that it is suitable for the type of client that is in front of you. This initial stage is often a good opportunity to deal with the formalities of the interview such as its cost and duration as well as the other requirements of Practice Rule 15 (discussed in detail in the section that follows).

With the preliminaries out of the way, you can move on to the questioning stage of the interview. It is often a good idea to start by inviting the client to provide further details of their problem: something along the lines of 'I understand you have had a problem with your neighbour. Perhaps you could tell me a little more about it' would suffice. Of course, if the client does not respond to this then you will need to use closed questions—questions that require a specific response such as 'how long have you lived in your house?'—to elicit details from the client. Using a combination of questioning and listening, you should gain a good insight into the client's problem. Reflect this understanding by summarising the essence of what they have told you and check to ensure that they agree that you have captured the central points. You are then ready to offer advice and consider a way forward for the client.

The stages of client interviewing

Client interviewing taught me to think ahead at the same time that I am listening to a client and to create a mental chronology of the client's story that helps me to ask sensible questions. I was really pleased to have the experience from the competitions when I started to deal with real clients in practice.

Beth, University College London

As with negotiation, there is a national client interviewing competition for law students and most internal competitions replicate the format and judging criteria of the national competition. The judging criteria identify 11 areas in which students are expected to be able to demonstrate proficiency. These skills are discussed in the sections that follow.

Establishing a professional relationship

The relationship between solicitor and client is governed by the rules set out in the Solicitors Regulation Authority *Code of Conduct*. This identifies ten 'mandatory' and 'all-pervasive' principles that 'define the fundamental ethical and professional standards' expected of solicitors. Chapter 1 deals with client care and sets out a series of outcomes that must be achieved to ensure that the client understands the service that will be provided, how it will be delivered, and what it costs. It also provides that the client must be made aware of the steps that they can take if they are unhappy with the service provided. It then identifies a series of indicative behaviours that show that these outcomes have been achieved. You will need to demonstrate these behaviours in establishing a relationship with the client. An extract from the *Code of Conduct* is provided in Figure 4.10 to give you an idea of what is expected but you should familiarise yourself with its full requirements and think about how you will satisfy these in your interview.

Dealing with the client's matter

IB(1.1) Agreeing an appropriate level of service with your client, for example, the type and frequency of communications.

IB(1.2) Explaining your responsibilities and those of the client.

IB(1.3) Ensuring that the client is told, in writing, the name and status of the person(s) dealing with the matter and the name and status of the person responsible for its overall supervision.

Fee arrangements with your client

IB(1.13) Discussing whether the potential outcomes of the client's matter are likely to justify the expense or risk involved, including any risk of having to pay someone else's legal fees.

IB(1.14) Clearly explaining your fees and if and when they are likely to change.

IB(1.15) Warning about other payments for which the client may be responsible.

Complaints handing

IB(1.22) Having a written complaints procedure which:
   (a) is bought to the client's attention at the outset of the matter.
   (b) is easy for clients to use and understand, allowing for complaints to be made by any reasonable means.
   (c) is responsive to the needs of individual clients, especially those who are vulnerable.

Figure 4.10 Extract from SRA *Code of Conduct*: Indicative Behaviours

There is often a distinct power imbalance in the solicitor–client relationship and the onus is on the solicitor, as the professional providing a service, to create an appropriate environment in which the client feels comfortable and which is conducive to the sharing of sensitive information. The ability to establish appropriate professional relationships with a range of different individuals will be important in any employment context, particularly one that involves dealing with clients outside of the profession in which you work.

Obtaining information

Without information, you cannot evaluate the client's problem, offer advice, or do any of the other things that are part of client interviewing. In essence, the interview will not work if you are not able to obtain information from the client. You need to be able to formulate a strategy for questioning the client that will obtain a clear and comprehensive picture of their problem. This will generally need to be a combination of open and closed questions:

- Open questions are those which invite a general response: in essence, they give the client space to talk and allow you to find out more about the issue at hand. They are often used at the start of an interview to obtain an overview of the client's problem that is then explored in greater detail with some follow-up closed questions. For example, you might ask 'what problems have you been experiencing with your neighbour?'.

- Closed questions are more specific and can only be answered with a narrow range of responses, usually by answering 'yes' or 'no' or by providing factual information. For example, you might ask 'how long have you lived at your current address?' or 'did anyone witness the altercation between you and your neighbour?'. These questions are useful for obtaining the specific details. They enable the interview to control the flow of information so can be a good way to elicit details from a client who seems reluctant to provide them or is hesitant about speaking but are also a useful method of quelling a stream of detail from an over-talkative client.

You can plan a line of questioning prior to the interview but you will need to be flexible in order to adapt to the client's manner and degree of engagement with the interview. You may also find that you need to formulate a different approach to questioning if the client's problem is not one that you have anticipated.

The key skill here is the ability to create a questioning strategy that elicits relevant information in an effective manner whilst still maintaining a professional and empathetic relationship with the client. You are demonstrating your ability to balance your goal in obtaining details of the client's problem with an awareness of the client as a person rather than as a source of information. This skill will be particularly valuable in a professional setting that involves dealing with clients on a regular basis.

Learning the client's goals, expectations, and needs

It is important that you do not get carried away with the niceties of the application of the law to the client's problems but that you take into account what the client wants to achieve. The most obvious legal solution is not necessarily the outcome that the client wants or needs so this aspect of client interviewing requires that you acknowledge the context in which the legal dispute takes place. Perhaps Geraldine could bring legal proceedings against her neighbours but will this ultimately make her relationship with them better or worse? What does she actually want—a court case or a quiet life? As part of the process of advising a client, you may need to modify their expectations of what a solicitor can achieve for them. You cannot allow a client to harbour an unrealistic expectation about the strength of their claim or the likely outcome of your intervention.

You must find out what the client wants, make sure that it is realistic and then respond by tailoring your advice to fit their objectives. In an employment context, this will demonstrate your awareness of the needs of others and your ability to evolve flexible solutions that adapt to their requirements.

Problem analysis

This is the stage of the interview at which you reflect your understanding of the client's problem based upon the information that you have elicited and your appreciation of what the client hopes to achieve. You should aim to recognise both the legal issues and the non-legal elements of the problem. Ideally, you should summarise the client's problem and check whether they agree that you have captured all the important points.

This is that stage of the interview at which you demonstrate that you have untangled all the detail and got to the heart of the problem. It demonstrates your ability to distinguish between key facts and peripheral detail and to provide a concise summary of complex events. Employers will value the ability to highlight the essential issue in a clear and concise manner.

Legal analysis and giving advice

This stage of the interview involves the application of the law to the facts of the client's problem. There is a limit to how much legal advice you would be expected to give at a preliminary interview but you should be able to identify the relevant area of law and explain this to the client in a way that can be understood by a layperson and without overloading them with detail.

In any industry involving interaction with customers or other non-experts, you may need to be able to explain specialist concepts to an audience of lay people. The key skills that you are demonstrating here is your ability to be understood by people who lack your level of knowledge or expertise.

Developing a reasoned course of action

All legal disputes involve at least two options—take legal action or do nothing—and most will raise even more possibilities so you will need to be able to set out the possible courses of action for the client. Not only will you need to explain these different options, you should also provide some brief insight into the strengths and weaknesses of each course of action for the client.

The skill here is to identify all the possible alternatives and to evaluate their relative merits. This is an analytical ability that can be divorced from a legal context and deployed in any professional setting.

Assisting the client to make an informed choice

Having set out the possible courses of action for the client, you should assist them to reach a decision as to which of these is preferable, taking into account their overall situation including their emotional needs. You cannot make the decision for the client neither should you leave them to make up their minds without support and guidance. You should be able to point out the wider implications of any particular course of action, advising not only on the legal dimension but also the economic, social, and psychological consequences of their choice.

This part of the interview demonstrates your ability to see the bigger picture as you look beyond the legal ramifications of a particular course of action to consider the overall impact on the client's life. You are also demonstrating your ability to guide and counsel the client as you assist them to reach a sensible decision about the way forward.

Concluding the interview effectively

The interview should end with the client feeling that they have received the assistance that they sought and that they have made a step forward with resolving the problem that led them to seek an appointment with a solicitor. They should have a clear idea about what will happen next so you will need to be sure that they know what you are going to do, when you are going to do it, and when they can expect to hear from you. You must also ensure that they have understood what is required if there is anything that you need them to do before your next meeting such as make a doctor's appointment or send copies of documents to you.

The end of the interview will shape the impression that the client has of the service that they have received so it should be courteous, efficient, and professional. The ability to establish and maintain appropriate professional relationships is an essential aspect of business practice.

Team work

It is usual for students taking part in a client interviewing competition to work in pairs so there will be an opportunity to develop your ability to work collaboratively with others. This should involve both the preparation and execution stages of the interview. Although you will be able to work out which of you will deal with particular aspects of the interview as part of the planning process, this should not be a hard and fast division of labour but one which adapts to the interview situation as it develops as it is often the case that a client will interact more effectively with one of the interviewers. Alternatively, it may be that you need to intervene to assist your partner if they are not having any success in eliciting facts from the client on a particular issue: perhaps, as the observer, you can think of an important question that your partner has not asked or you can see a way to approach an issue that is upsetting the client differently. Think carefully about how you will deal with intervention if it is necessary as it could undermine your colleague if you do it clumsily and it may alarm or confuse the client if they feel that they are being questioned by two people at the same time. Make sure you stay engaged with the interview when you are not talking to the client: look at whoever is speaking and make notes of any important points that are raised.

The ability to work with others in an effective and professional manner is a real asset in the workplace so you should take any opportunity that arises to develop these skills and to demonstrate your ability to cooperate and collaborate to potential employers.

Ethical behaviour

The client may disclose facts which raise moral issues that you will need to address, particularly as the client is aware that their discussions with you are confidential. You will need to recognise and address any ethical issues and deal with them in an appropriate manner without being judgemental or damaging your relationship with the client. For example, if your client says 'my neighbours have accused me of beating my children' then you should not ignore this and will need to ask 'do you beat your children?' as this raises a risk to the welfare of the children that may not be something that can be kept confidential.

Ethical issues can arise in any profession. Participation in client interviewing competitions will ensure that you encounter tricky moral issues and give you an opportunity to demonstrate your professionalism in addressing them and in asking difficult questions without losing composure.

Post-interview reflection period

After the interview is concluded and the client has left, the final stage of the client interviewing competition involves a period of reflection in which the students talk to each other (in the presence of the judges) about the interview. This is an opportunity to identify any limitations in the way that the interview was conducted and to consider alternative ways in which it could have been approached that would have been stronger and more effective. There should be an evaluation of the way in which the client's problems were handled and the extent to which the client's feelings were recognised and taken into account.

Employers are often interested in your ability to evaluate your own performance. This reflective stage of the client interviewing competition will enable you to demonstrate to employers that you are able to recognise your own limitations and identify ways of strengthening your own performance.

Figure 4.11 shows a simple schematic of the key steps in a client interview and the associated skills that are being used and developed at each stage.

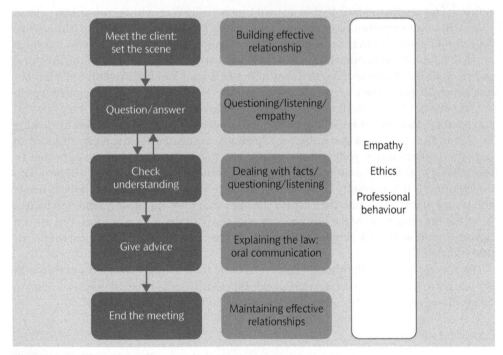

Figure 4.11 Client interviewing skills

What employability skills does client interviewing develop?

A client interviewing competition involves the use of a very general set of transferable skills in a legal setting. In other words, the skills at the heart of this activity have no necessary connection with the law or legal practice but will demonstrate your ability to deal with people and information in a way that could be adapted to any number of professional settings. This section highlights the way in which negotiation skills are relevant to employability by using the categories outlined in Chapter 1 that have already been discussed earlier in this chapter in the context of mooting and negotiation.

Practical skills

- **Numeracy.** The client's problem may require you to make financial calculations. For example, you may need to work out how much redundancy pay the client should receive or calculate the sum that they will receive if they have an entitlement to a particular percentage of profits.

Personal skills

- **Time management.** Participation in any extra-curricular activity will necessitate that you balance the time commitment involved with the need to keep up with the demands of your studies. There will also be a need to manage your time carefully in the interview itself to ensure that you conclude within the set time. This can be difficult if you encounter a particularly talkative client or one with a very detailed problem but it gives you good experience of achieving goals within tight time constraints.

- **Professional and ethical behaviour.** Client interviewing offers an excellent opportunity for you to understand and apply professional rules as you must work within the framework of the requirements of the SRA *Code of Practice*. It is also likely that you will have to address ethical issues as these are often included in interviewing scenarios.

- **Flexibility.** However well you plan your interview strategy, it is likely that you will need to adapt this to suit the needs of the client and the nature of their problem so it is a good opportunity to demonstrate your ability to be responsive and flexible.

Interpersonal skills

- **Team working.** The way in which you work with your partner will be a key component that determines the success of the interview. You need to strive for an even level of participation whilst also responding to any difficulties that your partner may encounter thus demonstrating your supportive approach to working with others.

- **Verbal communication.** Effective verbal communication is at the heart of a successful interview. You have to be able to ask questions that provide a framework for the interview and which elicit the information that you need whilst listening carefully to the detail of the answers provided. Your explanation of the law and the possible courses of action to the client need to be clear and easy for them to understand.

- **Customer service.** Interviewing is an opportunity to experience client care in action. You will have to develop a rapport with the client and ensure that you create an environment in which the client is comfortable to share sensitive information with you. The client must be treated in a professional and courteous manner that is in line with the requirements of the SRA *Code of Practice* and you should ensure that the client goes away from the interview feeling more positive than they were at the start and clear about what is going to happen next.

Professional skills

- **Legal problem solving.** Dealing with a client is the real world equivalent of writing an answer to a problem question. It requires you to focus on the relevant facts, match them to the correct area of law, and work out what will happen when the law is applied to the factual situation.

- **Interviewing.** The whole purpose of the competition is to give you an opportunity to develop your interviewing skills.

In conclusion, interviewing is not an essentially legal skill: it is a set of highly desirable employability skills that are exercised in a legal setting but which could be transferred to any situation that involves the use of questioning to elicit facts from a client. It is a valuable activity for students who wish to practise law because all solicitors and barristers have to deal with clients and to develop an effective method for extracting the relevant details of their case from them. For students who aim to work in a non-law profession, client interviewing is still a valuable activity as it provides an opportunity for you to experience fact-finding and to learn how to manage people.

Tell us

Tell us about your experiences with mooting, negotiation, and client interviewing. Did your involvement with these activities help you to get work experience or a training contract or pupillage? Perhaps you found the skills that you learned useful once you were working. Let us know at finchandfafinski.com/get-in-touch or @FinchFafinski on Twitter.

Finding opportunities to interview

As with negotiation, it is still sadly the case that some law schools do not provide any opportunities for students to learn interviewing skills or to take part in interviewing competitions. However, more and more universities are recognising the importance of client interviewing as a skills-rich extra-curricular activity so if it is not available yet at your university, campaign for it to be introduced or, better still, take the initiative and start it yourself. In the sections that follow, you will find information about internal client interviewing, including advice on how to start your own competition, and the national and international competitions.

Internal client interviewing competitions

If an internal competition already exists at your university, you should ensure that you take part. The process of eliciting information from a real person, analysing their problem and formulating some preliminary advice offers you an insight into the business of working within the legal profession and will help you to appreciate the real-world application of the law that you study. Negotiation is all about people and their problems, so being involved in a negotiation will make the law come alive to you in a way that purely academic study can never achieve.

Entry into an interviewing competition should not be too onerous in terms of the time commitment involved. You will need to ensure that you have a provisional structure in mind for the interview that covers matters such as costs, confidential and other professional matters as well as ensuring that you think about the way in which you will approach questioning but preparation is minor compared to mooting. It would be a good idea to get involved with the competition as early as possible in your academic career: consider that the first year is when you find out what it is all about and the second year is when you achieve success in the internal competition and the final year (or thereafter as a post-graduate) is when you intend to represent your institution in the national competition. Of course, it may not work out like this but it is a good objective. Alternatively, you might want to volunteer as a client in your first year so that you can see client interviewing from the 'other side of the table' as this will help you to understand what is required if you enter the competition the following year. Some students prefer to gain their practical skills experience during their first and second years to ensure that they have a wealth of experience to support their applications for work placements, training contracts, and funding for the postgraduate stage of legal education as well as leaving them time to really focus on their studies in the final year.

If no client interviewing competition exists, as with mooting and negotiation, the option is available to start one yourself which, again, shows your ability to create your own opportunities where none existed previously. Alternatively, you could raise support for the idea of a client interviewing competition amongst the student body and seek to persuade your law school to organise one for you. Either approach achieves your objective of creating an interviewing competition to enter but the first gives you more opportunity to develop organisational skills whilst the latter requires less time commitment from you.

Practical advice: organising an interviewing competition

An interviewing competition is based upon a simulated interview between two solicitors working together and a new client with a fictitious legal problem. As with negotiation, you will need scenarios, rules, judging criteria, and a judge plus you will also need someone to act as a client for each team of lawyers as well as someone to judge their performance.

⚫ You will find a pack of information about organising an interviewing competition with a selection of interview scenarios on the Online Resource Centre.

National client interviewing competition

There is a national client interviewing competition held each year and, in 2013, it attracted entries from 28 universities across England and Wales. The four highest scoring teams from two regional heats (held in London and Sheffield in 2013) are joined by a team from the institution of the winning team from the previous year's competition in the final.

Practical example: competition scenarios

The national competition focuses on a particular area of law each year to help students in their preparation. Students should think about the possible problems that could arise in relation to that area of law and decide what sorts of questions they may need to put to the clients that they encounter. This can be shaped by the memos that are sent to the teams prior to the competition in which they receive some indication of the nature of each client's problem.

For example, in 2013, the focus of the competition was serious violent crime and the client memos for the regional heats were as follows:

- You have an appointment to see Ed Barnes on Saturday 26th January. Her/his contact details: 14 Highlands Road, email address **edbarnes88@gmail.com**. S/he seems rather upset and worried. S/he says it is to do with the death of her neighbour.

> - I have made an appointment for you with Gerald/Geraldine Fisher. S/he wouldn't say exactly what was involved. However s/he did ask if you would be able to explain what was involved in being an accessory to an offence. I assured her/him that you would have that information at the interview.

The teams conduct two interviews with different clients in front of a panel of three judges who assess their performance on the basis of a set of criteria which take into account their interpersonal skills as well as their ability to handle a legal problem. The winning team will go on to represent England and Wales in the Louis M Brown and Forrest S Mosten International Client Consultation Competition. You will find further details about the national and international competitions on the following websites:

- **www.clientinterviewing.com/index.asp**
- **www.brownmosten.com**.

Skills summary

The practical legal skills activities covered in this chapter develop skills in many categories of your skills portfolio, as shown in Table 4.1.

Table 4.1 Skills portfolio: practical legal skills

Skill	Mooting	Negotiation	Interviewing
Practical skills			
Written communication skills	X		
Numeracy			
Problem solving	X	X	X
Use of IT			
Personal skills			
Time management skills			
Professional and ethical behaviour	X	X	X
Organisational skills			
Flexibility			
Planning			
Decision-making			
Interpersonal skills			
Team working	X	X	X

Skill	Mooting	Negotiation	Interviewing
Verbal communication	X	X	X
Customer service		X	X
Leadership			
Professional skills			
Legal research			
Legal problem solving	X	X	X
Drafting	X		
Negotiation		X	
Advocacy	X		
Knowledge of legal practice and procedure	X	X	X
Interviewing			X
Presentation skills			

WHERE NEXT?

Mooting, negotiation, and client interviewing offer enormous potential as ways of developing and demonstrating key employability skills. They will be of particular interest to prospective employers within the legal profession—in fact, there is rather an expectation amongst law employers that you will have done at least one of these activities during your degree—but they can be used to impress employers in any field of employment. The best advice that we can give is that you should aim to try each of these activities at least once and at the earliest possible point in your degree. This gives you plenty of time to continue with the activity if you are good at it—bear in mind that your application will stand out far more if you have represented your university in a national competition and it will take time to build up your skills to the necessary standard—and you can use it to help you get work experience in your first summer vacation if you take part in your first year. But it is never too late to get involved so make the decision to find out what opportunities exist to participate in these activities at your university and sign yourself up! If no opportunities exist, make your own by starting up an internal competition: this in itself will show your commitment to developing relevant legal skills and your leadership, organisation, planning, and team work skills.

Ethical theories

Key issues

- What are ethics?
- Is there a right answer to an ethical dilemma?
- How are lawyers' ethics different from general ethics?

Introduction

'Lawyers' ethics' has been described as one of the great oxymorons. Jokes about lawyers abound. Few are complimentary:

> The National Institutes of Health have announced that they will no longer be using rats for medical experimentation. In their place, they will use lawyers. They have given three reasons for this decision.
>
> 1. There are now more lawyers than there are rats.
> 2. The medical researchers don't become as emotionally attached to the lawyers as they did to the rats.
> 3. There are some things that even rats won't do.

At one time, three learned professions were seen as the pillars of society: doctors; clergy; and lawyers. While once the three most respected occupations in the land, a lively debate could now be had over which of these is held most in disrepute.

In a survey by the American Bar Association of public attitudes about lawyers, the following five were the most common responses:

- 'lawyers are too expensive';
- 'lawyers are greedy';
- 'lawyers are not honest';
- 'there are too many lawyers';
- 'lawyers are self-serving, don't care about clients'.

A survey in the UK found that only 42 per cent of respondents would trust a lawyer to tell the truth.[1]

---

[1] Legal Services Consumer Panel, *Annual Tracker Survey* (Legal Services Consumer Panel, 2013).

If lawyers seek to be held in high regard by society, it is crucial that there be a system of legal ethics that ensures that the public can have confidence in the legal profession. That is why the topic of this book—ethics for lawyers—is so important.

It is easy, however, to be starry-eyed about lawyers' ethics. Although people say that they want lawyers to be fair to both sides, to be scrupulously honest, and to put justice first, it is all rather different if they are talking about the lawyer who is representing them: in that event, they want their lawyers to do everything necessary to win the case. People want their opponent's lawyer to be fair and reasonable—but not their own!

Lawyers and legal ethics

As is well known, there are two primary branches of the legal profession: solicitors and barristers. Less well known is the fact that others play a crucial role in the provision of legal services, including legal executives, licensed conveyancers, will drafters, paralegals, and informal advisers. This book is primarily designed for law students who most commonly go on to seek work as solicitors or barristers, and so it will focus on these.

As we shall see later in this chapter, there has been a lively debate over whether or not legal ethics should be part of a law degree. We will explore the reasons for this later on. This book, however, will be designed to introduce students to the major issues around legal ethics. As well as setting out what are generally accepted as the ethical principles governing lawyers, it will also identify the different theories behind these principles.

The aim of this book is to introduce you not only to the rules of lawyers' ethics, but also, more importantly, to the principles behind the regulations. This is crucial because cases that can be dealt with under the rules are easy; hard cases are those in which it is not clear whether a rule applies or which of two rules apply. In these cases, it is necessary to know the principles behind the rules to assess the best way forward. Further, this book will explain alternative ways of examining ethical issues and criticisms of the current approaches. You should then be in a good position to take a sensitive and well-rounded approach to the rules.

Although the phrase 'lawyers' ethics' itself might bring a smile to the face of some, the issue is extremely important. The financial crisis of recent years can be blamed, in part, to ethical failures on the parts of the lawyers involved. Indeed, one of the major responses to the financial crisis has been to tighten the regulation and enforcement of ethics. If courts and the justice system are seen to lack an ethical foundation, society—that is, people—will lose respect for the law. A degree of respect for lawyers and the legal system is crucial for a well-functioning society.

This chapter will start by setting out some general theories about ethics. How do we judge what is the right thing to do? What makes a decision morally justifiable? What makes a person good? Of course, people disagree on these questions. There is no consensus on the correct answer to these questions and many books have been written on them.

It hardly needs to be said that lawyers are people and so are bound by these general principles just like anyone else. So lawyers must not kill innocent people—but that is true for everyone and so is not a special ethical obligation on lawyers. Because this book is about *lawyers'* ethics rather than general ethics, we need to go beyond the standard ethical rules and explore two questions, as follows.

1. Are there any additional ethical obligations that a lawyer has over and above the general ethical principles that apply to anyone else?

2. Are there circumstances in which lawyers are excused from the general ethical obligations that are imposed on others?

The first question considers whether, in addition to the general ethical principles (that is, 'do not kill', 'do not lie', among other things), there are special ethical obligations imposed upon lawyers. As we shall see, many people believe that lawyers have especial obligations to their clients that are more onerous than the normal obligations that people owe to each other.

The second question asks whether a lawyer may be excused from those ethical obligations that are imposed generally. A person who discovers that his or her friend is going to commit a crime may be under an obligation to report that friend to the authorities; a lawyer's special obligation of confidence may mean that the lawyer is not. Charles Fried, a leading legal ethicist, once asked: 'Can a good lawyer be a good person?'[2] The very fact that this question has been raised indicates that many believe that sometimes lawyers are asked to do things that, if they were done by a non-lawyer, would be seen to be wrong. A further interesting question is whether, in the interpretation and application of the law, lawyers have particular obligations. Lawyers are often called upon to interpret or apply the law. In cases in which the law is ambiguous, to what extent is the lawyer required to ensure that the law takes a moral approach?

These extra obligations arise because of the special position that lawyers have in relation to their clients, and in relation to society more generally. In relation to their clients, lawyers have a special relationship of trust. People will disclose to their lawyers highly personal information and give them highly valued property. There need to be legal and ethical obligations that protect those who put such trust in lawyers. This is important for clients, but also for lawyers. If lawyers cease to be trustworthy, people will no longer use lawyers in relation to their sensitive matters. This will be disastrous both for lawyers, who will lose business, but also for society more generally. It is widely thought to be beneficial that people can seek legal advice and engage in legal transactions. If people cannot find out what the law is and have no access to legal services to enforce their legal rights, the rule of law will break down.

---

[2] C. Fried, 'The lawyer as friend: The moral foundations of the lawyer–client relation' (1976) 85 Yale Law Journal 1060.

But there is a balance here. While we want people to have trust in their lawyers and to have an advocate who will represent them in legal proceedings, lawyers also have a special duty to courts and the justice system generally. If lawyers are seen to act immorally and to undermine the principles of justice underpinning the legal system, the legal system will fall into disrepute.

As we shall see as this chapter develops, many of the most difficult ethical issues for lawyers arise when there is a clash between their duties to their clients and their broader duties to the justice system, and to society more generally. Lawyers will disagree on where that balance should be and much academic debate centres on that question. It is one to which we will return repeatedly in this book.

The role of ethics

We need to say a little more about what is meant by 'ethics'. When we are undertaking an ethical analysis we are seeking to answer the question: 'What is the right thing to do?' Another way of putting the question is to ask: 'How would we want people to respond to this situation?'

Rosalind Hursthouse[3] has stated that there are no 'moral wiz-kids'. Her point is that while we might expect the very best physicist to discover the right answer to scientific questions, we do not expect the same of ethicists. Good ethicists are not necessarily correct, but should be able to explain their views in clear ways, with reasoned arguments. So we cannot expect ethicists to give us the 'right answer'; we have to work that out for ourselves. But we can expect ethicists to provide us with tools that we can use to reach reasonable answers. They can provide us with the tools to live good and virtuous lives. They can help us to understand which answers are consistent with certain values and which are inconsistent. Ethicists can therefore help us to find out the appropriate responses to dilemmas, once we choose which values we want to uphold.

The nature of ethics will become clearer if we distinguish ethics from some other things.

Norms and ethics

It is important to distinguish the 'norms' that govern lawyers and ethics. There may be certain norms that lawyers follow: they may wear suits; they may be in their offices by 9.30; they may like drinking coffee! But these are norms—that is, behaviour that is common, but which is not itself justified by an ethical principle. There is nothing unethical in not drinking coffee, even if it is uncommon.

Perhaps the best way of telling whether something is a norm or moral principle is looking at the reaction of others when the rule is broken. If a male solicitor were to turn up to work not wearing a tie, there may be a few eyebrows raised, but he would

---

[3] R. Hursthouse, *On Virtue Ethics* (Oxford University Press, 1999).

not be condemned—at least not in anything like the same way as he would had he revealed confidential information. This latter instance would lead to his investigation by the professional body and perhaps even by a court. It could lead to a punishment. His failure to wear a tie might, at most, lead to a quiet word in his ear. While breach of an ethical principle might indicate a character flaw, a breach of a norm would indicate only a need to be reminded of 'the way in which we do things'. It would be seen as a matter of ignorance or eccentricity rather than of immorality.

One way of determining the ethical obligations under which lawyers act is to look at what a lawyer did or did not do. In doing so, you might spot that, soon after meeting a client, the lawyer set out the arrangement for the payment of fees. But this, in itself, would not tell you whether this was because this was a norm or an ethical principle; you would also need to consider what would happen if the behaviour were breached. Who would respond to the breach and how? Social norms are typically enforced by people saying bad things about the transgressor or shunning him or her. Laws are enforced by courts by means of punishment. Professional regulations fall somewhere in between, with consequences that can be legal or professional, and which can ultimately result in the transgressor's removal from the professions.[4]

Law and ethics

Asking whether an action is 'legal' and whether it is 'ethical' are two very different questions. Something may be ethically, but not legally, required. Being polite to other people may be demanded by ethics, for example, but not by the law; adultery may be unethical, but it is not illegal. The law may require Person A to pay damages to Person B for a breach of contract or for causing Person B an injury, even though Person A is not morally to blame. Similarly, an act may be against the law even if it is not unethical. Such instances are rare, but a father who does not buy a parking ticket for a hospital car park because he has no change and has a seriously ill child whom he needs to take to the hospital may be behaving illegally, even if not unethically. Generally, however, the two are linked. It is relatively rare for people to be found to have breached the law in circumstances in which they have acted well in ethical terms. And most serious breaches of ethical standards will involve a breach of law of some kind.

The law tends to focus on matters that harm the public and are susceptible to proof. So a behaviour that is unethical, but does not cause a public harm (lying to a friend, for example) is unlikely to be unlawful. The harm is only to the other person and does not require societal condemnation by means of the law. Other behaviour that may cause a public harm cannot be readily susceptible to proof or definition. Malicious gossip might be an example. Even if we were to decide that gossip harmed the public good, it would be hard to define gossip in a way that would be sufficiently clear for the law. Also, the law tends to focus on behaviour that is seriously harmful.

---

[4] For more discussion, see H. Hart, *The Concept of Law* (Oxford University Press, 1961).

Unethical conduct that causes only minor harms may not be sufficiently serious to merit an official legal response.

Ethics and law are focused on different things. For law, the focus is on cases in which there is a sufficiently serious harm and a need for someone to be held to account in a public forum; for ethics, the focus is on whether the act is a good thing to do.

There is much more that could be said about the link between law and ethics, something that has generated substantial debate amongst legal philosophers.

Ethical disagreements

If you hope that ethicists and ethical analysis will provide you with the right answer to every difficult question, you will soon be disappointed. Ethicists disagree on what is ethical. This can be disconcerting. In this section, I will explore a little more why that may be and why it is that people disagree.

The overarching approach

As we set out some of the ethical approaches, it will be noted that they adopt a rather different style of approach to resolving ethical dilemmas and that this leads to different answers. Some of the different approaches are as follows.

1. *Rule-based approaches*—for example, deontology (considered later in the chapter)
   Some approaches seek to reduce ethical principles to a set of rules to follow. This has an appeal to lawyers, because they are familiar with the idea of applying rules to particular situations and following them. For supporters of this approach, the answer to the question 'What is the ethical response to this situation?' is 'Follow the rules'.

2. *Outcome-based approaches*—for example, utilitarianism (considered later in the chapter)
   Some approaches argue that the central issue in an ethical dilemma is to look to the consequences of the decision. To be ethical is to produce the best outcome. For supporters of this approach, the answer to the question 'What is the ethical response to this situation?' is 'Consider what will produce the best outcome'.

3. *Character-based approaches*—for example, virtue ethics (considered later in the chapter)
   Some approaches argue that ethics is about character. Ethics is about displaying certain virtues, such as honesty or kindness. So, for supporters of this approach, the answer to the question 'What is the ethical response to this situation?' is 'Act in a way that displays virtue'.

This book will not seek to judge between these general theories, which it will explore in more detail shortly. People will disagree strongly over which approach is preferable.

It is certainly not the purpose of this volume to persuade you of the benefits of one approach over another. It is hoped, however, that after reading this chapter you will be better equipped to explain your ethical reasons for acting in certain ways and to judge the decisions of others. It might also be that you will come to understand better why someone might take a completely different view from your own on what is ethically the appropriate thing to do in a given situation. It is not necessarily the case that the other person is wrong and you are right; rather, you might be asking different questions or starting from fundamentally different ethical points.

Minimum requirements or maximally ethical

One reason why people disagree on the answers to ethical dilemmas is that they may be asking different questions. When asking an ethical question, it is important to be clear whether we are asking 'What is the minimum standard that is ethically required?' or 'What is the best response?' Sometimes, an ethical dilemma raises two alternatives: action A or action B. However, more often there are a range of alternative courses of action. The answer is often far more nuanced than simply 'This is the ethical thing to do and that is not the ethical thing to do'. For example, it may be that there is an option that is ethically acceptable, but not as good as the ethically most desirable, or an option that is ethically good, but is not required. For example, if a lawyer engages in pro bono work, offering free legal advice to disadvantaged groups or charities, this may be required as an ethically good thing to do. But most people would not regard a lawyer who failed to engage in that work as acting in an ethically bad way. So it is important to be clear whether what is being asked is 'What is ethically acceptable?' or 'What is ethically the best?' When professional bodies set down ethical guidance, they are generally setting out the minimum requirements for lawyers.

Guiding me or judging others?

There is an important distinction between asking what is ethically the right thing for me to do and asking what is the ethically appropriate response to someone else's behaviour. 'Should I drop litter?' is a different question from 'How should I respond if someone else drops litter?', which is again a different question from asking 'How should the law respond if someone else drops litter?' In particular, it does not always follow from your own decision that it would be unethical for you to act in a particular way that you think that you and/or society should condemn a person who chooses to act in that way. There may be reasons peculiar to you that mean it would be wrong for you to engage in an action that would not be wrong for someone else. For example, if you were head of a campaign to encourage people to become vegetarian, that would give you a reason not to eat meat (that is, you would be being hypocritical if you were to do so) that would not apply to others. It is important to be aware of this distinction when reading academic writing. When lawyers discuss ethics, they are often discussing how the law should respond to the unethical behaviour of others, while philosophers are often discussing the way in which an ethical person should behave. These are different, although related, questions.

Ethics and regulation

In this book, we are talking about the ethical conduct of solicitors and barristers. In Chapter 3, we will be looking at how lawyers should be regulated in ethical matters. The issue of ethical regulation raises some special issues. The questions 'What is ethical?' and 'What should be included in ethical regulation?' are not the same, for two reasons.

First, ethical regulation must offer guidance. If we are to punish a lawyer for breaching professional ethics, that lawyer is entitled to know what the ethical requirements are. This requires the ethical guidance to be reasonably clear and capable of being applied. Consider, for example, a complex ethical dilemma involving a conflict of interest. A philosopher addressing the issue might produce a densely argued document covering many pages of analysis, teasing out numerous nuanced points that need to be put into balance. However, a lawyer in the throes of the ethical dilemma cannot be expected to undertake an analysis of that depth. This means that there is often a crudeness about the ethical guidance used in regulation. It offers clear concise guidance that can readily be applied, but it does so by sacrificing the sophistication that a deeply philosophical analysis would offer. Indeed, as we will discuss in Chapter 3, this leads to a lively debate over how detailed or how clear that regulation should be.

Second, the regulation must be capable of being enforced. Regulation would be a laughing stock if it were not enforceable. For example, let us say that you consider it to be unethical for a lawyer to look lustfully at a client. A regulation prohibiting lawyers from doing so would be impractical: we could never know what the lawyer was thinking. A better regulation might target matters capable of determination: whether the lawyer said anything inappropriate to the client, for example. So there may be some aspects of ethical behaviour that cannot be captured in a code of regulation because they could never be enforced.

People and acts

Codes of professional legal ethics focus mostly on acts, rather than character. They set out what actions are ethical or not. Not all philosophers agree with that approach. Some think that the better approach is to ask whether someone is a 'good person'— that we should be seeking to produce good lawyers, not only lawyers who do good things. Alice Woolley disagrees: '[L]egal ethics should never be concerned with the morality of *lawyers* or of *clients*; rather it should be concerned only with the morality of the acts lawyers or clients do (or propose to do).'[5]

[5] A. Woolley, 'Philosophical legal ethics: Ethics, morals and jurisprudence—Introduction: The legitimate concerns of legal ethics' (2010) 13 Legal Ethics 168.

The issue is not straightforward: what someone is and what someone does are closely related: you cannot really claim to *be* brave if you do not *do* brave things. Nevertheless, Woolley is right to emphasise that, generally, we are asking whether a particular act in a particular situation is justified, rather than making a general assessment of someone's life. In particular, if a lawyer has breached an ethical code, it will not be a defence to claim that, generally, he or she lives an ethical life.

General ethical principles

Here, we will describe some of the general ethical approaches that are taken to ethical dilemmas, before looking at some more concrete principles. We will start with perhaps the most popular ethical approach: **consequentialism**.

 Definition

> **Consequentialism** determines whether an act is morally justified or not, depending on whether it produces good or bad consequences overall.

Consequentialism

For a consequentialist, the key issue in determining whether an action is ethically appropriate is to consider its consequences. Quite simply, the action is right if, all things considered, the consequences are good; the action is wrong if, all things considered, its consequences are bad. This approach therefore tends to reject firm rules for ethics, such as 'Do not lie' or 'Do not kill', because it all depends on the circumstances. So if, in a particular situation, lying is going to produce an outcome that is more good than bad, then it is legitimate to lie.

Consequentialism requires a careful consideration of all of the consequences of an act. There may be some good and some bad consequences flowing from an act, in which case you need to determine whether, overall, more of the consequences are good or more are bad. So although it might be presumed that a particular lie will be good because it will make someone happy, a consequentialist would think about the possibility that he or she will be found out; in that instance, there will be more harm than good, and this will need to be taken into account.

It is not surprising that consequentialism is a popular ethical approach. It reflects how most people make many day-to-day decisions. When deciding what to watch on television, you are likely to think about which programme you will enjoy the most. If you are deciding what birthday present to buy a friend, you will consider what they will like the best. Most people want good things to flow from their actions, not bad.

 **Application**

You are acting for the prosecution of a man accused of murder. Conclusive DNA evidence has shown that he has committed the crime, but, owing to a technical violation of the rules, you cannot rely on that evidence and a conviction cannot be secured without it. A police officer offers to plant some incriminating evidence.

If you were a consequentialist, you might decide that the good of ensuring a conviction of a guilty person justifies planting the evidence.

Problems with consequentialism

At the heart of consequentialism is the claim that we must consider what will produce the most 'good'. But what does 'good' mean? One popular theory, known as 'utilitarianism', suggests that we should seek to increase the good. The greatest good is the largest amount of pleasure or happiness. But that may be problematic. Most people do not simply make decisions about what makes them happy: we may choose the television programme that is educational over one that is more fun; we may attend the lecture when we are tired, rather than sleep in late. Both of these may be seen as decisions to promote the 'good', but not necessarily happiness.

So perhaps consequentialism should not be restricted to happiness, but should include other kinds of goods? Suddenly, the approach becomes very vague. If I buy gym membership for my brother rather than buy him a cake, how can I weigh up the good of his health against the pleasure that the cake would have given him? Comparing the good of health with the deliciousness of cake is comparing incommensurables.

There are further uncertainties surrounding consequentialism. The approach all depends on predicting the consequences of our actions. But often we cannot do so. If I am not sure how people will react to my decision, it is difficult to work out whether it will produce good or not. Not only that, but how wide should the net of consequences be thrown? If I am considering driving to visit my mum next weekend, am I to consider the environmental consequences of the journey, or the impact on other road users of my erratic driving? And does a proper consequentialist analysis require me to compare the good produced by visiting my mum with the good that might be produced by visiting any of the other people whom I might see? A full consideration of all of the consequences might mean that I need to spend the whole weekend thinking it through! So the attractive simplicity of consequentialism becomes considerably more complex if we properly consider all of the outcomes of an action.

Others criticise consequentialism from other perspectives. One is that it places no weight on motivations. The act is justified under consequentialism if it produces good results, even if it is badly motivated. If a judge decides to acquit an innocent defendant because he finds her attractive, is that ethical? The result is good: the innocent defendant goes free, but has the judge acted ethically?

For others, the problem with utilitarianism is that it leads to unacceptable results. Imagine that a judge sentences an innocent, but unpopular, politician to prison for ten years. A utilitarian calculation might suggest that the joy caused to the public by the imprisonment is greater than the harm done to the politician and that the wrongful imprisonment is therefore justified. But is that right? Can good consequences (the happiness to the public) really justify injustice? Can a lawyer who runs off with his millionaire client's money really try to justify this by saying that he derived far more pleasure from the money than the millionaire would have done, and so has acted ethically?! Surely, the good consequences do not always justify the means?

 Scandal!

In 2010, the BBC[6] reported that a vicar, a lawyer, and a businessman had been convicted of helping people illegally to obtain permission to remain in the country in breach of immigration law. The vicar had undertaken 'sham marriages' to bypass immigration rules.

One can imagine, in cases such as these, defendants persuading themselves that they were doing good by helping those in a desperate situation. However, the courts will not allow a defence to a criminal offence to be based on a claim that, in this case, more good than bad was achieved.

These powerful concerns with consequentialism have led some commentators to develop an alternative approach: **rule consequentialism.**

 Definition

Rule consequentialism promotes the following of rules that will normally overall produce good consequences.

Rule consequentialism

Rule consequentialists argue in favour of developing rules that, if followed, will promote the best outcomes over the long run. So rule consequentialism asks 'Which general rules will promote the best consequences in the long term, assuming that everyone accepts and complies with them?'[7], rather than what will promote the most good in this particular case. So we might decide that the rule that lawyers should not steal their clients' money is a rule that, if followed, will promote the good, even if we might accept that there can be individual cases in which that is not so. Lawyers should follow the rule that promotes good generally, even if it does not do so in a particular

---

[6] BBC News, 'Sussex vicar guilty of immigration marriage scam', 29 July 2010, online at www.bbc.co.uk/news/uk-england-sussex-10781151

[7] W. Glannon, *Biomedical Ethics* (Oxford University Press, 2005), 5.

case. This makes it easier for people to follow guidance because they need only to follow the general rule, rather than to assess its usefulness in any particular case.

One benefit of the rule consequentialist approach is that, sometimes, there is a difference between what is good for an individual lawyer and what is good for lawyers as a group.[8] A good example may be that if one lawyer were to refuse to represent a man charged with rape, that would probably not cause any harm—but if all lawyers were to refuse to represent men charged with rape, that could be problematic.

Problems with rule consequentialism

Although rule consequentialism is popular, it too has difficulties. It is problematic for individuals seeking guidance on what to do in their particular situations. Working out the consequences of alternative courses of action as required for 'act utilitarianism' is difficult enough; attempting to work out what general rule to apply in cases of this kind would be very complex. Further, there is the issue of whether, within 'rule utilitarianism', the rules have exceptions, and if so, how these exceptions are to be calculated.

Other criticisms can include that, as mentioned earlier in relation to consequentialism, no account is taken of motive in rule consequentialism; nor does the rule utilitarian take account of special duties that we might owe to our children, for example. It does not provide sufficient scope for an actor to say that although generally this is a good rule, in the circumstances of this case, it will be improper to follow it.

Deontology

Deontology provides a quite different approach to ethics from consequentialism. A deontological approach holds that certain actions are good or wrong *in or of* themselves. It is, they say, right to tell the truth not because doing so makes people happy or because of other good consequences, but simply because telling the truth is a good. Immanuel Kant is widely seen as a leading proponent of this approach. One of his fundamental principles is well known: you should never use someone simply as a means to an end. This is important for lawyers because it shows that lawyers should not use clients to achieve their own goals, even if they believe that doing so will create more good.

 Definition

> **Deontology** states that there are certain moral rules that must be followed, regardless of the circumstances.

---

[8] A. Ayers, 'The lawyer's perspective: The gap between individual decisions and collective consequences in legal ethics' (2011) 36 Journal of the Legal Profession 77.

It is crucial for deontologists that a breach of an ethical principle cannot be justi-fied simply by referring to the consequences. Telling the truth might cause pain in some cases, but that is no justification for lying.

One of the great benefits of deontology is its clarity—at least as long as the rules are clear! There is no need to worry yourself about the consequences of your action; you simply follow the rule, come what may. Lawyers may be drawn to this approach because they are familiar with statutes or contracts setting out requirements that must be followed.

Deontologists often place much weight on duties. They emphasise the duties that parents owe to their children, or physicians to their patients, which are overlooked in utilitarian approaches. When making a decision about our children, we must take into account the duties that we owe them, not only the consequences for all children. Lawyers must acknowledge their special duties to clients and justice, and not consider only the consequences of their actions.

Problems with deontology

Consequentialists will question whether principles should be stuck to, come what may. Even if you are not an out-and-out consequentialist, you might ask: 'Should I not lie if doing so will save someone's life?' The classic scenario is the person in Nazi Germany, who is hiding a Jew escaping persecution, being asked by a soldier if he or she has any Jewish people in the house. In such a case, the deontologist must be truly committed to his or her principles to demand that the person should tell the truth despite the inevitable results.

Some deontologists are willing to give some flexibility. They accept that the prin-ciple must be followed unless there are overwhelmingly bad consequences that will flow from it. You should not kill, they say, although maybe if thousands of people were going to be saved as a result, it may be acceptable. Lawyers are familiar with this in terms of human rights. You must not discriminate against someone, but it might be possible to produce a very strong case for why discrimination might be justified. Those who are willing to accept this more flexible version of deontology face the prob-lem that doing so renders their approach less clear-cut: inevitable uncertainty will surround precisely how bad the consequences must be to justify interfering with the principle. They also face claims that once they are allowing consequences to override the rule, they are consequentialists in disguise.

Perhaps the central problem facing deontologists is to explain where their prin-ciples come from. Why should we not lie? One argument is that deontological prin-ciples are derived from rationality. Our rationality is what distinguishes us from animals and provides us with the means to develop moral principles. The problem is that people's rationality leads them to different conclusions on difficult moral issues.

It is not surprising that many (but by no means all) religious people take a deon-tological approach. For them, there are certain things that God has declared wrong. No explanation or justification is needed: God has spoken. Deontologists seeking to explain their principles in a non-religious way usually suggest that there are certain self-evident goods that are part of human flourishing: truth, knowledge, friendship, among other things. The difficulty may be that what is self-evidently good to some is not so to others. Is it self-evidently good that a child should be raised by his or her biological parents? Some would say so, but others would not. Another possible source of deontological principles is public opinion—yet history teaches us that the majority of people have followed some very unpleasant principles in the past. Also, why should the fact that most people believe X to be true make X an ethical principle? This different source of deontological principles is a problem for lawyers and for drafters of legal ethical principles. If the law wishes to take a deontological approach, whose deontological principles should the law adopt? Having said that, whichever theory is adopted, there will usually be a debate over which version of the theory is to be applied.

Applying deontology: principlism

A popular way of applying a deontological approach is through an approach known as **principlism**.

 Definition

Principlism involves applying a set of prima facie principles to an ethical dilemma.

Principlism avoids some of the grand themes that we have discussed so far and suggests that we can identify some key principles. Through considering an application of these to the issue at hand, the correct ethical approach becomes apparent. This approach has been particularly influentially put forward in a book by Tom Beauchamp and James Childress, *Principles of Biomedical Ethics*.[9] While written for medical law and ethics, it has been applied in a range of situations. It relies on four key principles:

- respect for autonomy;
- non-maleficence;
- beneficence; and
- justice.

If these were used more generally for legal ethics, they would require that, in any moral dilemma, a lawyer should consider the four principles to direct his or her action.

The four principles need a little more explanation.

[9] T. Beauchamp and J. Childress, *Principles of Biomedical Ethics*, 7th edn (Oxford University Press, 2013).

Autonomy

Autonomy is about allowing people to make their own decisions, unless their doing so harms others or the common good. Applying this in the legal context, lawyers should respect the decisions that clients make about what they want to do. For example, if a client asks a lawyer to draft a will giving particular gifts, the lawyer should respect the client's decision. It is not for the lawyer to tell the client to give more money to charity. This is not to say that the lawyer should not provide information or advice, but that the lawyer should acknowledge that the decision is the client's own.

In favour of emphasising autonomy is the view that lawyers have a central role in society in terms of helping people to achieve what they want in life. Lawyers play a positive role in helping people to reach their aspirations: to set up a company; to buy a house; or to get married. They also have a role in protecting clients from oppression and ensuring that clients are free to make their own decisions. The primary job for a lawyer under the autonomy principle is to help clients to realise their objectives.

There is one aspect of the autonomy principle that might appeal to some lawyers: that the lawyer is non-judgemental. The whole point of autonomy is that people are free to pursue their own visions of the 'good life'. It is not for lawyers to tell clients whether they are making bad decisions. In the past, it may have been that doctors, lawyers, and other professionals were seen as the experts to whom ordinary people deferred. Now, the relationship between professionals and clients has changed. People consulting lawyers on divorce would be astonished to hear their lawyers suggest that they change their minds and be reconciled with their spouses. The lawyer's job is to help the client to obtain the divorce, not to question the client's decision.

Non-maleficence

Non-malificence is the principle that a lawyer should not harm a client. An obvious example is that the lawyer should not steal his or her client's funds. This is a *negative* principle: it tells a lawyer what they should not do.

Beneficence

Beneficence is the related principle that the lawyer should seek to promote the well-being of the client. It is a *positive* principle, requiring action from a lawyer. The lawyer should seek to do his or her best to advance the client's cause and do as well as he or she can for the client.

Justice

The requirement of justice means that the lawyer must act fairly as between different clients and also to promote justice more widely. This may involve a commitment to the well-being of the legal profession[10] and to the justice system as a whole. Few would disagree with that principle. More problematic is the question of what is meant by

---

[10] D. Brindle and P. Curtis, 'Fight for equality that could put jobs at risk', *The Guardian*, 2 January 2008.

'justice'. At the heart of most theories of justice is the principle of formal equality: all equals should be treated equally and unequals should be treated unequally. The principle, so baldly stated, is perhaps uncontroversial—but its application causes difficulties: how do we know if two people are equal; and how do we know if treatment is equal?

Justice can be a slippery concept and there is no clear agreement about what it contains or involves. It comprises three aspects: the procedural; the substantive; and the social.

- The *procedural* aspects of justice require a proper hearing for disputes and that judges be free from bias. There should be an opportunity for each side to present its case and for reasons to be given for a decision. Procedural justice is not uncontroversial. Lawyers can get a bad name if they are seen to use procedural justice arguments to undermine substantive arguments. Claims that a case must fail because a particular form was not lodged at an appropriate time or in the correct way can appear to put technical requirements over and above finding a fair solution to a dispute. Yet there need to be rules about how claims can be made and how evidence is presented if there are to be fair procedures to deal with disputes. The difficulty is striking the balance in ensuring that these are complied with in a way that ensures fair outcomes.

- *Substantive* justice requires that the outcomes of legal disputes are just. What is a 'just' law is a huge question and beyond the scope of this book. Some lawyers believe that it is the job of Parliament and the courts to ensure that the content of the rules is fair. The lawyer will use the existing legal rules to pursue a client's case. If the content of the law is unfair, the blame for that rests not with the lawyer, but with the Parliament or courts.

- *Social* justice takes a broader view. Justice, it is said by some, is not only about having a fair legal system, but also about ensuring that society, generally, is fair. John Rawls suggested two key principles as aspects of the social dimension of justice: that offices and positions should be open to all, with fair equality of opportunity; and that the social system should act for the greatest benefit of the least advantaged of society. Not everyone will agree with these, by any means: here, we are entering political questions about the kind of society and government that we want.

Applying the principles

Having now explained the four principles, let us consider how they work in practice. Beauchamp and Childress[11] promote these principles because they represent a 'common morality'—that is, a set of principles agreed by people around the world and from a broad range of perspectives. They hope that everyone will agree that these

---

[11] See n. 9.

principles are good ones to follow. They also acknowledge that these are prima facie principles. In other words, they accept that there may be particular cases in which there are very good reasons why the principles should not apply.

They argue that, in approaching an ethical dilemma, we should consider what each of these four principles would have to say about how to act. Crucially, they do not rank the four principles. Importantly, this means that their approach does not provide an answer to a difficult dilemma. It provides us with tools to help us look at the issue, but does not give us the answer. It is easy to imagine cases in which respecting autonomy (doing what the client wants) conflicts with non-maleficence (not harming the client). Where there is a conflict, Beauchamp and Childress hope that a careful consideration of the application of these principles will lead to the solution becoming apparent.

The popularity of their approach lies partly in the fact that it provides a workable way of thinking through the issues. By taking each principle one by one and thinking through its significance, one is likely to consider most, if not all, relevant moral issues. Further, it provides an accessible language and tools with which to talk through issues with colleagues and, in doing so, highlight why there is a disagreement. It might, for example, become clear that the difference of viewpoints arises because one person is emphasising autonomy and another is emphasising non-maleficence.

Critics of principlism

Critics of principles argue that, in difficult cases, it does not really provide a clear approach, especially in cases in which the principles suggest different answers.[12] Suppose a client instructs a lawyer to act in a way that the lawyer judges will harm the client. For example, he or she asks the lawyer to institute proceedings, even though the lawyer thinks the case has no chance of success. In this instance, we have a clear clash between autonomy (complying with the decision of the client) and non-maleficence (not harming the client). Principlism does not tell us which principle to follow. Indeed, nearly all ethical dilemmas come down to a clash between two or more of these principles. Without an indication of which principle is to trump the other(s), they provide little help. Critics argue that there is a need for a unifying moral theory to justify these four principles, which would then provide a way of reconciling them in the event of a clash. Beauchamp and Childress do not claim that the principles provide the answers; rather, they provide an effective way of analysing an issue.[13] It may therefore be that principlism provides tools with which to think through an issue, rather than indicates the answer to be reached.

[12] A. Campbell, 'The virtues (and vices) of the four principles' (2003) 29 Journal of Medical Ethics 292.

[13] T. Beauchamp, 'Principlism and its alleged competitors' (1995) 5 Kennedy Institute of Ethics Journal 181.

Intuition

So far, we have been looking at forms of ethical analysis that promote rational ways of resolving dilemmas. They provide ways of thinking through the issues to determine what is the right thing to do. But maybe these are mistaken. Should we place greater weight on intuition[14]—that is, a gut feeling that something is right or wrong? Whatever logic or argument may suggest is right, 'our hearts' sometimes tell us that 'our heads' have got it wrong. These arguments are often particularly prominent in medical ethics. For example, many people feel that creating animal–human hybrids is wrong. They may not be able to articulate in a rational way *why* they think it is wrong; it simply *feels* wrong to many people.

Moral intuition can be important in practice. It is often intuition that alerts the practising lawyer to an ethical issue. He or she may realise that something 'does not feel right' and will then analyse the issue more carefully. Indeed, without intuition alerting lawyers to a potential issue, it is not clear that carefully drafted ethical guidance will be of help: the lawyers simply will not realise that they need to refer to it.

Alice Woolley argues that lawyers should acknowledge the importance of moral intuition. She argues:

> Moral decision making relies significantly on our intuition and moral emotions, the unconscious cognitive processes through which we perceive and respond to moral problems. Intuition and moral emotions are affected by reason—by our moral commitments, by our reasoned exchanges with others, and by our own reflections on what reasons matter most. Intuition and moral emotions are, though, nonetheless distinct and are themselves the primary operative feature in moral decision making, rather than reason itself. Knowing what to do in any particular case is not normally the direct product of an ex ante reasoned analysis.[15]

This view should not be dismissed too easily. While people articulate reasons for their ethical analysis, it may be that deeply held intuitions underlie these. It may well be that this explains why, when there is a disagreement over a moral issue, people rarely change their moral positions however much they may trade arguments. In other words, it may be that while people like to pretend that their moral views are the result of rational thought, in fact emotional responses and personal history play a bigger part than they like to admit. Their response to lying, for example, may be affected by experiences in the past of being lied to.

There is a further important point that Woolley makes. Successful ethics means not only that people will come to see the correct response, but also that they will be able to see that decision through to action. Ethics that talks to the 'head', but makes no

[14] G. Kaebnick, 'Reasons of the heart: Emotion, rationality, and the "wisdom of repugnance"' (2008) 38 Hastings Center Report 365; J. Niemela, 'What puts the "yuck" in the yuck factor?' (2011) 25 Bioethics 267.

[15] A. Woolley, 'Intuition and theory in legal ethics teaching' (2011) 9 University of St Thomas Law Journal 285, 287.

sense to the heart, may not work to help to prevent the lawyer being tempted to do the wrong thing. Principles that accord with a lawyer's moral values and deeply held commitments are more likely to be understood and complied with. As Woolley points out:

> In order to act ethically, a person must first perceive that the ethical problem exists; she must have moral sensitivity.... She must also have the judgment to know how to appropriately respond to the moral problem, to know which values or principles are relevant to it and to know which values or principles should be given priority given the context and facts.... Moral sensitivity and moral judgment allow an individual to know the right thing to do in a given situation; however, she must also be able to act on that knowledge. This additionally requires that the individual have moral motivation and moral will.[16]

Indeed, David Luban has gone so far as to suggest that the 'most important' aspect of ethical decision-making by a lawyer is 'the lawyer's moral sentiments', arguing that:

> ...the vaunted 'artificial reason of the law' is no substitute [in ethical decision-making] for the emotional responses that a lifetime of moral education provides us...no form of reasoning, artificial or not, can bear the burden of discerning right from wrong in particular cases. We just aren't that smart.[17]

Concerns with intuition

Many ethicists are sceptical of relying on intuition. Cynics may say that is because it would do them out of a job! More seriously, there is a concern that 'gut feeling' can simply be the result of prejudice or ignorance. History teaches us that what seemed in the past natural to some people, such as an opposition to mixed-race marriages, now looks like blatant prejudice. So while we should acknowledge the importance of intuition, we must make sure that this is justified on a rational and coherent basis. We cannot rely on intuition alone.

Further, our intuition is sometimes unclear. We may face a dilemma and have no clear intuition of what is the right thing to do. This might be because, for example, it is a brand new situation or a highly complex one that we have not come across before. Clearly, in such a case, an ethicist needs tools in addition to intuition on which to rely.

Hermeneutics

Hermeneutics provides a very different way of responding to ethical dilemmas from those discussed so far. At its heart is listening to the different points of view and the stories that people have to tell.[18] Through discussions with another and listening, the solution emerges. That solution will be the one that works for the parties involved.

---

[16] Woolley (n. 15), 295.

[17] D. Luban, 'Reason and passion in legal ethics' (1999) 51 Stanford Law Review 873, 876.

[18] K. Boyd, 'Medical ethics: Principles, persons and perspectives—From controversy to conversation' (2005) 31 Journal of Medical Ethics 481.

 **Definition**

Hermeneutics promotes listening and talking through problems. Through articulating the issues and discussing them, a solution will emerge.

Problems with hermeneutics

Hermeneutics can work well as an approach to resolving interpersonal conflict. Indeed, as we shall see in Chapter 10, it is at the heart of mediation. The approach, however, works less well when there are interests involved that are not restricted to the two parties. The lawyer and client may well reach agreement over how to proceed by means of a discussion, but that agreement may represent an unethical course of action, because of the impact of the decision on third parties. Further, hermeneutics is not an approach that provides a busy lawyer with clear, concise guidance about what to do in a particular dilemma.

Before dismissing the benefit of hermeneutics in the context of lawyers' ethics, however, it may be worth considering whether it could be seen as explaining the source of lawyers' codes. The different legal associations and organisations are forums in which professionals can discuss and debate issues before producing the codes that guide fellow professionals. That process of discussion and debate could be seen to be based on hermeneutic principles.

Casuistry

A defining feature of casuistry is that it avoids relying on grand principles and applying them to the facts of the case, as does, for example, principlism; instead, casuistry recommends dealing with cases one by one and relying on the agreed approach in other cases. Lawyers will feel familiar with this, because it has some similarities with the approach to precedent in common law countries. So, if faced with an ethical dilemma, a lawyer will ask how similar cases are dealt with and seek to find the correct solution in that way.

Problems with casuistry

The problem with the approach is that casuistry provides little guidance where there appear to be conflicting precedents or where there is a novel situation with no direct precedent. Without appealing to some kind of underpinning principle, it might be a difficult approach to take. Indeed, a danger with casuistry is that the result can be a set of inconsistent precedents that lack a logical basis.

 Alternative view

This criticism of the casuistry approach—that it can lead to a series of inconsistent rules with no logical basis—is generally assumed to be a bad thing. But that is not beyond doubt: many people hold a series of inconsistent political, religious, and immoral beliefs, which work for them, even if they do not fit together in an entirely logical way. If we were to produce a set of rules to govern lawyers' ethics that worked in the context of the chaos of everyday life in the lawyer's office, why should it matter so much if that scheme lacks intellectual coherence?[19]

Feminist ethics

Feminist approaches now play a major role in ethical analysis.[20] Although the issue is debated, it is probably incorrect to identify **feminist ethics** as offering a unified approach to ethical analysis.

 Definition

> **Feminist ethics** considers ethical dilemma within the context of gender. It is alert to ensuring that styles of thinking or outcomes do not disadvantage women.

Feminists fiercely disagree on the correct approach to some ethical issues, however. Two leading feminists have explained the major schools of feminist thought in the following way:

> Today, feminist legal theory has evolved into four major schools: formal equality theory, "cultural feminism," dominance theory, and post-modern or anti-essentialist theory. Formal equality theory, grounded in liberal democratic thought, argues that women should be treated the same as men, while cultural feminists emphasize the need to take account of "differences" between men and women. Dominance theory sidesteps both of these approaches, focusing instead upon the embedded structures of power that make men's characteristics the norm from which "difference" is constructed. Anti-essentialism, by contrast, contends that there is no single category "female," pointing instead to the varying perspectives resulting, for example, from the intersection of gender, race and class.[21]

Many feminists have been drawn to an 'ethic of care', which does provide a unified approach and which we will discuss later. However, not all feminists would support such an approach. What does unite the feminist approach is that it asks 'the woman question'.[22] It is highly aware that gender and sex play an important part in the distribution of power within society. Gender is often the basis of assumptions about and

---

[19] J. Dewar, 'The normal chaos of family law' (1997) 61 Modern Law Review 467.
[20] C. Grant Bowman and E. M. Schneider, 'Feminist legal theory, feminist lawmaking, and the legal profession' (1998) 67 Fordham Law Review 249.
[21] Grant Bowman and Schneider (n. 20), 250.
[22] K. Bartlett, 'Feminist legal methods' (1990) 103 Harvard Law Review 829, 837.

expectations of individuals. Feminism seeks to prevent the oppression of women and to promote equality regardless of a person's sex. That includes tackling not only practices that overtly disadvantage women, but also 'the gender implications of rules and practices which might otherwise appear to be neutral or objective'.[23]

Feminist analysis is therefore interested in how the regulation of the legal professions and their practice might work against the interests of women. It explores concerns over diversity among barristers and solicitors (see Chapter 14). But there is more to a feminist approach than pointing out examples of sexism within the legal profession.

Feminism also explores whether values are being promoted that reflect 'male' norms, which work against the interests of women or which do not reflect the values that women hold. Arguably, a culture of long working hours, an aggressive litigious attitude, and a strongly economic-based model might be seen by some as fitting that description.

Naomi Cahn, for example, has complained that standard approaches to legal ethics posit the lawyer as being separated from her client.[24] The debate then centres on whether the lawyer should act as simply giving effect to the client's wishes or direct the client what to do. These debates 'distance the lawyer from the client, they rhetorically exclude one of the two voices in the attorney/client relationship, and as a result, they limit the context in which to view the client's problems'. Cahn would prefer a more contextual approach, recognising the interests of both parties and their relationship, and encouraging them to work through these together. Such an approach would suggest, for example, that the lawyer disclose her own values and perspectives with a client just as the client does, and then find a way to move on. This kind of approach is based on an ethic of care, which will be explored shortly.

One issue on which feminists disagree, however, is whether female lawyers act differently from male ones.[25] This is something that we will explore further in Chapter 14.

Problems with feminist ethics

One concern is that not all ethical dilemmas contain a clear gender element. Is there a particularly feminist perspective on lawyers' fees or the law on confidentiality? Some feminist commentators will insist that gendered assumptions can be made even in relation to such apparently dry issues. Critics will argue that seeing gender inequality everywhere is a false picture of the world.

[23] Bartlett (n. 22), 837.
[24] N. Cahn, 'A preliminary feminist critique of legal ethics' (1990–91) Georgetown Journal of Legal Ethics 23.
[25] A. Bartlett and L. Aitken, 'Competence in caring in legal practice' (2009) 16 International Journal of the Legal Profession 241.

Even if one accepts that there is gender inequality inherent to a particular issue, feminists do not always agree on what is the correct response. If, for example, the reason why there are fewer women than men making the rank of partner in firms of solicitors is the caring responsibilities of women, is the solution to free women from their caretaking (for example by offering more childcare facilities) or is it to change the mindset among firms of solicitors so that someone undertaking care is not disadvantaged in her career? Feminists will not agree on that.

Ethics of care

Considerable attention has been paid to the **ethics of care** in recent years.[26] This approach is critical of traditional legal ethics, with its focus on rights, individual autonomy, and abstracted universal principles. Instead, it focuses on relationships and care. Rather than valuing individual freedom, it values the interdependency and mutuality in relationships.

 Definition

> The **ethics of care** sees care as the core ethical value. An ethical response to a dilemma
> is one that promotes good, caring relationships.

Susan Wolf has argued:

> By depicting the moral community as a set of atomistic and self-serving individuals,
> it [liberal individualism] strips away relationships that are morally central. This not
> only is impoverished, but may also be harmful, because it encourages disregard of
> those bonds. It is also inaccurate; developing children as well as full-grown adults
> are profoundly interdependent. Indeed, we are so interdependent that we cannot
> even understand the terms of moral debate without some community process and
> shared understanding.[27]

The ethics of care therefore tends to avoid using abstract principles as the primary tool of ethical analysis, seeking instead to find an approach that fits in with the needs and relationships of the individual case.[28] Hence the focus is less on questions such as 'What do I owe others?' and rather on questions such as 'How can I best express my caring responsibilities?' and 'How can I best deal with vulnerability, suffering and dependence?'[29]

---

[26] See, e.g., J. Herring, *Caring and the Law* (Hart, 2013); V. Held, *The Ethics of Care* (Oxford University Press, 2006); C. Menkel-Meadow, 'Portia Redux: Another look at gender feminism and legal ethics', in D. Carle (ed.) *Lawyers' Ethics and the Pursuit of Social Justice: A Critical Reader* (New York University Press, 2005).

[27] S. Wolf, 'Introduction: Gender and feminism in bioethics', in S. Wolf (ed.) *Feminism and Bioethics* (Oxford University Press), 17–18.

[28] J. Tronto, *Moral Boundaries: A Political Argument for an Ethic of Care* (Routledge, 1983), 21.

[29] J. Bridgeman, *Parental Responsibility, Young Children and Healthcare Law* (Cambridge University Press, 2009).

The following are some of the key themes that are found in much writing on care ethics.[30]

1. *The inevitability of interdependence* Caring is the essence of life. From the very start of life, we are in relationships of dependency with others. The law should therefore see caring relationships as of crucial social significance.

2. *The value of care* Care is not only an inevitable part of life; it is also a *good* part of life. The law should therefore value and encourage it.

3. *Relational approaches* The law should not treat us as atomistic individuals with individual rights and interests that clash with others. Rather, the focus should be on the responsibilities that flow from our relationship with others. Virginia Held makes the point by contrasting the ethics of care and an ethic of justice:

> An ethic of justice focuses on questions of fairness, equality, individual rights, abstract principles, and the consistent application of them. An ethic of care focuses on attentiveness, trust, responsiveness to need, narrative nuance, and cultivating caring relations. Whereas an ethic of justice seeks a fair solution between competing individual interests and rights, an ethic of care sees the interest of carers and cared-for as importantly intertwined rather than as simply competing.[31]

Applying this approach to lawyers is likely to lead to greater emphasis on developing a good relationship, based on mutual respect, between the lawyer and client in which care is emphasised as the good that we are aiming to promote. Such an approach will move away from general principles, considering instead what response will fit best in the context of the particular relationship between this lawyer and this client.

A care-based approach would challenge some key features of traditional ethics. Is the preference for clear general rules desirable, or should we find the solution that fits with the caring responsibilities and clients involved? Should the lawyer whose child is sick at home leave a client in the hands of a colleague while he or she meets these caring responsibilities? Does the notion of a 'caring lawyer' involve some element of emotional bond between lawyer and client? How should the lawyer balance a caring obligation to the client with others?

Stephen Ellmann argues:

> The lawyer must care for every member of the community, each person in the web of interconnection, including those people who have manifested indifference or antagonism toward this very idea of mutual responsibility—manifested it, perhaps, by frauds, or crimes, or simple lack of caring for their fellow community members. To say that the lawyer should care for everyone regardless of character or conduct is rather like saying that everyone is entitled to exercise his or her legal rights regardless of character or other conduct—a quintessential claim of rights morality.[32]

---

[30] Herring (n. 26), ch. 3.   [31] Held (n. 26), 94.
[32] S. Ellmann, 'The ethic of care as an ethic for lawyers' (1993) 81 Georgetown Law Journal 2665, 2684.

Ellmann goes on to argue that the ethic of care cannot require an equal caring for all, because that would be impossible; rather, it requires that people take on special obligations to individuals. This can apply to the lawyer. Abstract principles about what lawyers must do for their clients do not acknowledge the competing claims that lawyers may face in their everyday lives.

Problems with ethics of care

Ethics of care approaches have, inevitably, received their fair share of criticism. First, it has been argued by feminists that its glorification of caring and dependency is likely to be harmful to women. The role of women as carers and dependants has led to their oppression and subordination.[33] To elevate and promote such a role is therefore harmful. Supporters of ethics of care would reply that the way ahead for women is not to seek to live the lives of independent, autonomous, un-obligated individuals that some men appear to live, but rather to promote these values of care and dependency.

A second concern is that the notion of care is too vague.[34] It might be pointed out that not all caring relationships are good ones: some may involve manipulation and oppression. Without a far clearer concept of what 'good care' is, care cannot form the basis of an ethical approach. Many supporters of an ethic of care would accept that more work needs to be done to 'flesh out' the concept and that it is in its relatively early days of development.[35]

Virtue ethics

Virtue ethics goes back to the writings of Socrates and Aristotle. It emphasises that, in assessing what is the morally correct thing to do, it is not the consequences of your actions that matter, but rather the attitudes (virtues) motivating your actions.[36] It is the character of an individual, not the consequences of his or her actions, that is more important. Virtues are good habits that will direct human nature towards good actions. James Rachels suggests that a virtue is 'a trait of character, manifested in habitual action, that it is good for a person to have'.[37]

 ## Definition

> **Virtue ethics** promotes the development of good characteristics that are seen to promote human flourishing. Ethical analysis should encourage us to be virtuous people, rather than to seek the solution to particular dilemmas.

[33] Wolf (n. 27), 9.

[34] P. Allmark, 'Can there be an ethics of care?', in K. Fulford, D. Dickenson, and T. Murray (eds) *Healthcare Ethics and Human Values* (Blackwell, 2002).

[35] C. Smart and B. Neale, *Family Fragments* (Polity, 1999).

[36] P. Gardiner, 'A virtue ethics approach to moral dilemmas in medicine' (2003) 29 Journal of Medical Ethics 297.   [37] J. Rachels, *The Elements of Moral Philosophy* (McGraw-Hill, 1999).

This opens up an interesting way of approaching ethical questions. We can ask 'How would an honest lawyer act in this scenario?', 'How would a just lawyer respond?', and so forth. Some people find this way of asking ethical dilemmas more helpful than considering how abstract principles apply. A further advantage of this approach is that it reassures those nervous about whether they are acting in the right way. If they are motivated by compassion or justice, they are displaying these virtues and need not worry about the consequences. That can be reassuring. It acknowledges that while we may seek to do the right thing, sometimes bad things happen.

Virtue ethics provides a useful way of guiding lawyers. It seeks not only to produce lawyers who comply with the rules, but also lawyers who display good character. We seek the just lawyer; the caring lawyer; the devoted lawyer. We move from act criteria to character tests.

There is disagreement among virtue ethicists over whether the consequences of an action are relevant to its ethical value. Some argue that as long as the act is virtuously motivated, the consequences are irrelevant. Others disagree, believing that the bad consequences can render a well-motivated act unjustifiable.[38]

One concern with virtue ethics is how we should decide what are 'good virtues'. In such a diverse society, there is little agreement on what makes a 'good person'; there are many different ideas of what makes a 'good life'. It may be that, in Western society, keeping fit or eating moderately would be regarded as a virtue, but it is unclear whether in other societies this would be so. But virtue ethicists often argue that there are moral values that are essential for any decent society: love, friendship, truth-telling, faithfulness, and wisdom would be accepted around the world as virtues.

So which virtues might be included within virtue ethics? We might include politeness, fidelity, prudence, temperance, courage, justice, generosity, compassion, mercy, gratitude, humility, simplicity, tolerance, purity, gentleness, good faith, humour, and love.[39]

Problems with virtue ethics

Critics of virtue ethics complain that appalling activities can be justified under virtue ethics. Consider the wicked doctor killing lots of elderly patients, believing that they will be better off dead than infirm, or the suicide bomber killing many to show a love of God: both might be well motivated, but their actions are clearly immoral. Of course, others would say that they were not actually acting virtuously, but only *believed* that they were doing so.

There is also a concern that virtue ethics fails to provide clear guidance on what precisely to do in a given situation. True, we are told to behave as virtuous people do—but if it is a novel situation, such advice might provide little practical guidance.

---

[38] P. Foot, *Natural Goodness* (Oxford University Press, 2001), 43.
[39] A. Compte Sponville, *A Short Treatise on the Great Virtues* (Heinemann, 2002); A. Woolley and B. Wendel, 'Legal ethics and moral character' (2010) 23 Georgetown Journal of Legal Ethics 1065.

A further problem is that there is little consensus on what makes a virtuous character. Asking people who are their moral heroes might soon reveal diversity of opinion. In the context of legal ethics, there may be concerns that the approach fails to acknowledge how easy it is for people to delude themselves into thinking that they are acting virtuously when they are not. It seems to be human nature for people to pretend that they are acting virtuously when they are not. A clear set of regulations telling lawyers what they can or cannot do may therefore be needed, rather than general guidance that lawyers must 'act honestly'.

Relativism

It is quite common to hear people say that, on moral questions, there is 'no right or wrong answer' and that 'Your view is as valid as mine'. Sometimes, when discussing ethics, people may say something like 'Personally, I think X is wrong', indicating that they are simply making a claim about what is wrong for them and that they are not saying that those who disagree are necessarily wrong. This view of ethics is known as 'relativism'. It is a claim that there are no right and wrong answers to a moral problem. An extreme relativist view would claim that there are never absolute right or wrong answers to a moral dilemma. A more moderate view would be that there is nearly always a range of acceptable moral answers and that we cannot choose between them.

The issue has become more prominent with recognition of cultural diversity. Are ethics developed in the West also based on a 'Western mindset'? We in the West tend to focus on individual rights, while concepts of community, tradition, and relationships may be neglected. Are these ethical principles no more than a reflection of certain Western norms, based on an assumption that the individualist lifestyles of the West are best?[40]

This view, in effect, suggests that we should, in terms of professional guidance, place little weight on ethical dimensions, or least accept that the guidance represents a choice between equally valid perspectives. We cannot ascertain what is good or bad—indeed there is no 'good' or 'bad'—and so we should focus on producing guidance that promotes efficiency, rather than goodness.

Problems with relativism

Although this is a popular perspective, in fact very few people really are extreme relativists. Whether rape is wrong is not really a matter of opinion. More realistically, people might claim that although there are some general moral precepts on which we can all agree, there are plenty on which there is no consensus. On these, we might take a guess at what is morally right, while accepting that we might be wrong. A person

---

[40] K. Bowman, 'What are the limits of bioethics in a culturally pluralistic society?' (2004) 32 Journal of Law, Medicine and Ethics 664.

might decide not to drink alcohol, while not necessarily saying that he or she thinks others should not do so. But in a way, even a view such as this is not relativist, because it takes a distinct view on the moral issue—namely, that there is no right or wrong answer. Further, in the context of legal ethics, if part of their role is to instil public confidence in the legal profession and protect clients from being taken advantage of, we cannot simply say that all ethical views are equally valid.

Are lawyers' ethics special?

A key issue is whether lawyers' ethics are any different from others. This issue will become apparent when we look at four viewpoints.

1. Lawyers' ethics are no different from general ethical foundations. So the principle that lawyers should keep clients' information confidential is no different from that which applies to any person given private information in a confidential setting. It may be that lawyers are given confidential information more commonly than other people, but the basic moral principles governing lawyers are the same as others.

2. Lawyers apply the same basic principles as other people, but the role of the professional means that they are applied in a particular way. So although the basic idea of confidentiality applies to all, there is an enhanced obligation for lawyers. Similarly, everyone must be honest, but lawyers are expected not only to be honest, but also to appear to be honest and to have the highest standards of honesty.

3. Lawyers apply the same basic principles as others, but have special exemption by virtue of their professional status. So although, generally, people must tell the truth, the special requirement of lawyers to do all that they can to promote their clients' well-being means that they are permitted to subvert that principle if necessary.

4. Lawyers' ethics are independent of the principles that apply to most people. The special obligations that lawyers have reflect their unique position for society. Lawyers' ethics should not, then, be seen simply as an enhanced form of general ethics, but as having their own special basis.

The debates between these views will be explored next and will be returned to throughout this book. They underpin many of the debates around lawyers' ethics.

The role of the lawyer

At the heart of many debates over legal ethics is the role of lawyers. For some commentators, the notion of partisanship is central to the role of the lawyer. The lawyer must show 'hyper-zeal' in pursuing a client's case, even if that means acting in a way that might otherwise appear unethical.[41] For such commentators, it is the duty of the

---

[41] Fried (n. 2).

lawyer to do everything that he or she can for the client that is the central moral claim. For others, the lawyer has commitments to the overall legal system, and to moral principles generally, that severely restrict the extent to which a lawyer can exercise hyper-zeal. The debate between these perspectives is reflected in the debates over a large number of the ethical issues that lawyers face.

Partisanship

One of the more controversial principles highlighted is partisanship—that is, the idea that the lawyer's primary role is to defend a client's rights and to put forward the best case possible. This must be done with no consideration of the impact on others. The lawyer defending the hospital trust against a personal injury claim brought by the parent of a paralysed child, for example, must put forward the best arguments for the trust and not be swayed by sympathy for the condition of the child. It is the job of the other party's lawyer to put forward the child's case.

Quite how far partisanship takes us is a matter for debate. Clearly, it could never require the lawyer to engage in illegal activity. No one suggests that. However, whether it requires the lawyer to use arguments of little moral merit with all zeal may be more debatable. A good example might be whether a barrister representing a man charged with rape should cross-examine the complainant with full rigour, even if doing so will cause the complainant severe distress and serious harm. We will consider some of these views further.[42]

Hyper-zeal

The argument in favour of 'hyper-zeal'—that is, that the lawyer should go 'all out' for his or her client—is as follows. A client has legal rights, but typically lacks the knowledge to assert these rights. If we believe that people should have the ability to access their rights, then access to lawyers is crucial. If a client wants his or her rights enforced, the lawyer must help the client to achieve this, even if others might think that the client should not assert these rights. The man accused of rape has a right to cross-examine the complainant fiercely and the lawyer has the obligation to enable the client to exercise his right. Once we start to say that the lawyer should not do everything that he or she can do for a client, we are, in effect, depriving people of access to their rights. Perhaps worse: we may be allowing people to exercise only the rights that their lawyers think they should exercise.

Lord Brougham's ancient statement is often quoted as summarising the position:

> An advocate, in the discharge of his duty, knows but one person in all the world, and that person is his client. To save that client by all means and expedients, and at all hazards and costs to other persons... is his first and only duty; and in performing

---

[42] T. Schneyer, 'The promise and problematics of legal ethics from the lawyer's point of view' (2004) 16 Yale Journal of Law & the Humanities 45.

this duty he must not regard the alarm, the torments, the destruction which he may bring upon others.[43]

Supporters of this view will accept that this can involve lawyers acting in ways that may seem disreputable. However, if this is unacceptable, then the problem lies in the law, not with the lawyer. If we think that a company should not be able to impose a contract with unfair terms on consumers, then any complaint lies with contract law, not the lawyer who advised the company as to its legal rights and drafted the contract.

Daniel Markovits argues that at the heart of the legal system is the separation of adjudication and advocacy.[44] The role of the lawyer is not to judge the merits of a client's case; that is the job of the courts. The lawyer makes the case for the client and the court decides if it is legitimate. This leads to what Markovits sees as the fundamental obligations placed on every lawyer—namely, loyalty, respect for the client's determination of ends, and legal assertiveness on behalf of clients. He accepts that this might lead a lawyer to lie—defined as 'asserting a proposition that one privately (and correctly) disbelieves'—and to cheat—that is, 'to exploit others by promoting claims or causes that one privately [and correctly] thinks undeserving'. These are justified because the lawyer is playing a role in a legitimate process. Indeed, properly understood, the lawyer is not lying or cheating, but faithfully presenting what his or her client wants to say and pursuing the client's case in a non-judgemental way. Lawyers, Markovits argues, should be seen as 'self-effacing', in that they put the interests of clients and presentation of the clients' cases first. He is, however, concerned that lawyers are not understanding their role and not appreciating the justification for what they are doing.

A linked argument is that if lawyers start to fail to disclose certain parts of the law from their clients because they think that doing so will not promote justice, then, in effect, the lawyers are changing the law. If, for example, under contract law, a company is allowed to put a punitive exemption clause in its contracts with consumers, but the lawyer decides not to tell the company about the existence of such clauses, it would be, in effect, as though the law had prohibited the use of these clauses. That would be improper: it should not be for lawyers to fashion their legal advice based on their own perception of fairness.[45]

Moderate zeal

Other commentators argue for a 'moderate zeal'. Tim Dare argues that lawyers should act with zeal, but not hyper-zeal.[46] There should, he argues, be limits on how far a lawyer seeks to act for a client. W. Bradley Wendel draws an interesting distinction

[43] J. Nightingale (ed.) *The Trial of Queen Caroline, Vol. 2* (Albion Press, 1820–21), 8.

[44] D. Markovits, *A Modern Legal Ethics: Adversary Advocacy in a Democratic Age* (Princeton University Press, 2010).   [45] Markovits (n. 44), ch. 1.

[46] T. Dare, *Counsel of Rogues? A Defence of the Standard Conception of the Lawyer's Role* (Ashgate, 2009).

between a lawyer protecting a legal entitlement of a client and a lawyer promoting a client's interests.[47] While lawyers are entitled to do all that they can to protect clients' legal entitlements, they do not need to do all that they can to promote clients' interests. Wendel suggests that lawyers should be competent and diligent in acting for their clients, and not necessarily zealous.

Dare suggests that 'institutions may be justified by appeal to ordinary or general morality, but that the conduct of those within those institutions is to be governed not by the original moral considerations but by the rules of the institution'.[48] He is therefore clear that because the legal system that we have is legitimate and because it depends on lawyers zealously presenting their clients' cases, any apparent immorality is justified. He emphasises the importance of pluralism: the idea that, within the constraints of the law, people are able to pursue what they think is good. Lawyers are needed to allow clients to exercise their choices and to follow their consciences, even if others (even the lawyers themselves) disagree with what the clients wish to do. However, Dare accepts that there are limits on this: the lawyer can put the client's immoral case even without being required to do everything possible to promote it.

Criticism of zealousness

Critics of zealousness argue that the role of the lawyer does not justify engaging in lying, cheating, or trickery. We see people who exploit the ignorance, poverty, or weakness of others for gain as acting immorally. This should be the case whether it is in the context of litigation or not.

There are a number of ways of pursuing the objection. The first is that arguments made for zealousness assume the justifiability of the current legal system. It is because the current system is legitimate that the lawyers' role within it is justified. However, we may question whether our current legal system—which seems to privilege the rich, who can afford the best lawyers and protracted litigation; which seems often designed to protect the interests of the advantaged rather than the marginalised; in which access to justice is denied to many—is a legitimate one. If it is not, then it cannot provide a justification for the lawyers' role within it.

Even accepting the legitimacy of the current legal system, it may be argued that the conception of zealousness emphasises autonomy too much. Yes, we do treasure the ability of people to pursue their own values, but autonomy can be used for good and bad. It is one thing to say that we should allow someone to pursue an immoral lifestyle if he or she so wishes; it is another to say that we should help him or her to do so. The legal system may allow large companies to exploit consumers, but this is not the same as saying that the law should help them to do that. Further, we need to weigh up

---

[47] W. Wendel, 'Legal ethics', in H. LaFollette (ed.) *The International Encyclopaedia of Ethics* (Blackwell, 2013).   [48] Dare (n. 46), 24.

the autonomy of different people: allowing one person to exercise his or her autonomy should not be at the expense of restricting another's.

Charles Fried has supported the zealous role of a lawyer, arguing that the lawyer should be like a good friend.[49] Because friendship is regarded as an intrinsic good and friends are zealous in promoting their friends' interests, so should a lawyer. But many have questioned this: is not a role of good friends to question your judgement if they think that you have made a mistake and even to stand in your way? Loyalty to a friend does not mean blind or complete loyalty. In any event, the analogy between a lawyer and a friend does not convince everyone. For a start, lawyers would stop being a client's 'friend' pretty quickly if they were not being paid. If a friend were to give you poor advice, you might forgive your friend fairly quickly, but you would not forgive your lawyer. The idea that lawyers are driven by the kind of long-term relationship that friends have seems false.[50]

It is interesting that much of the writing in support of a zealous approach assumes that clients want to win their cases at all costs and that lawyers should help them to do so. In fact, it may be questioned how many clients take that view. Indeed, it may be the role of a lawyer to point out the disadvantages to the client of winning—at least if that can be achieved only by humiliating a rival, ruining the other party's reputation, or acting against the client's deeper values. In a divorce case, a client may feel like doing all that he or she can to humiliate and ruin the ex-spouse, but that may well be contrary to the client's long-term interests.[51]

A final concern has been voiced by Naomi Cahn, who is critical of the traditional approach, which sees lawyers as mere conduits of legal advices.[52] She argues that, in fact, lawyers are inevitably influenced by their own reaction to a case: 'By defining a legal role in which lawyers must be neutral partisans on their clients' behalf, legal ethics ignores the lawyer's legal and non-legal experiences that influence how she approaches any legal problem and represents a client.' It may therefore be more honest to encourage lawyers to be open with clients about their own reaction to cases than to assume a facade of neutrality.

Digging deeper

This debate reflects a wider argument over the nature of law. When a judge decides a case, is the judge only to apply 'the rules' or also to seek to draw on the broader principles underpinning the law? For some, the judge applies the rules, and should not seek to go beyond these and draw on grander principles. For others, it is proper for the judge to

---

[49] Fried (n. 2).
[50] E. Dauer and A. Leff, 'Comment on Fried's lawyer as friend' (1976) 85 Yale Law Journal 573.
[51] Cahn (n. 24).　　[52] Cahn (n. 24).

develop the principles on which the law is founded and to rely on these, even if doing so requires stretching the rules or even bypassing them. This is similar to the debate over whether the lawyer, in upholding the law, is permitted to use the legal rules to a client's advantage, however much that might seem to undermine the fundamental values that the law protects.

In *Spaulding v Zimmerman*, the hyper-zeal approach was followed.

 Key case

Spaulding v Zimmerman, 116 N.W. 2d 704 [Minn. 1962]

In this notorious American case, a child was injured in a car accident. The driver's lawyer obtained a medical report on the child, which disclosed that the child had a potentially fatal heart condition (unknown by the child's family), which may have been caused by the accident. The case settled and the defendant's lawyers never disclosed the report. The matter later came to court, where the judge found that the defence lawyers had not acted improperly. They had no duty to disclose the report and were acting in their client's interests.

Neutrality

The principle of neutrality requires that lawyers should not prefer one client over another. All clients need lawyers and it would be undesirable if the man charged with child abuse could not find a lawyer to represent him. This is best represented by the 'cab-rank rule': the barrister must accept clients in the order in which their briefs are presented. This reinforces the idea that the lawyer must represent a client however much the lawyer may disagree with the case, and must do the best that he or she can. This will be explored further in Chapter 3.

There is another aspect to the principle of neutrality and that is that lawyers must give impartial advice. Their advice should not be tempered by emotion, but should be cool and dispassionate. It may be that the lawyer needs to tell the client what the client does not want to hear and that the client might even be upset by the lawyer's advice.

There is a third issue here that might be raised. As we have seen, it is sometimes said that lawyers must put aside their own moral views. They must present their clients' case forcefully, with no thought of their own views. There is, for example, no equivalent for lawyers of the conscientious objection protection that doctors have under the Abortion Act 1967, whereby the doctor can refuse to be involved in, for example, an abortion on account of a moral conviction. A lawyer does not have a statutory right to refuse to defend a doctor on the basis that the doctor engaged in abortions. Why this lack of regard for lawyers' moral sensitivities?

Others have suggested that, in fact, it is wrong to think that lawyers should set aside their own human or moral feelings. Indeed, a lawyer who does not deal on an emotional level with the issues that a client is facing may not be giving the best advice. It has been suggested that the kind of neutrality traditionally advised has caused 'debilitating psychic tension',[53] and it has even been linked with high rates of drink and drug misuse among American lawyers.[54] Approaches based on an ethic of care would argue that good lawyer–client relationships must be built on honesty and mutual respect. Where a lawyer cannot relate to a client, they cannot enter into a good lawyer–client relationship and so the lawyer should be free not to act.[55] One concern about such an approach, however, is that it may mean that unpopular clients (for example people accused of child abuse) will not be able to find a lawyer to represent them.

Justice

For William Simon, the primary duty of a lawyer is to pursue justice.[56] Often, presenting a client's case will promote justice, but not always. If a lawyer is asked by a client to do something that will promote injustice, then the lawyer is not obliged to act. Some may go further and say that the lawyer *must* not act in a way that will promote injustice. However, Simon argues that this is only in cases in which there is clear injustice—and here lies the uncertainty: how is a lawyer to know what justice is? Supporters of the zealousness approach would say that the law provides the answer and that, as long as the client's request is compliant with the law, this should be sufficient.[57] Opponents argue that lawyers are moral agents and must justify their acts. They cannot justify promoting injustice by saying that they were simply following their clients' instructions. It was the 'following orders' mindset that explains the role that lawyers played in the financial crisis of the first decade of this century.[58]

Donald Nicolson has argued that this commitment to justice has a wide-reaching significance and is tied to the idea of being a professional:

> I . . . ground this sense of professionalism in the personal ethical duties of practitioners and argue that individual lawyers have moral duties to ensure that legal services extend beyond those who can pay or qualify for legal aid. In other words, law involves a calling to devote one's training, skills and privileges to assist those

---

[53] L. Fisher, 'Truth as a double-edged sword: Deception, moral paradox and the ethics of advocacy' (1989) 14 Journal of the Legal Profession 89.

[54] P. Goodrich, 'Law-induced anxiety' (2000) 9 Social and Legal Studies 143.

[55] Cahn (n. 24).

[56] W. Simon, 'Legal ethics should be primarily a matter of principles, not rules' (2010) 15 Legal Ethics 200.

[57] B. Wendel, 'Razian authority and its implications for legal ethics' (2010) 13 Legal Ethics 191.

[58] K. Hall and V. Holmes, 'The power of rationalisation to influence lawyers' decisions to act unethically' (2008) 11 Legal Ethics 137.

who require law's benefits or protections, and hence a true legal professional is a lover of justice.[59]

We will be exploring in Chapter 13 the argument that lawyers owe special obligations to the justice system and to the broader social good.

 What would you do?

You are advising a company defending against a claim for sexual harassment brought by an employee who cannot afford a lawyer and so has brought the proceedings herself. It is clear from your investigations that the claim is justified and that a serious wrong has been done to the employee. However, you notice that, in the paperwork, the claimant has made a technical error on which the company could rely to make a legal defence.

What would they do?

This 'What would you do?' scenario is accompanied by a podcast in which current law students debate the issues and articulate their own responses to the ethical questions that it raises. The podcast is available online at www.oxfordtextbooks.co.uk/orc/herringethics/

Care

We have already mentioned the ethics of care. Various writers have sought to apply this approach to legal ethics. Christine Parker and Adrian Evans explain how this might work:

> [T]he ethics of care for lawyers focuses on trying to serve the best interests of both clients and others in a holistic way that incorporates moral, emotional and relational dimensions of a problem into the legal solution. It is particularly concerned with preserving or restoring (even reconciling) relationships and avoiding harm. It sees relationships, including both the client's network of relationships and the lawyer's own relationships with colleagues, family and community, as more important than the institutions of the law or systemic and social ideas of justice and ethics.[60]

In Chapter 3, we will explore further the potential implications of such an approach. One interesting aspect of it is that it opens up the idea that lawyers' ethics should focus

[59] D. Nicolson, 'Calling, character and clinical legal education: A cradle to grave approach to inculcating a love for justice' (2013) 16 Legal Ethics 36, 48.

[60] C. Parker and A. Evans, *Inside Lawyers' Ethics* (Cambridge University Press, 2009), 33.

not only on the obligations of lawyers, but also on the lawyer–client relationship as a whole. It is therefore arguable that clients should have obligations to their lawyers.[61]

Application

Christine Parker and Adrian Evans helpfully set out a three-step process that can be used in address an ethical issue.[62] It involves asking three key questions and considering further questions in light of each of these.

The following is an adapted version of their process.

- *Step one*: What ethical issues have arisen or might arise in the future in this situation?

  Consider the following questions.

  - Whose interests are affected?
  - What values and interests are at stake for those affected?
  - Is there a conflict between these interests?
  - What are your own interest and values?

- *Step two*: What ethical principles should be used to resolve the issues in this scenario?

  Consider the following questions.

  - What do the codes of conduct say?
  - What general ethical principles apply to this scenario?
  - Are there any special responsibilities that lawyers have because of their role as lawyers?
  - How are the conflicts between these principles to be managed?

- *Step three*: How might the ethical thing to do actually be put into action in the current situation?

  Consider the following questions.

  - What actions can feasibly be done?
  - What will be the consequences of different alternatives?
  - What resources are needed from others to do the right thing?
  - How can we prevent this dilemma from arising again?

Should law degrees include ethics?

At the time of writing, legal ethics is not a compulsory part of the law degree. It is covered in the Legal Practice Course (LPC) and the Bar Professional Training Course (BPTC)

---

[61] D. Wilkens, 'Do clients have ethical obligations to lawyers? Some lessons from the diversity wars' (1998) 11 Georgetown Journal of Legal Ethics 855.   [62] Parker and Evans (n. 60).

to some extent.[63] In recent years, there has been an increased interest in making ethics part of the law degree. Kim Economides and Justine Rogers' 2009 report to the Law Society, *Preparatory Ethics Training for Future Solicitors*, recommended that 'awareness of and commitment to legal values and the moral context of the law, [be] mandatory in undergraduate law degrees'.[64] Professor Andrew Boon was then asked to produce a model curriculum.[65] The aim was to develop training to encourage students to learn about ethics, but also to reflect on the nature of legal ethics and to become involved in the formation of legal ethics in the future. These reports led to the Legal Education and Training Review (LETR),[66] which was set up by the Solicitors Regulation Authority (SRA), the Bar Standards Board (BSB), and the Institute of Legal Executives (ILEX).[67] The LETR report sees the need to 'strengthen requirements for education and training in legal ethics, values and professionalism, the development of management skills, communication skills, and equality and diversity'.[68]

The LETR is clear that achieving 'appropriate learning outcomes in respect of professional ethics, legal research, and the demonstration of a range of written and oral communication skills' must be part of legal education, training, and research.[69] Indeed, in its survey of lawyers asking what training was important, 'ethics and procedure came out above all other areas, having been rated "important" or "somewhat important" by over 95% and 94% of respondents, respectively'.[70] However, the LETR noted that there was 'no majority support for the introduction of professional ethics as a new Foundation of Legal Knowledge for the QLD [Qualifying Law Degree]/GDL [Graduate Diploma in Law]',[71] and so that was not recommended.[72] In short, although the LETR found it crucial that ethics should be a part of legal training, it did not make a clear recommendation as to where in the training process that should occur.

It is perhaps surprising that, in England, legal ethics are not yet an established part of a law degree. In other countries, notably the United States, the teaching of legal ethics is a standard part of a law degree. Why has there been a reluctance to include legal ethics in a law degree? There are a number of reasons, including, first, that academic lawyers have insisted that the law degree is not simply a preparation to be a lawyer. Only a minority of those completing law degrees become lawyers.[73]

---

[63] L. Webley, 'Legal ethics in the academic curriculum: Correspondent's report from the United Kingdom' (2011) 14 Legal Ethics 132.

[64] Law Society, *Preparatory Ethics Training for Future Solicitors* (Law Society, 2009), 3.

[65] A. Boon, *Legal Ethics at the Initial Stage: A Model Curriculum* (Law Society, 2010).

[66] P. Leighton, 'The Legal Education and Training Review (LETR), 2011–2012' (2011) 45 The Law Teacher 361.

[67] Law Society, *Response to Discussion Paper 02/2012* (Law Society, 2012).

[68] Legal Education Training Review, *Setting Standards* (LETR, 2013), ix.

[69] LETR (n. 68), xiv.   [70] LETR (n. 68), 33.   [71] LETR (n. 68), para 7.10.

[72] LETR (n. 68), para 7.89.

[73] S. Mayson, 'The education and training of solicitors: Time for change' (2011) 45 The Law Teacher 278.

Many law graduates do not go on to pursue a career as a solicitor or barrister and legal academics see themselves as not simply preparing students to be lawyers, but as providing a critical and philosophical approach to the study of law. This has meant that some academic lawyers are wary of teaching the law degree as simply a preparation to become a lawyer. Indeed, much research produced by legal academics is not read by practitioners, precisely because it is not seen as being directly relevant to the day-to-day practice of lawyers. Legal academics have been keen to assert their autonomy to decide the nature of law degrees and have resisted attempts by the professions to regulate too strictly the content of law degrees. On the other hand, it is important to law schools that the law degree is seen as a good first step towards the legal profession. There is no doubt that is what motivates many students to apply for a law degree in the first place. The tension between the academic aims of a law degree and the professional bodies is mitigated in part by the year of professional training at law school or Bar school, where the more practical skills—such as drafting, advocacy, and negotiations—are taught. Traditionally, many academics have felt that training on professional ethics fits into that part of the process better than the university part.

Second, there are few legal academics who feel equipped to teach legal ethics. There is a shortage of staff for many courses, and universities are under pressure to find staff to teach core subjects, or popular courses, rather than to create a new course on legal ethics.

A third argument that is sometimes put forward is that ethics 'cannot be taught'.[74] The basic principles of honesty and integrity are an ingrained part of character. In short, ethics are seen to be 'common sense' and there is little that one can do if a student has no appreciation of their significance. If a lawyer is corrupt, no amount of legal ethics training will change this.

A fourth concern that has sometimes been raised is whether it is possible to assess ethical reasoning. Ethical views may be seen as a matter of opinion and there are even concerns that lecturers may seek to impose their personal ethical opinions on their students.

None of these arguments are, I suggest, convincing.[75] As to the first, it will be clear that the role of lawyers and the regulations governing their behaviour are central to how the law operates in practice. A detailed academic study of the law must include a consideration of how the law works in practice, and that involves an investigation into the restrictions placed on and values found among lawyers. They play a central role in how law works in the real world.

As to the third and fourth points, there is plenty of academic writing on legal ethics in the United States and England showing that there is ample scope for reasoned academic debate and analysis. It is no more 'a matter of opinion' than many other areas of the law.

[74] A. Paterson, 'Legal ethics: Its nature and place in the curriculum', in R. Cranston (ed.) *Legal Ethics and Professional Responsibility* (Oxford University Press, 2006).

[75] Mayson (n. 73).

That leaves only the argument about resources. It is always difficult to know how law schools should focus their resources, but the study of the principles guiding lawyers as they negotiate on behalf of their clients and advise them in non-adversarial matters is essential, given that the vast majority of cases are resolved outside the courts, with legal advice.[76]

 Application

Professor Andrew Boon has drafted a list of what might be included in a legal ethics course as part of a law degree.[77] He defines the course as: 'The study of the relationship between morality and Law, the values underpinning the legal system, and the regulation of the legal services market, including the institutions, professional roles and ethics of the judiciary and legal professions.'

He proposes the following objectives for the course:

Objectives that are consistent with these aims are that the ethics curriculum should:
a) further appreciation of the relationship between morality and law
b) promote understanding of the role of the legal profession in supporting democracy and protecting justice and the rule of law
c) provide opportunities for ethical decision-making
d) promote understanding of the importance of values, including justice, honesty, integrity, critical self-reflection and respect for others
e) stimulate reflection on the ethical challenges of practice and lay a foundation for ethical behaviour[78]

Professional codes

It is one of the marks of a profession that it produces guidance for its members. The Bar Council has produced the Bar Council Code of Conduct (the Bar Code). The Law Society has produced the Guide to the Professional Conduct of Solicitors. These codes seek to set out how members of the profession ought to behave. They include general ethical principles, advice on the application of these to particular contexts, and an explanation of the particular legal obligations that are at play.

It is interesting to note that both of these codes came late to the professions. The Solicitors Regulation Authority (SRA) Code of Conduct was first produced in 1960 and the Bar Code in 1979. In part, the reticence was a feeling that the ethical principles

---

[76] R. Burridge and J. Webb, 'The values of common law legal education: Rethinking rules, responsibilities, relationships and roles in the law school' (2007) 10 Legal Ethics 72.

[77] Boon (n. 65).   [78] Boon (n. 65), 14.

could not be readily reduced to a single document. But perhaps there was also an assumption that the professional did not need to be told what ethical principles bound him or her because her or she knew that all too well. However, a range of pressures led to the production of these codes, including recognition of the complexity of work that lawyers had to enter into and of the ethical issues raised.

The codes have been controversial. One issue is that they tend to use vague language. In a way, this is inevitable. They are not, generally, setting down legislation that it is expected will be followed to the letter; rather, they are seeking to articulate principles. The professional bodies do not want someone who has clearly behaved in an inappropriate way to be able to claim to have complied with the letter of the code and so be blameless. However, this vagueness leads others to claim that what are left are statements of the obvious, or rules of etiquette.[79]

The status of the codes is somewhat ambiguous. At one level, they are not law as such. They are enforced by the professional bodies and sanctions are imposed by those bodies. However, a lawyer who breaches a professional code may find that fact being relied upon by a court. A client who claims that his or her lawyer was negligent would have the case greatly strengthened if it could be shown that the lawyer breached ethical codes. Similarly, a lawyer facing a criminal charge of fraud would face problems if it were established that he or she had breached a code. So even if the codes are not enforced by the courts as such, they will be taken into account when the courts consider how the general law applies to lawyers.

A crucial point is that few would see a professional code as saying all there is to say about ethics and lawyers. There are many things that the codes do not mention that lawyers would accept as being moral obligations. Inevitably, the codes cannot cover every scenario that a lawyer might face; in order to deal with such cases, a lawyer is likely to turn to some key values or ethical principles, described in this chapter.

We will look in detail at the form of regulation in Chapter 3, but some general points can be made now. The SRA Handbook took a new approach in its 2011 edition. It took an 'outcomes-focused approach' (OFA) to regulation.[80] The SRA explains that this OFA is 'a regulatory regime that focuses on the high level Principles and outcomes that should drive the provision of services for clients'. So rather than seeking to set out detailed guidance on specific issues, the SRA Code emphasises general points of principle, which it then leaves to solicitors to apply in the circumstances that they face.

The new Code focuses on ten key Principles.

[79] A. Ayers, 'What if legal ethics can't be reduced to a maxim?' (2013) 26 Georgetown Journal for Legal Ethics 1.

[80] Solicitors Regulation Authority, *Outcomes-Focused Regulation at a Glance* (Solicitors Regulation Authority, 2013).

Follow the Code

The following are the ten key Principles outlined in the SRA Code:

You must:

1. uphold the rule of law and the proper administration of justice;
2. act with integrity;
3. not allow your independence to be compromised;
4. act in the best interests of each *client*;
5. provide a proper standard of service to your *clients*;
6. behave in a way that maintains the trust the public places in you and in the provision of legal services;
7. comply with your legal and regulatory obligations and deal with your regulators and ombudsmen in an open, timely and co-operative manner;
8. run your business or carry out your role in the business effectively and in accordance with proper governance and sound financial and risk management principles;
9. run your business or carry out your role in the business in a way that encourages equality of opportunity and respect for diversity; and
10. protect *client* money and *assets*.

The Code states that it 'empowers' solicitors to determine the appropriate application of these Principles in the cases before them. Deliberately, there is 'more flexibility in how you achieve the right outcomes for your clients, which will require greater judgement on your part'.[81] This means that, rather than 'prescriptive rules', there are 'mandatory outcomes' and 'non-mandatory indicative behaviours'. The mandatory outcomes 'describe what you are expected to achieve in order to comply with the Principles in specific contexts, as set out in the different chapters in the Code'.[82] The indicative behaviours are not mandatory; they are 'examples of the kind of behaviours which may establish whether you have achieved the relevant outcomes and complied with the Principles'.

Because these indicative behaviours are not mandatory, it may be possible for a solicitor to demonstrate that he or she has not met the indicative behaviour, but has complied with the Principles by other means.

Digging deeper

The new SRA Code takes a particular stance over ethical issues, from which the following themes might be drawn out.

[81] SRA (n. 80), 2.   [82] SRA (n. 80), 2.

- The Code supports the use of general principles. There is therefore a degree of principlism indicated in the Code. However, these principles are mostly not abstract, but applied.
- The Code acknowledges that the application of principles might work out differently in different contexts. There is therefore an acceptance that the ethical approach must involve a careful appreciation of the particular set of facts. This might suggest support for those ethical approaches, such as the ethics of care, which seek to tailor the ethical solution to the facts of the particular case. However, there is a limit to that. The mandatory principles show that there are some bright lines that must not be crossed.
- The Code, interestingly, accepts that there is a degree of judgement involved in the application of the principles. This suggests that there is, in some cases, a range of acceptable views about what might be an ethical approach in a context and that the SRA will respect that. That is hardly full-blown relativism, but an acknowledgement that there is not always a single correct solution in ethically complex issues.
- The Code acknowledges that small firms and large firms, or solicitors with different kinds of clients, may respond differently to an ethical dilemma.

The Bar Code is, in some ways, more like the traditional approach to setting out ethical guidance in that it sets out what barristers must or must not do. It reads more like the traditional 'rule book' approach than does the SRA Handbook. That said, it would be wrong to exaggerate the differences between the two. The Bar Code is replete with sufficiently vague commands that leave quite some discretion to their interpretation. What is most notable is that the SRA Code is explicit about only providing general guidance.

Follow the Code

The key principles outlined in the Bar Code are that a barrister must not:

(a) engage in conduct whether in pursuit of his [or her] profession or otherwise which is:
  (i) dishonest or otherwise discreditable to a barrister;
  (ii) prejudicial to the administration of justice; or
  (iii) likely to diminish public confidence in the legal profession or the administration of justice or otherwise bring the legal profession into disrepute;
(b) engage directly or indirectly in any occupation if his [or her] association with that occupation may adversely affect the reputation of the Bar or in the case of a practising barrister prejudice his [or her] ability to attend properly to his [or her] practice.

Digging deeper

A couple of things to notice about the Bar Code principles: notice that these are a list of 'Thou shalt not's, rather than a list of things to which a person should aspire. Are ethics about not doing bad things or about doing good things? Further, the list seems to focus not on following ethical principles because they are good things to do in and of themselves, but on doing so because they produce bad consequences: discrediting barristers; prejudicing the administration of justice; or reducing confidence in the Bar or its reputation. Using the terminology considered earlier in the chapter, the Bar Code looks like a set of utilitarian principles, rather than deontological ones.

Conclusion

This chapter has introduced some of the key themes that will be explored in the book. It has sought to explain what ethics is: an attempt to find what is the right course of action. It has set out some general ethical theories that have been developed to resolve ethical dilemmas generally. It has then gone on to explore whether lawyers have special ethical obligations over and above the obligations of ordinary citizens. Finally, it has considered how legal training and legal practice has taken the ethical obligations of lawyers more seriously.

Some readers may feel frustrated that this chapter has not provided a single correct answer on how to resolve ethical dilemmas.[83] That is deliberate: there is no agreement over what is the best way in which to deal with ethical issues. You will need to develop your own way of thinking through the issues. Most commentators agree that there are some issues on which only one ethical response is justified: child abuse is wrong and there are no two ways about it. However, on other issues, reasonable people may disagree. This chapter has provided tools that you can use to find out what you think, but also to understand why other people may disagree.

Further reading

The following are some books that are useful on general ethical issues:

T. Beauchamp and J. Childress, *Principles of Biomedical Ethics*, **7th edn (Oxford University Press, 2013).**

P. Benn, *Ethics* **(Routledge, 1997).**

N. Biggar and L. Hogan, *Religious Voices in Public Places* **(Oxford University Press, 2010).**

[83] Ayers (n. 79).

R. Dworkin, *Taking Rights Seriously* (Harvard University Press, 1977).

J. Raz, *The Authority of Law* (Oxford University Press. 1979).

The following are some of the leading works on ethics as applied to lawyers:

R. Abel, *American Lawyers* (Oxford University Press, 1989).

A. Boon and J. Levin, *The Ethics and Conduct of Lawyers in England and Wales* (Hart, 2008).

T. Dare, *The Counsel of Rogues? A Defence of the Standard Conception of the Lawyer's Role* (Ashgate, 2009).

C. Fried, 'The lawyer as friend: The moral foundations of the lawyer–client relation' (1976) 86 Yale Law Journal 1060.

D. Luban, *Lawyers and Justice: An Ethical Study* (Princeton University Press, 1988).

D. Luban, *Legal Ethics and Human Dignity* (Cambridge University Press, 2007).

D. Markovits, *A Modern Legal Ethics* (Princeton University Press, 2009).

D. Nicolson and J. Webb, *Professional Legal Ethics* (Oxford University Press, 2000).

C. Parker and A. Evans, *Inside Lawyers' Ethics* (Cambridge University Press, 2007).

S. Pepper, 'The lawyer's amoral ethical role: A defense, a problem, and some possibilities' (1986) 11 American Bar Foundation Research Journal 613.

D. Rhode, *In the Interests of Justice* (Oxford University Press, 2000).

T. Schneyer, 'Moral philosophy's standard misconception of legal ethics' [1984] Wisconsin Law Review 1529.

W. Simon, *The Practice of Justice* (Harvard University Press, 1998).

K. Tranter, F. Bartlett, L. Corbin, M. Robertson, and R. Mortensen, *Reaffirming Legal Ethics: Taking Stock and New Ideas* (Routledge, 2010).

B. Wendel, *Lawyers and Fidelity to Law* (Princeton University Press, 2010).

A. Woolley and B. Wendel, 'Legal ethics and moral character' (2010) 23 Georgetown Journal of Legal Ethics 1065.